Living Reptiles of the World

Living Reptiles

of the World

by KARL P. SCHMIDT

Curator of Zoology Emeritus, Chicago Natural History Museum

and ROBERT F. INGER

Curator of Reptiles, Chicago Natural History Museum

Photographs by

ROY PINNEY

JOHN MARKHAM

HAL H. HARRISON

CY LA TOUR

ERICH SOCHUREK

and others

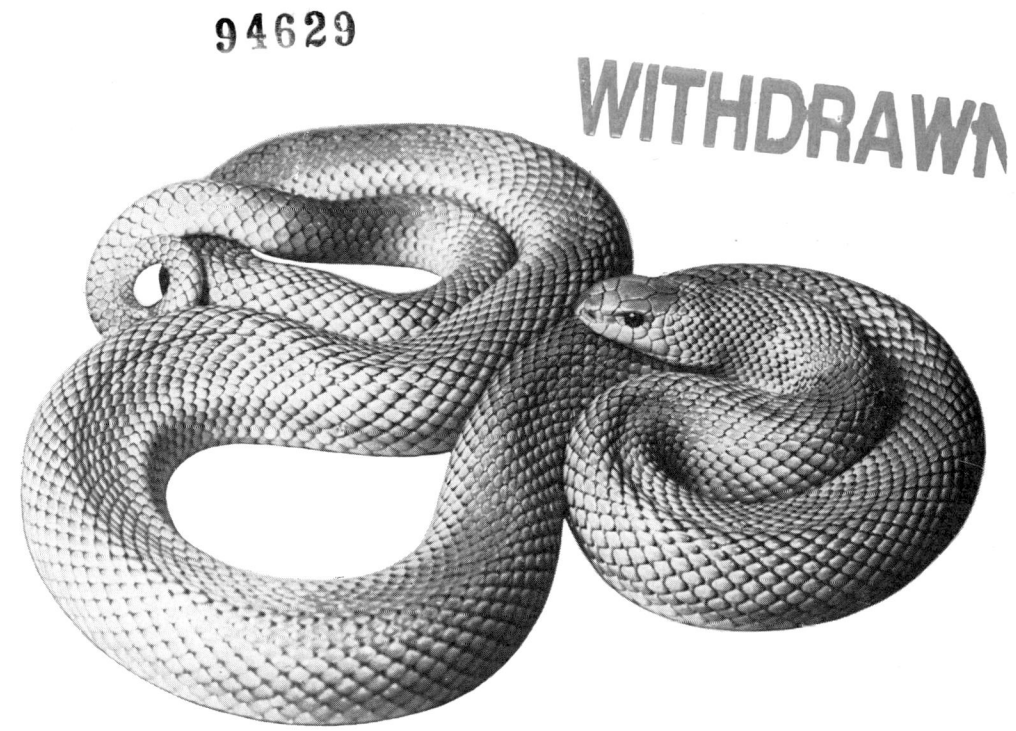

A CHANTICLEER PRESS EDITION

DOUBLEDAY & COMPANY, Inc.

Garden City, New York

THE WORLD OF NATURE SERIES

Living Mammals of the World by Ivan T. Sanderson

Living Reptiles of the World by Karl P. Schmidt
and Robert F. Inger

Living Birds of the World by E. Thomas Gilliard

Living Insects of the World by Alexander B. Klots
and Elsie B. Klots

*The Lower Animals: Living Invertebrates of the
World* by Ralph Buchsbaum and Lorus J. Milne,
in collaboration with Mildred Buchsbaum
and Margery Milne

Living Fishes of the World by Earl S. Herald

Living Amphibians of the World by Doris M. Cochran

Library of Congress Catalog Card No. 57–9783

Preface

BOOKS about reptiles intended for the general public begin with Aristotle, who put all that was known to him about the crocodile of the Nile, the various turtles of Greece, and lizards and snakes into his *Historia Animalium*. Since Aristotle's time, there has been a flow of books and other publications about salamanders and frogs, lizards and snakes, and turtles and crocodiles, many directed strictly to professional zoologists, but always some with the object of popular instruction or entertainment—or both. No period has seen such an upsurge of interest in reptiles and such a volume of publications about them as the first part of the present century. This has furthermore been especially a feature of North American natural history and has been fostered by American zoological gardens and museums.

The American books were at first mainly descriptive works, beginning with the many volumes by Raymond Lee Ditmars. With the growth of a large group of professionally trained herpetologists, a greater range of interests has come to be emphasized even in the most popular works. The younger generation of American naturalists is fortunate to have such introductory works as Clifford Pope's *Snakes Alive and How They Live,* and at another level, James A. Oliver's *The Natural History of North American Amphibians and Reptiles.* The present volume is one of a series in which the colored illustration now made available by photography affords an essential supplement to the existing works.

Information concerning any animal group or, indeed, any aspect of nature, is accumulated slowly through the careful and serious work of literally thousands of scientists, most of whom will never be known to the public at large. Like the authors of previous books on reptiles, we are indebted to a host of colleagues, both those long dead and those who are still very much alive, for the fund of knowledge on which we have drawn.

We have seized the occasion for a new review, at the descriptive level, of the reptiles, which are the great central stock, ancestral to both mammals and birds and themselves derived from the amphibians. Some knowledge of the reptiles is important to everyone who wishes to understand something of "man's place in nature."

KARL P. SCHMIDT
ROBERT F. INGER

April, 1957

Contents

PREFACE   PAGE   5

INTRODUCTION   11

THE TURTLES (*Order Chelonia*)   13

The Snapping Turtles (*Family Chelydridae*)   14
The Mud Turtles and Musk Turtles (*Family Kinosternidae*)   16
Central American River Turtle (*Family Dermatemydidae*)   17
Big-headed Turtles (*Family Platysternidae*)   17
Common Fresh-water Turtles (*Family Emydidae*)   18
The Land Tortoises (*Family Testudinidae*)   27
The Leatherback Sea Turtle (*Family Dermochelidae*)   30
The True Sea Turtles (*Family Chelonidae*)   31
The Soft-shelled Turtles (*Family Trionychidae*)   36
The New Guinean Plateless Turtle (*Family Carettochelidae*)   37
The Hidden-necked Turtles (*Family Pelomedusidae*)   37
The Snake-necked Turtles (*Family Chelidae*)   38

THE TUATARA (*The Tuatara Order, the Tuatara Family and the Tuatara*)   41

THE ALLIGATORS, CROCODILES AND GAVIALS (*Order Crocodilia*)   44

The True Crocodiles (*Family Crocodylidae*)   47
Alligators and Caimans (*Family Alligatoridae*)   66
The Gavial or Gharial (*Family Gavialidae*)   68

THE LIZARDS AND SNAKES (*Superorder Squamata*)

THE LIZARDS (*Order Sauria*)   69

The Geckos (*Family Gekkonidae*)   69
The Flap-footed Lizards (*Family Pygopodidae*)   76

THE LIZARDS AND SNAKES (continued)

The Agamids (*Family Agamidae*)   PAGE   77
The Chameleons (*Family Chamaeleonidae*)   90
The Iguanids (*Family Iguanidae*)   96
The Night Lizards (*Family Xantusidae*)   124
The Skinks (*Family Scincidae*)   124
Skink Relatives (*Families Anelytropsidae and Dibamidae*)   134
The Girdle-tailed Lizards (*Family Cordylidae*)   135
The Gerrhosaurids (*Family Gerrhosauridae*)   136
The Teiid Lizards (*Family Teiidae*)   137
The Lacertids (*Family Lacertidae*)   140
The Worm Lizards (*Family Amphisbaenidae*)   161
The Anguid Lizards (*Family Anguidae*)   163
The Legless Lizards (*Family Anniellidae*)   166
The Xenosaurids and Shinisaurids (*Family Xenosauridae*)   167
The Gila Monsters (*Family Helodermatidae*)   167
The Monitor Lizards (*Family Varanidae*)   169
The Earless Monitor (*Family Lanthanotidae*)   173

THE SNAKES (*Order Serpentes*)   175

Giant Constricting Snakes (*Family Boidae*)   175
The Python Family (*Family Pythonidae*)   179
Blind Burrowing Snakes (*Families Typhlopidae and Leptotyphlopidae*)   183
More Burrowing Snakes (*Families Anilidae, Uropeltidae, and Xenopeltidae*)   185
The Oriental Water Snakes (*Family Acrochordidae*)   186
The Colubrid Snakes (*Family Colubridae*)   187
The Cobra and Coral Snakes and Their Relatives (*Family Elapidae*)   232
The Sea Snakes (*Family Hydrophidae*)   238
The True Vipers (*Family Viperidae*)   240
The Pit-Vipers (*Family Crotalidae*)   264

INDEX   281

Living Reptiles of the World

Introduction

The Place of Reptiles in the Animal Kingdom

IN THESE days, when "dinosaur" has become almost a household word, most people realize that there was a great Age of Reptiles, long ago, when gigantic four-footed creatures with long tails and necks splashed and fed in the swamps, and great flesh-eaters stalked the land, walking erect on their hind legs, to prey upon the lesser types. The vast array of other kinds of reptiles that lived in that age—the Mesozoic—is still mostly unfamiliar except to students and to those children and parents who are confirmed museum-goers. There were long-necked plesiosaurs, short-necked ichthyosaurs, slender mosasaurs, incredible placodonts, and gigantic paddle-limbed turtles in the seas; and on land multitudes of smaller reptiles lived beside the dinosaurs.

It was from the more ancient types, long preceding the dinosaurs, that mammals (and thus we ourselves) took their origin. Birds evolved from some small dinosaur stock that had taken to life in the trees, quite as many modern lizards do. Fishes maintained their dominance of the sea, but as the birds and mammals underwent their great evolution into varied types in the Tertiary Era, the reptiles declined. The living reptiles are a mere remnant of the innumerable ancient kinds, an unknown number of which remain undiscovered, locked as fossils in the rocks or lost by erosion into later seas.

Only the turtle group is really ancient, as ancient indeed as the earliest reptiles, surviving as a cohort of about two hundred kinds. The crocodilians, with only twenty species or so, give us a good idea of what some dinosaurs must have been like, but they are a uniform lot, without anything of the vast diversity of the dinosaurs. Still more obviously a remnant held over from the Mesozoic is the tuatara, the lizardlike creature of New Zealand that stands alone as a single species of beak-headed reptiles, whose ancestors flourished at the beginning of the Age of Reptiles. Lizards and snakes we have in modern times in great numbers, some two thousand kinds of each, and in sufficient variety of habitat and habits to give us a picture of the deployment of their groups into terrestrial, subterranean, arboreal, and aquatic types, evolving in the past into close adjustment to every niche in the environment where food was available and where a cold-blooded creature could live.

If there is a theme in our book, it lies in the contrast between the modern and still-evolving snakes and lizards and the relict types that are plainly survivors from a time long past. And this theme finds fulfillment in the account of the evolving adjustment of individual forms, not only to the major habitats, but also to very specific roles in the economy of nature, often illustrated by species that exhibit in their shapes and colors the stamp both of their special environment and of their evolutionary history.

Snapping Turtle (*Chelydra serpentina*)

The Turtles

IN CONTRAST with their attitude toward most of the major groups of reptiles and amphibians, few people look with aversion on turtles or think of being afraid of them. It does not excite surprise to find these creatures kept as children's pets, and the larger ones are favorites in zoological gardens. Almost all turtles are eaten by primitive peoples, and a good number of different species are highly regarded as food among civilized nations. Even English-speaking peoples, who are inclined to disdain many sea foods enjoyed in the countries bordering the Mediterranean (and in more remote regions) eat the marine green turtle; and in North America the snapping turtle has been added to the list of regularly eaten forms. The diamondback turtles of the brackish-water marshes along the Atlantic and Gulf Coasts are regarded as a special delicacy, and a very costly one.

On account of our great familiarity with them, we are inclined to forget that turtles are really the oldest type of living reptiles, vastly more ancient in lineage than the fossil dinosaurs and most of the other extinct forms. The turtles really deserve the name of "living fossils" much more than do some of the creatures to which it is commonly applied. There are only twelve families among the existing turtles, and a few more than two hundred species. It is fortunate for those who study them that these existing forms include almost all of the types of turtles, extinct as well as living.

The earliest turtles, at the very beginning of the Age of Reptiles, were already characterized by the bony, boxlike shell that encloses the shoulder and hip girdles and all of the internal organs, and serves as a very effective protection against more active predators. From this "box" the head and neck and forelimbs project through an opening at the front, and the hind limbs and tail at the rear. Swift locomotion and agility on land are quite impossible with such a structure. The shell is made up of an inner layer of regularly arranged bony elements and an outer layer of horny shields that overlap the bony plates. The possession of so effective a protective shell is accordingly directly correlated with the turtles' proverbial sluggishness of movement and in-offensiveness of disposition. Metaphorically, peace has been the keynote of their evolution through some hundreds of millions of years, and their reliance, in a world filled with predacious enemies, has been on passive defense. It is all the more clear that the main theme has been defense when we find that, in the less sluggish types, more active habits have been correlated with reduction of the shell, and that this has gone hand in hand with enlargement of the limbs, or of the head and limbs together.

The importance of the protective shell in evolution is shown by the development of all sorts of devices for its more complete closure; they are variations on the theme of defense. For this effect, either the front or rear lobe of the lower shell (the plastron), or both, may be hinged so as to close the front and rear openings of the box. An irregular but effective hinge is developed even in the upper shell (the carapace) of an African land turtle, so that its posterior part can be drawn down over the opening for hind feet and tail. The typical land turtles both large and small (to which the term "tortoises" is now restricted in the American language) close the openings neatly with the armored surfaces of their limbs. Such complete closure of the shell by secondary modification has been attained at least a dozen times in quite different and unrelated types of turtles. We shall return to this subject again and again in describing the living turtles family by family.

Four great lines of evolution are immediately recognizable among living turtles. There is the gigantic leatherback of the sea, one of the largest of modern reptiles, with a most extraordinary type of shell; then all the rest of the sea turtles, quite unrelated to the leatherback but quite closely related among themselves; then the curious side-necked turtles of the southern continents, all extinct in the Northern Hemisphere; and lastly the hidden-necked turtles, in which the head is completely withdrawn into the shell by a vertical flexure of the neck. All of the familiar land and fresh-water turtles of the northern continents belong to this last-named type.

The words "turtle" and "tortoise" are a source of confusion in the English language, for originally neither applied to the group as a whole. The word "turtle," in Great Britain, applies properly only to the sea turtles, like the herbivorous green turtle, prized as food, and the carnivorous loggerhead turtle, which is less esteemed. In England, then, the word "tortoise" is applied to all members of the order Chelonia, and these include fresh-water tortoises, soft-shelled tortoises, side-necked tortoises, and land tortoises. When the English settlers came to America they found a bewildering variety of such "tortoises." There had been no native fresh-water or land tortoises at all in Britain, except occasional specimens from the Continent or from North Africa, kept as pets. The most conspicuous of the new types in America, in both size and abundance, was the snapping turtle; to this species the term "turtle" was almost automatically applied, instead of tortoise, perhaps because it was also edible. In America, after this initial extension of the meaning of "turtle," the word has gradually become current for the group as a whole, while "tortoise" has come to be more and more restricted to the turtles with high-domed shells that live on land. In the United States, no one now thinks of saying "water tortoise," although this would still be correct usage in England.

The Snapping Turtles
(*Family Chelydridae*)

Nothing seems more exclusively North American to a herpetologist than the common snapping turtle, *Chelydra serpentina*. This is the most widespread, and in many waters the most abundant, of turtles in the United States, ranging all the way from the Atlantic seaboard to the Rocky Mountains and from Canada to Florida. One learns with a little surprise that a form barely distinguishable from the northern one is found in Central America, and that another closely related kind ranges from Panama to Ecuador, west of the Andes. The snapping turtles of the Florida Peninsula are slightly different from those of the rest of North America. It is even more surprising to learn that fossil snapping turtles readily recognizable as the close relatives of the North American forms should be found in the Miocene beds of Europe, where they seem to have become extinct long before the Ice Age.

The snapping turtle, by being so much an exception to the "theme of defense," illuminates our remarks on that subject. Instead of taking to a defensive posture when approached, the snapper squares away, faces an aggressor, lunges and bites savagely at him, and may even advance to the attack. A large snapping turtle with a shell a foot or more in length, lunging at one's hand or foot with open jaws that close with a snap like that of a steel trap, is really a somewhat frightening creature. A snapper may be held safely by the tail, and can be carried along if it is held away from one's leg.

Hand in hand with the agressive behavior goes the modification of the anatomy. The large head and broad neck are too bulky for complete retraction into the shell, and so are the powerful limbs and long tail. The tail, by the way, bears a crest of enlarged scales on its upper edge, somewhat like those of an alligator. The shell, too, seems to have been modified away from its defensive role, since, far from being able to contain the big head and limbs, the lower shell (the belly shield or plastron) is much reduced in width. With aggressiveness goes the capacity for great activity on land and in the water. Once the animal is in the water, the aggressive behavior disappears, and the snapper appears to be a rather poor swimmer, walking on the bottom instead of swimming in open water, and lying in wait for its prey instead of engaging in active pursuit. Instead of basking on logs as so many turtles do, the snapping turtle basks in shallow water, with most of itself buried in the mud. The rough and dull-colored shell, often overgrown with algae, is very well camouflaged in this situation.

The snapping turtle feeds on any living thing it may capture, but it also takes some vegetation and steadily patrols the bottoms of the ponds and lakes and streams in which it lives for dead animal matter. It thus plays an important role in nature as a scavenger. Snapping turtles have been thought to have an adverse effect on game-fish populations,

Snapping Turtle

but careful studies by Karl Lagler, in Michigan, seem to indicate that this is negligible. The carrion-feeding habit was used in an extraordinary way by an elderly Indian in Indiana, who was long known for his ability to find the bodies of drowned persons when all other means had failed. He appears to have kept a very large snapping turtle, which he could take to the lake in question, where he would release it from a boat after attaching a long wire. After allowing the turtle time for exploration, the wire would be followed up, and the turtle would be found to have located the body.

The egg-laying of the common snapping turtle is often accomplished at some distance from the water. The mother turtle searches for a suitable place, sometimes in a nearby cornfield, or in any open area. What makes one place suitable and a hundred others just like it less so is somewhat mysterious. Once a spot is selected, the earth is excavated by digging with the hind limbs in alternation, to a depth of several inches and to the width of perhaps a foot at the bottom. The eggs in a single clutch usually number about twenty, but as many as forty may be laid by a large individual. When laying is completed the hole is filled in, and surface material is scratched over it with the hind limbs. All sorts of varied nesting sites may be chosen, among them the heaped-up mounds of vegetation made by muskrats. How the hatchling baby snapping turtles find their way to the water is not evident, and has been the subject of some study. Like the sea-turtle babies, they seem to head toward the more open sky, which would of course usually take them lakeward or riverward. Hatching takes place relatively late in summer, after a period of ten weeks or more for development. Eggs laid too late in June, or delayed by a cool summer, may have their development arrested by cool weather in fall, and then usually hatch safely in the spring. Nests of snapping turtle eggs, with fully developed young, have been found in the course of early spring plowing. One may speak quite properly in such cases of hibernation in the egg. The baby snapping turtles have a rough and wrinkled shell, and their tails are relatively longer than those of the adults. Odd appearance and eagerness to feed makes these little creatures pleasing inhabitants of a terrarium; but they cannot, of course, be kept with fishes.

The common snapping turtle often grows so large that really big ones, weighing more than sixty pounds, quite deserve to be called giants. They are giants until one becomes acquainted with their truly gigantic relative, the alligator snapping turtle, *Macrochelys temmincki,* of the rivers of the south-

Snapping Turtle hatching

eastern United States, especially the lower Mississippi and its tributaries. This creature is one of the largest fresh-water turtles in the world and grows to a weight of at least two hundred pounds. Like other large reptiles, the alligator snapper is long-lived, one specimen at the Philadelphia Zoological Garden having lived in captivity for fifty-seven years.

The alligator snapper lies concealed in the mud of river bottoms and preys on passing fishes much more effectively than does the common snapping turtle. It is camouflaged by its color and by its rough three-keeled shell, which may bear a dense growth of algae. The dark inside of the mouth is relieved at the front edge of the tongue by a bright pink appendage under muscular control. This structure moves back and forth for all the world like a crawling worm, a veritable animated fish lure. Its effectiveness as bait has often been observed in captive turtles.

In former times the alligator snapper ranged far to the northwest of the region it now inhabits, for a related extinct species occurred in South Dakota in Miocene times. This fossil form is named *Macrochelys schmidti* (for the senior author of this book).

The principal range of the alligator snapper is now the Mississippi basin, as far north as central Illinois. It is found also in the streams of the Gulf of Mexico drainage, from northern Florida to central Texas.

The nest and eggs of the giant snapper are much like those of the common snapping turtle. It does not wander as far from the water, but otherwise the nest-digging and egg-deposition follow the same pattern. The depth of the excavation may be as much as twenty inches. The eggs are nearly round, about an inch and a half in diameter, and somewhat variable in this dimension. The number of eggs in a single clutch varies from seventeen to forty-four.

Both the common and the giant snapping turtles are eaten in the eastern and southern United States. "Snapper soup" is a specialty in many restaurants in Philadelphia, where the market price of snapping turtles, alive, is at this time about forty cents a pound.

The Mud Turtles and Musk Turtles

(*Family Kinosternidae*)

The smallest of the water turtles of eastern North America, very abundant in sluggish streams and ponds, are of two kinds: the mud turtles, with hinged lobes of the plastron; and the musk turtles, with a much reduced plastron without hinges. These turtles seem to be the nearest relatives of the snapping turtles and are known only from the Western Hemisphere.

The musk turtles have such a strong smell that fishermen in the southern United States, who often catch them on hook and line, call them "stinkpots." The common musk turtle, *Sternotherus odoratus* (Plate 3), is found from southern Maine westward through southern Ontario, Michigan, and Wisconsin, and southward through all of the Atlantic and Gulf states, westward to eastern Texas. It is a small turtle with a rather high but elongate shell usually less than five inches in length. The plastron has

Musk Turtle (*Sternotherus odoratus*)

HUGH SPENCER

the shields well separated on the mid-line by soft skin. It is usually seen crawling about on the bottom mud of ponds or sluggish parts of small streams, especially where there is abundant plant growth. That it is one of the most thoroughly aquatic of turtles is shown by the fact that it lives well in an aquarium without opportunity to leave the water. It seems to come out on land only rarely, aside from the necessity for egg-laying.

There are striking differences between the sexes. As in most turtles, the plastron of the male becomes concave in the adult. The areas of soft skin that separate the shields of the plastron are wider in the male. The most remarkable feature is a pair of opposing patches of horny scales on the inside of the hind limb. These apparently aid in holding the female during copulation. They were once thought to form a stridulating organ, to produce sounds to attract the female during courtship. Both sexes seem to be provided below the edge of the carapace with glands that secrete the strong-smelling musk from which these turtles receive their common name.

The egg-laying habits of the musk turtles are remarkable in being more varied than are those of most of the members of the turtle group. The number of eggs laid varies from two to seven. They measure a little more than an inch in the longer diameter, and about two-thirds of an inch in the shorter. They are remarkable in having a hard and brittle shell. They may be deposited in a regular nest excavated in soft soil; but eggs have often been found on the surface, or covered with a thin layer of leaf mold, or even laid in the rotten wood of a tree stump. Muskrat nests are favorite egg-laying sites. In Florida, the eggs are often deposited between the buttress roots of cypress trees.

The food of the musk turtle consists mainly of small animals, together with a small amount of vegetable matter. Any bodies of dead fishes, crayfishes, or snails are devoured when encountered. Like the snapping turtle, these small creatures play an important role as scavengers, preventing the fouling of ponds and pools by dead animal matter.

The keel-backed musk turtle, *Sternotherus carinatus,* is a distinct species found in the southeastern United States. Both the common and scientific names refer to a sharp ridge running along the mid-line of the upper shell, which is steep-sided. A form living in Georgia and Florida has an additional keel on each side. The keeled-back musk turtle, unlike the common stinkpot, suns itself a great deal and will climb stumps and cypress knees in order to reach a suitable basking site.

The second group of kinosternid turtles, the mud

turtles (genus *Kinosternon*), is much more widely distributed, with numerous forms in Mexico, Central America, and South America, as well as in the United States. These turtles have a broad, solid middle portion of the plastron firmly anchored to the carapace on each side. The front and rear lobes of the plastron are hinged by tough connective tissue to this central bridge, and operate like valves to close the openings of the shell at front and rear when the head, limbs, and tail are withdrawn.

The eastern mud turtle, *Kinosternon subrubrum,* reaches a shell length of little more than four inches. The shell in the young bears three blunt keels that gradually disappear with age. Although much less confined to water than the musk turtles, the mud turtles are certainly mainly aquatic. In fact, mating usually takes place in water. Like the common musk turtle, the male has an opposing pair of patches of horny scales on the inside of the thigh and lower leg behind the knee. A turtle of this species was reported to have lived in captivity for thirty-eight years. The eggs are elongate, little larger than those of the musk turtle, few in number, and often deposited in or beneath rotten logs or stumps of trees. We know astonishingly little about the natural diet of the eastern mud turtle, as common as it is. It has been seen eating dead fish and insects, but, judging from the way captive individuals eat anything offered them, the diet is probably much more varied.

There are four additional species of the genus *Kinosternon* in the United States, and no less than eleven in Mexico and Central America. The somewhat larger South American mud turtle, *Kinosternon scorpioides,* has an astonishingly wide distribution from Panama through the Guianas and Brazil. This species has the hinged lobes of the plastron much enlarged and accurately fitted to the carapace, so that the protection of the head and limbs is perfected. Two additional South American species of this genus live on the Pacific slopes of Colombia.

Two more Central American genera add greatly to the range of structure within the family Kinosternidae. One of these, the narrow-bridged mud turtle, *Claudius angustatus,* looks very much like an ordinary mud turtle from above, but when turned over proves to have a greatly reduced plastron, somewhat like that of a snapping turtle, connected to the carapace by a narrow bar of bone known as the bridge. The second type, the three-keeled Central American mud turtle, *Staurotypus,* is a much larger form, reaching a shell length of seven or eight inches. With its generally flat shape and high keels, this turtle presents a bizarre appearance. Almost nothing is known of the habits of these tropical turtles.

Central American River Turtle
(*Family Dermatemydidae*)

The Central American fauna includes a large fresh-water turtle that by itself forms a complete family. It is found in the coastal rivers from central Vera Cruz to northern Guatemala. It is characterized by having a large and heavy shell, much like that of an ordinary terrapin, but with a row of small plates on the bridge between carapace and plastron, which relates it to the snapping turtles. Numerous extinct forms are known from fossils found in Europe, Asia, and North America. The living species is known as *Dermatemys mawi.*

The species is eaten in Guatemala, and it is therefore somewhat remarkable that so little is known of its habits. Although it is rarely seen in zoological gardens or public aquariums, there was a very large one in the aquarium in the Munich Zoo in 1950, and one individual lived in the London Zoo for eight years.

Big-headed Turtles
(*Family Platysternidae*)

The big-headed turtles of southeastern Asia bear the appropriate scientific name *Platysternon megacephalum,* meaning "the flat-plastroned big-head," which is highly descriptive. The head is much too large to be retracted into the shell. The single genus and species is found in southeastern Asia, from Burma to the island of Hainan and in the states of southern China.

During his stay on Hainan Island in 1925, Clifford H. Pope obtained a series of specimens and learned something about the habits of the big-headed turtle. This is a relatively small kind of turtle, with a shell about six inches long (maximum seven inches), and with a strikingly long tail nearly as long as the shell. The whole body is much flattened. The plastron is rather large and entirely without any development of hinges for moving the lobes. Nothing is known of its food habits. The species is unlike most turtles in that it lives in rocky mountain streams, where it clambers out on stones to sun itself. The females lay only two eggs at a time.

Common Fresh-water Turtles

(*Family Emydidae*)

Of the 66 genera of living turtles, 25 belong to the family Emydidae, and these include 76 of the total of 211 full species. Enumerating all recognizable forms of turtles, there are, as of 1956, 332 species and subspecies; and 136 of these are emydids. Thus, on all counts, the hard-shelled, mainly aquatic turtles of this family compose the majority of turtles—the majority, that is, in the Northern Hemisphere. In Australia there are none; in Africa they are confined to the Mediterranean border. In South America a few species enter at the northwest. A species of the genus *Pseudemys* occurs in Uruguay, so widely separated from its relatives that it must have been distributed early enough (presumably when South America, after long separation, was reunited with North America) to have become well differentiated. Europe and western North America have remarkably few emydid turtles—two in each area (see remarks below on the pond turtles of the genus *Clemmys*).

The emydid turtles all tend to have an oval, streamlined shape, only a few forms having a high-domed shell resembling that of the quite closely related land turtles of the family Testudinidae. All except the few land-dwelling forms sun themselves on logs or rocks that project from the water, or bask on the banks of the lakes or rivers in which they live. Most of them leave the vicinity of water only for egg-laying. Otherwise, the water is their invariable refuge when they are approached.

The American name "terrapin," for the large emydid turtles, is derived from an Algonquin Indian root. It corresponds to what an Englishman would call a "water tortoise." In the southern United States there are other widely used general terms, especially "cooter" and "slider."

The life history of one of the common North American species has been thoroughly studied by Fred Cagle. Information about other North American species is summarized in *Turtles of the United States and Canada* (1939) by Clifford H. Pope, and in *Handbook of Turtles* (1952) by Archie F. Carr.

How the tortoises, which are primarily land animals and even live in deserts far from water, could be derived from the terrapins is shown by the adoption of land-dwelling habits by the North American box turtles, the Southeast Asian box turtle, and by a species of an otherwise aquatic genus, *Geoemyda*, in Panama. A few other forms also plainly tend toward land-dwelling habits. These will be commented on below. It seems most desirable to treat this great complex of rather closely related forms in geographic order—first North America north of Mexico, then tropical America, then Europe, and finally Asia.

It is usual to begin the North American list of emydid turtles with a little group of the genus *Clemmys,* commonly known as the pond turtles, which have relatives in eastern Asia and in Europe. The American forms are sufficiently familiar to have received widely current popular names for each species. The spotted turtle, *Clemmys guttata* (Plate 6), is well named, for it has sharply defined bright yellow or orange spots. It is a small turtle, with shell length well under five inches. The somewhat larger wood turtle, *Clemmys insculpta* (Plate 5), with shell length up to eight inches, is also happily named, for it is found mainly near woodland streams and may wander far from water to feed. Its carapace is roughly sculptured, and thus very different from the smooth surface of the spotted turtle. The young have a strikingly long tail, about as long as the shell. The wood turtle takes a much larger proportion of vegetable matter in its normal diet than does the spotted turtle. The little Muhlenberg's turtle, *Clemmys muhlenbergi,* named for a pioneer American botanist, is usually only about three and a half inches in shell length, with a maximum of four. This species is mainly found in boggy places, sometimes in widely separated areas, from northern New York to North Carolina. The fourth American *Clemmys* is the common pond turtle of the Pacific slopes, which region is surprisingly deficient in turtles and shares this deficiency with Europe. The Pacific pond turtle, *Clemmys marmorata,* reaches a length of about seven inches. This turtle was formerly regularly collected for the markets in California cities, and brought prices of three to six dollars a dozen as lately as the 1920's. It is not surprising, therefore, that it is now rare or extinct in populated areas.

The age records of turtles of the genus *Clemmys* are surprising, in view of their small size. The spotted turtle seems to have reached an authentic age of forty-two years, and one wood turtle is known to have lived fifty-eight years.

Blanding's turtle, *Emys blandingi,* confined mainly to the Great Lakes region in North America, is the sole American representative of the genus *Emys.* The American species has a European counterpart in the European pond turtle, *Emys orbicularis* (Plate 4). There are no other species of the genus. This widely separated occurrence of related forms is referred to as "disjunct distribution," and is always a subject for speculation as to the causes that might have produced it and for search for paleontological data that might cast light upon it. Blanding's turtle has a limited distribution in North America, in an east-west zone from southern Minnesota and Iowa through Illinois and Wisconsin, eastward to Massachusetts and New Jersey. Its occurence eastward of Indiana becomes more and more sporadic. The European form has a somewhat similar east-west range in southern Europe, western Asia, and North Africa. It ranged north as far as England and Scandinavia in relatively recent times, but is now entirely absent north of Poland.

Blanding's turtle is sometimes called the "semibox turtle," to contrast it with the true box turtles. In the adult Blanding's turtle, the plastron has a single transverse hinge, and the openings of the shell at front and back may be closed quite tightly. The hinge develops during growth, after hatching. The carapace is more highly domed than in more aquatic forms, but less so than in the box turtles. The shell is oblong, with the sides nearly parallel. The coloration is very distinctive, the carapace being dark brown with light yellow speckling, the plastron yellow with a large black blotch on each shield. The dark upper side of head and neck meet the yellow throat and chin in a sharp line. The upper jaw is conspicuously and deeply notched.

Blanding's turtle is mainly carnivorous, but takes some vegetable matter; the great bulk of its food consists of crustaceans and insects. Six to seven eggs are laid in June or July, and they may not hatch until late September. The hatchling is about as broad as long, with a surprisingly long tail.

The box turtles (genus *Terrapene;* Plate 1) are almost as terrestrial in habits as are the land tortoises proper. The several species inhabit the eastern United States, ranging from New England and Wisconsin to Florida and Texas, with additional quite distinct species in Mexico as far south as the Yucatan peninsula. Their common name is singularly appropriate, for the plastron has a crosswise hinge, and the two lobes are so adjusted to the openings at front and back that the closure of the shell is all but airtight. The species are all relatively small, being five to six inches in shell length. The relatively high dome of the carapace resembles that of the true land turtles, the "tortoises." It may well be that the high shell makes the tightly closed box, with the turtle meat inside, more difficult to crush, and thus a still better defensive retreat. The principal predators against which this defense was needed during the evolution of the box turtle were

Blanding's Turtle (*Emys blandingi*)

the puma and the wolf, the bobcat and the fox.

Dr. Carr reports that hounds, in the South, may become so habitually interested in box turtles that their effectiveness in deer-hunting is reduced. He writes that they "often carry turtles for long distance, stopping once in a while to gnaw ineffectually at the high, smooth shells and usually at last burying them in the ground. Individual hounds may become addicted to carrying box turtles . . . and one hound of my acquaintance habitually brought them in and buried them around camp." Bird dogs quite frequently point box turtles, to the great disgust of the quail-hunter, and to the evident shame of the dog when he discovers his mistake.

The eastern box turtle, *Terrapene carolina,* is a singularly beautiful creature. The brown horny plates of the carapace bear symmetrical yellow or orange markings that are very variable in extent and form. The lower shell is likewise variable in coloration, mostly dark with yellowish outer border. The head of the male is larger than that of the female, and the iris is bright red, contrasting with gray or brown in the female.

The box turtle mates soon after emergence from hibernation in the spring. The male courts the female by following her about and biting at the edges of her shell and at her head and neck. When the female is ready for copulation, the male mounts her from behind, hooks the claws of his hind feet under the edge of her carapace, and leans backward to a position somewhat beyond the vertical. Only in this position can effective contact with the anal opening of the female be made. Nesting takes place in June and July in the northeastern states and a month earlier in the Southeast. The excavation in the soil is made with the hind limbs, as is the case with all turtles, to a depth of three inches or more, scooped out at the bottom to a flask-shaped expansion in which two to seven eggs (usually four or five) are laid. The covering of the eggs and filling of the hole is an elaborate procedure, the whole process often extending over several hours. The egg-laying time is in late afternoon, and may continue to midnight. Hatching usually takes place in September or October, but hibernation in the egg may delay emergence until spring, and the hatchling young may hibernate in the nest.

The common box turtle eats both animal and vegetable food—a great variety of the former, and of the latter, notably mushrooms and berries. This makes it an animal easy to feed in captivity, and it lends itself well to the role of a children's pet. Astonishingly little is known about the habits and behavior of the young during their first two years. An ingenious means of learning a good deal about the typical day in the life of a turtle was invented by Dr. C. M. Breder, Jr. It consists in attaching a two-hundred-yard spool of thread with a wire axle to the rear of the turtle's shell (by drilling a hole in it), and letting the turtle go, preferably just where it was found. The spool unrolls as the turtle walks along, and leaves an exact record of its movements —where it stopped to eat a snail, with telltale fragments of shell, or a mushroom; how far it moved during the day; and where it spent the night.

The box-turtle group is decidedly interesting in its geographical distribution. A subspecies of the common box turtle, *Terrapene carolina bauri,* inhabits the Florida Peninsula. A somewhat larger form with the carapace flared at the rear, *Terrapene carolina major,* is found along the Gulf coast from the Florida Panhandle to eastern Texas. The three-toed box turtle, *Terrapene carolina triunguis* (Plate 7), ranges very widely in the Mississippi valley. The western box turtle, *Terrapene ornata* (Plate 2), is the common form of the plains region, overlapping the range of the common box turtle

Diamond-back Terrapin (*Malaclemys terrapin*)

in the states bordering the Mississippi. In northern Illinois it occurs in isolated populations in sandy areas along the Rock, Illinois, and Kankakee rivers, and there is a further population at Lake Maxinkukee in northern Indiana. To the west this species reaches the foothills of the Rocky Mountains. With a quite invariable complex network of yellow on its brown plastron, this species is extremely easy to distinguish from all of the forms of *Terrapene carolina.* Its habits in general are not very different from those of the Eastern species.

Nothing seems to be known of the habits of the Mexican species, *mexicana, nelsoni,* and *coahuila.*

The diamondback terrapin (*Malaclemys*), so called from the bold sculpturing of the plates of the carapace, is famous as a delicacy for the table, and pound for pound the most expensive turtle in the world. It was originally so abundant that during the eighteenth century it was fed to slaves, who once struck for relief from a diet too heavy in terrapin. The diamondback gradually found a place on the tables of the privileged, and about the end of the nineteenth century it came to be extremely fashionable. Dr. Carr remarks that "the difference between a seven-dollar diamondback and a forty-cent soft shell of the same weight is to a considerable degree a difference in the state of mind of the consumer." The fact that the prices received for this turtle by the owners of the marshes where it was collected reached ninety dollars a dozen in 1920 (when the dollar was worth a good deal more than it is today) naturally led to great interest in its artificial propagation. This in turn led to government experiments that have given us a large amount of information as to its breeding habits and rate of growth. The market price of diamondback terrapins has declined, and in the 1950's they have been quoted at thirty dollars a dozen, but with greatly reduced demand.

The average size of the fully adult diamondback may be set at eight inches in length of carapace for the female and six inches for the male. This is the greatest disparity in size between the sexes known among turtles. The hatchling young measure about one and one-fifth by one inches, and females reach sexual maturity and a salable size of about five inches in five years. The potential longevity in this species is reckoned at forty years, for old wild-caught specimens have lived seventeen years in captivity. Since the diamondback has been the subject of breeding experiments, it is well known that the females continue to produce fertile eggs for at least three years after they have been separated from the males. This is, however, a general phenomenon among turtles and apparently among

Two-headed Diamond-back Terrapin (young)

snakes; the sperm is stored in the ovarian tissues of the female.

The diamondback turtles are distributed along the Atlantic and Gulf coasts of the United States from Cape Cod to southern Texas (and perhaps farther to the south on the Mexican coast). They are quite strictly creatures of tidal waters and salt marshes, never found much farther inland than the brackish water of the coastal marshes, estuaries, bays, and sounds. In this long, narrow band of geographic range, six forms are reasonably well distinguished.

We may close our account of the most famous of turtles in gastronomic lore with the recipe for "Terrapin à la Maryland" from the *Boston Cooking-School Cook Book.**

TO PREPARE TERRAPIN for cooking, plunge [alive] into boiling water and boil 5 minutes. Lift out of water with skimmer and remove skin from feet and tail by rubbing with a towel. Draw out head with a skewer and rub off skin.

TO COOK TERRAPIN. Put in a kettle, cover with boiling salted water, add 2 slices each of carrot and onion, and a stalk of celery. Cook until meat is tender (35 to 40 minutes) which may be determined by pressing feet-meat between thumb and finger. Remove from water, cool, draw out nails from feet, cut under shell close to upper shell and remove. Empty upper shell and carefully remove and discard gall bladder, sandbags, and thick, heavy part of intestines. Any of the gall bladder would give a bitter flavor to the dish. The liver, small intestines, and eggs are used with the meat.

To three-fourths cup of white stock (for each turtle) add one and a half tablespoons of wine, and add the turtle meat with bones cut in pieces and the entrails cut in smaller pieces. Cook slowly until liquor is reduced one-half. Add liver, separated into pieces, and salt, pepper, and cayenne to taste.

Cream together a tablespoon each of flour and butter (or a little more), one half cup cream, the yolks of two eggs slightly beaten, and one teaspoon of lemon juice. Cook until thickened, add one tablespoon sherry, and serve in a deep dish, garnished with toast or puff-paste points.

The addition of a half-cup of chopped mushrooms for each turtle makes "Washington Terrapin."

* From *The Boston Cooking-School Cook Book*, by Fannie Merritt Farmer, revised edition copyright 1918 by Cora D. Perkins. Reprinted by permission of Little, Brown & Company, publisher.

The map turtles and sawbacks, genus *Graptemys,* are little differentiated from the diamondbacks, but inhabit fresh water. They have a quite different head coloration of yellow lines or angulate spots. The several species are distributed through the eastern United States to eastern Nebraska and central Texas.

The common map turtle, *Graptemys geographica,* has a wide range in the northern and central states; it is replaced in the Gulf states by other species. This turtle, which reaches a shell length of eleven inches, is strikingly a mollusk-eater, and the surfaces of both upper and lower jaws are correspondingly broad and flat.

The remaining species of this group have a more distinctly keeled shell, the keel often being raised into sharply marked knobs on each of the vertebral shields, so that it is sawlike when viewed from the side. This gives rise to the common name of "sawback." The more general term "geographic turtle," and hence "map turtle," is derived from the conspicious and intricate pattern of light markings on the shields of both carapace and plastron.

The painted turtles (genus *Chrysemys,* Plate 8) are the most abundant of the small pond turtles found in the northern United States and in the

Red-eared Terrapin (*Pseudemys scripta*)

adjacent southern parts of the provinces of Canada, from Maine and Nova Scotia to Washington and British Columbia. There is only a single species, but this has four subspecies, with quite distinctive areas of distribution. *Chrysemys picta picta,* with unmarked yellow plastron, is found on the Atlantic coastal plain; *C. picta dorsalis,* likewise with unmarked plastron, is found in the Mississippi valley from southern Illinois to Louisiana; *C. picta marginata,* with a central black marking on the under shell, ranges from the Alleghenies to the Great Lakes; and *C. picta belli,* in which the black marking extends along the margins of all the plates of the plastron, spreads through the northern plains and reaches the Pacific coast in Washington and British Columbia. The last-named subspecies is spread along the eastern face of the Rockies to New Mexico and into southeastern Arizona and adjacent northern Mexico. The occurrences to the west of the Cascades, along the Pacific coast, are sporadic, and are probably the result of introductions by man.

In these handsome small turtles, yellow bands cross the dark olive carapace, the shields along the margin of the shell are brightly marked with red, the limbs are marked with narrow red bands, and the head and neck have a pattern of sharply marked yellow lines.

The most abundantly represented genus of emydid turtles in North America is *Pseudemys* (Plate 10). These are known throughout the South as terrapins. They are clearly the close relatives of the little Northern painted turtle, broadly overlapping its geographic range. Their distribution extends far beyond the other familiar types of American emydid turtles into Mexico and even South America.

The abundant Middle Western forms of the species *Pseudemys scripta,* known as Troost's terrapin and the red-eared terrapin, or as "sliders," have had a curious history of confusion with related forms for a hundred years because the males may become black with increasing age. Once this was properly understood, the related forms could be discerned as a chain, from *P. scripta scripta* on the Atlantic coastal plain, through *P. scripta elegans* in the Mississippi valley and *P. scripta troosti* in the upper reaches of the Cumberland and Tennessee rivers to *P. scripta gaigeae* in western Texas. The females and young of both *elegans* and *troosti* have an elongate bright red band behind the eye, which provides occasion for the name "red-eared terrapin." Dr. Fred Cagle has made a special study of these turtles, and the following account of a typical emydid life history is drawn largely from his papers.

Dr. Cagle examined more than 8000 specimens of the form *elegans*. The largest populations develop in quiet waters full of vegetation. Smaller numbers are found in waters with little natural plant or animal food; they are able to feed on leaves and other vegetable matter dropping in from above. The species feeds on both animals and plants, taking what is most available. The drying up of ponds may cause extreme concentrations of turtles, for they do not readily undertake land journeys. During spring and late summer, however, there is a tendency to disperse over land, so that all suitable waters are likely to be reached. Juveniles are most abundant in shallow water and in small ponds. The older and larger individuals tend to move into larger and deeper bodies of water.

Each adult turtle has a home range, to which it attempts to return if it is removed. When turtles are studied by trapping, the same individual will be caught repeatedly. The individual home area seems to be about a hundred feet in diameter (or in width along the shore). These turtles compose the great majority of the fresh-water turtle populations in the Mississippi valley.

The elaborate courtship performance takes place in spring and fall. The sexually mature male engages in an active search for a female partner, and takes no interest in other males or in young individuals. Just how the adult males are infallibly able to distinguish these undesired partners is not known. When a female is encountered, the male maneuvers himself in the water to a position directly in front of her and facing her; he then places the forefeet close together and vibrates his claws against the female's head. She swims slowly forward against the vibrating claws and feet, so that the male must back away by means of reversed swimming motions of his hind feet. When the female is receptive to the male's advances, she sinks slowly down; the male swims over her and mounts her from behind, grasping her shell with the claws of all four feet. Union is effected by the tail of the male being curved down and brought beneath that of the female. This pattern of behavior is quite different from that of other turtles found in the same waters.

The egg-laying period is mainly from mid-June to early July. The nest is a hole in the soil, dug with the hind feet, usually not far from the water. When the soil is hard, the female softens it by means of fluid from the cloacal bladders. The time required for excavating the nest varies greatly, ranging from thirty minutes to more than three hours, though the longer time may have been the result of the turtle having been disturbed by the observer. The eggs, averaging about nine in number but vary-ing from two to twenty-three, are laid at regular intervals in the bottom of the flask-shaped hole. The hole is then filled by means of the hind limbs, the soil being further moistened by the fluid from the bladders. Kneaded and pushed into place, the earth fill looks like a mud ball thrown against the ground. Such nests are easily recognized by the turtle-egg collector with a little experience.

Incubation requires about ten weeks, but the temperature of the summer season affects the time, so that the last of the eggs to be deposited in July may not reach the hatching stage before the onset of cool weather in the fall. The eggs may then carry through the winter with the embryos near full size, and hatch the following spring. The turtle accomplishes hatching by pushing forward against the front of the shell, which may be cut by the "egg tooth" or by the claws, or may merely be forcibly ruptured. Once its head is free, the baby turtle remains in this position and makes pumping movements with the head and neck. It is thought that this may aid in drawing the contents of the yolk sac into the body through the umbilical opening, and this process may require twenty-four hours or more. The hatchlings ordinarily do not feed during the few weeks they are active in the fall after emergence, the yolk supply in the intestine being sufficient to carry them through the winter.

The hatchling turtles measure a little more than an inch in length of carapace, which is nearly as wide as long. Once feeding begins in spring, growth is rapid, though variable. Specimens three inches long are two or three years old, as shown by their growth rings, and subsequent growth is at the rate of about a half-inch per growing season. Sexual maturity is reached by males at a length of plastron of about four inches, females at six inches.

The daily activities of a red-eared terrapin outside the breeding season are feeding, basking, and sleeping. Food is taken at various times during the day, though mostly in early morning and late afternoon. Basking is at its height in the mid-forenoon and late afternoon. In order to bask, the turtle climbs out of the water onto a log or rock or muskrat nest, or even just onto the bank. Then it stretches the front legs well out to the sides and the hind legs well to the rear. Basking serves two functions: the raising of the body temperature, which increases the rate of digestion; and the drying of the skin, which is thought to cause the leeches, which attach themselves where the skin is softest, to drop off. The broad dark shell absorbs heat rapidly in the sun, and the turtle returns to the water when its optimum temperature has been reached. Turtles confined and exposed to the midday sun would be killed. Sleeping

Chicken Turtle (*Deirochelys reticularia*)

is quite different from basking, for the eyes are closed and a sleeping individual may be approached, whereas basking turtles are alert and slide off their log at the slightest disturbance.

Everywhere in the United States the red-eared terrapin has a winter hibernation period; this is of three to four months' duration in Louisiana and of five to six in Illinois. The emergence from hibernation is quite strictly controlled by the water temperature, which must be above 50 degrees Fahrenheit to bring the turtles out. The optimum temperature seems to be about 85 degrees Fahrenheit, to judge from the behavior of captive turtles and from the numbers caught in traps on days with varying water temperature. In the northern part of the range of this turtle, as in Illinois, there are two well-marked breeding seasons, in May and September, and in these months the adult turtles in the population seem to move about much more actively than during the intervening period.

The physiological meaning of the hibernation of aquatic turtles underwater is not yet clarified, and it is not certain at what temperature and for what lengths of time the breathing of air may be suspended. Doubtless some oxygen is obtained through the skin from the gases dissolved in water.

The capacity to eat a great variety of animal and vegetable food is of great significance in the evident success of the red-eared terrapin. In captivity it eats almost all leafy vegetables and most fruits, and literally any animal food offered. Its food in nature consists of tadpoles, crayfishes, mollusks, larvae of aquatic insects, and small fishes.

In the northern part of their range the adult sliders have few enemies other than man, who may destroy them in the mistaken notion that they are harmful to fish populations. In the Gulf states the alligator and the alligator gar prey on these turtles to a significant extent. The hatchling young and the first-years crop of juveniles are much more vulnerable to predation. The destruction by predators naturally begins with the eggs, which are devoured by snakes and by all predaceous mammals. In northern Louisiana we found the intestines of a water moccasin packed with the horny plates of baby turtles, evidently from a concentrated diet of hatchlings.

Slider turtles or red-eared terrapin are the most abundant turtles in ponds, ditches, lakes, and quiet streams throughout their range. In bodies of water examined by Dr. Cagle the sliders comprised 71 to 87 per cent of all turtles found there.

The last of the types of North American turtles of this family is the chicken turtle, *Deirochelys reticularia,* which is distributed along the Atlantic and Gulf coasts to eastern Texas, and to the north through Louisiana into Arkansas. It is thought to be more closely related to the painted turtle than to the terrapins. The chicken turtle has an elongate shell, with nearly straight sides sloped together toward the front as seen from above or below. The carapace is olive or olive-brown, with a very distinctive wide-meshed reticulation of narrow, light lines. The plastron is almost unmarked yellow. Carr reports a hatchling from Louisiana as having a carapace one and one-tenth inches long and one inch wide.

The chicken turtle is essentially a species of quiet waters. Little is known of its habits, but it has been demonstrated that it wanders rather freely on land (as shown by the number of crushed shells found on highways), and it does not appear to have a fixed breeding or egg-laying season.

In the Americas outside the United States several species of the terrapin genus *Pseudemys* are to be found in Mexico and through Central America to Colombia, with one in far-off southern Brazil, Uruguay, and adjacent Argentina, as remarked above. The quite distinct genus *Geoemyda,* which is well represented in southeastern Asia, is also found in tropical America, from southern Mexico to Ecuador and Venezuela.

Turning from the Americas to the Old World, the remarkable impoverishment of the fresh-water turtle fauna of Europe requires consideration. Southeastern Asia and eastern Asia have a rich variety of turtles, including no less than seventeen genera of the family Emydidae—even more, therefore, than the nine types of emydids in southeastern North America. Europe, with only two genera and three species, compares with western North America, where the sole fresh-water turtle is *Clemmys mar-*

morata. The European turtles are the pond turtle, *Emys orbicularis,* and an eastern and western species of *Clemmys, C. caspica* in the southeast and *C. leprosa* in Spain and Portugal.

The turtles of southeastern Asia, from India and Ceylon through the East Indies, and those of eastern China and Japan, would be difficult to describe were it not for the excellent review by Malcolm Smith in the second edition of the reptile volumes of the *Fauna of British India.* We are thus adequately provided with means of identifying and naming the Asiatic turtles; but our knowledge of the habits of these creatures is extremely deficient. Some of the larger forms exceed the largest American turtles of this group in length of carapace (rarely more than sixteen inches in our species), the four largest Asiatic forms reaching seventeen, eighteen, twenty-three, and twenty-four inches.

The first of the genera, *Cyclemys,* is found in Assam, Burma, and eastward to the southernmost Chinese territory, the island of Hainan, and through Sumatra and Borneo to the Philippines. These turtles have a solid bridge between plastron and carapace in juvenile specimens. With age, the bridge is invaded by tendinous tissue, and a somewhat imperfect single hinge develops between the pectoral and abdominal plates, involving the suture between the hypoplastral bones.

In the related genus *Cuora* the hinge across the bridge is present from hatching, and the two lobes of the plastron can be tightly closed over the openings at front and back. This corresponds strikingly with the box turtles of eastern North America and thus clearly illustrates a parallel evolution of such hinge development. There are four species of Asiatic box turtles: one widespread, ranging from Burma to the Philippines; two in southern China, Formosa, and Hainan; and one in the Chinese province of Yunnan. The common Malayan box turtle, *Cuora amboinensis,* inhabits lowland areas: ponds, marshes, and flooded rice fields. It feeds entirely on vegetable matter. It is of a timid and quiet disposition, and when first caught and kept in a terrarium is excessively shy, closing the shell as soon as it is approached. It seems to eat only small amounts of food at a time. It lays only a few eggs, which are of relatively large size. A turtle with a carapace eight inches long lays eggs measuring one and four-fifths inches long by about one and two-fifths inches broad.

The next genus, *Geoemyda,* is represented in tropical America as well as in Asia. It includes species that have taken to terrestrial life as well as forms that are typically riparian and aquatic. There are six American species and nine in the Oriental Region. The mainly terrestrial forms are easily recognizable by hind feet that are more or less club-shaped, with webbing greatly reduced between the toes, whereas in the aquatic forms the feet are flattened and the webs well developed.

The aquatic forms are *G. trijuga,* widespread in India and Ceylon, and *G. grandis,* which has a more eastern range in southeastern Asia. The latter species is one of the regular inhabitants of the "Tortoise Temple" in Bangkok. *Geoemyda trijuga* is divided into five well-defined subspecies: one in the central part of the Indian Peninsula, one in Travancore, one in Ceylon and the southeastern tip of the Peninsula, one to the northwest of Calcutta, and the last in Burma. The Burmese form is reported to feed on water plants, especially on *Vallisneria* (eel grass). The form in Ceylon is said to exhibit great adaptability in its habits. Some specimens are commonly found in ponds, basking on logs or stones that project above the surface. If disturbed, they take immediate refuge in the water. Other individuals are more terrestrial in habits, and wander well away from water. As far as is known from examination of stomachs, this species is exclusively vegetarian, but there are reports of scavenging and omnivorous food habits.

The genus *Geoclemys,* which has only the single species *hamiltoni,* occurs in northern India from Sind (now in Pakistan) to Bengal. It is said to be abundant in the lower Ganges. Its habits are carnivorous. *Damonia* (for which the substitute name *Malayemys* has been proposed) has also only a single species, *subtrijuga.* This species is found in Siam, Indo-China, the Malay Peninsula, and Java. The broad crushing surfaces of the jaws are associated with the carnivorous diet, in which mollusks are reported as a considerable element.

Hieremys, again with a single species, *annandalei,* is one of the larger forms, with a maximum known carapace length of eighteen inches. This species is abundant in Siam, where it inhabits marshes and the slower-flowing reaches of the rivers. It ranges farther into Cambodia and the northern part of the Malay Peninsula. In captivity this turtle is easily tamed. It feeds on water plants, fruits, or almost any vegetable. Dr. Smith reports:

Numbers of them are usually to be seen in the Tortoise Temple in Bangkok, an honour which they share with *Geoemyda grandis,* a species of much the same size and general external features. No particular form of worship is attached to these tortoises. They are presented to the temple in accordance with the tenets of the Buddhist religion, by which a life saved gains merit for the saver in the next world.

Having saved the life of the tortoise, the obligation ceases, and no particular care is taken of them in the temple afterwards.*

Notochelys platynota, which takes its name from the flattened form of the carapace, is still another monotypic genus of Asiatic emydid turtles, split off from the older *omnium gatherum Cyclemys.* This species is found in southern Indo-China and the Malay Peninsula and through the Malayan islands. Major Flower writes of it that it lives in ponds and swampy jungles. When alarmed, it hisses after the manner of tortoises in general, and like many of them voids its excrement when picked up. In captivity, however, it quickly becomes tame and soon discards this disagreeable habit. It feeds voraciously on almost any vegetable, but prefers fruit, of which it will get through a large quantity in a day.

The black pond turtle, *Geoclemys hamiltoni,* is descriptively named, for it is black above, and the yellow plastron of the young has a dark pattern that gradually increases in proportion to the yellow. It is a small species, being less than seven inches in length of carapace. It ranges from southern Burma

*From *Fauna of British India: Reptilia and Amphibia,* Vol. I, by Malcolm Smith, 1931.

eastward and southward to Cochin China and to the larger East Indian islands.

The species of *Clemmys* in the Oriental Region are *mutica* of southern China, Formosa, and Hainan, and *bealii,* of much the same region. To the north there are *japonica* in Japan and *nigricans* in China. Beal's *Clemmys* has a striking head coloration, with red longitudinal lines on the neck and two pairs of yellow, black-centered eye marks on the back of the head.

The common small emydid turtle of China, *Chinemys reevesi,* scarcely reaches a length of carapace of five inches. It ranges northward from southern China to Japan. This small creature lays from four to six eggs, usually in sandy localities. Its close relative in South China, *Chinemys kwangtungensis,* has only two eggs in a clutch. A second common Chinese turtle is *Ocadia sinensis,* ranging a little farther to the south, into Hainan and Indo-China.

The next group of Asiatic emydids is *Morenia,* with two species, *ocellata* and *petersi,* the first from Burma and the second from Bengal. The Burmese species reaches a length of a little more than eight inches. Theobald (an early collector in the Oriental Region) reports that this form is strictly aquatic, "but that it is often left dry by the drying up in hot weather of the inundated plains, in which

Turtles sunning on a log

MASLOWSKI AND GOODPASTER: NATIONAL AUDUBON

situations incredible numbers are captured for food by the Burmese, who fire the grass for the purpose."

Another genus with a single species, *Hardella thurgi,* reaches a length of carapace of about twenty inches in females, with the males much smaller. This species is found in the Ganges and Brahmaputra river systems in India. It frequents slow-moving and stagnant waters, and feeds entirely on vegetation. Large numbers are brought to the market in Calcutta for food. The turtles are caught by diving for them and feeling for them in the bottom mud, where they live with soft-shelled turtles and with *Kachuga tectum.*

The genus *Kachuga,* with six forms, is confined to northern India and Burma. The three-lined kachuga often exceeds a length of twenty inches in females, the males being somewhat smaller. All of these turtles appear to be purely herbivorous.

The wide-ranging monotypic *Batagur baska* is found in Bengal, southeastern Asia, the Malay Peninsula, and Sumatra. It is the largest of the Asiatic emydids. The length of the carapace may reach at least twenty-three inches. It is herbivorous and entirely aquatic. The breeding habits of this species have been reported by Maxwell in an official report of turtle-egg collecting on the sandbanks of the Irrawaddy delta. As recounted by Malcolm Smith, the laying season lasts from the beginning of January to early March, and every day, regardless of the tide, the tortoises come out of the sea and sun themselves on the sand from about 2:00 P.M. until dark. They assemble in herds of from one to five hundred, lying quite close to one another. "Every night," Dr. Smith writes, "some of them lay their eggs, between ten and thirty in number, in the sand of the beach, digging a hole for them from 1½ to 2 feet deep, above the influence of the tides. On no consideration will the tortoises allow themselves to be approached: directly they wind a human being they disappear into the sea. After the tortoises have been laying for about six weeks, a raid is made on the banks, and men poking about with sticks easily find the nests and take the eggs." He further reports that they measure about three inches in length and a little more than half that in breadth and weigh about three ounces. The period of incubation is said to be seventy days.

About fifty eggs are laid by each female. They are deposited in three lots at intervals of about two weeks. During this period the turtles eat nothing, so that on their return to the tidal estuaries they are ravenously hungry. There they are trapped in large numbers by the Burmans for the sake of their flesh. The chief method employed is a form of basket trap baited with the leaves of the thamé tree.

The Land Tortoises
(*Family Testudinidae*)

In the quotations from Malcolm Smith anent the water turtles of southeastern Asia, "tortoises" appears repeatedly as their common appellation. It will evidently be a very long time before the English language as a whole can be brought to adopt "tortoise" exclusively for the club-footed and dome-shelled land forms that come to water only to drink or bathe. Nevertheless, in view of the greater variety of species found in America, British English must be brought to the use of *turtle* for any member of the group, not merely for the paddle-limbed marine forms. And the next step, which now also seems inevitable, is the restriction of "tortoise" to the family Testudinidae.

As indicated above, the tortoises (in this specific sense) are adapted to walking on land by their club-shaped feet, in which the toe bones of the middle toes are reduced to two. The limbs are covered with hard scales that often have a bony core. The shell is high-domed in all but a very few forms. The openings at front and rear of the shell are usually neatly closed by the retracted limbs, on which the enlarged scales may be defensively mingled with still larger spines. The head is entirely withdrawn, and the elbows meet in the middle in front of it; the claws of the forelimbs overlap the posterior edge of the opening at the front, and the hard-scaled soles of the hind feet are presented at the openings at the rear. One form has the front lobe of its plastron hinged.

There are about forty different kinds of land turtles that may properly be called land tortoises or

Texas Gopher Turtle (*Gopherus berlandieri*)

ISABELLE HUNT CONANT

Gopher Tortoise (*Gopherus polyphemus*)

just tortoises, and these have been classified into seven genera. Of these, *Gopherus,* including the three gopher tortoises, is found in the southern United States and adjacent Mexico. One, *Pyxis,* is confined to Madagascar. *Testudo,* which includes the gigantic island forms of the Galapagos Islands and of the islands in the Indian Ocean (*T. gigantea,* Plate 15), is found also in South America (*T. denticulata,* Plate 14), southern Asia (*T. elegans,* Plate 9), Africa, and Madagascar. The remaining genera, *Geniochersus, Homopus, Malacochersus,* and *Kinixys* (Plate 11) are exclusively African.

We may begin with an account of the tortoises of the principal genus, *Testudo.* There are several small forms in southern Europe and North Africa that are familiar throughout Europe and the British Isles as pets, often acclimated in walled gardens to a life of relative freedom. These are the common European tortoise (unhappily misnamed *graeca*); Hermann's tortoise (Plate 13), found in both southeastern and southwestern Europe; and the margined tortoise, *Testudo marginata,* which appears to be confined to Greece.

Tortoises have become symbols of leisurely movement, of persistence, as in Aesop's fable of the hare and the tortoise, and of longevity. The small European tortoises share the capacity for living to great age for which the giant island forms are especially famous. Major Flower has searched the longevity records for the common tortoise, *Testudo graeca* (Plate 12), of which a specimen is known to have been kept by Archbishop Laud in the garden of Lambeth Palace, and another by the Bishops of Peterborough. In both cases, the actual records available prove to be contradictory.

So far as the records for Archbishop Laud's tortoise go, an old label is attached by a string to a shell preserved in Lambeth Palace. Although almost illegible, it can be deciphered. It states: "The shell of a Tortoise which was put into the garden at Lambeth by Abp. Laud in the year 1633, where it remained until 1753, when it was unfortunately killed by the negligence of a gardener." A second label states that the tortoise died in 1730 (at the age of 107 years). Its death was caused by frost, for "a labourer in the garden . . . for a trifling wager, dug it up from its winter retreat and neglected to replace it."

The Peterborough tortoise had been commonly reported to have lived for 220 years. The records are again conflicting and inadequate; they are connected with a well-mounted specimen kept in a glass case in the hall of the episcopal palace. When everything is considered, this tortoise lived at least from 1757 to 1819, or 62 years; on the other hand it may have lived from 1747 to 1839, or 92 years. The mounted specimen in question is a remarkably large *Testudo graeca,* the length of carapace in a straight line being ten inches.

The most notable and charming account of such a tortoise naturalized in an English garden is that of Gilbert White in his classic *Natural History and Antiquities of Selborne.* He gives a good account of its feeding habits, daily activities, and annual hibernation.

The Seychelles Islands of the Indian Ocean and other islands to the south, toward Madagascar, were the homes of at least three races of gigantic tortoises, well named *Testudo gigantea.* The largest known shell measures forty-nine and one-half inches in length (in a straight line). This came from the island of Saint Anne in the Seychelles, where it is reasonably certain to have lived for about sixty-eight years. The longest life of any tortoise of which there is authetic record is that of "Marion's Tortoise," a *Testudo gigantea* taken when full grown from its native island to the island of Mauritius, where no tortoises occur, by the French explorer Marion de Fresne, in 1766. When the British captured Mauritius in 1810, a large tortoise, which was quite certainly the survivor of the five specimens that had been brought by Marion de Fresne, was officially handed over to the British troops by the surrendering French forces. This tortoise continued to live in the artillery barracks at Port Louis until 1918, when it fell through a gun emplacement and was killed. It had exhibited signs of advanced age since 1891, and was completely blind at the time of its death. Its shell and stuffed skin are preserved in the British Museum (Natural History) in London. This turtle, then, provides an authentic age record of 152 years; since it was an adult at the time of its capture, in 1766, its actual age may be estimated at not less than 180 years.

The populations of the huge turtles that are still found on the Galapagos Islands are very much reduced in numbers. The ten forms (or perhaps more) are each found on a single island or are confined to one or another of the nearby isolated volcanoes of the largest of the islands, Albemarle, which appears to have become a single island by the flowing together of lava from the craters of the five volcanoes that compose it. In the seventeenth century, when the islands were first discovered, the number of tortoises seems to have been almost unbelievable. The slopes of the great volcanoes were said to have been black with them. Speaking of this island in his *New Voyage around the World* (1617), William Dampier declared that "the land-turtles are here so numerous that five or six hundred men might subsist on them for several months without any other sort of provisions. They are so extraordinarily large and fat, and so sweet, that no pullet eats more pleasantly." Charles Darwin spent some five weeks there in the year 1835 in the course of the voyage of the *Beagle*. His observations on the birds and reptiles of the islands were of crucial importance in turning his thoughts toward the "origin of species," for in these islands he recognized that species had been developed from island to island and in adjustment to different modes of life on a single island. It has gradually become evident that each of the islands is inhabited by a distinct form of tortoise. It has been very difficult to decide on the earliest name for these island forms, and the latest authors have assembled them under the single species *Testudo elephantopus,* regarding the ten island forms as representative "subspecies." Other authors, however, reckon the Albemarle Island populations as representing five distinct forms (or even six), and, giving more weight to the differences between the various forms, regard them all as "species." Under either classification the turtles remain the same.

Specimens of the Indefatigable Island tortoise have relatively the broadest shells among the Galapagos forms, and may reach the largest size. Two such tortoises, which weighed thirty pounds each when brought to the Brookfield Zoo near Chicago in 1929, had grown to nearly four hundred pounds in 1955.

The near-extermination of the giant tortoises of the Galapagos Islands is a sad chapter in the history of man's destruction of the wildlife of the world. Charles Darwin's visit to the archipelago occurred at the height of the great era of American whaling in the eastern Pacific, which was interrupted by the

BOB EAST : GILLOON

Galapagos Tortoise (*Testudo porteri*)

American Civil War and which came to an end with the development of the petroleum industry. The whaling voyages with sailing vessels required absence from the home port for three and even four years; fresh meat on such a voyage was of the utmost importance to the health of the men and the success of the enterprise. The giant turtles were palatable, and had the great advantage that they could be kept alive in the hold of the ship for months. In order to make use of this food supply, great numbers of the turtles were taken on shipboard from the islands. Dr. C. H. Townsend examined the logbooks of old-time whaling vessels and found records of more than 10,000 large "turpin" taken by the whalers from 1831 to 1868 in a total of 189 visits to the islands. This is obviously only a small fraction of the turtles taken during the century or more of whaling in the waters off western South America.

Far more directly destructive was the exploitation of the turtles for their oil by the Ecuadorians in the twentieth century. But neither the whalers nor the oil-gatherers were the most destructive. The earliest human settlements on the islands were made from Ecuador, with a penal settlement founded on Charles Island in 1832, with colonies on Chatam, Albemarle, and Indefatigable, with attempts at agricultural development and at establishment of fisheries. These colonies brought domestic dogs and cats, together with mice and rats, and, to some islands, cattle, donkeys, and horses. Of these, the cats and dogs promptly took to life "on their own" and spread over the islands. Of course they could not harm the big turtles, but alas, they could search out the eggs and eat them, and the feral dogs, nearly as big as coyotes, could prey on the baby turtles. The one large island, Narborough, that has never had a human colony has none of these feral domestic animals; on it the great lava flow of 1825 must have nearly exterminated the native race of turtles, known only from a single specimen collected by Rollo H. Beck in 1906 in an almost superhuman exploit that took him to the interior of the island over the still-fresh and incredibly rough lava.

The Leatherback Sea Turtle

(Family Dermochelidae)

To turn from the dome-shelled land tortoises to the sea turtles is to present the extremes of adjustment to life in the sea on the one hand and life on land on the other. There are two very distinctive families of sea turtles. The first of these is represented by only the giant leatherback, *Dermochelys coriacea,* which is found in all tropical seas and strays out of the warmer zones to the coasts of England and Maine, South Africa and the Argentine. In the tropics its breeding places are for the most part unknown. The only records for the Atlantic available to us are the old one for the coast of Jamaica (in 1846) published by Philip H. Gosse in *A Naturalist's Sojourn in Jamaica* (1851), and the Florida record for June, 1947, reported by E. Ross Allen to the principal American authority on turtles, Archie F. Carr.

This remarkable creature reaches a far greater length and weight than does any land tortoise or fresh-water turtle. It is said to approach a ton in weight, and an over-all length of ten feet; but really authentic measurements seem to indicate that this is an exaggeration, and that a seven-and-a-half-foot specimen weighing twelve hundred pounds is very large indeed.

The leatherback is very much like the other sea turtles in general body form and especially in the form of the forelimbs, which are converted into enormous flippers, with a spread of about nine feet in a seven-foot turtle. Otherwise, the smooth skin without any external shell and the seven lengthwise ridges on the back contribute to its streamlined appearance. There is a bony shell consisting of irregular platelets of bone embedded in the skin. The hatchling specimens have the top of the head, the flippers, the back, and the underside covered with small scales. Those along the dermal ridges and the

M. W. F. TWEEDIE

Leather-back Sea Turtle (*Dermochelys coriacea*)

ridges that correspond to the phalanges buried in the webs are enlarged and in regular series, those between quite irregular.

The nesting and egg-laying of the leatherback appear to provide the only occasion on which individuals of this species come to land. The digging of the hole for the eggs and the deposition of a clutch of about eighty are not especially different from the processes in other sea turtles (see below) or indeed in turtles in general.

The peculiarities of structure of the leatherback shell are such as to have given rise to a variety of theories as to its relations to other families of turtles. One theory is that it is an independent adjustment of an ancient fresh-water type to life in the sea, and that all of the resemblances to other sea turtles are the result of the molding influences of the stresses of continuous swimming, which are alike in the two groups. Other anatomists regard the leatherback as an aberrant offshoot of a generalized ancestral sea-turtle stock.

The leatherback affords an extraordinarily difficult problem for museum preservation. The flesh and skin, and even the skeleton, are so saturated with oil that it is extremely difficult to degrease them. A mounted specimen may drip oil for years and is presently "grease-burned" and ready for the incinerator. By far the most elaborate study of the leatherback is that of P. E. P. Deraniyagala, Director of the Colombo Museum in Ceylon. He made a fortunate find of a nest of fresh eggs, and described the development of the embryo in a series of papers in the *Ceylon Journal of Sciences,* beginning in 1930, which were summarized in a fat volume, *The Tetrapod Reptiles of Ceylon,* in 1939.

The True Sea Turtles

(*Family Chelonidae*)

The green turtle, the loggerhead, the olive-backed turtle, and the tortoise-shell turtle are true denizens of salt water, and, like the leatherback, come ashore only to lay eggs. Curiously, however, the green turtle may come ashore to bask, almost like the fresh-water turtles on a riverbank, on remote and uninhabited islands.

These turtles all have true shells, in which the horny plates and the bony ones beneath them correspond to those of other turtles. They are all streamlined in so far as a turtle can be, and swim by means of powerful flippers in front. The head is too large

to be withdrawn beneath the shell, but the vertebrae of the neck show that they belong to the vertical-withdrawal type.

The best known of the sea turtles is the green turtle, *Chelonia,* which has been esteemed as food for centuries. It is mainly confined to tropical waters, and the populations of the Pacific and Atlantic are regarded as distinct races. The great number of eggs laid, and the correspondingly large number of hatchling turtles, do not seem to prevent the steady decline of the sea-turtle populations. Even on the remote Galapagos Islands we found every single turtle nest dug out and the eggs devoured by feral dogs. The female turtle, moving inland to find a site above the tidemark for her eggs, leaves behind a trail like that of a small caterpillar tractor. Thus by walking along the beach we could see every egg-laying site, and they had all been dug out. Only on short beaches enclosed between walls of rough lava and on the beaches of little offshore islands were the turtle eggs safe for development and replenishment of the population. The number of eggs laid is very large (up to two hundred), and it is not surprising that they should be highly esteemed for food. They are somewhat objectionable to most North Americans or Europeans because the albumen, or "white," does not coagulate in cooking but remains clear and jellylike. The taste is unexceptionable, but we do not ordinarily eat eggs with the white apparently uncooked and the yolk coagulated. There is, however, no disagreeable flavor. The number of eggs that may be collected on the beaches of offshore islands in the tropics is astonishing. The reports of the turtle-egg industry on the little islands of Talang Talang, off northwestern Borneo, include an account of the whole process of egg-laying and breeding. Edward Banks reports as follows in the *Sarawak Museum Journal* for 1937:

> With the exception of one or two visits yearly from the Hawksbill Turtles (*Chelone imbricata*), valued for its Tortoiseshell, the only species to visit the islands is the Green or Edible Turtle (*Chelone mydas*) and it is an eerie sight on a moonlight night at high tide to see scores of these four-hundred-pound monsters emerge from the sea, black and shiny like so many enormous leeches or slugs, struggle slowly up the beach before depositing their eggs in the sand above high-water mark.

Both the modification of the limbs for life in the sea and the tremendous weight are serious handicaps to the female green turtle as she struggles over the beach. Gripping the sand with fore and hind flippers, she shoves and pushes herself forward a few feet, then stops and heaves what can only be

described as a tremendous sigh. The labored breathing is caused by two factors: first, the great effort required to drag her hundreds of pounds against the friction of the sand; and secondly, the effort required merely to raise the heavy body so that the lungs can be expanded and filled. As a matter of fact, the work involved in just breathing is so great that captive green turtles kept out of water die of suffocation if not turned over on their backs.

When the turtle has passed the high-tide mark, she scrapes a shallow depression, scattering the sand with fore and hind feet. Then the digging of the nest begins in earnest. Using the hind feet alternately as scoops, she digs a flask-shaped hole roughly eighteen inches deep. After the hundred or more eggs are laid, the nest is filled merely by pushing sand in with the hind feet. Once more the turtle begins a laborious trip across the beach, but, before doing so, she scatters sand in every direction with her flippers to obliterate surface indications of the nest.

By dawn the female is once more in the comfort and safety of the sea. Usually many males are swimming immediately offshore, and one of these will mate with the female just as soon as she leaves the nesting beach.

The harvesting of the turtle eggs is now a Sarawak government monopoly and is strictly regulated to insure that many of the eggs hatch, sustaining the turtle population. The natives who dig the eggs have an almost superstitious regard for the turtles. Indeed, the suggestion that one of the females be killed is greeted with the horror that should have met the idea of killing the goose that laid the golden eggs. Nevertheless the number of eggs harvested at Talang Talang is astronomical.

Egg-laying there takes place throughout the year, but with a well-marked seasonal cycle. The minimum number of eggs taken in a month in 1933 on one of the islands was 8401. This occurred in January, the number rising month by month to the astonishing total of 147,259 in August, and then dropping off again steadily to the mere 25,831 of December. The largest number of eggs recorded for this island for a single month during the period from 1927 to 1936 was 423,048 (in July, 1934). In 1934 the total of turtle eggs collected was given as 1,790,370.

The loggerhead (genus *Caretta*) is distinguished from the green turtle by its much larger head and by details of the skeleton and of the external plates of the shell. In its streamlined form, its oarlike flippers, and its mode of swimming, it is much like the other marine turtles. Unlike the leatherback, both loggerhead and green turtle seem to come ashore to

Green Turtle depositing eggs

sun themselves, in addition to laying eggs. The carnivorous feeding of the loggerhead perhaps gives it the reputation of being less desirable for human food than the alga-eating green turtle. As in the green turtle, there are distinctive differences between the Atlantic and Pacific populations. As the gigantic green turtles of more than five hundred pounds in weight seem to be a phenomenon of the past, so is the size of the loggerheads now reduced, and even a weight of three hundred pounds is rare. The loggerhead is distributed farther to the north and south, out of the tropics, both in its general range and in actual breeding range, for it formerly nested as far north as Virginia. The usual breeding season on the Florida and Georgia beaches seems to be at about the "first full moon in June," but early nests may be found in April and late ones in August.

The nests are placed above high-tide mark, and salt water may destroy those that are accidentally placed too low. The sand is excavated by the use of the hind flippers alone, cupped so as to make effective scoops, and dug down to a depth of one and a half or two feet. The tail and cloaca are then placed over the hole, and the eggs are extruded at the rate of a dozen or more a minute. The number of eggs in a single laying varies from a low of 60 to more than 150. The duration of incubation varies with the site of the nest and the season, ranging all the way from thirty to sixty-five days. The hatchlings rest briefly in the shell and then pour out of

←

Green Turtle preparing to lay eggs (*Chelonia mydas*)

the nest in a mass and head toward the most open horizon, and downhill. What becomes of the vast numbers of the juveniles that reach the water is not exactly known, but we may guess that almost every predaceous creature in the sea takes a toll of them. Very few young or small-sized specimens are found.

The poor reputation of the flesh of the loggerhead as food is scarcely deserved. It is said to be tough and stringy in adults, but it can be ground and then forms an acceptable substitute for ground beef. The prejudice does not extend to the eggs, which are eaten everywhere in the West Indies, and were formerly sold, in season, in the streets of Savannah and Charleston, where they were especially valued for cake-making.

If this great visitor to the Atlantic and Gulf coast is to be preserved, it is urgent that effective measures for its protection should be devised and enforced.

The third type of sea turtle of the family Chelonidae, the ridley or bastard turtle, seems at first glance very similar to the loggerhead. With more careful examination, it is convincingly distinguished by the gray color of the shell and upper parts of the limbs; the four enlarged marginals on each side, each with a pore at the rear; the two pairs of prefrontal shields on the top of the head; and the rounded instead of elongate shape of the shell as seen from above. From the green turtle it is distinguished by the five (or more) pairs of the lateral shields of the carapace.

It is surprising to find that this turtle is almost entirely limited in distribution to the Gulf of Mexico. It reaches both coasts of Florida, but in spite of entering the Gulf Stream at the Florida Straits, it is unknown in the Bahamas. So many young ridleys are carried by the Gulf Stream that individuals stray out of it to the coast of New England, while others are carried on across the Atlantic to the shores of the British Isles and Europe.

The ridley is the smallest of the sea turtles, reaching maturity at a length of shell of about two feet, and the record shell length of the Atlantic ridley is only twenty-eight inches. Even more remarkable is the fact that almost nothing at all is positively known of the breeding habits of this turtle. The Florida fishermen regard it as a hybrid between the loggerhead and the green turtle (or perhaps the tortoise-shell turtle), and a kind of "mule" that does not propagate its own kind. This makes no sense when it is remembered that the Atlantic ridley is the representative of the much larger Pacific form, which ranges from Ceylon and the East Indies to the Pacific coasts of the Americas. These two species, or three if the East Indian one proves to be distinguishable from the one on the American Pacific coast, compose the genus *Lepidochelys,* distinguished es-

pecially by the pores on the marginal shields. In the East Indies the species *Lepidochelys olivacea* appears to be more abundant than the loggerhead.

The distribution of the sea turtles is little understood, but they all seem to reach such remote islands as the Midway chain in the Pacific and Ascension in the South Atlantic. The Atlantic and Indo-Pacific forms seem to be potentially in breeding contact around South Africa, certainly not around Cape Horn. But this potential does not seem to be realized with the present zonation of the sea in temperature belts, for the Atlantic forms are clearly distinguishable by minor features of color and shape and shell characteristics.

Three hundred years ago, when all of the sea turtles were vastly more abundant, their migration to and from breeding grounds was a conspicuous phenomenon. The reader should refer to Archie Carr's *The Windward Road* for an account of personal experiences during explorations undertaken to study the problems of numbers and migration of these giant reptiles of the sea.

The fourth and last of the principal kinds of sea turtles is as famous as the green turtle, but for quite a different reason. It is the tortoise-shell turtle, *Eretmochelys,* which is valued for the translucent and variegated plates of the shell, which can be molded and carved into ornamental objects, from combs to jewel boxes. Like most of the others, this turtle is found in all tropical seas. The size range is only a little larger than that of the ridley, with a maximum shell length of somewhat less than three feet, and a length at maturity of about two feet.

The plates of the carapace are strongly overlapping in young specimens, but gradually come to meet at the edges—more nearly like those of other sea turtles—in very old individuals. Like the green turtle, the tortoise-shell turtle has four lateral plates on each side of the carapace. This turtle may properly be called the hawksbill, a name descriptive of its hooked and elongate jaws.

The great vogue of tortoise shell for ornamental combs dated from ancient times nearly to the twentieth century. The development of celluloid, in which the peculiar marbled pattern of various colors and the deep translucence of the plates of shell could be accurately imitated, and then of various other plastics, has gradually diminished the demand in Europe and America. The former center of the tortoise-shell industry was in the East Indian islands and Ceylon. The turtles are caught in nets, often with the crudest of decoys made of boards, which attract either sex during the breeding season aggregations. The flesh of this turtle is widely eaten in the Caribbean region.

⟶

Green Turtle returning to the sea

The Soft-shelled Turtles

(Family Trionychidae)

The most exclusively aquatic of all the groups of cryptodire turtles (i.e., those that withdraw the head into the shell by a vertical bending of the neck), the superfamily Trionychoidea, is composed of two families. The soft-shelled turtles proper have lost the horny plates of the shell entirely. The bones of both carapace and plastron are embedded in thick and tough dermal tissue, and there is a cartilaginous rim in which marginal bones may be present. The lips are fleshy, quite unlike the horny beaks of other turtles, and the snout is drawn out into a fleshy proboscis, which serves as a breathing tube, a little "snorkel." Thus these soft-shelled turtles, which are confined to fresh water, are immediately recognizable as one of the most distinct of the types of turtles. The most widespread single genus of soft-shelled turtles is *Trionyx* (Plate 16), which is found abundantly in North America, eastern and southern Asia, and in Africa as far as the Congo. It was abundant in Europe in Tertiary times, as shown by fossil remains. These turtles are remarkably active and quite belie the reputation of the turtle group for sluggishness.

In North America the spiny soft-shelled turtle, *Trionyx spinifera* (Plate 17), is the most widespread. It is named for the spinelike but soft tubercles that rim the shell in front. This turtle is common in the rivers of the Mississippi and Saint Lawrence basins, ranging westward to the Rocky Mountains. Its shell reaches a length of sixteen inches, but the average is very much smaller. The upper side of the carapace is grayish olive, with numerous dark spots, which are often little dark circles (ocelli). In old females this pattern tends to be lost, and the carapace may be blotched or mottled with dark and light areas. As in all the soft-shells, the hind feet have much elongated fourth and fifth clawless toes, webbed to the tips, forming powerful paddles.

Hatchlings and juveniles are astonishingly active little creatures, with shell length about an inch and a half at hatching. On land they stand high on their feet and tend to run, not walk, to the nearest refuge. Though so thoroughly aquatic, the adults often lie out on logs or riverbanks to bask in the sun.

The food of this turtle is almost exclusively water insects and crayfish. It has been unjustly accused of preying on food and game fishes to a damaging degree, but careful studies show that fishes of all kinds compose only a minor fraction of its food. It is, of course, a competitor of the game fishes in its feeding habits. This is at least counterbalanced by the fact that it is itself one of the most highly esteemed of turtles for human food.

The larger relative of the soft-shell, the Florida soft-shelled turtle, *Trionyx ferox,* reaches a larger average size and a somewhat greater maximum length of shell. The old males may develop extremely wide crushing surfaces on the jaws, presumably associated with mollusk-eating habits.

A very distinct species, the spineless soft-shelled turtle, *Trionyx muticus,* has a geographic distribution curiously restricted to the mid-continent of North America. It ranges from Pennsylvania to Illinois in the Ohio drainage, northward along the Mississippi to Minnesota, and westward in the Missouri and Arkansas and Red rivers, but is not found in the streams that enter the Gulf of Mexico nor in the lower Mississippi. This turtle has a much more flattened form than the *spinifera-ferox* series, and it does not have the soft spines that border the shells of that group. It differs also in a detail of the tubular nostrils; the other soft-shells all have a projecting ridge on the septum that separates the nasal tubes, and this is absent in *mutica.* The bony internal carapace and plastron of the spineless soft-shell are distinctive, and can be discerned among fossils as early as the Cretaceous Age.

The soft-shelled turtles of Asia and Africa are much more varied. There are six distinct genera, differing in development of the plastral bones. There are, however, no less than ten species that are placed in the same group with the North American forms. As already mentioned, the genus *Trionyx* was represented in Europe in mid-Tertiary times. Of the ten living species, one is the common soft-shelled turtle of the Nile, which ranges from the Nile through the Congo basin and is found also in some of the small coastal streams of Palestine. This species, *Trionyx triunguis,* is one of the largest forms of the genus, with dorsal shell often two feet or more in length. This turtle exhibits the same dimorphism in jaws as does the American *Trionyx ferox,* with broad crushing surfaces in the mollusk-eaters and sharp cutting edges in the fish-eaters. It may be presumed that this is also correlated with age and sex in the African species. Another species of *Trionyx* is found in the Euphrates. Peninsular India has no less than four species, with three more in Burma and southeastern Asia, and one more spread over the whole of eastern China. Some of these are very strikingly marked with two pairs of large black eyelike spots on the upper side of the shell.

Of the remaining genera of these turtles, one of the giants is the Malayan soft-shell, *Pelochelys bibroni,* whose shell may exceed two feet in length. This species also has a very wide geographic range, from southern China through the East Indies to the Philippines and New Guinea. Its wide distribution indicates either that it can pass naturally through salt water (which is unlikely) or that it has been carried about for food by the Malays (which is probable). Another large form, the long-headed soft-shell, *Chitra indica,* is found in North India, Burma, Siam, and the Malay Peninsula. It has an extraordinarily elongate and narrow head, with a long neck. It reaches a shell length of more than thirty inches. A third form, *Dogania,* is a smaller form, with a ten-inch shell, and is also widespread in southeastern Asia.

The remaining Asiatic soft-shell is *Lissemys,* which may be referred to as the Indian flap-shelled turtle. A pair of strong, hinged flaps at the rear of the plastron close over the hind limbs when they are withdrawn, and the head and front limbs are likewise completely concealed by a closure of the anterior opening of the shell, accomplished by drawing down the edge of the carapace and drawing up the front lobe of the plastron. This soft-shell has the bony shell remarkably well developed, with marginal bony plates along the rear of the carapace and large rough callosities over the bones of the plastron. It ranges through India, Ceylon, and Burma.

The two remaining genera of soft-shelled turtles are both African, and both have valvelike flaps on the plastron to close the openings when the limbs and head are withdrawn. They are the Senegal soft-shelled (*Cyclanorbis*) and the African flap-shelled turtles (*Cycloderma*).

The New Guinean Plateless Turtle

(*Family Carettochelidae*)

Throughout the system of classification of the animal kingdom, there are existing forms (and even more numerous extinct types) that represent links between one large group and another. It is curious that the term "missing link" should have made so great a popular impression and should have found a place in the dictionary, for the world is full of links that are not missing. The New Guinean soft-shell (*Carettochelys*) is such a link between the

common and widespread group of true soft-shelled turtles on the continents of Asia, Africa, and North America, and the main stock of cryptodire turtles.

In *Carettochelys* the bony carapace is complete, and the marginal bones meet the rib plates as in most turtles, so that "soft-shelled turtle" is a misnomer. The plastron is composed of nine bones and does not have the central opening of the true soft-shells. The limbs are developed as paddles and have only two claws. What links this strange creature to the soft-shelled turtles is the fact that it has no horny plates on the shell, which is covered by a thin layer of soft skin.

Little is known of the habits of the New Guinean soft-shell, and it has long counted as one of the rarest of living turtles. Fortunately, enough specimens have reached museums to make a very complete description possible. Almost nothing is known of its habits in nature, but it is found in the largest river of southern New Guinea, the Fly, and is obviously a powerful swimmer. It does not seem to be present in tropical northern Australia.

The Hidden-necked Turtles

(*Family Pelomedusidae*)

The method of concealing the head beneath the front edge of the shell by bending the neck sidewise is in sharp contrast with the method employed by the cryptodire turtles, which bend the neck vertically as the head is withdrawn into the shell. In many ways it is a more primitive and less efficient apparatus; but the side-necked turtles, primitive or not, are in no way ancestral to the cryptodires. It is remarkable that the two families of side-necks, the hidden-necked turtles and the snake-necked turtles, are confined to the southern continents, South America, Africa, and Australia. The vertebrae of the neck are provided with lateral processes for the attachment of the muscles that bend the neck sidewise.

Although the bending of the neck sidewise is a less efficient mode of withdrawing the head beneath the shell than the vertical bending of the cryptodire turtles, the first of the families of side-necked turtles accomplishes the withdrawal of the head beneath the skin. There are three types, of which the African pelomedusas (using the generic name *Pelomedusa* as the common name) give their name to the family;

the almost equally widespread African box turtles *Pelusios* are confined to Africa; the third type is the river turtle *Podocnemis* of South America and Madagascar, which reaches a large size. The South American ones are of great importance in the economy of the Indian tribes of the Amazon and Orinoco regions.

Pelomedusa subrufa is a small turtle with a length of shell rarely exceeding twelve inches, and is spread all over Africa south of the Sahara wherever it can find water. There are numerous subspecies. These creatures are dull gray in color and somewhat resemble the plain-colored *Clemmys* until one notices the sidewise-bending neck. Though mainly aquatic, they wander rather freely over land, which helps to explain their wide distribution. They are mainly carnivorous but take some plant food. The dry season in South Africa, when the water holes dry up completely, is spent in aestivation, i.e., in dormancy, in the mud at the bottoms of the pools of the rainy season.

The second African genus of pelomedusids, *Pelusios,* includes several distinct species. These turtles have the front lobe of the plastron hinged to the solid shell, so that the anterior opening can be tightly closed. This is a remarkable development of the hinged-lobe shell-closing device, astonishingly like that of *Emys* and *Terrapene* and the true *Sternotherus* of North America. All of these turtles are river and lake inhabitants, and do not differ greatly in habits from other kinds of turtles.

The headquarters of the genus *Podocnemis* is tropical South America, with no less than seven species in the Magadalena, Amazon, and Orinoco river systems, and in the Guianas and northern Brazil. None occurs in Africa, but one is found in Madagascar. The reason for this remarkable distribution appears to lie originally in a wide dispersal of the ancestral marine forms through shallow coastal seas. At any rate, fossil forms related to *Podocnemis* are found in Europe and Africa in Eocene deposits, and in North America in the Cretaceous. We may suppose that these marine forms entered the rivers, and that the great modern families of sea turtles took over the marine habitat and left the modern remnants of the great *Podocnemis* group as exclusively fresh-water forms. Their extinction in the fresh waters of Africa is not readily explainable.

The largest of these South American river turtles, *Podocnemis expansa,* grows to a shell length of thirty inches. Vast numbers of these turtles assemble at relatively few islands in midstream in both the Orinoco and Amazon for their egg-laying. From time immemorial the Indians in these areas have depended on the turtle eggs for a large share of their annual food supply. The gathering of the eggs and the preparation of the turtle-egg oil from them have been highly organized activities, even as long ago as the 1860's, when they were described by the great English naturalist Henry W. Bates in *The Naturalist on the Amazons.*

At that time the local governments saw to it that no collecting of eggs began until after all the female turtles had left the sand islands. The turtles, which came ashore in such numbers as to blacken the sands, would climb toward the center of each island, a height of roughly twenty to thirty feet above the river level. This elevation protected the incubating eggs from water even in the event of floods. Finally the Indians formed a large circle around each laying site, and at a prearranged signal all began digging. Bates estimated that 48,000,000 eggs were gathered annually. Not only that, the Indians killed innumerable adult turtles in the rivers around the nesting sites, and finished by catching and eating hordes of hatchlings from the eggs that had been overlooked.

This clearly wasteful procedure, so different from the conservative methods practiced on the turtle islands off Borneo, could have only one result. In Bates' own words, "The universal opinion of the settlers on the Upper Amazons is, that the turtle has very greatly decreased in numbers, and is still annually decreasing."

The Snake-necked Turtles

(*Family Chelidae*)

The distribution of the Pelomedusidae is, as we have seen, limited to Africa, Madagascar, and South America. The second family of side-necked turtles, the Chelidae, is found in greatest variety in South America, where six genera occur. A considerable number of very distinctive forms, referred to four genera, live in the rivers and swamps of Australia and New Guinea. All of these turtles conceal the head, really only the nose, in the loose skin in front of the shoulder, leaving the neck exposed beneath the overhanging front of the carapace.

The best known of the Australian forms is a long-necked creature appropriately named "snake-necked turtle," *Chelodina longicollis.* It is a small turtle, measuring about five inches in length of shell. This species lives well in captivity and is active by day. It feeds mainly on small fishes, and these are captured by a snakelike forward stroke of the long neck. These creatures are quite inoffensive and are not known to bite, however roughly handled. The bright yellow iris gives them a peculiar physiognomy. Seven related species occur in New Guinea and the rest in northern and western Australia.

The genus *Elseya* has only the single species, *dentata,* which is confined to northeastern Australia. Like the emyduras to be mentioned below, this turtle has a much shorter neck than *Chelodina.* The third genus, *Emydura,* has seven species in New Guinea, only one of which reaches northeastern Australia. Two more species are found in Western Australia. Still another Australian side-neck is placed in a genus by itself, *Pseudemydura,* but even the part of Australia from which the first specimen came is unknown, and it has not been subsequently reported.

The much greater variety of genera of the Chelidae in South America includes much larger turtles than any of the Australian types. One of the most bizarre of all turtles, the matamata, *Chelys fimbriata,* has a shell as much as sixteen inches long, with three broad keels on the back produced by the raised costal and vertebral shields. The neck is longer than the backbone within the shell, and its skin is produced into frayed lappets that give it the name

Australian Snake-necked Turtle (*Emydura macquari*)

Matamata (*Chelys fimbriata*)

"*fimbriata,*" meaning "fringed." The head is unique among turtles, for the jaws are weak, the lower jaws consisting merely of a pair of rods. The jaws extend backward to the ear, and the mouth is accordingly very large. This is associated with a mode of feeding more commonly found among fishes than in turtles. The matamata opens its mouth very wide and very suddenly whenever a food animal such as a fish, tadpole, or crustacean—perhaps baited by the moving lappets of skin on the head and neck—approaches; the prey is carried into the gaping mouth cavity with the inrush of water, and the jaws are closed upon it. It seems evident that the prey is swallowed whole. The bizarre appearance of the matamata is heightened by a long proboscis, which forms a "snorkel."

Another South American side-neck, the otter turtle, is known as *Hydromedusa.* There is an Argentinian and Paraguayan species, called *tectifera,* and another in southeastern Brazil, called *maximiliani.* These two forms have very long necks, the head and neck being much longer than the backbone; and thus they are especially "snake-necked."

The other South American side-necked turtles have the neck shorter than the backbone. One of the species of *Hydraspis* reaches a shell length of sixteen inches or more. The species of *Platemys* have the front end of the carapace extended forward, so that it protects the exposed head and neck somewhat more effectively. The remaining genera are *Mesoclemmys, Phrynops,* and *Batrachemys,* each with only a single species.

The Tuatara

(*The Tuatara Order, the Tuatara Family, and the Tuatara*)

AMONG existing types of reptiles the lizardlike tuatara (Plate 18) of New Zealand represents a very special and distinctive group, one of the five main divisions of living reptiles. It thus constitutes a separate order within the class Reptilia, and therefore likewise a family by itself. It is often referred to as a "living fossil," and this term in fact fits it very well, for it is the sole survivor of a group of very ancient reptiles, the beak-heads (order Rhynchocephalia), which flourished in the Triassic and Jurassic Periods at the very beginning of the Age of Reptiles. In that remote time, contemporary with the ancient turtles and long before the rise of the great dinosaurs, the beak-heads developed into an astonishing variety of forms, known from fossils found in South Africa, southern South America, and Eurasia. Some of these were of much larger size than the tuatara, but the largest were far from the size of even medium-sized dinosaurs, reaching an estimated length of five or six feet.

After the Jurassic Period, during the times when the dinosaurs were evolving their giant forms, the group steadily declined. Unlike the dinosaurs, one member of the group escaped extinction, lived through the Tertiary (without leaving a fossil anywhere so far as yet known), and survived into modern times in remote New Zealand. There it affords a unique glimpse in the flesh of a reptilian type of the Mesozoic Age. The scientific name of this unique creature is *Sphenodon punctatus;* it was named by the English zoologist John Edward Gray from a specimen received at the British Museum in 1831. Gray supposed it to be a new type of lizard; the discovery that this inhabitant of far-off New Zealand was not a lizard at all, but was related instead to extinct creatures whose fossil remains were known from the ancient sandstones of England and Scotland, was made by Dr. Albert C. L. G. Günther, Gray's successor at the British Museum. The tuatara *is* lizardlike in external features, and it is only when its anatomy is examined that we find the distinctions that place it in a different order.

The first of these distinctions is an additional bar of bone in the side of the skull; this anchors the quadrate bone (to which the lower jaw is hinged) solidly in place. The quadrate bone is free at its lower end in lizards, and it becomes a part of the expansible jaw apparatus in snakes. Quite as remarkable is the absence of any male organ of copulation; this is the more unexpected, since the paired organs of lizards and snakes are so elaborately developed and so unique among vertebrates. Even in the turtles, which are as ancient in their origin as the beak-heads, and which are even more closely related to the first reptiles that arose from the amphibia, there is a well-developed intromittent organ.

The "third eye" or "parietal eye" of the tuatara, situated on the top of the head, has attracted much attention among anatomists. It is not, however, one of the distinctions of the beak-heads or of the tuatara, for this curious structure is shared with many types of lizards. In younger specimens of the tuatara the third eye may be distinguished externally by a translucent scale with an opening in the roof of the skull beneath it. Then come vestiges of a lens and retina, but no iris, and this structure connects with a glandular body in the brain, which corresponds with the pineal body of higher vertebrates. In adults the skin thickens over the opening in the skull, and it is not likely that any sensation of light from the external world is conducted to the brain. Sensitivity to light of the corresponding structure in lizards has been demonstrated. The anatomy of this remarkable structure has been described in great detail.

If one holds a living tuatara in one's hand, the big brown eye that one sees seems very lizardlike until one sees the wink of the third eyelid, the nictitating membrane familiar in birds. This moves outward from the inner corner of the eye, wipes the surface of the lens, and is then slowly withdrawn.

The teeth of the tuatara are firmly set along the edges of the jaws, much as in the agamid lizards, and there is a pair of much enlarged upper teeth in front.

The lizardlike external appearance of the tuatara is produced by its body form and the general proportions of limbs and tail. The crest of enlarged flat spines along the neck and back is like that of many large agamid and iguanid lizards. The scales covering the body are unlike those of most lizards and are entirely without overlapping or free edges. There are no little bony cores in the tuatara's dermal scales. Its tail has a curious superficial resemblance to that of the common American snapping turtle. The plates of the belly are larger and more regularly arranged than those of the back and sides.

The general color is brownish olive, with a small yellow spot on each scale. Younger specimens are more greenish, and hatchlings are brownish pink. The long scales of the crest are yellow. The skin is shed in patches; the yellow spotting is brightest just after the skin is shed, and it becomes obscure as the skin becomes old.

The habits of the tuatara in nature are not fully known. It became extinct on the main islands of New Zealand by the middle of the nineteenth century, but it has persisted on the waterless offshore islands, sometimes in considerable numbers. On these islands it escapes the hosts of rats, mice, weasels, feral cats, and pigs-run-wild that inhabit the bush of the mainland, the plagues of introduced mammals brought by the English immigrants to New Zealand during the first decades of their settlements. The tuatara is positively known from thirteen of the offshore islets, and since it is protected by the government from molestation of any kind, the species will survive as long as the peculiar conditions of the island environment can be preserved.

The associations of the tuatara on its island homes are very remarkable. These islands are the nesting grounds of great colonies of various kinds of shearwaters or petrels, called mutton-birds by the New Zealanders, which nest in underground burrows. The shearwater burrows are shared by the tuataras, for the most part on quite amicable terms. The islets inhabited by the mutton-birds and tuataras, when no sheep or goats are kept on them, develop a remarkable soil and vegetation. Beneath the canopy of the leaves and branches of a species of low tree of the genus *Coprosma* there is a deep humus layer, the surface of which is essentially bare. The burrows of the birds are so numerous, with about three to every square yard of suitable surface, that this whole humus layer is riddled with the underground tunnels. A constant wind sweeps falling leaves and twigs into the openings of the burrows. These are constantly being worked over by the burrowing of the birds and lizards, with the result that the whole upper layer of soil to a depth of from eighteen to twenty-four inches is uniform in color and composition. The protection of the tua-

tara accordingly requires the protection of the *Coprosma* cover, and likewise the protection of the birds that are the main agents in mixing the leaves, twigs, feathers, eggshells, and bird and tuatara remains to produce the loose upper layer of soil. The principal hazard to the vegetation cover is the introduction of goats, and this, fortunately, is now fully realized by the New Zealand conservationists; the government has engaged in exterminating goats on some of the islands where they had been introduced in the past.

That the tuatara can also burrow for itself is quite evident. On Stephen Island the senior author observed a thirty-inch individual, a giant among tuataras, living in a hole beneath an almost impenetrable clump of the thistlelike soldier plant. Other individuals lived in their own burrows quite near a lighthouse, where the birds did not venture. Morning and evening, these tuataras were seen to bask in the sun for a short time at the mouths of their burrows. The general opinion that the tuataras are lethargic in both temperament and physiology is not borne out when they are observed at night. It has been shown, however, by careful taking of temperatures of the tuataras on Stephen Island by Mr. William Dawbin, that these creatures are active at about 52 degrees Fahrenheit, the lowest temperature recorded for normal reptilian activity.

A curious observation bears on the extraordinary insensitivity of the tuatara. The living specimen received by the Chicago Zoological Society in 1952 had a broken femur when it arrived. In spite of its injured leg it took food readily, and when the leg was X-rayed the animal did not flinch while it was manipulated. Instead of knitting, the bones developed a kind of false joint at the break.

The food of the tuatara under natural conditions consists mostly of insects, especially beetles and the large wingless grasshopper known throughout New Zealand as the "weta." An occasional lizard is doubtless eaten, and earthworms and snails also form a part of the nocturnally captured food. Petrel eggs and sometimes a small nestling petrel are taken on occasion.

The eggs of the tuatara are laid in shallow excavations, sometimes near the mouth of the burrow, but more commonly well away from the usual home. They are laid in the New Zealand spring, September to October, and do not hatch until the following spring, often requiring more than a full year for the development of the embryo.

This remarkable reptile often lives well in captivity, the age record being that of a specimen reported by William Dawbin, of Victoria University College, Wellington, New Zealand, as having lived in confinement in New Zealand for more than fifty years. A specimen kept in Sweden was in good health at the end of twenty-eight years, and one in the Dublin Zoo lived at least twenty-five years. The tuatara adapts readily to a diet of lean beef or horse meat. James Oliver, curator of reptiles at the New York Zoo, reports that their captive specimen croaked softly when held in the hand, with a voice somewhat like that of a frog. The long-enforced prohibition against the export even of single specimens to zoological gardens in Europe and America was relaxed in 1952, and four specimens were sent to the zoos in London, New York, Chicago, and San Diego. Unhappily, none of these survived long. The Chicago specimen died during a sudden heat wave when the curator was unexpectedly absent. The London specimen had a badly injured pelvic region from bruises received during its journey, and lived less than a year. The San Diego specimen died after two years, apparently from mouth rot;

autopsy showed that the internal organs were affected. The New York specimen, which arrived in good health and was provided with a specially air-conditioned cage, lived very well for seven months and then quite unaccountably refused food, sickened, and died. New specimens were received in London and New York in 1955.

Nothing is yet known of the courtship habits of the tuatara. Estimates of the populations on the various islands where it occurs are to be desired. Some authors believe that there are distinct races on certain of the islands, but this requires verification. Renewed studies of the life history of this remarkable creature were initiated by the senior author in company with Mr. William Dawbin in 1949, by a visit to Stephen Island in Cook Strait. These have since been carried on by Mr. Dawbin, and we may now hope that the habits and behavior of the tuatara will become as well known as its anatomy.

The Alligators, Crocodiles
and Gavials

(Order Crocodilia)

THE LIVING kinds of alligators, crocodiles, and gavials, taken together, are all properly referred to as crocodilians, and constitute (with numerous extinct related forms known from fossils) the order Crocodilia. This is a fairly compact group, and the twenty-odd living forms are sometimes thought of as all of the same family, the Crocodylidae. It seems more logical to group the several forms into three families: the Crocodylidae for the true crocodiles, dwarf crocodiles, and the false gavial; the Alligatoridae for the alligators and three genera of caimans; and the solitary gavial, which forms a family (Gavialidae) by itself.

The group as a whole is a mere remnant from the Age of Reptiles, when there were many kinds of crocodilians, including such spectacular forms as *Phobosuchus,* which had a skull six feet long and must have preyed upon young dinosaurs, and the wholly marine teleosaurs, which became extinct along with the dinosaurs. The crocodilians are all amphibious and essentially riparian, by which we mean that they are more or less bound to a life on the banks of the lakes, streams, and swamps in which they swim and seek their food. All of the forms are egg-laying, some depositing their eggs in shallow excavations on sandy shores, others placing them in a nest of piled-up vegetation made by the mother. In such nests, the heat of decomposition of the nest material promotes the incubation of the eggs. All crocodilians swim by means of the tail, holding the legs close to the body. On land, they usually lie on their bellies, but can raise themselves high on their legs in a curiously dinosaurlike pose. For short distances they can make a considerable show of speed on land. Except for egg-laying and nest-guarding, they lie out of water mainly as sun bathers, and present a curious spectacle when their mouths are held wide open.

The anatomical adjustments to swimming and floating at the surface of the waters in which they live form remarkable features that distinguish the group from all other reptiles. The skin of the head is directly attached to the pitted bones of the elongate skull, with no muscular padding and without fleshy lips. Thus no watertight closing of the jaws is possible. For breathing at the surface of the water, where these creatures spend so much of their time, the throat is provided with a broad fleshy valve that closes it tightly. The skull is adjusted for breathing in this situation by the bone-walled air-passage that extends from the nostrils to an opening behind the throat valve. The nostrils are placed on top of the snout, and, as in other animals that float at the water's surface, the eyes, ears, and nostrils are so placed that they are at the same level and project slightly out of water in the resting position. The ears are closable by means of a strong hinged valve. The nostrils are also provided with valves, and the eyes have well-developed upper and lower lids and a nictitating membrane.

Crocodiles and alligators habitually attack creatures too large to be swallowed whole, and the larger ones have a gruesomely efficient means of tearing up a good-sized animal. They have the capacity to rotate the body rapidly on its longitudinal axis; thus when they seize the leg of an animal in their powerful jaws with their long, strong teeth, they can spin the body and literally tear the victim limb from limb. Such larger prey includes water birds, land mammals that come to the water to drink, and a surprisingly large proportion of the young of their own species. Young and medium-sized individuals, however, feed heavily on fishes, and the very young eat many water insects and crustaceans.

A few of the larger species of true crocodiles occasionally attack man; very large individuals may become habitual eaters of domestic animals, even of full-grown cattle. Sizable creatures—for example, antelopes and deer—are seized by the snout when they come to drink, and are pulled beneath the surface and drowned.

All crocodilians appear to be long-lived, and astonishing claims are often made for age records where these creatures are exhibited to the public.

American Alligator (**young**) (*Alligator mississipiensis*)

American Alligator

A group of Moslem fakirs in Pakistan maintain a pit in which the common Indian marsh crocodile is kept as an attraction for pilgrims to the nearby holy places. They claim the largest of them to be centuries old. The very same claims may be heard at snake and alligator "farms" in Florida (really the American version of the Oriental snake-charmer show). There one may hear the reptile patriarch declared to be "a thousand years old."

The truth about the longevity of the various crocodilians is interesting enough, even without exaggeration. From 1925 to 1937, Major S. S. Flower brought together age records from the zoological gardens of the world, studied and sifted contradictions, and reduced what is actually known about the potential length of life of reptiles to a set of tables. As to crocodilians, we learn that the two alligators, the American and the Chinese, appear to be much more long-lived than the true crocodiles or any other members of the group. Individuals of

both kinds of alligators have lived for more than fifty years. Of twenty individuals of the American alligator that averaged thirty-three years in captivity, eleven were still alive. Among the various species of true crocodiles, an Orinoco crocodile is known to have lived twenty-two years, and a Nile crocodile twenty. We may estimate the potential length of life at a higher figure, but the sluggish alligators do apparently long outlive their more active crocodile cousins.

Since reptiles continue to grow throughout life, though more and more slowly as they become older (and finally very slowly indeed), it is not easy to establish the normal adult length of the various species. There are, however, dwarf species, medium-sized species, and gigantic forms, though the estimates of thirty feet for the East Indian salt-water crocodile and the gavial appear to be entirely unsubstantiated. The following table gives a rough summary of the average and maximum

Species	Range	Approximate adult length	Maximum known length
Broad-nosed caiman	Eastern Brazil	6 feet	6 feet 9 inches
Paraguay caiman	Paraguay River system	6–7 feet	8 feet
Spectacled caiman	Amazon and Orinoco	5–6 feet	8 feet 6 inches
Central American caiman	Central America and Colombia	4–5 feet	6 feet
Black caiman	Amazon basin and Guiana region	10–12 feet	15 feet
American alligator	Southeastern United States	8–10 feet	19 feet 2 inches
Chinese alligator	Eastern China	4–4½ feet	5 feet
Smooth-fronted caiman	Amazon basin	4 feet	4 feet 8 inches
Dwarf caiman	Amazon basin	3½ feet	4 feet
West African dwarf crocodile	West Africa	5 feet	6 feet
Congo dwarf crocodile	Upper Congo	3½ feet	3 feet 9 inches
Nile crocodile	Africa and Madagascar	12 feet	16 feet
African slender-snouted crocodile	Congo basin	6 feet	8 feet
Mugger or marsh crocodile	India and Ceylon	10 feet	13 feet
Siamese crocodile	Southeastern Asia and Java	10 feet	12 feet
New Guinean crocodile	New Guinea	8 feet	9 feet 4 inches
Australian crocodile	North Australia	6–7 feet	8 feet
Philippine crocodile	Philippine Islands	5–6 feet	8 feet
Salt-water crocodile	Southeastern Asia and East Indies to Australia	12–14 feet	20 feet
Cuban crocodile	Cuba	6–8 feet	12 feet
Morelet's crocodile	Southeastern Mexico and eastern Guatemala	6–7 feet	8 feet
American crocodile	Central America, West Indies, Florida, Colombia	10–12 feet	23 feet
Orinoco crocodile	Orinoco basin	10–12 feet	23 feet
False gavial	Malay Peninsula and East Indies	9–10 feet	16 feet
Gavial	India	12–15 feet	21 feet 6 inches

length of the twenty-five different kinds of living crocodilians.

It is quite likely that the Ceylonese form of the marsh crocodile could be distinguished as an addition to the above list of names, and there appear to be one or more well-distinguished subspecies of the spectacled caiman in northern South America that remain to be described and named.

The True Crocodiles

(*Family Crocodylidae*)

The genus *Crocodylus* includes the largest of the crocodilians and several of the best-known forms. The common African crocodile, which occurs throughout southern and tropical Africa wherever there is a watercourse, even in oases in the southern Sahara, ranged northward to the lower Nile in historic times, and even along the shores of the Mediterranean to Palestine. It swims freely into salt water, and is accordingly present on many offshore islands and on Madagascar. This is the crocodile of classical literature, for it is described at length by Herodotus, who gave currency to the story that the crocodile opens its mouth by having the upper jaw move on the skull instead of the lower. This is not true; the lower jaw is hinged to the skull quite as in other animals. It is easy to understand, when one sees an open-mouthed crocodile sunning on a riverbank, that an uncritical observer might think that it was the upper jaw that had been raised, for the lower jaw is laid flat on the sand. Opening the mouth in this position is accomplished by raising the rest of the head, and not the upper jaw alone. Among reptiles it is really only the snakes that have their upper jaws separately hinged to the skull. Heredotus likewise observed the Nile plover apparently picking the crocodile's teeth, running unharmed in and out of the open mouths of the giant reptiles basking in the sun. Aristotle seems to have known the crocodile only from the account by the "father of history," for he repeats Herodotus' fallacy that this creature has no tongue.

The African crocodile, *Crocodylus niloticus* (Plate 20), attacks human beings in some areas and not in others. This is somewhat mysterious, or at least has not been explained satisfactorily. In some native villages it is necessary to build a stockade at the edge of the river to enable the women to fill their water jars without being attacked. In others the children splash and swim fearlessly in the water and are not molested. It appears that very old and large individual crocodiles may become habitual eaters of domestic animals and attackers of human beings. The same differences of behavior of the crocodiles in different rivers are reported from Madagascar.

The African crocodile takes its scientific name, *niloticus,* from the classical accounts. The species is one of the largest of crocodilians, with apparently authentic records of lengths up to sixteen feet, which would correspond to a weight of at least a ton. The age to which these creatures live is often greatly overestimated; well-fed specimens kept in zoological gardens grow as much as a foot a year up to the length of six or eight feet, after which the rate of growth becomes progressively slower. The eggs, usually thirty to fifty in number, are laid in sandy spots on the riverbanks, and the spot is somewhat loosely guarded by the mother, who opens the nest when she hears the peeping of the young about to hatch. The young within the egg are able to make sounds for as much as three days before hatching, and do so in response to any disturbance of the soil above them, such as would be made by the return of the mother after a trip to the river.

The smaller species of true crocodiles are often strictly fresh-water forms, or inhabit smaller bodies of water, or are otherwise not in contact with the larges species, which prey upon the smaller ones when they can. Two dwarf forms in Central and West Africa are sufficiently distinct from the common crocodiles to be placed in a separate genus, *Osteolaemus,* a name that refers to the bony shields of the belly. The West African form is commonly seen in zoological gardens. Africa also has a fourth distinct species of crocodilian, one of the long-snouted species, *Crocodylus cataphractus.*

The salt-water crocodile of the Indian and East Indian region, *Crocodylus porosus,* is even more famous as a man-eater, and is perhaps greater in average size than the larger African species. Sixteen-foot specimens are well known, and careful measurements of a jaw fragment in the Chicago Natural History Museum indicate that it came from a specimen about eighteen feet long. The jawbone in question was that of a crocodile that was killed by a stick of dynamite in the Solomon Islands after a long career of cattle-stealing.

This Oriental species is sharply distinguished from all of its fellow crocodilians by the absence of the crossrows of enlarged plates, known as the occipital scutes, just behind the head. Its common name of salt-water crocodile is appropriate, for this species swims freely from island to island in the Malay Archipelago. Stray specimens have even arrived at the remote Fiji Islands, and a specimen is known

West African Dwarf Crocodile (*Osteolaemus tetraspis*)

to have landed on Cocos-Keeling Islands in the Indian Ocean, more than six hundred miles from the nearest larger island. In 1929 there was a large old specimen that had long been resident on the island of Espiritu Santo in the New Hebrides, but it was apparently also a solitary stray.

It was a salt-water crocodile that attacked the well-known entomologist, Philip J. Darlington, Jr., during his service in the Army Medical Corps in New Guinea in World War II. As reported by Arthur Loveridge in *Reptiles of the Pacific World,* Captain Darlington was engaged in collecting mosquito larvae in connection with the control of malaria. He had worked his way out along a partly submerged log at the edge of a swamp, and was dipping a test tube in the clear water to obtain mosquito larvae, when he saw a crocodile rise. He started to retreat along the log, but slipped and plunged into the water. As he came to the surface the ten-foot saurian seized him by the arms and employed the customary crocodilian tactic of rolling over and over while backing into deeper water. Dr. Darlington, six feet tall and weighing about 170 pounds, remembers being twisted about in the water as he was carried to the bottom. He struggled and

kicked, but found it impossible to exert any force in the water. After what seemed like an hour but could only have been a few seconds, the crocodile opened its jaws and released him, perhaps in response to a lucky blow on its belly. The captain struggled to the surface and swam to the edge of the pool. Only when he had pulled himself out did he realize the severity of his wounds: his left hand had been punctured by several teeth; there was a dislocation and compound fracture of the left ulna; and the muscles and ligaments of his right arm were torn.

The vast tropical area south of the Himalayas, extending eastward through the East Indies to the Philippines and Celebes, is known as the Oriental Region to the student of animal geography. This part of the world is especially rich in crocodilians. In addition to the salt-water crocodile along its coasts, the peninsula of India has a large fresh-water crocodile, the mugger or marsh crocodile, *Crocodylus palustris*. The population of this crocodile in Ceylon has been described as a distinct geographic form by Dr. Deraniyagala, the director of the Colombo Museum. It is this crocodile that is regarded as sacred in parts of India. As we have

[48]

[continued on page 65]

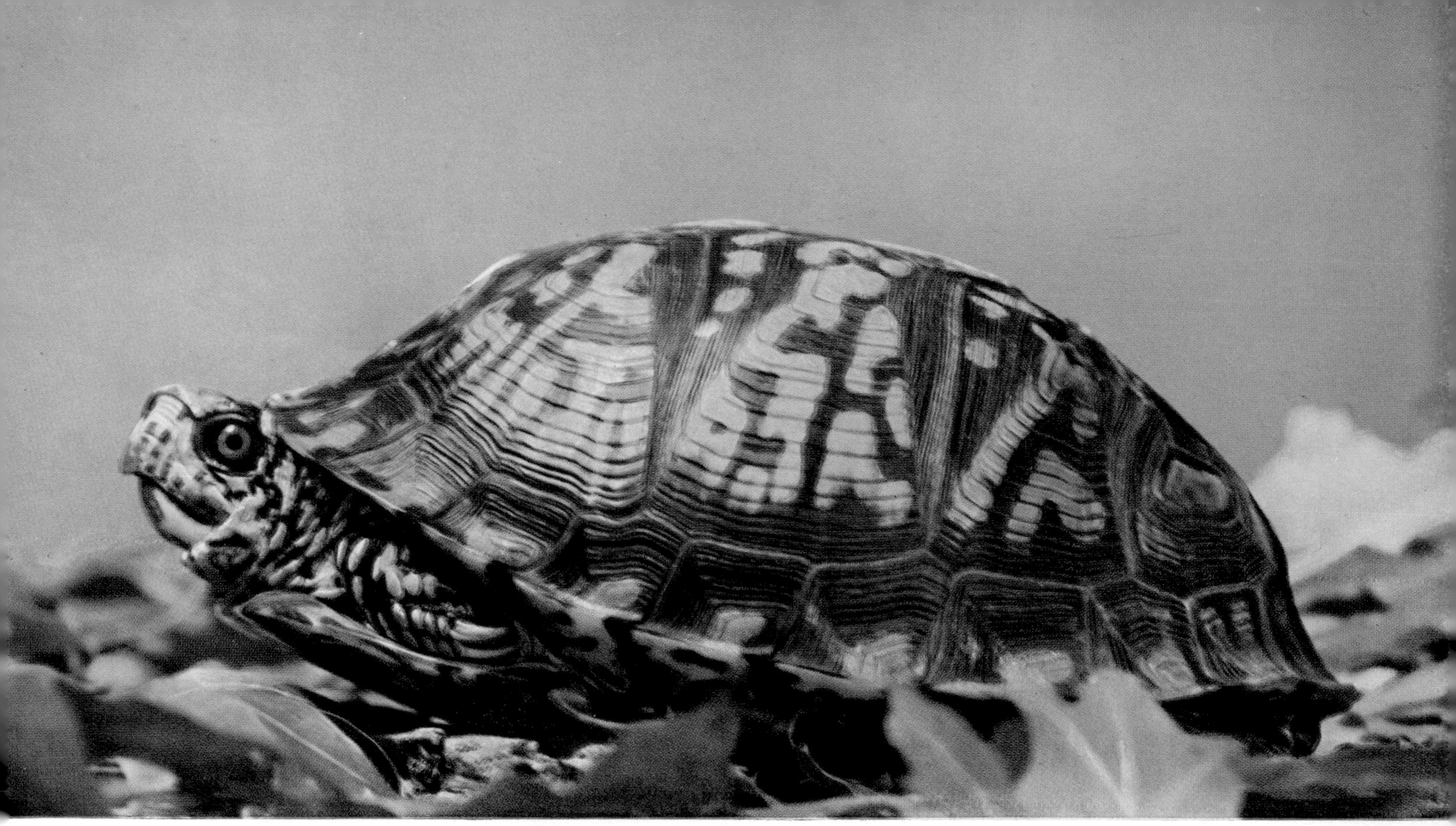

1. Eastern Box Turtle (*Terrapene carolina carolina*)

[ROY PINNEY]

2. Western Box Turtle (*Terrapene ornata*)

[H. A. THORNHILL : NATIONAL AUDUBON]

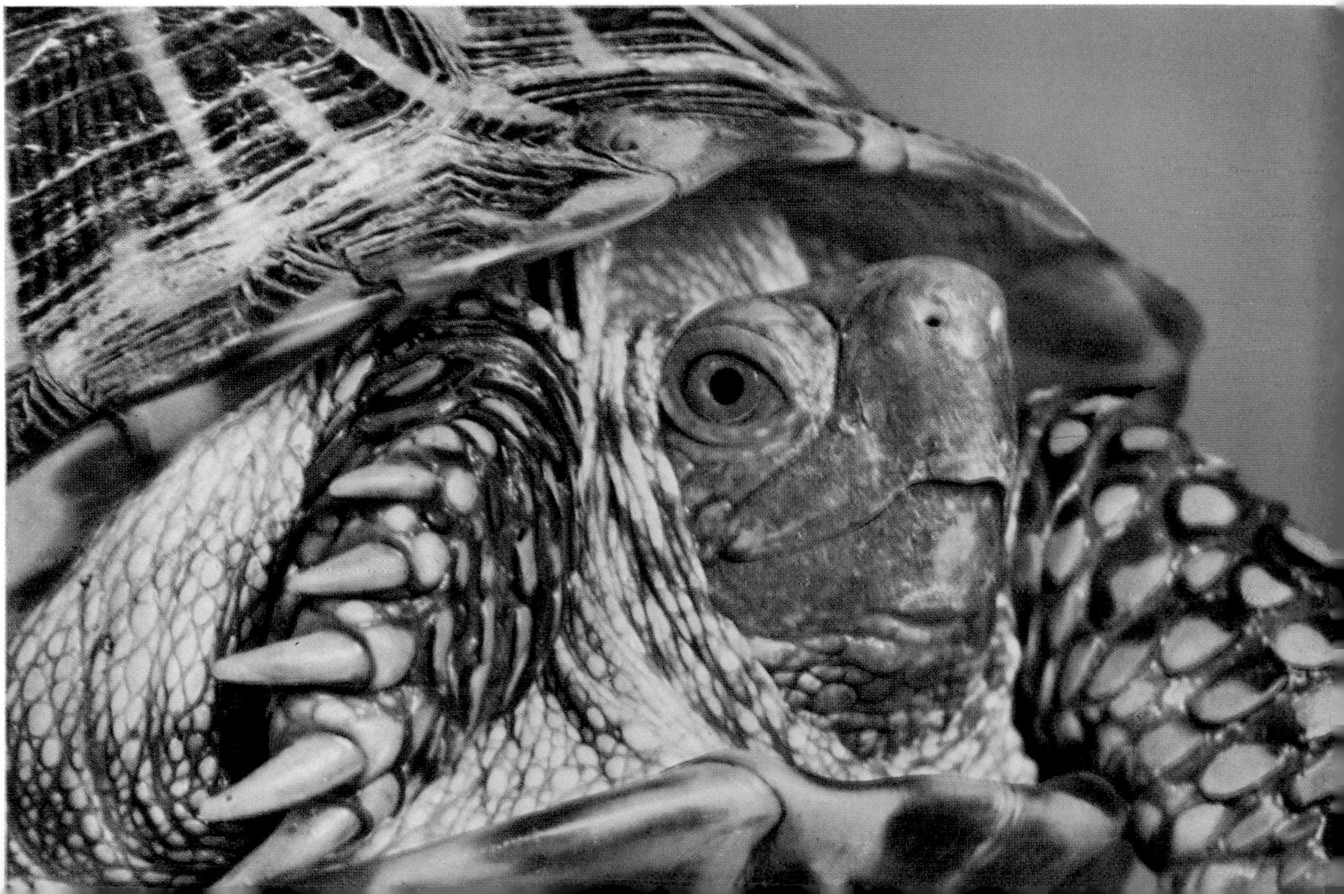

3. Stinkpot
(*Sternotherus odoratus*)

[HAL H. HARRISON :
NATIONAL AUDUBON]

4. European
Pond Turtle
(*Emys orbic-
ularis*)

[JOHN MARKHAM]

5. Wood Turtle
(*Clemmys
insculpta*)

[HAL H. HARRISON :
NATIONAL AUDUBON]

6. Spotted Turtle (*Clemmys guttata*)

7. Three-toed Box Turtle
(*Terrapene carolina triunguis*)

9. Star Tortoise (*Testudo elegans*)

8. Painted Turtle (*Chrysemys picta*)

10. Red-eared Turtle
or Pond Terrapin
(*Pseudemys
scripta elegans*)

[JOHN MARKHAM]

11. Forest Hinge-back Tortoise (*Kinixys erosa*)

[JOHN MARKHAM]

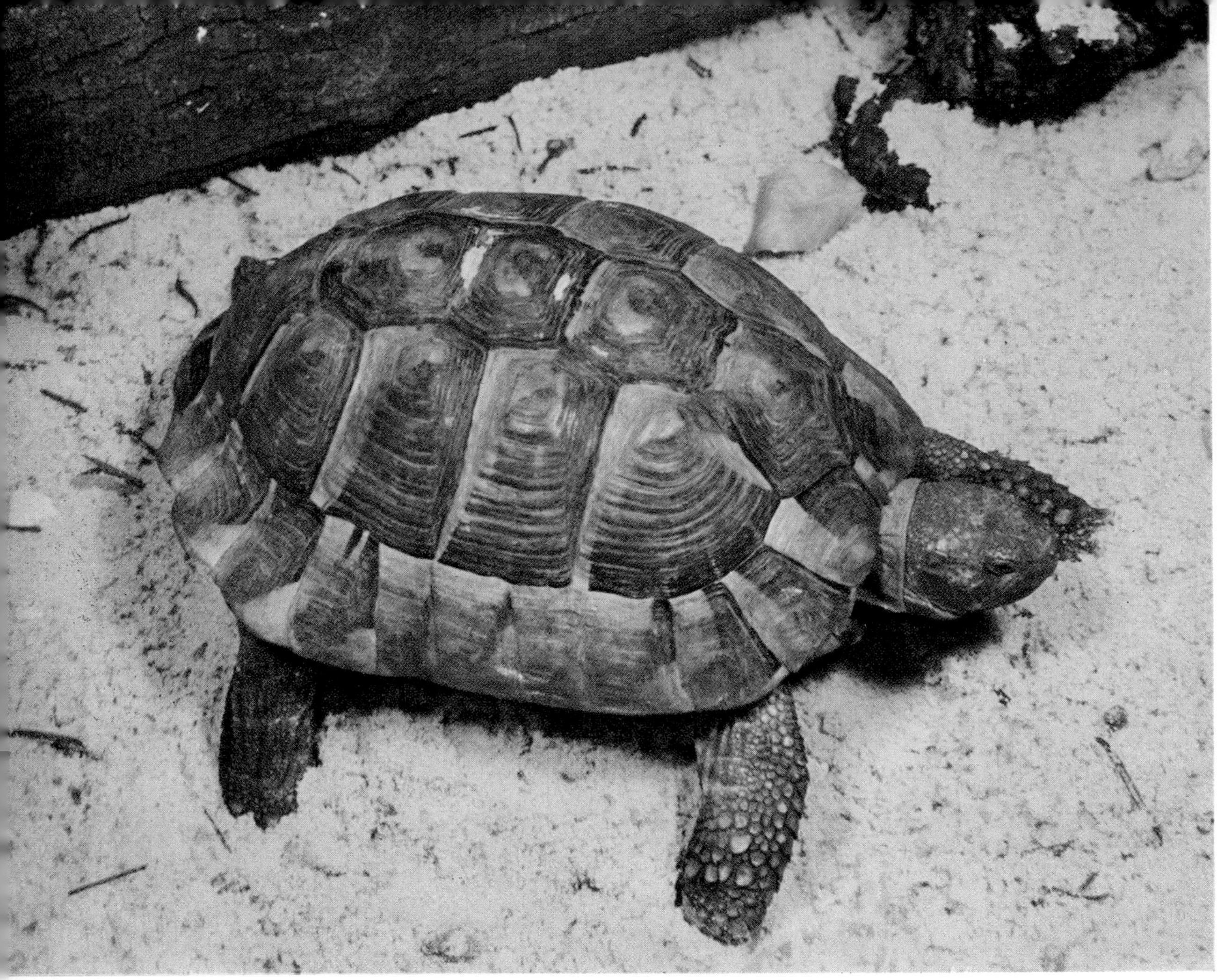

12. European Tortoise (*Testudo graeca*)

[JOHN MARKHAM]

13. Hermann's Tortoise (*Testudo hermanni*)

[JOHN MARKHAM]

14. South American Tortoise (*Testudo denticulata*)

[JOHN MARKHAM]

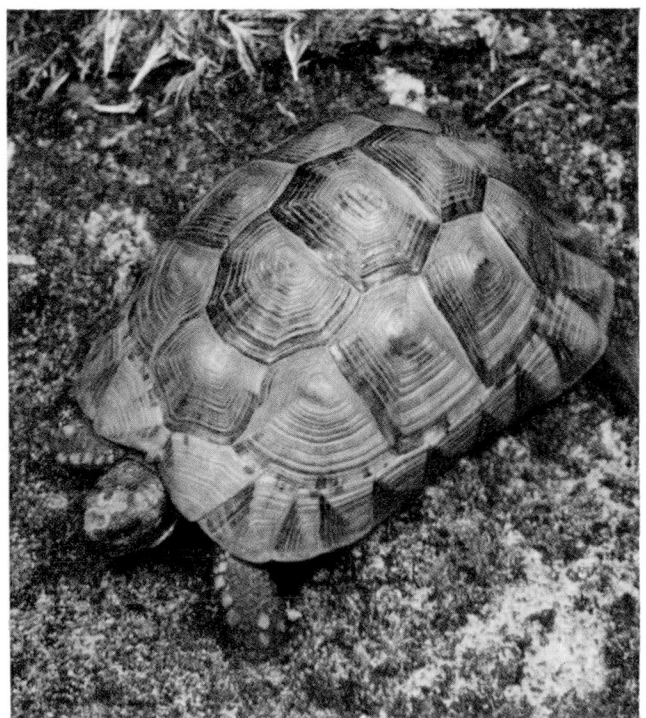

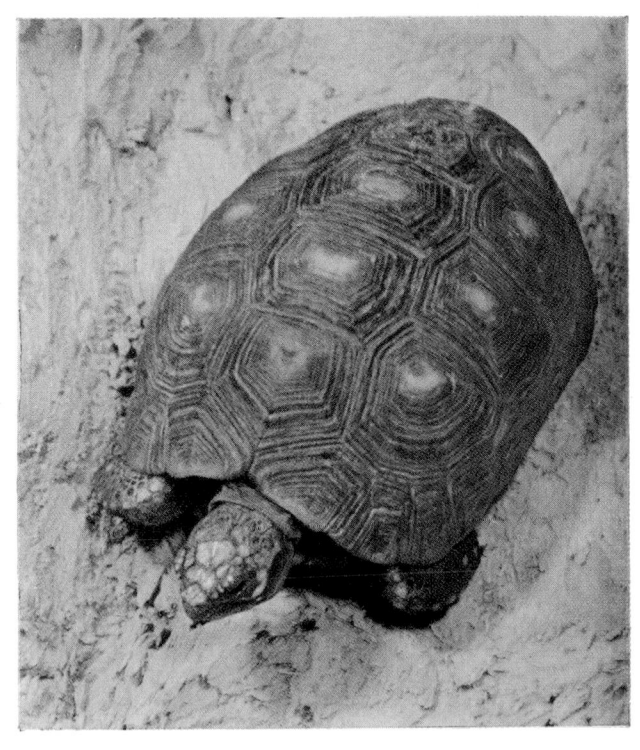

15. Aldabra Giant Tortoise
(*Testudo gigantea*)

16. Eastern Spiny Softshell Turtle (*Trionyx spinifera*)
[CHARLES HACKENBROCK]

17. Eastern Spiny Softshell Turtle
[HAL H. HARRISON : NATIONAL AUDUBON]

18. The Tuatara (*Sphenodon punctatus*)

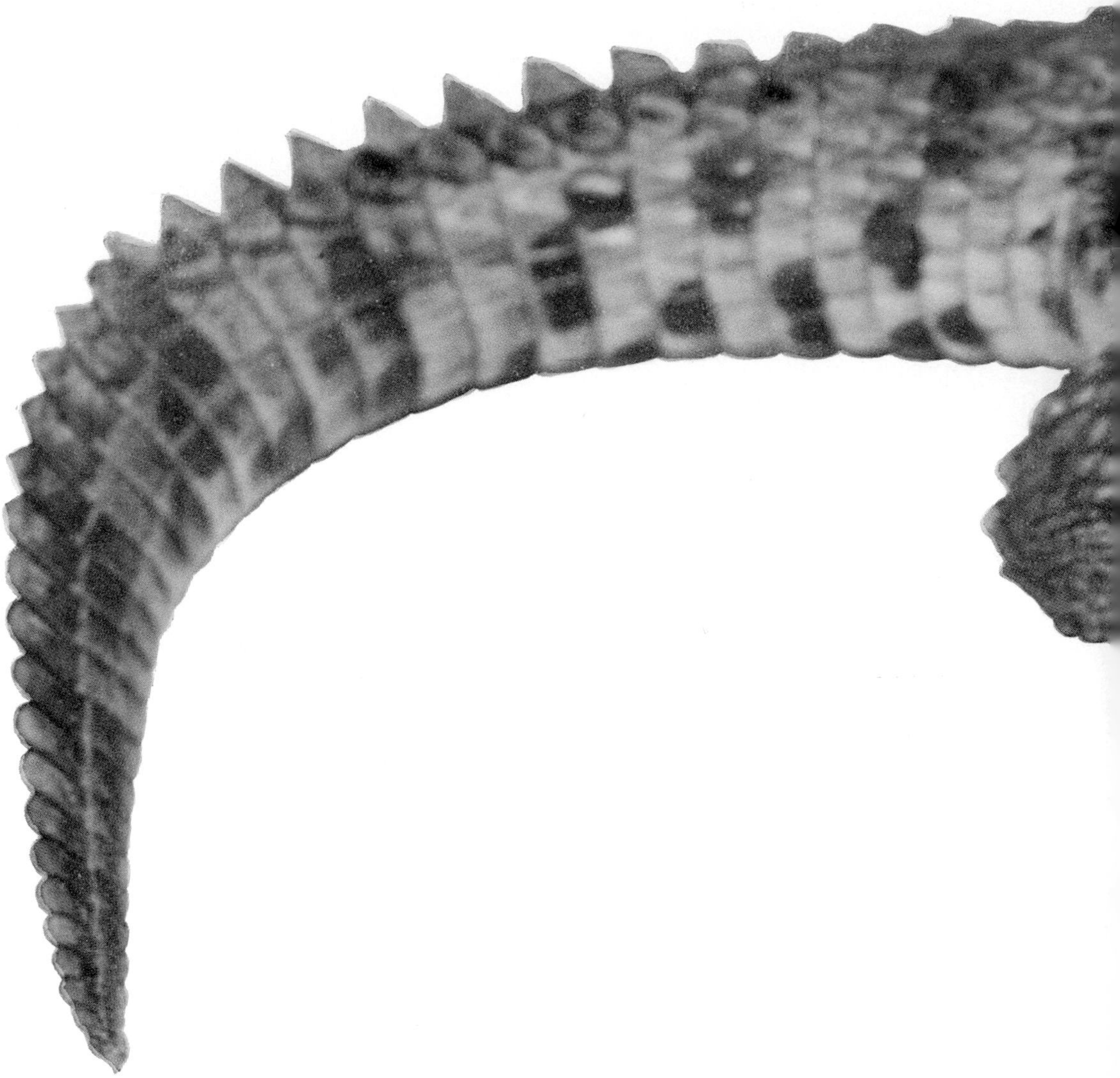

19. Spectacled Caiman
(*Caiman sclerops*)

[ROY PINNEY AND PHILADELPHIA ZOO]

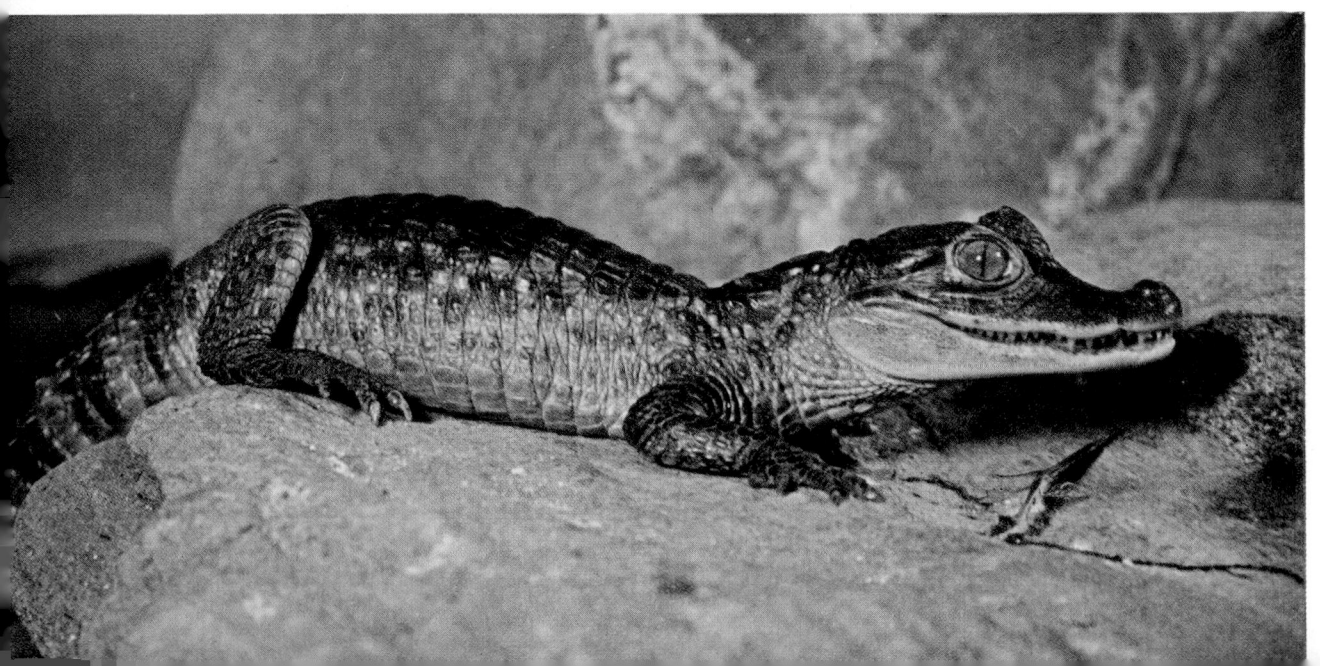

20. African Crocodile
(*Crocodylus niloticus*)

[ROY PINNEY]

21. Siamese Crocodile
(*Crocodylus siamensis*)

[JOHN MARKHAM]

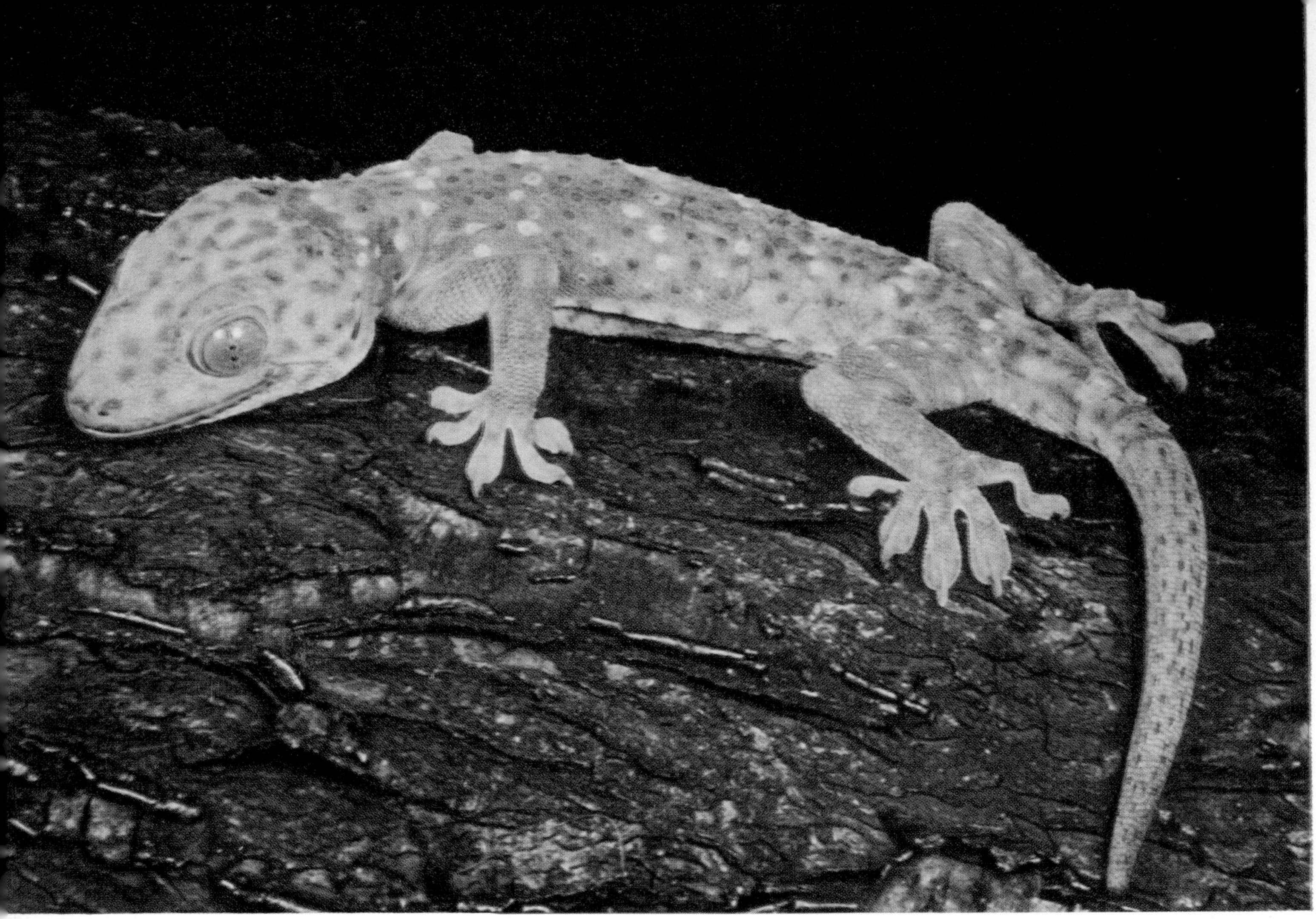

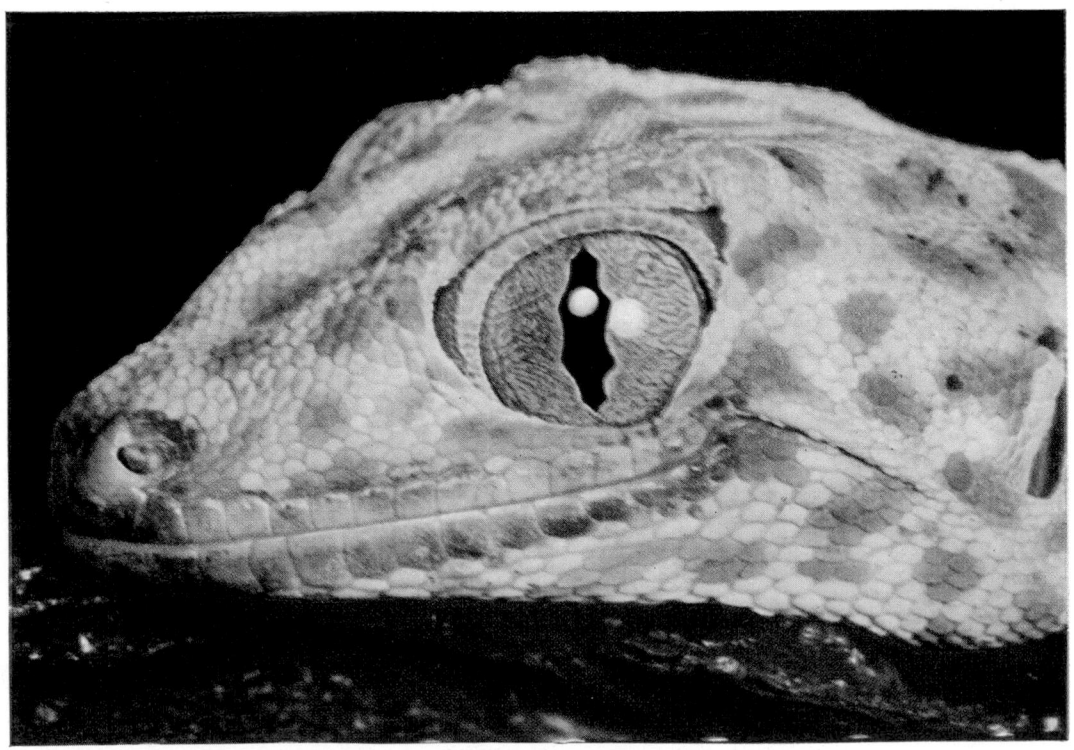

22. Tokay Gecko (*Gekko gecko*)
[NATHAN W. COHEN]

23. Tokay Gecko
[NATHAN W. COHEN]

24. Wall Gecko (*Tarentola mauretanica*)
[JOHN MARKHAM]

→

28. Hardun
(*Agama stellio*)

[JOHN MARKHAM]

→

25. Banded Gecko
(*Coleonyx varie-
gatus bogerti*)

[HAL H. HARRISON :
NATIONAL AUDUBON]

26. Spiny-tailed Agamid
(*Uromastix acanthinurus*)

[JOHN MARKHAM]

27. Lesueur's Water Lizard
(*Hydrosaurus lesueuri*)

[JOHN MARKHAM]

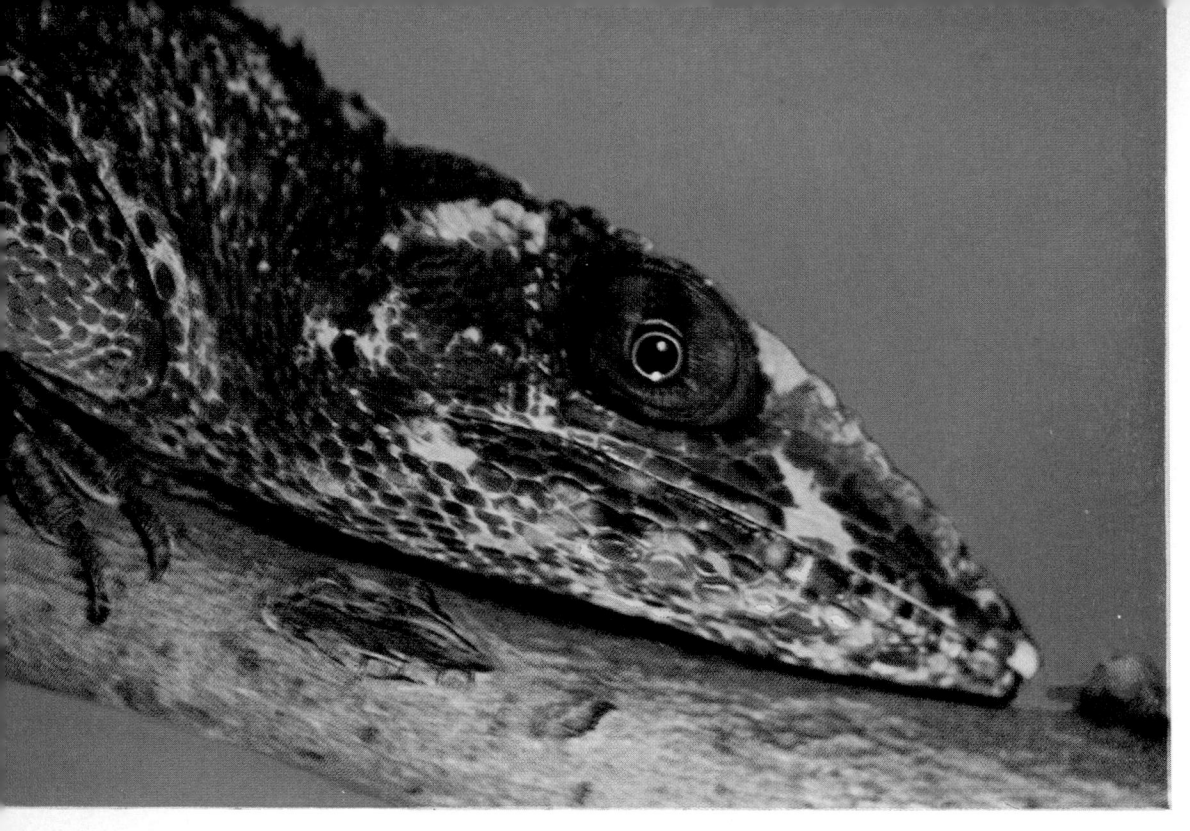

29. Knight Anole
(*Anolis equestris*)
[CY LA TOUR AND SAN DIEGO ZOO]

30. Knight Anole
(*Anolis equestris*)
[CY LA TOUR AND SAN DIEGO ZOO]

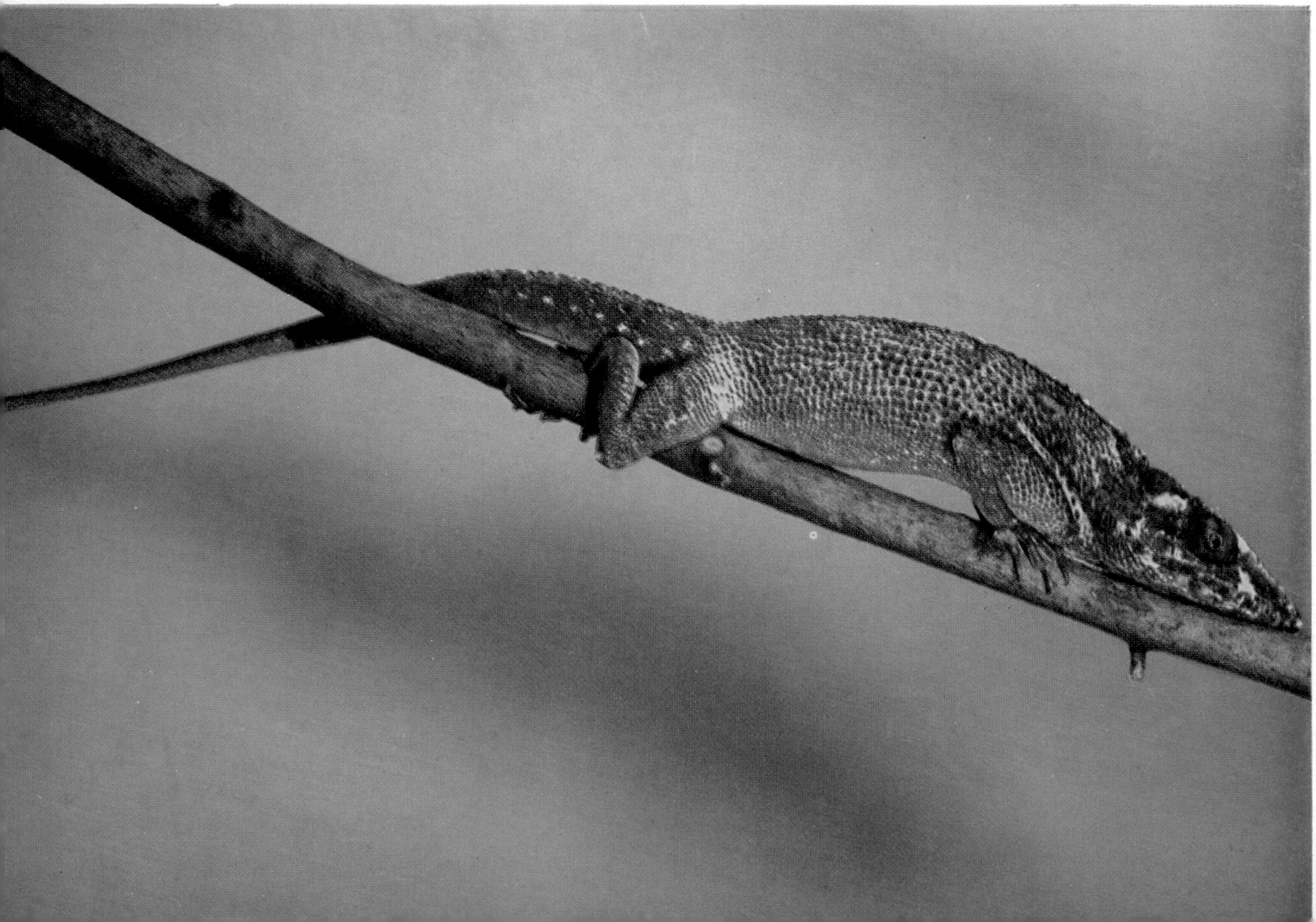

[continued from page 48]

already mentioned, there is a famous crocodile tank in the vicinity of Karachi in Pakistan. About fifty large specimens of the mugger are kept confined here, with one exceptionally large individual in a separate tank, no doubt to prevent its eating the smaller specimens. The crocodiles are in charge of a priest, and pilgrims going to pray at the holy places of Karachi pay their respects to the crocodiles as they pass. They contribute to the support of the crocodiles by the occasional purchase of a goat, which is slaughtered and cut to pieces for the big saurians, who come at the call of the attendant. The tameness of these crocodiles is attested by the fact that verses of the Koran are painted on their bony heads.

The mugger has the distinction of being the most broad-snouted of all true crocodiles. Also broad-snouted, but less extremely so, is the Siamese crocodile, *Crocodylus siamensis* (Plate 21), which occurs to the east of the range of the mugger. This species is the common form of the Irrawaddy, as the mugger is of the Ganges. It has a sharply defined median keel on the head, between the eyes, as its distinguishing mark.

Still farther to the east, the Siamese crocodile is replaced by the Philippine species, *Crocodylus mindorensis,* which has a still more pointed snout and is perhaps more nearly related to the salt-water crocodile. This is replaced, in its turn, by the New Guinean crocodile, *Crocodylus novae-guineae.* Finally, in this series, there is the slender-snouted fresh-water crocodile of northern Australia, *Crocodylus johnstoni.*

The false gavial of Borneo, Sumatra, and parts of the Malay Peninsula is misnamed, for it is definitely more closely related to the true crocodiles than to the gavial. It is, however, the most slender-snouted of the forms in the crocodile family, and is distinguished as *Tomistoma schlegeli.* The two halves of the lower jaw are united as far back as the fourteenth or fifteenth tooth, whereas in the narrow-snouted species referred to the genus *Croco-*

Mugger Crocodile (*Crocodylus palustris*)

[65]

dylus this union extends at most only to the eighth tooth from the front. The false gavial is not often seen in zoological gardens. Old specimens may exceed fifteen feet in length. The probable reason for the tendency to elongation of the snout will be discussed in connection with its even more extreme development in the gavial.

The common American crocodile, *Crocodylus acutus,* like the crocodile of the Nile and the salt-water species of the East Indies, freely enters salt water, and this accounts for its wide range. From the mainland of Central America it extends southward along the Pacific coast to Ecuador, and northward to western Mexico; it ranges through the Magdalena River drainage in Colombia, thence widely through the larger islands of the West Indies, reaching the southern tip of Florida.

One of the largest of crocodiles is found only in the basin of the Orinoco River. The lengths of specimens observed in this area by the great naturalist-traveler Alexander von Humboldt are recorded as having been twenty to twenty-four feet. The Orinoco crocodile, *Crocodylus intermedius,* is long-snouted, like the African species *cataphractus* and the Australian *johnstoni.* Elongation of the snout evidently represents independent evolution of this feature in these widely separated regions. The extreme within the crocodile family is reached in the false gavial; and the extreme in the group as a whole is of course the parallel-sided snout of the true gavial.

There are two smaller closely related species of true crocodiles in the Americas. The Cuban crocodile, *Crocodylus rhombifer,* is found only in the Zapata swamp on the south coast of Cuba. Morelet's crocodile is confined to the Gulf coast of Mexico, ranging through northern Guatemala to British Honduras. This species was duly described in 1851 from specimens collected for the Museum of Natural History in Paris by the French traveler Morelet; but when no further specimens had been discerned for some seventy years, the existence of the species began to be doubted, with the supposition that there might have been confusion with Cuban specimens of *rhombifer* in the original material. It was thus a considerable success of the 1923 expedition of the Chicago Natural History Museum to rediscover this species in the swamps inland from Belize, British Honduras. An adult specimen and a series of young were collected, quite enough to restore *Crocodylus moreleti* to its proper status.

Alligators and Caimans
(*Family Alligatoridae*)

The fact that a large crocodilian, the common American alligator, *Alligator mississipiensis* *, inhabits the swamps and rivers and lakes of the southeastern United States, from the Carolinas to Texas, makes this species perhaps the best known of all crocodilians. The most frequent question asked of the reptile department in any museum is likely to be the distinction between an alligator and a crocodile. The distinction is not, in fact, a very great one. In the crocodiles the teeth of upper and lower jaws are more or less in line, and the enlarged fourth lower tooth fits into a notch in the side of the upper jaw and is plainly visible from the side when the jaws are closed. This notch produces a constriction of the snout at this point. In the alligators and caimans, the upper row of teeth is placed *outside* the lower. Thus the enlarged fourth lower tooth fits into a pit in the upper jaw and is quite invisible when the jaws are closed.

For some reason this simple distinction between the true alligator and the true crocodile, although written down and diagramed hundreds of times, is still not really well known. In almost any part of the world where there is more than one kind of crocodilian, one is likely to be called an alligator, and the other a crocodile; and wherever English is spoken, the word "alligator" is likely to be applied to the nearest convenient species of crocodilian, regardless of relationship. In Cuba, the larger and more active species, the American crocodile, is called the "lagarto" (the Spanish word which, in the form "el lagarto," gave origin to the word "alligator"). The broader-snouted Cuban crocodile, *Crocodylus rhombifer,* is called the *"cocodrilo."* It is perhaps a general rule of language that a name deeply rooted in usage tends to be used for something, however different the new object may be from the one to which it was originally applied. The birds called "robins" in New Zealand, for example, are black.

The American alligator has been so persistently hunted for its skin, from which ornamental leather is made, that there now appear to be none of the gigantic specimens of former times left. The record length of an American alligator is nineteen feet two inches, claimed for a Louisiana specimen shot by the

---

* The scientific name of the American alligator illustrates the rule of zoological nomenclature that the original spelling of any name (on its first appearance in print) is to be followed in all subsequent usage, even when misspelled.

father of E. A. McIlhenny, of Avery Island, Louisiana. Mr. McIlhenny's book, *The Alligator's Life History,* published in 1955, remains the most comprehensive account of the species.

The food of the American alligator changes decidedly with age. The young feed primarily on water insects and crustaceans; as they grow older they take any larger animals that become available, especially frogs, snakes, and fishes. Older specimens, still with a diet basically of fishes, take some larger animals such as young pigs, muskrats, and other mammals of the marsh and riverbank, and even some waterfowl. Very large individuals, finally, may occasionally pull into the water and drown a larger mammal, such as a deer or cow, that comes to the water to drink.

There has been in the past a large trade in baby alligators sold as pets to the children of tourists in the Gulf states and Florida. The great decline in numbers of alligators in Florida in recent decades has led to complete protection of the species, with the abolition of this trade in baby 'gators. An unexpected result was the prompt replacement of the baby alligators by baby caimans from South America. Naturalists are inclined to expect that one or another of these South American forms will sooner or later escape from captivity and establish itself as an addition to the United States fauna in the South. Juvenile alligators (or caimans) make interesting animals for the home zoo, but they are scarcely suitable for pets.

The alligator is one of the crocodilians that make a large nest-mound for its eggs. The mud for the mound is scooped up with the broad jaws, and is mixed with mouthfuls of marsh vegetation, until the structure is about three feet high and some five to seven feet wide at the base. The eggs are deposited in a hollow made in the center of the nest, which is then smoothed over and filled out with material from the rim of the nest. The whole is smoothed and shaped by crawling over and around it. The eggs number from about twenty to about seventy. They are hard-shelled and of about the size of a goose egg. When the young are ready to emerge they peep loudly, and the mother, who has been on guard for the nine to ten weeks required for incubation, tears open the nest and helps in the release of the hatchlings. These measure about eight inches in length, and it seems impossible that so large a creature could have been coiled up in the three-inch egg.

The nearest living relative of the American alligator is the Chinese alligator, which was made known to the western world in 1879. It appears in Chinese writings for centuries before that date. It is in fact a very distinct species, which reaches a maximum length of only about five feet. Mr. Clifford H. Pope collected a series of nineteen specimens near the city of Wuhu, a short distance up the Yangtze River from Nanking, in 1925; they were dug from shallow burrows in which they were in hibernation. Their food habits and rate of growth correspond in essential respects with those of other crocodilians.

South America is so rich in species of crocodilians of the alligator family that this must have been a special center of evolution of the group during the long ages when the southern American continent was cut off from the rest of the world. The two true crocodiles have been described. In addition, there are three quite distinct genera of the broad-snouted and alligatorlike caimans, namely the spectacled caimans (genus *Caiman*), the black caiman (*Melanosuchus*), and the smooth-fronted caimans (*Paleosuchus*).

The most abundant and best-known of the South American caimans are the three species of spectacled caiman: one, *Caiman latirostris,* in the rivers of eastern Brazil, one, *Caiman yacare,* in the Paraguay River, and one much more widespread, ranging through all of the Amazon and Orinoco basins, the Guiana region, and northeastern Brazil, the common spectacled caiman, *Caiman sclerops* (Plate 19). This species, whose length rarely exceeds six feet, is present in enormous numbers in all favorable waters, and it varies geographically, with distinct subspecies in different parts of its range. The Paraguay caiman has been shown to feed very largely on the giant water snails of that region, for masses of the horny opercula (which close the openings of the snail shells) are found in their stomachs.

The black caiman, *Melanosuchus niger,* ranges beyond the Amazon basin to the Orinoco basin and the Guiana region. It is the giant among caimans and thus become dangerous to larger animals. For this reason great caiman drives are made every year on the large island of Marajo at the mouths of the Amazon, in which great numbers of caimans, large and small, are killed.

The spectacled caimans are so called because a curved ridge of bone connects the eye sockets, and this is thought to resemble the nose bow of a pair of spectacles. The two species that do not have this ridge are named the smooth-fronted caimans. These are the smallest of all crocodilians; they are very much alike but are completely distinct species, for the most part inhabiting the same vast Amazonian region, which they share also with the more abundant spectacled caiman. Dr. Fred Medem of the Instituto de Ciencias Naturales in Bogota, Colombia, traveled to the upper Amazon region of Colombia;

and his observations in the field revealed that there is a sharp difference in habitat between the spectacled caimans, which are creatures of sluggish streams and bayous with mud banks and muddy bottoms, and the smooth-fronted caimans, which live in swifter waters, often with rocky banks and rock-bottomed stream beds. The smooth-fronted caimans, as an adjustment to their rocky environment, are the most completely armored of all crocodilians. Their armor protects them when they are thrown against the rocks in rapids.

In all crocodilians, pitted bony plates underlie the large horny scutes of the back and tail; the number and position of these bones vary widely, and greatly affect the value of the skins for leather. The American alligator does not have bony elements in the scales of the belly, and for this reason its skin was especially valued for leather when it was sufficiently abundant to provide a steady supply to the hunters and to the alligator-leather industry. The bony scutes in the armor of a smooth-fronted caiman actually interlock on both back and belly, so that their complete skeletons resemble those of some ancient extinct similarly armored forms.

The Gavial or Gharial

(Family Gavialidae)

The crocodile and alligator families are quite connected by fossils in the long history of the group. There are no such connecting links with the gavial, whose fossil history goes back to the beginning of the Tertiary in Europe and Asia—but the group, somewhat surprisingly, has not been found in American fossil beds. The Indian gavial is abundant in the Indus, Ganges, and Brahmaputra rivers, and it reaches the coast of Burma.

The gavial, *Gavialis gangeticus,* is another of the crocodilians whose name is a matter of nomenclatorial confusion. The colloquial name in India is "gharial." The first specimens brought to Europe were described in the scientific literature as *Gavialis;* as result, "gavial" became the common name in English, except that purists continue to insist that this is a misnomer and that "gharial" must be employed. "Gavial" has, however, long since won this contest in English and German alike.

The extremely elongate snout of the gavial is associated with an almost exclusive diet of fishes, and of living fishes caught in the water by a sidewise sweep of the head and jaws. One need only try to move a stick rapidly sidewise in the water to realize the enormous physical advantage of slenderness versus breadth in such a motion. The correlation between resistance of the water and increased dependence on the capture of fishes as food must be the explanation of the independent evolution of slenderness of snout in so many crocodilians. In the gavial this evolution took place long ago, and it reaches its extreme for the whole group in the living gavial.

The gavial is not known to attack man, though it grows to very large size. There are records of bracelets and necklaces and rings found in the stomachs of gavials, but these are without doubt the result of the eating of the corpses of human beings set afloat in the Ganges at the end of burial ceremonies.

The greatest size on record for a gavial appears to be twenty-one feet six inches. For a long time the species was short-lived in captivity, but more recently zoological gardens have been successful in keeping gavials. In 1937 a specimen that had been in captivity twenty-four years was still alive.

The Lizards and Snakes

(Superorder Squamata, Orders Sauria and Serpentes)

APPROXIMATELY 95 per cent of living reptiles belong to this superorder, divided almost equally between lizards and snakes. The group, therefore, may be considered far and away the most successful of reptiles under present conditions. The roughly 5700 species of snakes and lizards have spread to every continent except Antarctica and have evolved forms adapted to almost every conceivable mode of life available to vertebrates. As a group they are aquatic, terrestrial, subterranean, and arboreal. Only true flight has been beyond their evolutionary capacities, although one genus glides as skillfully as flying squirrels.

Very likely activity is the keynote to the success of lizards and snakes, for activity is required if an animal group is to compete with the energetic, quick-moving mammals and birds. The turtles and crocodilians are slow and inactive by comparison, the turtles presumably surviving only because of their protective armor and the crocodilians seemingly headed for extinction, while the tuatara is protected only by its remoteness from the continental faunas.

Anatomically these scaly, active creatures differ from all other vertebrates in the possession of paired copulatory organs, the hemipenes. As a group the Squamata have rather flexible skulls, another distinguishing characteristic that has been carried to an extreme in the snakes (order Serpentes). The snakes also differ from the lizards in the absence of forclimbs and in the almost universal absence of hind limbs, although as will be seen later certain lizards have evolved in this direction too. Another snake characteristic is the absence of a movable eyelid, the eye now being covered by a clear scale, the "spectacle," derived from the lower eyelid. But this structure, too, has been evolved in certain lizards. The snake's highly extrusible tongue and very flexible lower jaw are also distinguishing features approached by a few lizards.

Despite the difficulties of making ironclad definitions, the two groups are clearly distinguishable. Equally clear is their close relationship to one another. These relationships are expressed by grouping them under the superorder Squamata but recognizing them as separate orders.

The Geckos

(Family Gekkonidae)

Reptiles are for the most part strangely silent. Male alligators bellow to warn one another to stay in their own territories; a few snakes hiss, and others rattle their tails. But this is a feeble assortment of sounds compared to the calls of birds, or of frogs and toads, or even of fishes. In this respect the only reptiles that will bear comparison with these other vertebrates are the lizards known as geckos.

Throughout the warmer parts of the globe, these small to medium-sized lizards (rarely over six inches) liven up their surroundings with a variety of calls running the gamut from feeble chirps and croaks to loud, nerve-wracking barks. In many cases the sounds give the geckos their local common names, as, for example, "cheechak" (*Hemidactylus frenatus*) and "tokay" (*Gekko gecko*). Indeed, the word "gecko" is based on the call of a common North African species. A newcomer to the tropics of southeastern Asia is not likely to forget the first time he is awakened by the stentorian "to kay" of a gecko that has taken up its abode on the ceiling right above him.

Houses seem to be a favorite habitat of certain species, and watching these little lizards scamper across the ceiling after insects or listening to them chirp to one another is one of the most entertaining pastimes of the tropics. The first sight of a three- or four-inch reptile running or standing upside down on a plastered ceiling causes astonishment and then speculation as to how the creature can do it.

Many lizards are excellent climbers, as we shall have occasion to note in later pages, but only among

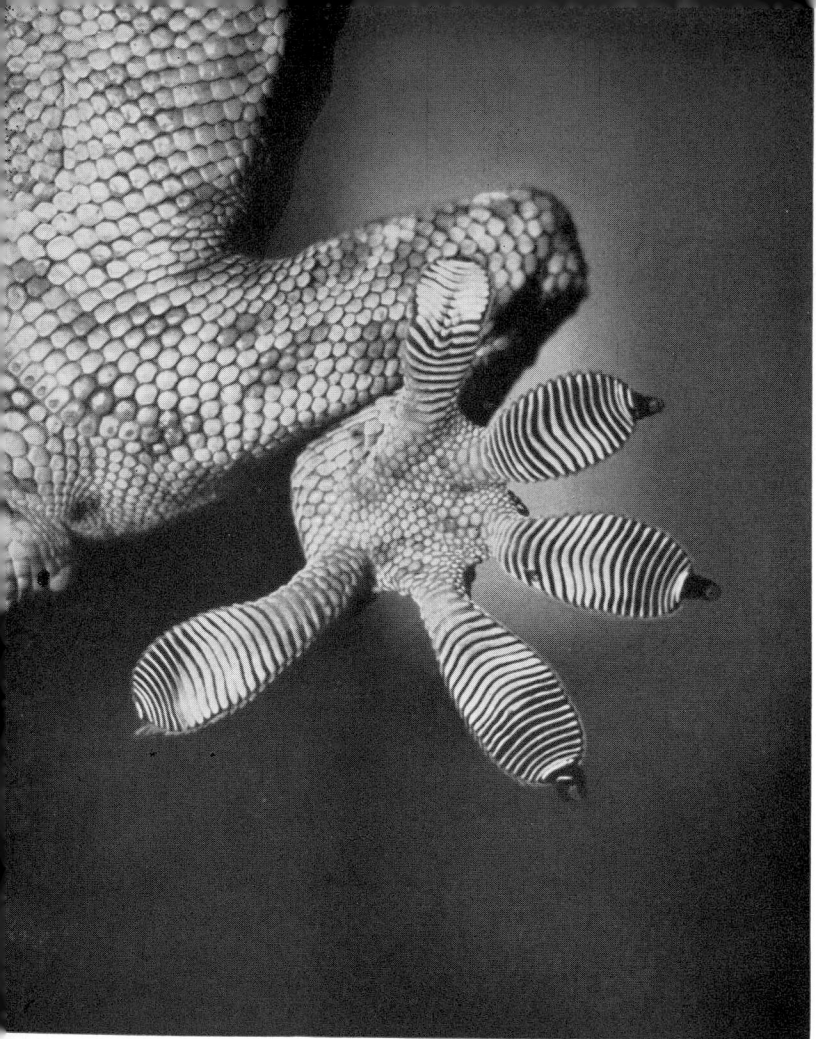

Tokay (underside of rear foot) (*Gekko gecko*)

Most geckos are too small and too fast to permit easy observation of the action of the feet. But the tokay of Malaya is large enough and deliberate enough in its locomotion to enable the detailed movements of its feet to be followed. Before a foot is raised and moved forward, the ends of the toes are curled upward and held in that position until the foot is put down. To disengage its foot from a tree trunk, a cat cannot simply pull straight out but must release its claws by a reversal of the way in which they were hooked into the bark. Similarly, since the hooklike cells of the gecko's toe pads point downward and to the rear, curling the toes upward from the tips releases the hooks. Thus, in running up a wall or tree, a gecko must curl and uncurl its toes with every step, actions that ordinarily are far too fast for the human eye to follow.

One of the most remarkable things about gecko toe pads is their great variety. These differ so from group to group that they simplify the task of classifying and identifying geckos. The plates of the pad may be arranged fanwise at the tip of the toe or distributed in rows along the entire underside of the toe. The plates may extend across the width of a toe or be divided in the center. And, perhaps most astonishing of all, a clinging pad is found at the tip of the tail in one group of African geckos. The picture is rounded out by the geckos, of which there are a number, that have no clinging pads.

The interest attached to the clinging pads tend to draw attention away from the sharp claws on the fingers and toes. The claws are as important as the pads in climbing on trees and other very rough surfaces. In this respect geckos are no different from many other climbing lizards.

Boys in Malayan towns sometimes take advantage of the strength in gecko claws and pads. A favorite trick is to lower a large gecko by means of a string from a roof or second-story window onto the hat of a passer-by. The gecko instinctively grabs hold with pads and claws as soon as it touches the hat. At that precise moment, the boy starts pulling up the string, only he then has not only a gecko at the end, but also a hat.

The tails of geckos, which are almost as interesting as their feet, present a bizarre array of types for which we still know no function. Most lizards have round, tapering tails. And some geckos have this simple type. But in other geckos the tail is slightly flattened. Then, if we arrange all geckos into a sequence based on tail shape, the tail develops next a fringe of scales along the margin, and finally a flap of skin that may be scalloped or lobed. The flattened tail has also evolved in this family into a shape like an apple leaf. But not all gecko tails are

the geckos do we find species that are able to walk on apparently smooth, hard ceilings. This ability depends on the unique development of special clinging devices under the toes. The undersides of the digits of most geckos are dilated along some portion of their lengths. Basically the dilated areas or "pads" consist of plates each of which bears a great many microscopic, hooklike cells that catch in the slightest irregularity of any surface. Even ordinary glass is sufficiently rough to afford a purchase for these amazing structures.

A great deal of confusion has surrounded the functioning of the clinging pads. They have been called suction devices, but no suction is involved. They have also been called adhesive, but no sticky substance is necessary to their operation. Probably the best evidence that the pads hook into irregularities of the substrate is the observation that geckos cannot cling to highly polished surfaces. The extreme smoothness of such surfaces would be no hindrance to the working of a suctorial or adhesive structure.

flat. Some have become excessively swollen and shortened into a form resembling a turnip. In fact the tail of the largest Central American species has given it its scientific name, *rapicaudus,* meaning "turnip tail." This type of tail reaches its oddest form in certain Australian geckos (*Nephrurus*) that have a small knob at the end of the "turnip."

Like other lizards, geckos have the ability to shed their tails, even the most elaborate ones, if attacked by an enemy. The lives of geckos must be full of danger and excitement, for often most adults in an area show signs of having lost their tails. The stump heals, and a new tail is grown. The replacement or regenerated tail is usually roughly the same shape as the original, especially if the original tail is the cylindrical, tapering kind. But at least one African gecko develops a wider replacement tail. If the original tail has a peculiar shape, its replacement is likely to be simpler in outline and in scalation.

Sometimes the tail breaks, yet remains attached to the base by a strip of skin. In this case a new tail will regenerate, but the old one will heal and become firmly reunited with the base. Eventually the gecko may have two full-length tails. Museum collections even contain geckos with three tails!

Geckos are outstanding for four things: voice, feet, tails, and eyes. Unlike most lizards of other families, the great majority of geckos have no movable eyelids. The true eyelids, now found only in a few primitive species, have fused in the course of evolution, and the eye of the vastly more numerous, advanced geckos is covered by a transparent "spectacle" or scale derived from a windowlike clear area in the lower lid.

By and large, geckos are inactive during the day. The eyes of the few that engage in daytime activities have circular pupils and show no specializations. On the other hand the nocturnal geckos—and this includes over three-fourths of the species—have modified eyes. Certain of these modifications, such as a change in the type of retinal cells and the loss of a retinal focal point (the fovea), are not readily seen. But the specialization of the pupil is perfectly apparent. The nocturnal geckos have vertical pupils. Some have smooth-sided pupils like cats, whereas others have pupils that are lobed on one or both margins. In still others the pupil has a bulge in the center of each margin. In bright light all of these vertical pupils contract. The smooth-sided type contracts to a vertical slit like a cat's pupil. But the lobed type is unique; it closes to a vertical series of four pinholes. Each pinhole is capable of focusing an image on the retina at the back of the eyeball, and the four images are superimposed. In the dim-

ness of dusk or night, a single image may not have enough light to stimulate the retina, but the combined light from the four pinholes can activate the visual cells. A larger pupil opening would accomplish the same purpose so far as amount of light is concerned, but the focusing advantages of a pinhole would be lost. In the terminology of photography, the lobed pupil provides the depth of focus of an f22 lens opening in light that would ordinarily require an f4.5 opening.

All geckos, except several New Zealand species, lay eggs. The usual number in a clutch is two, although certain geckos from the Greater Antilles lay just one. The eggs have a tough white shell and are laid under stones, behind window shutters, or under bark. Their incubation period may last several months.

The long incubation, the tough shell, and the fact that the eggs are laid under bark all help to explain how five geckos—the scaly-toe, *Lepidodactylus lugubris;* the half-toe, *Hemidactylus frenatus;* the oceanic gecko, *Gehyra oceanica;* the waif gecko, *Hemiphyllodactylus;* and the Pacific gecko, *Peropus mutilatus*—have managed to spread throughout the island world of the South Pacific. Eggs may have been laid under the bark of a log that a storm subsequently washed to sea. Once in the ocean currents, the log could drift to another island. Though the trip might last several months, the eggs would still be incubating and the embryos living on yolk. Of course, it is more likely that the log would disintegrate before making a landfall in the vastness of the Pacific, and the geckos thus would not have been transported to another island. Or other accidents might befall the log and the geckos be lost. But these little lizards are so numerous wherever they occur that the chances of successful "waifing," as this kind of dispersal is called, are increased, especially if considered over a span of thousands of years.

Other scaly-toed geckos are found closer to the mainland of Asia in the Philippines and the East Indies, where they, together with the half-toes, are the common geckos in houses. As soon as night falls and the lights begin to attract their insect food, the three- to four-inch "cheechaks," as these geckos are called by the Malays, emerge from their resting places and start the evening's activities of chirping, feeding, and mating on the walls and ceiling. If anything should disturb them, each scampers back to his own resting place—a crack in the wall, the rear of a picture frame or other wall ornament, etc.

The half-toes live throughout southern Asia and all of Africa. In southeastern Asia they are joined by the tokay, *Gekko gecko* (Plates 22 and 23), the giant of the geckos by virtue of its length of ten to fourteen inches. The red- or orange-spotted tokay not only has a bark as loud as that of a dog, but also a bite like that of a small dog, as we can attest from personal experience. Even in large cities such as Singapore and Bangkok, the tokay is found in buildings; indeed, we have one report that at the turn of the century the clatter of billiard balls did not disturb the tokays living in the game room of one of Bangkok's hotels.

The tokay is considered by many Malayan people to be a symbol of good luck. The length of time intervening between the completion of a new house and the first call of a tokay in it is thought to be a measure of the good fortune the home-owner can expect. Similarly, the bark of a tokay shortly after the birth of a child is said to signalize a happy life for the youngster.

But if superstition surrounds the tokay with a happy aura, it does not treat other geckos so kindly. A Dyak was horrified one night to see us reach for a bent-toed gecko (*Cyrtodactylus*) on a tree trunk in the Bornean jungle. "Its bite is poisonous!" Of course it was nothing of the sort. No gecko is poisonous. Nonetheless, the bent-toe is interesting because it belongs to a group of geckos having no toe pads. The digits of this black-and-gray cross-banded lizard are bent sharply upward near the base and then downward near the tip, so that the claws are permanently set at a right angle to any surface on which it walks. Despite the absence of clinging pads, the bent-toe is enabled by its claws to climb trees or rocks with ease.

One other gecko of the Orient merits attention. Many geckos have a narrow lateral fringe on the sides, but this particular species, named *Ptychozoon* or "fold animal," has a wide flap of skin half the width of the body on each side of the trunk. Not only that, but there are similar though narrower flaps on the sides of the head and along the hind margins of the limbs. The toes are completely webbed, and the tail is flattened and bears wide, scalloped margins. Herpetologists have speculated about the function of all this excess skin, but only within the last few years has a definite solution to this puzzle been found. If this gecko is dropped or made to jump from a height of twenty feet or more, its limbs and tail are stiffly outstretched and the flaps along the sides are spread, all the expansions acting as planing surfaces as the animal glides to the ground. To call it a "flying gecko" is perhaps an exaggeration, but it gets the point across.

One of the speculative explanations for the flying gecko's skin flaps had been that if the flaps were pulled down against a limb on which the lizard was at rest, the body would cast no shadow and the animal would thereby be camouflaged. The flaw in this suggestion was that the body flaps are not spread when the animal is at rest. As a matter of fact, its coloration, consisting of wavy cross-bands of

Malayan Bent-toed Gecko (*Cyrtodactylus pulchellus*)

lighter and darker shades of brownish gray, was sufficient to camouflage it when it was quiescent.

The same type of coloration is found in many geckos, including one of the common house geckos of Africa, *Hemidactylus mabouia*. This gecko, which reaches a maximum length of seven inches, will eat any living creature it can overpower. Although its diet usually consists of moths, crickets, cockroaches, and other household insects, it has been observed eating such tidbits as other geckos, large centipedes, and driver ants. Should a large insect try to put up a fight, the house gecko, while retaining a grip with its mouth, beats the unfortunate prey against the wall or ground until resistance ends.

The house gecko is only one of a large clan. We have already referred to Oriental species of this genus (*Hemidactylus*). No less than forty-one species occur in Africa alone. Many live on the ground, hiding under rocks and debris by day and foraging at night. Other species are arboreal and are confined to the forested portions of Africa. Approximately six African species are frequently found in and around houses.

Africa is also the home of the garrulous gecko, *Ptenopus garrulus*, which lives in sand dunes in the dry southwestern part of the continent. This small (three inches), gregarious creature digs narrow, vertical burrows about a foot deep in the sand. Each individual occupies its own burrow, and sticks its head out in the late afternoon to chirp at its neighbors. So many may live in one place that the noise has been described repeatedly as "deafening." Fortunately for campers, the "talking" ends abruptly at nightfall.

In North Africa, Spain, and on the Dalmatian coast of Yugoslavia, the wall gecko, *Tarentola mauritanica* (Plate 24), is a conspicuous element of the fauna because of its daytime activities. It turns up in a few cities of southern France, where it is undoubtedly brought in by ships from Algeria. In these ports the wall gecko is found only around the docks. Transportation by boat may partially account for the presence of geckos in the isolated islands of the South Pacific. It is almost certainly the explanation for the presence in the West Indies of the African house gecko, *Hemidactylus mabouia*, and the Turkish gecko, *Hemidactylus turcicus*.

In addition to these introduced species, the West Indies and the Caribbean lands have their own native geckos. In fact one of the principal divisions of the family is limited to this area. The five genera and about fifty species of this group are evidently voiceless, which would be enough to distinguish them in this noisy family. But those species about which we have information also differ from other

HANS ROSENBERG

Fan-footed Gecko (*Ptyodactylus hasselquisti*)

geckos in laying only one egg at a time. One of these species, *Sphaerodactylus elegans*, shares with a chameleon the title of the smallest living reptile. As one herpetologist puts it, this gecko, which reaches a maximum total length of one and a third inches, is shorter than its own printed scientific name. All the members of this genus, though equipped with clinging pads, spend as much time on the ground as in climbing about in vegetation.

South America has only five genera in addition to the five Caribbean ones, a small number in comparison to the twenty-three found in Africa. Wall's gecko (*Wallsaurus*) and the half-dozen or so species of naked-toed geckos (*Gymnodactylus*) have no clinging pads; instead, like those of the bent-toed geckos of the Orient, their digits are bent upward at the bases and downward at the tips.

The largest South American gecko, the turnip-tail, *Thecadactylus rapicaudus*, which averages about six inches in total length, ranges far up into Central America. In Honduras we were solemnly assured by the natives that this lizard was among the most deadly creatures alive. How people who live close to nature in a country that contains rattlesnakes, relatives of the fer-de-lance, coral snakes, and scorpions can be genuinely afraid of such a harmless animal as the gecko surpasses understanding. We caught these geckos barehanded, and that was twenty years ago; if the species was poisonous, the effects have been a long time coming.

Three of the West Indian geckos, with the help of man, have recently invaded the United States. The yellow-headed gecko, *Gonatodes fuscus,* the ashy gecko, *Sphaerodactylus cinereus,* and the reef gecko, *Sphaerodactylus notatus,* are now living in the Keys or tip of southern Florida. The much-traveled Turkish gecko, *Hemidactylus turcicus,* has also arrived in southern Florida, not directly from the Old World but by way of the West Indies. Unfortunately, these interesting, lively lizards will probably not be able to move much farther northward in the United States because of low winter temperatures.

No other geckos are found in the United States until we come to the Southwest. In extreme southern California, just across the border from Mexico, the leaf-fingered gecko, *Phyllodactylus tuberculosus,* lives in dry, rocky country. Its common name refers to the leaf-shaped or fan-shaped clinging pads at the tips of the fingers and toes. With the help of these devices, it scampers over boulders at night, hiding by day under rocks and in crevices.

The banded gecko, *Coleonyx variegatus* (Plate 25), has a much wider distribution in the United States, living in the desert areas from southern California to southern Texas. This gecko resembles the leaf-fingered gecko (and at least three-fourths of all geckos) in its diet of insects and its nocturnal habits. But the banded gecko has no clinging pads. Nevertheless it manages to climb over rocks with the use of its claws, although most of its time is spent on the ground.

This pretty gecko, which is three to four inches long, has a slender, tapering tail lacking the odd adornment of some members of this family. But what the tail lacks in form it makes up for in action. As the banded gecko stalks a cricket, it raises itself

BERNARD GREENBERG

Banded Geckos mating (*Coleonyx variegatus*)

high on its legs, cocks its head, and twitches its tail nervously, catlike, just before making the final lunge on the prey. In courtship, too, the tail is waved, though only by the male as he approaches the female. The uses of the tail may not be unique to the banded gecko; we merely happen to have the benefit of some intensive study of this species. Perhaps we will learn in time that many geckos use their tails in these ways.

Yet the banded gecko has one feature that is most remarkable in this family of lizards, one that is found in only about a dozen species—true eyelids. And all twelve or so species lack clinging pads. The banded gecko, ranging from the southwestern United States to Panama, is the only member of this most primitive group of living geckos found in the Western Hemisphere. Other species of this group live in West Africa, in East Africa, in southwestern Asia, and in certain of the islands along the Pacific coast of Asia.

The geckos of two regions of the world have yet to be mentioned. One of these regions, Madagascar, is relatively small compared to the continental areas, but it has a remarkable fauna and will pop up repeatedly in our discussions of other lizard families. No less than twelve genera (about fifty species) of geckos are found in Madagascar, only one less than occur in the entire Western Hemisphere. In terms of faunal relations, Madagascar and several groups of small islands of the Indian Ocean, the Mascarene Islands and the Seychelles Islands, are usually considered as forming a unit. Seven of the genera mentioned above are found nowhere in the world but on Madagascar and these smaller islands. One odd thing about this assemblage of geckos is that it does not include a single primitive species or a single species without clinging pads.

Probably the most extraordinary group of Madagascar geckos are the day geckos (genus *Phelsuma*). The fact that these lizards are active exclusively during the day is itself unusual in this family and is very likely connected with another surprising characteristic, namely, their bright green color. As we have suggested earlier, geckos run to dull colors, predominantly various shades of gray and brown, in patterns that tend to camouflage the animal, though only if it remains quiet. The activity of an animal that scurries around in broad daylight will destroy any concealing effect its coloration might have. Many songbirds are in this situation; they have gone to the opposite extreme and have developed bright flashes of color that make them conspicuous and recognizable to other members of their own species. The day geckos seem to fit this tend-

ency of the songbirds. The flat-tailed day gecko, *Phelsuma laticauda,* for instance, has a bright green head and body splashed with red spots, and a light blue tail. And they seem to recognize their own species, judging by the way they fight.

Other Madagascar residents include the leaf-tailed geckos (*Uroplatus*). As the name implies, their tails are broad and flat. The sides of the body and limbs have peculiar fringes of scales. The eye has the lobed, vertical type of pupil. Indeed, we might almost say that the leaf-tailed gecko has so many peculiarities that it is scarcely noticed in this family.

One gecko is found in so many places that enumerating them is almost boring. The common half-toed gecko, *Hemidactylus frenatus,* originally lived

Australian Leaf-tailed Gecko (*Phyllurus platurus*)

Australian Spiny-tailed Gecko (*Diplodactylus spinigerus*)

in Southeast Asia and the East Indies but has now spread to Africa, Guam in the mid-Pacific, and Mexico. It is no surprise that it turns up in Madagascar.

The common half-toe has also reached Australia, the other region we have not discussed. But Australia has its share of native geckos as well. This small continent has fourteen genera and about fifty species, of which eight genera do not live elsewhere. About one-fourth of the Australian species lack clinging pads. Among the native geckos are some with fancy tails. The fat-tailed geckos (genus *Oedura*) are just that. The appendage swelling out behind the body gives the impression of some malignant tropical growth, but of course it is as normal for these geckos as the split clinging pad at the tips of their digits. Some of the fat-tailed geckos are common in houses.

Among other weird tails are those carried behind the Australian leaf-tailed gecko, *Phyllurus cornutus,* which is probably the largest gecko in Australia (eight inches), and the kidney-tailed gecko (*Nephrurus*), the knob at the end of the latter apparently having reminded the herpetologist who named the genus of a kidney.

Even in Australia the myth that geckos are poisonous hounds these inoffensive lizards. Size has nothing to do with the fable, since the stone gecko, *Diplodactylus vittatus,* which is often called the stone adder and considered to be deadly venomous, is only three and a half inches long. It is a perfect example of ignorance filling the world with uncalled-for fears.

The Flap-footed Lizards
(*Family Pygopodidae*)

One of the recurrent evolutionary themes among lizards is the tendency to lose the limbs. The flap-footed lizards (family Pygopodidae) of Australia, Tasmania, and New Guinea constitute a prime example of this. The slender, snakelike members of this small family of about twenty species have lost completely all traces of forelegs. The hind limbs are represented by small scaly flaps on the sides of the body near the anus, giving these lizards their common name as well as their technical name, which means "hip foot." The legs, which scarcely deserve the name, are oblong in shape, with no outward evidence of joints or toes. The flaps are held pressed against the sides and, since they are small to begin with, usually escape notice, so that these lizards are often mistaken for snakes. In fact, the scaly-foot (*Pygopus*) is sometimes called the "salt-bush snake" or "jumping snake" by people who believe it is actually a snake.

Although small in all flap-footed lizards, the length of the flap varies in the family. The limbs reach their maximum length in the scaly-foot, in which the flaps are a little less than half an inch in an animal two feet long, and amount to between 1 and 2 per cent of the total length. Even in the "giant" of the family, the two-and-a-half-foot Jicar's lialis, *Lialis jicari,* from New Guinea, the legs are never over one-fourth inch long. The limbs are almost nonexistent in one of the smaller species, the pretty flap-foot, *Aprasia pulchellus;* all that is left of them in this six-inch lizard is a small scale and a minute bony spur.

This last structure represents part of the pelvic or hip girdle, and appears in the same form and relative size in most species of the family. Other parts of the skeleton are concealed in the flap feet. For example, in the scaly-foot, which has the best-developed limbs, several leg bones and the bones of four or five toes are recognizable. Only one leg bone can be found in Jicar's lialis and none at all in the pretty flap-footed lizard.

Lizards, like mammals, use their limbs for locomotion, among other things. But the legs of the flap-footed lizards are so ridiculously small that they cannot conceivably be used to help propel the body. Nevertheless, the flap-footed lizards seem to get around reasonably well despite this handicap. Several species, including the pretty flap-foot, are burrowers. The majority, however, live on the surface of the soil, taking refuge under rocks or low-growing vegetation. Locomotion is accomplished by a sidewise undulation, which of course only adds to the snakelike impression these lizards give. At least one species, Jicar's lialis, is said to use this wriggling motion in order to "swim" over tall, thick grass for short distances. For the most part, however, the lialis moves on the ground in the way its relatives do.

The long, muscular tail, which is as thick as the trunk and about twice the length of head and trunk together, is important in locomotion. Propulsion by means of this horizontal undulatory movement depends upon a part of the body pushing backward against a rough spot on the ground—a lump of earth or a rock—and so shoving the body forward. The short trunk of the flap-footed lizards does not provide nearly as many opportunities to utilize such purchase points as does the long tail. Although these lizards are able to break off parts of their tails to confuse enemies, the primary function of their tails is locomotion.

The superficial resemblances of the flap-footed lizards to snakes is carried one step further by their lack of movable eyelids. As in most geckos, the eye is covered by a large transparent scale or "spectacle" evolved from a clear area in the lower eyelid. Again as in most geckos, the pupil of the eye is vertical, but its edges are always smooth.

The resemblance to snakes comes to an abrupt end as soon as one looks at the rear of the head of a flap-footed lizard. The opening of the external ear is a typical lizard character and is found in all but four species of Pygopodidae. These four species are specialized burrowers, and their loss of the ear opening may be considered part of their specialization. The same loss occurs in other burrowing lizards as, for example, the worm lizards (family Amphisbaenidae). As an additional modification the four burrowers have pointed, awl-like heads with sharp snouts projecting beyond the lower jaws. Whether it is another adaptive feature or only coincidence, these burrowers have the smallest rudiments of hind limbs among the entire family; in fact, one has lost all external traces of legs.

Reproduction among the Pygopodidae is typical of lizards. They all lay eggs, but the number laid by each species is not yet known.

The insect diet of the flap-footed lizards is also characteristic of lizards in general. The teeth are bluntly pointed except in the two species of *Lialis.* The latter have sharply pointed, backward-curved teeth, and their diet of relatively large lizards also departs from the norm of the family.

In general appearance and behavior, the flap-footed lizards seem to be as unlike geckos as lizards can be. To be sure, both groups lack movable eyelids and both usually have vertical pupils. But the modes of life of these two families are radically different, reflecting to a very great extent the marked difference in the development of the limbs. Nevertheless anatomists have found such significant similarities in the skull and in the sense organs between these two families that the flap-footed lizards must be considered as probably more closely related to geckos than to any other living family of lizards.

The Agamids

(*Family Agamidae*)

The approximately three hundred species of agamid lizards live in the Old World, where they are much more abundant in the tropics than in temperate areas. The majority of agamids are medium sized, four to six inches being the average length of head and trunk, behind which the tail usually stretches for another eight to twelve inches. At one extreme, the giant of the family, the water lizard (*Hydrosaurus*) of the East Indies and New Guinea, reaches a total length of slightly over three feet, while at the other several of the toad-headed agamids (genus *Phrynocephalus*) never exceed five inches.

The agamids are typical lizards. They are scaly,

have four well-developed limbs, and usually have a moderately long tail. Roughly cylindrical bodies and tails and short, broad heads are the rule. Some groups of species, however, have bodies flattened above and below (e. g., the spiny-tailed agamids), and others have bodies flattened from side to side (*Calotes*). Nevertheless, the over-all impression is of a relatively uniform body shape.

But when we move our eyes past the trunk to the tail, we find one or two strange developments. The oddest tails of the family are owned by the spiny-tailed agamids (genus *Uromastix*). Unlike most agamids, whose slender, tapering tails ordinarily make up over half of the total length, the spiny-tailed agamids have thick tails that are shorter than the rest of the body; the head and trunk usually measure six to eight inches and the tail about an inch less. But the outstanding feature of the tail is its armor of large, hard, and pointed scales arranged in rings. These whorls of spines provide these non-aggressive lizards with their principal means of defense.

The spiny-tails are burrowers in the steppes and deserts of Central and West Asia and North Africa, and each lizard has its own burrow. Caught away from their underground homes, these lizards are relatively defenseless. Naturally, they head for home when danger looms. If attacked by a snake or small mammal, a spiny-tail ducks into its hole, leaving part of its tail protruding. If the enemy persists in its attack, the lizard swings its tail violently from side to side. A few blows from this heavy, spiny club usually discourage small enemies.

But when applied to large enemies, this defensive behavior sometimes leads to the downfall of these lizards. The people of northwestern India trick a spiny-tail into sticking its tail out of a burrow by brushing twigs across the ground near the entrance to imitate the noise of a snake moving through dry vegetation. The hunter then grabs the tail with one hand and pries the lizard out of its hole with a stick. The tail, once the spiny skin is removed, is said to be a delicacy.

Almost nothing is known about the function, if any, of the other outstanding agamid tail, that which belongs to the island water lizard, *Hydro-*

East Indian Water Lizard (*Hydrosaurus amboinensis*)

saurus amboinensis. Although thick and cylindrical at the base, this lizard's tail becomes progressively flattened from side to side toward the tip. The crowning glory of this appendage is the high crest it sports on its basal half. Supported by long bony processes from the tail vertebrae, the extremely flattened crest rises about two and a half inches, more than equaling the depth of the tail base. As its common name indicates, the water lizard is aquatic and lives among forest streams. It is a strong swimmer, propelling itself through the water by sidewise undulations of its tail. The flattening of the tail away from the base converts it into a more efficient paddle. Perhaps the high crest is a part of this same adaptation. Unfortunately, the observations of water lizards either free or in captivity have been too few to determine the exact use or uses of the "sailfin" tail.

The water lizard has another, though much lower, crest down the center of its back from the base of the tail to the nape. But this crest consists of scales only and is not unique among agamid lizards. Indeed, if any adornment is characteristic of the family, it is a scaly crest on the back. Typically, the crest consists of long, pointed scales that give it a jagged appearance. A hint of the function of these crests is provided by the fact that they are usually higher in males than in females.

Male lizards, including those of many agamids, are extremely combative, and competition for the females most often takes the form of fights in which bluff is the dominant element. When two males meet, they turn broadside to one another, so that each presents the largest surface to his opponent. Apparently the bigger they are the more successful the bluff. Males of certain other families commonly flatten their bodies and thus deepen and enlarge their appearance in side view. This flattening behavior has not been reported of any agamid, but the same effect is obtained by having a crest sticking up along the back. And in many male agamids, such as the Bornean angle-headed agamid, *Gonyocephalus liogaster,* the height of the crest may equal two-thirds of the depth of the body.

In connection with the crest, we should also mention the throat dewlap or fan so common in agamids and other lizards. This appendage of scaly skin under the throat is better developed in males or present only in them. The hyoid or tongue bones run through the dewlap, and by contraction of the proper muscles the lizard can expand or "flash" the fan at will. When expanded, the dewlap, like the crest, increases the surface area in side view.

Now, when two male agamids—for example, two Indian bloodsuckers, *Calotes versicolor*—approach one another, a more or less stereotyped ritual is performed. Each inflates his throat dewlap and turns sideways, so that his rival gets the full view of crest and dewlap, and bobs his head up and down. The nodding often involves the whole fore part of the body; the lizard bends his forelegs, then straightens them, repeating the cycle until a new phase of the "fight" is reached. If the fearsome display of crest and dewlap and the threatening bobbing gestures do not frighten away one of the combatants, they move closer and may get close enough to bite. But even the biting has overtones of sham, for, though the grip is strong and may be maintained a few moments, there is rarely any gore, and usually one bite is enough. One male retreats, and the fight is over.

Another element of these combats is color change, a common thread running through many groups and families of lizards. Although the word "chameleon" pops into our minds in this connection, the ability is also found in geckos, agamids, and iguanids. The technical name of the Indian bloodsucker, *versicolor,* means "changing color." Incidentally, *"versicolor"* is a much more appropriate name than "bloodsucker," for, of course, this lizard is no such thing. Possibly the common name was given it because of the reddish color assumed by victorious males. Ordinarily these lizards are brownish or grayish olive, with irregular dark brown spots or bars. During the course of a combat, the males change color rapidly, becoming lighter and darker, with the victor finally turning red and the vanquished remaining brownish or grayish. The final coloration of the loser is very much like that of a female.

Oddly enough, a male courting a female goes through many of the same actions as when fighting. This is true not only of the Indian bloodsucker and its relatives, but also of lizards in other families. A male bloodsucker, after spotting a female, will turn broadside to her and expand his throat dewlap. He becomes pale yellowish or flesh-colored, with a conspicuous black patch on each side of the throat. Then, just as in fighting, he bobs his head and forequarters. If the female appears to be receptive, the male moves a few steps closer and goes through his performance again. This process is repeated until the two are close enough to mate. The male approaches the female from one side and grips her neck with his jaws. With the hind leg closest to her, he clasps the top of her leg across her back and twists the hind end of his body under her. The female raises her tail and twists it away from the male. Then, as they bring their vents together, the male inserts a hemipenis. The pair usually remain together about two minutes.

Sometimes the female initiates the courtship. A flirtatious female of the common agama, *Agama*

agama, will run up to a male and raise her tail in front of him. Then he pursues her until, we presume, she lets him catch her. Of course, if the female is not in breeding condition, she does not court the male, nor can he mate with her even if he begins the courtship. He may bob in front of her or chase her until exhausted, but there will be no mating.

Posturing, display of throat fan, and color change are not restricted to activities centering around reproduction. Both males and females may defend certain home territories that are usually maintained for feeding purposes. If a female moves into the territory of another female, the occupant will turn sideways, puff out her throat, and change color. We watched such a performance put on by two females of a relative of the bloodsucker, *Calotes cristatellus,* in the Bornean jungle. The two lizards were in a low bush about two feet apart. One, dark brown with its small expanded dewlap almost black, was slightly above the other and bobbing its head. The other lizard, perched motionless, was a leafy green with vertical rows of turquoise spots. After watching them a while, we collected them, and the dark female immediately turned the same shade of green as the other.

The changes in color are obviously related to change in emotional state. Although generally associated with fighting over mates or feeding grounds, a shift in pattern or hue may also take place with fear of a predator, as in the case of the Bornean lizard's reaction to us. The bearded lizard of Australia, *Amphibolurus barbatus,* when teased turns bright yellow barred with orange; when relaxed this lizard is dark olive-brown. Sometimes agamids if threatened will flash a color not ordinarily visible. For example, one of the African species, *Agama atricollis,* a foot-long arboreal animal, is ordinarily brown mottled with silver-gray, sepia, bluish green, and yellow. But it will turn to face an intruder with head held high, and open its brilliant orange mouth.

Australian Bearded Lizard (*Amphibolurus barbatus*)

South African Agama (*Agama atricollis*)

This method of defense depends partly on surprise but primarily on bluff, a technique common throughout the animal kingdom and well developed among the agamid lizards. The Australian bearded lizard, though only a foot and a half long, can put on a fearsome display. The "beard" consists of a great many pointed scales on the throat and sides of the neck. When molested, the bearded lizard faces the enemy with mouth open, but the effective part of the display is accomplished by greatly distending the throat not only downward but sidewise as well, which stretches the mouth opening. The pointed scales of the "beard" then appear as a fringe of spines. What the enemy sees is a lizard whose head has suddenly grown twice as large as it was a fraction of a second before, and an enormous mouth fringed with spines. If the enemy is not much larger than the lizard, the ferocious display may turn his interests to other places and other food. The display may also cause an inexperienced boy to hesitate in his tormenting of the lizard just long enough for the animal to escape.

Another Australian agamid, the frilled lizard, *Chlamydosaurus kingi,* uses a variation of this technique. A scaly membrane or frill extends backward about two and a half inches from the throat and sides of the neck of this lizard. Most of the time the frill lies thrown in folds against the body, but by contracting the muscles attached to the tongue bones, which run out into the membrane like struts, the frill can be held out perpendicular to the body. The span of the frill may be seven inches in a lizard that has a head and trunk length of eight inches. Like the bearded lizard, the frilled lizard opens its mouth and raises its frill, and thus can confront an enemy with a head suddenly appearing several times its previous size.

The great majority of agamids feed exclusively on insects and other small invertebrate animals. These are run down, grabbed between the jaws, and broken up by the long row of rather sharp, compressed teeth. Some agamids, such as the toad-headed lizards (*Phrynocephalus*), though mainly insectivorous, include a few flowers, fruit, and leaves in their diets. The spiny-tailed agamids (*Uromastix*) are completely herbivorous, and their teeth are accordingly modified. Young spiny-tails have the usual sharp agamid dentition, but as they age the two front upper incisors drop out and are replaced by a broad downgrowth of the upper jawbone. The two lower incisors gradu-

ally fuse, so that the lizard eventually has two broad, bladelike "teeth" for nipping off bits of vegetation. The real chewing of the food, however, is done by the rear of the tooth row, where the teeth have developed broad-crowned grinding surfaces.

The agamid lizards live in many kinds of habitats. Many are arboreal, living in bushes and trees. Most of these climbers, like the bloodsucker and its relatives (genus *Calotes*) and the angle-headed agamids (genus *Gonyocephalus*), seem to have no special adaptations for this mode of living, clinging to the vegetation by means of their claws, which are well developed in all agamids, ground-dwellers as well as climbers. Generally, the arboreal groups have bodies that are compressed sidewise, and this shape, by keeping the weight centered along the midline and thus over the twig on which the lizard is perched, may be adapted to their mode of living. Some of the climbing agamids do have special aids to a life in trees. For example, the deaf agamids (genus *Cophotis*) have prehensile tails.

But the outstanding adaptation for arboreal life among agamids, and perhaps among all lizards, is the possession of a genus of small lizards (genus *Draco*) living in the forests of southeastern Asia and the East Indies. The appearance of one of these lizards clinging to the trunk of a forest giant is quite ordinary. After all, a slender eight-inch lizard hanging onto the bark with its claws is what one expects to see in the jungles of Sumatra or Borneo. Its colors are pleasing but neither brilliant nor camouflaging. The head, body, and limbs are forest green crossed by olive-colored bars. Then the lizard jumps out into space and is transformed into something as wonderful as it had seemed ordinary before, for it suddenly looks like a beautiful giant butterfly with black-spotted orange wings gliding to another tree thirty or forty feet away.

This is one of the remarkable flying lizards. Actually the common name is somewhat misleading, as they are able only to glide like "flying" squirrels, as distinguished from the true flight of bats and birds. The "wings" are broad scaly membranes reaching from front to hind legs, supported by five or six long ribs that grow out of the body. At rest, the wings are folded against the sides. In flight, the wings give the impression of flapping, but it is only the fluttering of their rear margins caused by the force of the air flowing past.

Probably no agamid lizard could be more different from the flying lizards than the spiny-tailed agamids (*Uromastix*) mentioned earlier. Large and heavy instead of small and slender, living in dry plains and deserts instead of humid green forests, burrowing in the ground instead of gliding through the air, the spiny-tailed agamids are at the opposite end of the spectrum. The family Agamidae has relatively few burrowers and none that lead a truly subterranean life. The spiny-tails tunnel with their strong claws for eight or nine feet and as deep as five feet, but these burrows are used for protection only—protection against animal enemies and against the radical daily temperature fluctuations so characteristic of dry, treeless country. They must leave their burrows to obtain food, which consists of grass, flowers, fruit, and leaves.

The toad-headed agamids (genus *Phrynocephalus*) are also pronounced burrowers. Unlike the much

Arabian Toad-headed Agamid (*Phrynocephalus nejdensis*)

←

Frilled Lizard
(*Chlamydosaurus
kingi*)

**Arabian Toad-headed
Agamid burrowing**
STANDARD OIL COMPANY

larger spiny-tailed agamids, these small (total length four to eight inches) inhabitants of the steppes and deserts of Central Asia have bodies flattened from top to bottom and slender, tapering tails. In addition to digging short tunnels a few inches long, the toad-headed agamids that live in sandy areas can bury themselves in sand by wriggling their flat bodies from side to side. This motion, which enables them to disappear from sight very rapidly, crops up again in the horned toads of our southwestern states and will be described in detail later. A burrowing life in dry soil presents some danger to the eyes from loose particles, but the toad-headed agamids successfully protect their eyes with strongly projecting scaly "eyebrows" that form what we might call eaves. In addition the eyelids have a fringe of long scales, and it is not stretching a point to draw a parallel between these scales and our own eyelashes. The projecting "eyebrows" protect the eyes from the pressure of soil, and the fringed eyelids flick away loose particles that may be blown against the lizard above ground in the windy deserts.

A good proportion of agamids have no specializations for life either in trees or underground. Nevertheless, they make a living scampering on the surface of the ground, climbing over rocks, and occasionally getting into low shrubs. The true agamas (genus *Agama*) fit this pattern. This large genus, which contains about fifty species, ranges from central India westward to extreme southeastern Europe, but has its real home in Africa, where it is found throughout the continent and where most of the known species live. With respect to body form, this is a rather undistinguished lot of lizards. The head is broadly triangular, with at most a poorly developed throat dewlap. Some species have clusters of small spines around the ear; in others, the spines occur but are shed seasonally. If a crest is present on the neck or back, it is usually low. The tail is always much longer than head and trunk and gradually tapered from the base. A few species grow to eighteen inches, but the usual size is around one foot. The agamas might almost be called the average lizards.

But the average lizard is an interesting creature—active, agile, and conspicuous. The common agama, *Agama agama*, for example, can be seen chasing insects around houses, sunning itself on stones, or courting and fighting in bush and grasslands over most of Africa. Its adaptability to the artificial conditions created by man has enabled the common agama to invade the dense rain forest wherever man has made a clearing for a village or plantation. This gray or blue lizard with its bright red or yellow head not only adds color to African villages, but it also earns its way by feeding so voraciously on insects. The great collector Herbert Lang, now research associate of the Transvaal Museum, saw a twelve-inch agama kill a four-inch grasshopper and then scare off a chicken that wanted a share of the prize. Although they conduct their affairs in plain view around houses, one false move and these lizards disappear, each into his own retreat, to reappear one at a time after danger seems to have passed. They frequently adopt the squirrel's habit of dodging behind a tree and moving so as to stay on the far side. The common agama has a good reason to be wary of man: its head is used by some Africans as a love potion.

A related lizard, the desert agama, *Agama mutabilis,* lives in the dry country of North Africa. It apparently avoids bare sand, preferring areas with scattered bushes. In such places it is abundant and, like so many desert lizards, feeds primarily on grasshoppers. Again like most desert lizards that are active by day, the desert agama dashes from bush to bush or from one cover to another. Relative speed is necessary not so much to escape enemies or to catch food, but to get out of the scorching sun. Because reptiles have no internal safety mechanism for regulating body temperature the way we mammals do, a reptile exposed to the blazing desert sun for even a short time, say about ten minutes, will be killed by the uncontrollable rise in its body temperature. It is true that desert lizards usually can tolerate higher temperatures than most reptiles; nevertheless even they cannot absorb the sun's heat for very long. During the cold desert night, a lizard becomes stiff and, with the sunrise, moves slowly into the sunlight to absorb enough heat to fire the engine, as it were. Then, once the body temperature reaches the most efficient level for the particular species, away it goes, hunting, courting, mating, and fighting, but always trying to stay in those parts of the environment with the most suitable temperature.

Another true agama, the hardun, *Agama stellio* (Plate 28), is one of the commonest lizards of the Nile delta. Every garden wall and every stony slope around Alexandria has its head-bobbing hardun. Not so long ago the excrement of the hardun was a highly prized cosmetic in the Near East, but times change. In general shape this foot-long lizard resembles all of the true agamas: broad and rather short head, thick body, and well-developed legs. But the tail is another matter. Instead of the usual overlapping, flat scales, the hardun's tail has rings of pointed and raised scales, bringing to mind the appendage of the spiny-tailed agamids. The hardun, however, still has the relatively thin, tapering tail of a true agama.

The wicked appearance of the appendage of the

spiny-tailed agamids, *Uromastix acanthurinus* (Plate 26), belies their rather docile behavior. This combination makes them sure-fire successes in traveling magic shows in Egypt. The spectators are fascinated by the vicious-looking tail, while the magician knows he has nothing to fear. All eleven species of *Uromastix* are inhabitants of very arid country and as a group are found from north central India to extreme northeastern Africa. Throughout this range they feed on vegetation.

Africa has only one other genus (*Aporoscelis*) for a total of three, a very low number compared to the twenty living in Asia. This ratio is a good measure of the difference in the variety of the two faunas. The genera *Agama* and *Uromastix* occur in Asia as well as Africa. *Aporoscelis* is restricted to Arabia and Northeast Africa, and it is very similar to the spiny-tailed *Uromastix*. Asia, excluding the rich East Indies, has nine genera found nowhere else, and its fauna runs the gamut from the burrowing, almost obese, spiny-tailed agamids to the small, slender, and graceful flying lizards.

The Asiatic agamid fauna is mostly concentrated in India and the tropical areas of Southeast Asia. Besides the true agamas and the spiny-tails, only the toad-headed lizards (*Phrynocephalus*), which mainly live in arid southwestern Asia, and one or two of the japalures (genus *Japalura*) occur outside of the tropics.

The largest tropical Asian group is the genus *Calotes,* the arboreal lizards including the Indian bloodsucker and its relatives. Twenty-three species of these usually green, long-legged, and long-tailed lizards live in India and Southeast Asia. Several species spill over into the East Indies and reach the southern Philippines. The accounts of behavior and color change given above for the Indian bloodsucker and a Bornean species apply equally to all members of this rather uniform group. Two or three species reach a length of two feet, of which as much as four-fifths may be tail, but the majority are between a foot and a foot and a half long. All live in bushes and trees, feed on insects and other small invertebrates, and lay six to twelve eggs. Differences between species usually involve arrangement and number of scales.

The rather heavy-bodied smooth-scaled agamid, *Leiolepis belliana,* of southeastern Asia contrasts sharply with the preceding genus. Where *Calotes* has large keeled scales, *Leiolepis* has minute smooth ones; whereas the body of *Calotes* is flattened from side to side, that of the smooth-scaled agamid is flattened from top to bottom. But the significant differences are in their modes of life. The smooth-scaled agamid is as terrestrial as *Calotes* is aboreal. In fact the former digs three- or four-foot burrows that serve as individual retreats. Unlike *Calotes, Leiolepis* eats as much vegetation as insects.

The coloration of the smooth-scaled agamid is attractive: the head and back are grayish or olive with black-edged yellow spots and stripes arranged longitudinally; the sides have bluish black and orange bars. During the breeding season, the neck and hind limbs of males become reddish and the throat and belly acquire blue markings. Fighting males flatten and distend the body by means of long, movable front ribs, and thus suddenly flash the brilliant colors of the flanks.

A naturalist of the last century claimed that these lizards could spring into the air while running and, by flattening their bodies, sail over the ground for twenty yards or more. According to this writer, the smooth-scaled agamid uses this aerial act when fleeing from enemies. The story is very dubious because, in the first place, in a glide such as this was supposed to be, the speed would decrease through the length of the flight and the animal could make better time on the ground. In the second place, many of these lizards have been collected in the seventy-five years that have passed since the original report without anyone's having seen them glide.

Southern Asia has some very odd-looking agamids, several of them found only in Ceylon. The three Ceylonese horned agamids (genus *Ceratophora*), for example, have a flexible, pointed spike or horn composed of one or several scales on the tip of the snout. Otherwise these are ordinary agamids with a coarsely scaled body, long tapering tail, and a low crest on the neck, and with the usual agamid habits of laying eggs and feeding on insects. What use these lizards make of their horns is not known. The fact that the horn is larger in males than in females suggests a courtship function, but this is pure speculation.

Another Ceylon lizard, the lyre-headed agamid, *Lyriocephalus scutatus,* is noteworthy because of the peculiar shape of its head. On the customary short, triangular agamid head, this lizard has superimposed a sharp bony crest above each eye and a globular lump about the size of the eye on the end of the snout. We know no more about the function of this lump than we do about the spikes of the horned agamids.

India and Ceylon are the home of Sita's lizard, *Sitana ponticeriana,* named after the wife of the Hindu hero-god Rama. Males of this agamid have an extremely long throat dewlap that, when folded, extends back almost to the middle of the belly. But Sita's lizard is most interesting because it is the only member of the family Agamidae showing any sign of degeneration of the limbs—it has four toes instead of five.

Though all of these Asian lizards have enough interest to warrant much more study than they have received, to us personally they are simply not in the same class with the flying lizards (*Draco*). The fifteen or so species are found from Burma and Indo-China southward and eastward through the Malay Peninsula and the East Indies to Celebes and the Philippines. One species, isolated from the rest of the genus, lives in southern India. For grace of form and movement and beauty of color, these lizards are matchless. Their fluttering, gliding flight has been described above. The coloration of the upper surfaces of the body is not spectacular, being green or grayish green in most species. The brilliant colors are confined to the wings, the throat dewlap, and flaplike wattles at the sides of the neck. Depending on the species, the tops of the spread wings are orange spotted with black, or reddish brown with black stripes and a broad maroon edge, or purplish black with light spots, or a mottled brown with white lines. The undersides of the wings are generally lemon-yellow or bluish. The neck wattles are often scarlet underneath, while the dewlap may be yellow, red, blue, or jet-black, again depending on the species.

Like many arboreal animals, *Draco* has the habit of moving around on a tree so that the trunk is always between the lizard and an animal it recognizes as a potential enemy. This trick can be maddening if one of the aims of a zoological expedition that has gone halfway around the world to the East Indies is to observe these creatures. On one occasion, however, we had an unobstructed view of the social activities of these lizards in a forest on a small island just off Celebes. Because of a steep slope, it was possible to look straight ahead at the level of the lizards well up on the trunks of trees only thirty feet away. A female with wings folded, clinging to the tree about twenty feet above ground, was being courted by a head-bobbing male. As he moved head downward toward her, his brilliant lemon-yellow dewlap and orange wings were extended. This bobbing display had gone on for only a minute when a second male glided over from another tree, and the two began to fight. They shook one another so vigorously that they fell off the trunk, separated in mid-air, and glided away to different trees.

Several other groups of Asian agamids live in the East Indies. We have already mentioned the bloodsuckers and allies (*Calotes*). Another large genus, the angle-headed agamids (*Gonyocephalus*), has half a dozen species in southeastern Asia and about twenty in the East Indies. Altogether thirteen genera

of agamids live in the East Indies (excluding New Guinea from this geographic division), and five of them are confined to this region. One of the natives, the hook-nosed agamid (genus *Harpesaurus*), has a rather long scale sticking up from the end of the snout. This upright, curved scale, which may equal one-fourth the combined head and trunk length, recalls the Ceylon horned agamids. One characteristic almost all East Indian agamids have in common is their arboreal habit, and no wonder, as the only nonforested areas in the East Indies are those cleared by man and those at the tops of mountains.

This major region of forest laps over into the next geographic division south and east of the Indies, but is interrupted by large natural grasslands in New Guinea and is still further reduced in Australia, with the result that some of the agamids have had the opportunity to develop into strictly terrestrial animals. Only two of the genera living in the East Indies reach the Australian region (in which we place New Guinea). One of these is the angle-headed agamid (*Gonyocephalus*), an arboreal group, and the other is the water lizard (*Hydrosaurus*). A third Australian genus (*Physignathus,* Plate 27) has one species living in Southeast Asia. The other six Australian genera are found nowhere else.

Bell's Angle-headed Agamid (*Gonyocephalus belli*)

M. W. F. TWEEDIE

Several of the native agamids are rather nondescript and are distinguished by structural details of interest to the specialist only. But Australia and New Guinea are also the homes of the frilled lizard (*Chlamydosaurus*) mentioned earlier. This lizard is interesting because of its ability to run on its hind legs with tail and forelegs off the ground, as well as the frill and its defensive use. Writers occasionally say that the bipedal running of the frilled lizard reminds them of pictures of dinosaurs, and rightly so, since those pictures were at least partly based on the locomotion of *Chlamydosaurus* and other nonrelated lizards with the same running posture.

The bearded lizard, *Amphibolurus barbatus,* whose fearsome display of expanded throat and mouth has been described, is also a native of Australia. Other species of the same genus do not have the distensible throat of the bearded lizard but do have the habit of turning on an attacker with open mouth. One of them, the Australian bloodsucker, *Amphibolurus muricatus,* though spending most of its time in bushes and low trees, will get up and run on its hind legs like the frilled lizard if it is pursued on the ground.

Another Australian agamid, the moloch, *Moloch horridus,* is probably the most grotesque of all lizards. This orange-and-brown, eight-inch inhabitant of sandy places is covered with spines arising from conical mounds so numerous as to be almost in contact with each other. A large knob bearing a spine over the eye enlarges the appearance of the small head. Slow and deliberate in its movements, the moloch is as different in temperament from its bloody namesake as is possible. Far from demanding human

Frilled Lizard (*Chlamydosaurus kingi*)

FRITZ GORO : *Life* MAGAZINE

JOHN WARHAM

Moloch (*Moloch horridus*)

sacrifices, this inoffensive creature merely requires a diet of ants, which it laps up with rapid flicks of the tongue. It has been estimated that a thousand to fifteen hundred small ants are consumed at one meal. Like other agamids, the moloch lays eggs, which in this case are slightly less than an inch long.

Before leaving this family, we must compare its range with that of the geckos. The latter are found all over the world in warm climates, the Agamidae only in the Old World. Furthermore the agamids have not been able to colonize the islands of the Pacific as the geckos have. Considering the difficulties of movement to these tiny dots of land, that is not surprising.

But it does seem strange that agamids, found throughout Africa, have not reached Madagascar, which stretches along the east coast of Africa for one thousand miles. We have already commented on how poor the African agamid fauna is compared to that of Asia. Only one genus, the true agamas (genus *Agama*), is found in tropical and southern Africa. And that fact contains the clue to the problem of their absence from Madagascar. Probably the agamids have reached Africa only in recent geologic

times from their ancestral home in Asia, and simply have not been there long enough to develop as many diverse types as are found in Asia or to jump the water gap to Madagascar.

One last comment: as we shall see in a following section, the distribution of the agamids complements that of the family Iguanidae. Where one family lives, the other does not.

Moloch (close-up)

JOHN WARHAM

The Chameleons

(Family Chamaeleonidae)

If there is any one fact that everyone knows about reptiles, it is that chameleons have the ability to change color. Here in the United States even the word "chameleon" acquired the meaning "to change color," with the result that the name was wrongly applied to our little anole, *Anolis carolinensis*, which is an iguanid lizard and not at all closely related to the true chameleons.

The true chameleons are found only in the Old World. Approximately half of the eighty species live in Africa south of the Sahara and the other half in the neighboring island of Madagascar. Only four chameleons live elsewhere. The common chameleon, *Chamaeleo chamaeleon,* lives on the southern fringe of the Mediterranean from Palestine eastward along coastal North Africa to southern Spain and, as a consequence, is the species most often kept alive in Europe, thus accounting for the "common." Two other species occur in the southwest corner of the Arabian Peninsula and one in India and Ceylon.

To return to color change, there are several popular misconceptions about chameleons' abilities in this matter. These are mentioned in connection with the anoles, but require mention here too. The first is that they change color to match their backgrounds and, as a corollary, that they can assume almost any color. As a matter of fact, while these abilities are remarkable enough without exaggeration, each species has a limited range of color change, and the changes are elicited not by background colors, but by other circumstances in the environment. Such factors as changes in light intensity or in temperature will result in the chameleon's becoming lighter or darker.

Ordinarily the Ituri chameleon, *Chamaeleo ituriensis,* a seven- to ten-inch species from the Congo first described by the senior author of this book, is forest green with large, irregular black spots on the body. From this it can pass gradually through lighter stages until it is very pale yellowish green without the dark spots, and, at the other end of its color range, it may become a distinct olive-green marked with black, or a very dark brownish green in which all traces of the dark spots are obliterated. Now, green and brown are the commonest colors in tropical rain forests, so that the Ituri chameleon stands a good chance, by coincidence alone, of resembling some portion of the low bushes in which it usually is perched. But, just as in the case of our little anole, color change in true chameleons is also governed by the lizard's emotions, and as a consequence of victory or defeat in a fight with a relative a chameleon may be pale green when brown would be better camouflage or brown when pale green would be better.

Common Chameleon (*Chamaeleo chamaeleon*)

Certain species, such as the three-horned chameleon, *Chamaeleo oweni,* of the Congo forest, have a more extensive color repertory. To the greens, browns, and blacks of the Ituri chameleon, the three-horned species adds white, yellow, and light reddish brown. On the other hand, some of the stump-tailed chameleons (genus *Brookesia*) can merely fluctuate between fawn brown and ashy gray.

But the ability to change color is just one characteristic of the chameleons and, to us at least, is one of the less striking things about these fascinating little beasts. After all, some iguanids, some agamids, and even geckos can change color. In size chameleons reach a maximum of little more than two feet, and two or three Madagascar species are said to be adult at the remarkably small size of one and a half inches. Most chameleons have an over-all length of eight to twelve inches. The facts that all chameleons have scaly skins and have bodies flattened from side to side are hardly worthy of mention. However, beyond these common lizard traits, chameleons are anything but ordinary.

The more remarkable aspects of chameleons fall into three categories: those that are connected with feeding, those that have to do with arboreal habits, and those that go under the heading of ornamentation. Taking these in order, the chameleons are the sharpshooters among the reptiles, using a common part of the anatomy, the tongue, in a unique fashion. Other lizards may depend on their tongues to pick up the scent of prey (e. g., monitors and Gila monsters); others may extend their tongues to lap up food the way we occasionally use our own tongues. But only chameleons shoot their tongues out for a distance, hit their prey, and quickly retract tongue and prey. This weapon, propelled at extreme speed often to a distance exceeding the combined length of head and body, is thrust forward by the sudden contraction of circular muscles and pulled back in by central longitudinal ones. The club-shaped end is coated with a substance sticky enough to cause the prey to adhere to the tongue.

Most chameleons feed on insects and other small invertebrates, food appropriate to lizards with bodies between four and six inches long. They make very interesting pets, and since World War II we have had many of them alive in our laboratory. During the summer we fed them on grasshoppers, flies, and other insects. In winter earthworms and mealworms were the staple food. Chameleons are voracious feeders, and, to avoid spending countless man-hours gathering food, one live-animal collector in Africa hit upon the scheme of dangling pieces of decaying meat six inches or so from branches to which his chameleons were tied. The meat attracted flies, and the chameleons perched there popping off flies all day.

Because it was a giant Madagascar chameleon, *Chamaeleo oustaleti,* twenty-two inches long, one of our pets posed a serious supply problem. A chameleon this size requires a great number of grasshoppers or mealworms, and somehow we had to keep it satisfied. The bright idea of tempting it with a half-grown mouse struck us. The mouse was no sooner put in the cage than the big chameleon was all interest. But could the tongue pull in such large prey? Nothing to it! From its perch on a branch, while still a foot away, the chameleon shot out its tongue, and the next instant the mouse was being crushed in the chameleon's jaws. After that we saved much of our time by feeding it young mice regularly. Meller's chameleon, *Chamaeleo melleri* (Plate 62), a big African species, is known to feed on birds.

Despite its usefulness, a chameleon's tongue has its limitations. We learned, for instance, and quite by accident, that it cannot pick up wet objects. Customarily the earthworms we fed our chameleons were washed after being removed from an earth-filled jar and then dried before being placed in the cages. On one occasion a small amount of water in the feeding dish of a ten-inch O'Shaugnessy's chameleon, *Chamaeleo oshaugnessyi,* escaped notice, and an earthworm was dropped in it. As usual the chameleon turned toward the food, aimed, and fired the tongue from the normal range of six inches. But the earthworm did not stick to the tongue. The chameleon moved a half-inch or so closer and tried again. Still no success. This process was repeated about ten times, the chameleon moving a little closer each time, until finally it was only an inch away. Then the chameleon leaned forward and picked up the earthworm with its jaws, employing the age-old, nonspecialized, lizard method of getting food.

The ordinary lizard technique of grabbing prey with the jaws does not involve the animal in problems of range estimation. But range estimates are as important to a chameleon as they are to naval gunners. If a fly is six inches away, the tongue must be shot out that far. Five and a half inches will not do. The distance to a food object cannot be determined merely by its apparent size, since the fly may be a big horsefly or a small housefly. To estimate the distance to an object we need to use both eyes, providing ourselves with a stereoscopic picture. A chameleon, though depending on the same basic effect, improves the accuracy of its stereoscopic view by rocking the fore part of its body, so that it looks at its prey from several angles.

Aside from providing the good vision basic to the chameleon's method of catching food, its eyes are remarkable for other reasons. The first thing that strikes us about these rather large and bulging eyes is that they are almost wholly covered by thick lids, leaving only a small peephole exposed. Backward, forward, up, down, the eyes (or at least the openings in the lids) are able to swivel in a complete hemisphere. And each eye moves independently of the other.

Now, suppose you are putting a grasshopper on the floor of a chameleon's cage. As you do, the chameleon has its back to you, but not its eyes, which are both pointing at you so that they are oriented 180 degrees from the direction of the snout. Then a slight movement of the grasshopper attracts the chameleon, and the near eye swivels to focus on this new interest. With the other eye still pointing at you, the chameleon swings around on its branch to face the grasshopper. Finally, its suspicions allayed, the chameleon turns the second eye on the grasshopper and moves forward on its perch. The end of the branch is just a little too far from the grasshopper, so the chameleon grasps the end with its hind feet and tail. Then with its body stretched forward into space, it rocks jerkily from side to side getting the range accurately, opens its mouth slightly, and in a split second the tongue is shot out and retracted. And our chameleon is contentedly munching on a grasshopper.

But we have left the lizard dangling off the end of its perch. How does it manage to get back, and how did it get into that position in the first place? This brings us to the second category of chameleon adaptations—those connected with an arboreal life. In the lizard families discussed so far, we have

South African Chameleon and young (*Chamaeleo pumila*)

seen two basic climbing modifications of feet, namely the strong claw and the toe pads. But the chameleons have their own unique specialization. The toes are united into two opposing bundles on each foot, two toes on the outside and three on the inside on the front feet and three on the outside on the hind feet. Only the last joints and the claws of each toe are separate. Thus the feet have been changed into clasping tongs strong enough to support the body when only the hind feet are engaged.

The finishing touches to the clasping, climbing mechanism are provided by a strong prehensile tail. In other families of lizards, one or two arboreal species have developed prehensile tails, but only among the chameleons has this type of appendage become the rule. Furthermore, the chameleon's tail is so inclined to curling around twigs that, when at rest and not wrapped around anything, it often coils up tightly like a watch spring.

Quite aside from anatomical features, chameleons behave in a way that is associated with arboreal lizards. When on a bush and stalking an insect, a chameleon does not move forward swiftly to within firing range. Instead one forefoot is lifted, moved forward, and stopped just short of clasping the twig, all at a painfully slow pace. Then the chameleon rocks back and forth, and finally the raised foot grasps the twig. Next, the opposite hind foot is lifted and moved forward at the same very slow rate, the body rocks, and the foot comes down. And, when a moving chameleon does not seem to be going anywhere in particular, the slowness with which the feet move is unbelievable.

Now, obviously a hungry chameleon does not attempt to run its food down. Stalking, which is the chameleon's forte, depends on slow movements, and a chameleon is an expert at that. But stalking also involves concealment. A cat crouches so that grass stems and low herbs will hide it. Apparently a chameleon achieves the same end by acting like a leaf. Its compressed body has a rough resemblance to the shape of a leaf, and the jerky, rocking movement that accompanies each step may be likened to the action of a leaf disturbed in a breeze.

Slow and painfully deliberate motion among lizards seems to be associated with arboreal habits. Apart from the chameleons, the only lizards that behave this way are several arboreal iguanids. Having just claimed this habit for tree-dwellers, we must point out that the small stump-tailed chameleons (genus *Brookesia*), a group of about twelve species, are often found on the ground yet retain the family gait, and may be seen rhythmically rocking their slow way down a forest trail.

Occasionally a chameleon will abandon its slow movement in order to escape an enemy. But even when fleeing, most chameleons could not challenge the speed of the proverbial tortoise. At least one chameleon, the three-horned chameleon, *Chamaeleo oweni,* of the African rain forest, is capable of jumping, though its leaps are usually downward and less than two feet long.

Despite the ornamental and sometimes bizzarre assortment of spines and scales we have seen in certain agamid and iguanid lizards, their ornamentation is not in the same class with that of the chameleons. Helmetlike crests, movable scaly flaps, bony horns, and wartlike projections on the snout adorn the heads of chameleons, though usually not all in combination. The commonest and simplest development consists of a scale-covered, bony crest or casque at the rear of the head. Typically, as in the Indian chameleon, *Chamaeleo zeylanicus,* the casque rises sharply in an arc on the mid-line immediately behind the eyes. Movable scaly flaps at the rear of the head are well developed in the widespread African flap-necked chameleon, *Chamaeleo dilepis* (Plate 63). In certain species, Labord's chameleon, *Chamaeleo labordi,* of Madagascar, for instance, both a casque and a horn growing out from the snout are present, whereas in the short-horned chameleon, *C. brevicornis,* also of Madagascar, the scaly flaps are added to the assortment.

Easily the most striking development, the "horns" take a variety of form. Perhaps the simplest condition is found in the short-horned chameleon, which has merely a scale-covered knob at the end of its snout. From this starting point, the horns, though always growing on the snout, vary in several directions, the principal types being those that are covered with scales and those that are not. Among the former type, we find species with one horn, others with two, and, somewhat surprisingly, some species (*Chamaeleo furcifer,* the forked-nosed chameleon, for example) with a single but forked projection. Probably the ultimate of the single scaly type occurs in a species from Madagascar, *Chamaeleo gallus,* which has a broad, flattened, bladelike projection about as long as the head itself and recalling a rooster's comb except that it is in the wrong place.

Actually, because of their flattened shape and frequent flexibility, many of the scaly projections should not be referred to as "horns." However, the second type, the one lacking scales, is rigid, pointed, and cylindrical, and can be called a "horn" with less stretching of the word. Chameleons with this type of projection may have short horns or long ones. And, even more interesting, different species are characterized by one, two, three (e.g. Jackson's Chameleon, Plate 61), or four horns.

All of the bizarre decorations of chameleons are either the exclusive possessions of the males or are better developed in the males. The horns without scales, for instance, are found only in the males, and this has given rise to the belief that males use them for fighting. The thought of a three-horned chameleon, for example *Chamaeleo oweni,* which looks like a miniature *Triceratops* dinosaur, charging one of his fellows is all but irresistible. Of course a chameleon charge is likely to be carried out in slow motion, destroying some of the romance, but it is still a fascinating idea. One live-animal collector decided he would treat himself to one of these bouts, and put two of his recently captured three-horned chameleons on an isolated branch. They immediately bore down on one another, but combat was not the purpose, for they merely climbed over one another, each heading for the other end of the branch.

The rather dull fact is that there is no evidence that the horns are used in fighting. Male chameleons do fight, but it would be better to refer to this behavior as a challenge, since they rarely make physical contact. Just as is the case with many other lizards, male chameleons attempt to bluff a rival.

The body is inflated with air, the throat is puffed out, the mouth opened slightly, and the whole animal turned broadside to the other male, giving him an exaggerated idea of its size. Possibly the horns, by adding to the outline, play a part in this bluff.

Males tend to establish territories that they try to keep free of other males. They will even exhibit this behavior if a number of them are kept in a large cage. With their swivel eyes, male chameleons are well equipped to keep watch on their territories —up and down, forward and to the rear. Of course, females are free to move into the territories of the males; otherwise the species might fail to reproduce.

Most species of chameleons are oviparous, and this poses a problem for the females. Chameleons are not built for squeezing under bark or any other confined space that might be suitable for secreting eggs above ground. Furthermore, the number of eggs laid is often large—say thirty to forty—adding to the difficulty of finding a good place for them in a tree or bush. As a consequence the females are obliged to descend to the ground, a dangerous and apparently uncomfortable place for arboreal creatures, in order to lay their eggs.

The Indian chameleon, *Chamaeleo zeylanicus,* a moderately large species with a body length of

Fischer's Chameleon (*Chamaeleo fischeri*)

ERICH SOCHUREK

eight inches, leaves her bush at laying time and digs a hole in the ground. One observer said that the digging reminded him of that of a terrier, because the chameleon tore into the earth with its forefeet and kicked the loose dirt to the rear with its hind feet. After the eggs are laid, the female turns around and pulls the earth back into the hole with her forefeet and tamps it with her hind feet. One particular female required three days at the job, two to dig the hole and one to lay the eggs and cover them. Chameleons are so completely diurnal that this female—and we presume this would be true of them all—worked only during the day and climbed up into her bush each night. The eggs, numbering thirty-one in this case and measuring just over half an inch, were buried at a depth of twelve inches.

This example is typical not only of the Indian chameleon but also of many other species, the differences in details being very slight. For instance, the common chameleon of the southern half of Africa, *Chamaeleo dilepis,* usually digs a hole only eight inches deep and lays thirty-five to forty eggs. The eggs of this species take approximately three months to hatch. Chameleons that live in the African rain forest often take advantage of the abundance of rotting logs and lay their eggs in this soft material, thus avoiding the hard work of digging in the earth.

The perils of a descent to the ground are escaped by a few chameleons that are viviparous and are therefore able to carry out all reproductive functions in the relative safety of bushes and trees. So accustomed were we to the idea that most chameleons lay eggs that we began to plan a special sand bottom for the cage of our captive two-lined chameleons, *Chamaeleo bitaeniatus.* As we stood there discussing the matter, a large female, who we thought was about ready to lay eggs, proceeded to give birth to her young right before our eyes.

The membrane encasing the newborn chameleon is sticky and adheres to the twigs it contacts. For a moment the young chameleon struggles, rupturing the membrane; then with eyes swiveling at all the strange sights, he clutches the twig with his tonglike feet and prehensile tail and is off to seek his fortune.

The viviparous chameleons are species that live throughout South Africa or in the mountains of other areas. Seven of the nine species in South Africa are live-bearers. But whether found in the mountains or in South Africa, the viviparous chameleons live in cooler climates than the species of lowland Central Africa. This pattern resembles that of the iguanids, in which the viviparous species tend to be mountain-dwellers. In the lacertids we find live-bearing in the species living farthest north.

Jackson's Chameleon (*Chamaeleo jacksoni*)

Practically all we have written so far of chameleons applies to the genus *Chamaeleo,* which includes about five-sixths of all the species. The most distinctive features of chameleons—the projectile tongue, the rotating eyes, the tonglike feet, and the generally compressed body form—are common to the other three genera of the chameleon family. But they differ from *Chamaeleo* in several ways. For one thing, none of the three has prehensile tails.

The stump-tailed chameleons (genus *Brookesia*), for example, have short tails capable of curling slightly at the tip but not of coiling around twigs. However, this is only a minor handicap to these chameleons, because they are not only terrestrial, living on forest floors, but are also able to climb bushes using their remarkably modified feet. About half of the species of stump-tailed chameleons live in Madagascar, the rest in Central Africa. These small chameleons—none of them is over four inches long—are oviparous, the number of eggs per clutch varying from two to eighteen.

The remaining two genera are confined to Madagascar and include only four species. One, the armored chameleon, *Leandria perarmata,* a four- to five-inch lizard, has a double row of spines run-

[95]

ning down the back and out the tail. It is unfortunate that next to nothing is known of the habits of the dwarf chameleons (genus *Evoluticauda*), the last three species, for, on the basis of present information, they are just about the smallest living reptiles. Of course there is always the possibility that after more dwarf chameleons have been collected we may discover that our inch-and-a-half specimens are merely half grown.

The Iguanids

(*Family Iguanidae*)

Despite much diversity in body form, all iguanids have a scaly body, four well-developed limbs, movable eyelids, and usually a moderately long tail. In size they range from the six or seven feet of the common iguana, *Iguana iguana,* down to the four or five inches of the Texas tree uta, *Uta ornata*. The majority are between eight and fifteen inches long. Most of the iguanids feed on insects and other small invertebrates, and most of them lay eggs. In all of these characteristics, the iguanids come close to the average for all lizards, just as do the agamids. In fact the Agamidae and Iguanidae are very similar.

The iguanids, which include about seven hundred species, are distributed from southern Canada (British Columbia) to southern Argentina, with many species in the West Indies. The great majority of the lizards in North America belong to this family. Outside of the Western Hemisphere, the Iguanidae are found only on Madagascar (seven species) and the Fiji Islands of the South Pacific (one species). At the end of the section on agamids, we observed that where one of these two families lived, the other did not. Africa has agamids but no iguanids; nearby Madagascar has iguanids but no agamids; Asia, the East Indies, and Australia have agamids but no iguanids; the Americas have iguanids but no agamids. In some way we still do not understand, these two families must compete with one another to such an extent that one (presumably the Agamidae) always drives out the other.

A comparison between the agamids and iguanids discloses some curious resemblances. Each family has produced corresponding odd types. For example, the iguanids have developed a group of South American species (genus *Urocentron*) that have the same thick body and, more interestingly, the same kind of prickly tail found in the spiny-tailed agamids (*Uromastix*). The East Indian water lizard (*Hydrosaurus*), an agamid, has its counterpart in the iguanid basilisks (genus *Basiliscus*) of tropical America. Both the basilisks and the water lizard live close to water on riverbanks; both have a high, flat crest on the basal half of the tail; both have fringes of scales on the sides of the toes; and, most remarkable of all, both can rear up and run on their hind legs, and in this semierect posture can actually run over the surface of water for short distances.

Both families have given rise to some grotesquely spinous lizards: the Agamidae have their moloch, *Moloch horridus,* of Australia, and the Iguanidae their horned toads (genus *Phrynosoma*) of the southwestern United States. The horned toads further resemble the moloch in preferring semiarid and arid country and in feeding almost exclusively on ants.

With so many similarities between the two families, why have herpetologists considered them distinct? Why not put all of these lizards in one world-wide family? The basic difference lies in the teeth. The agamids have teeth seated on the crests of the jawbones, whereas those of iguanids are set on the inner sides of the jawbones. As the iguanids wear out or lose teeth, they are replaced; but the agamids do not have replacement teeth. These may seem like trivial differences. Yet, when all of these Old World lizards (with the exception of the seven on Madagascar) have one kind of dentition and all in the New World the other, regardless of the peculiarities of body form, this difference takes on significance.

The evolution of similar types in the two families, such as the water lizard and the basilisk, falls under the heading of "convergence," and can be explained on the basis of there being an opening in the environments of both the Old and New Worlds for the particular types. The forests of the East Indies and Central America, for example, apparently had room for a rather large aquatic lizard, and each family evolved one to fill the niche. On the other hand, because there is an opening, it does not necessarily follow that an animal will evolve to fill it. Presumably a flying lizard, like those of the East Indies, could make the grade in the vast rain forests of the Amazon, but none has evolved there.

The iguanids have two main types of body form, the one flattened from side to side and the other somewhat flattened from back to abdomen. The first type is characteristic of arboreal iguanids, just as in the Agamidae, and is best exemplified by the helmeted iguanids (genus *Corythophanes*) and the long-legged iguanids (genus *Polychrus*) of tropical America. In general, the iguanids with bodies flattened above are ground-dwellers, like our earless

[continued on page 113]

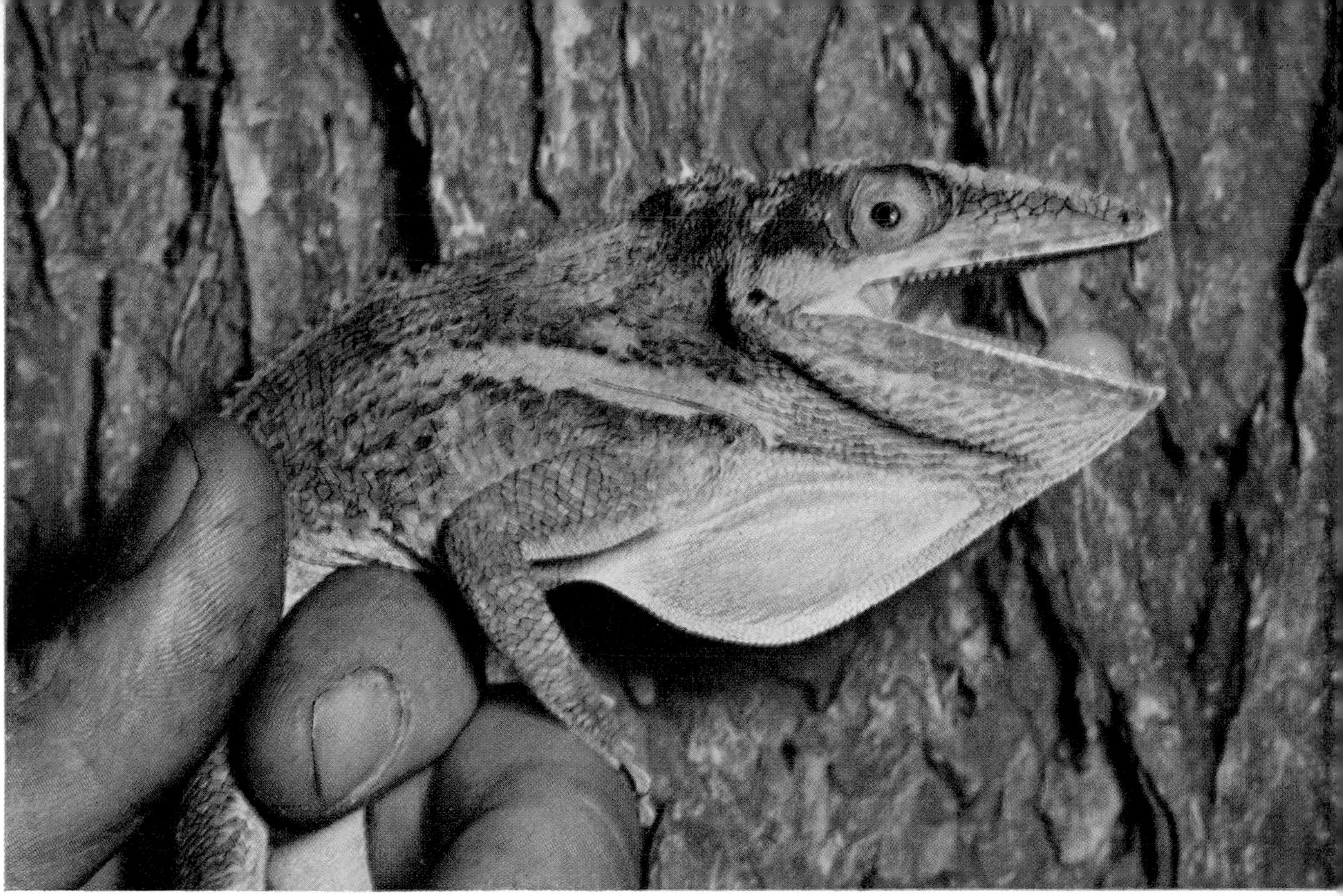

31. Knight Anole (*Anolis equestris*)

[CY LA TOUR AND DETROIT ZOO]

32. Green Anole (*Anolis carolinensis*)

[L.W. RAMSEY]

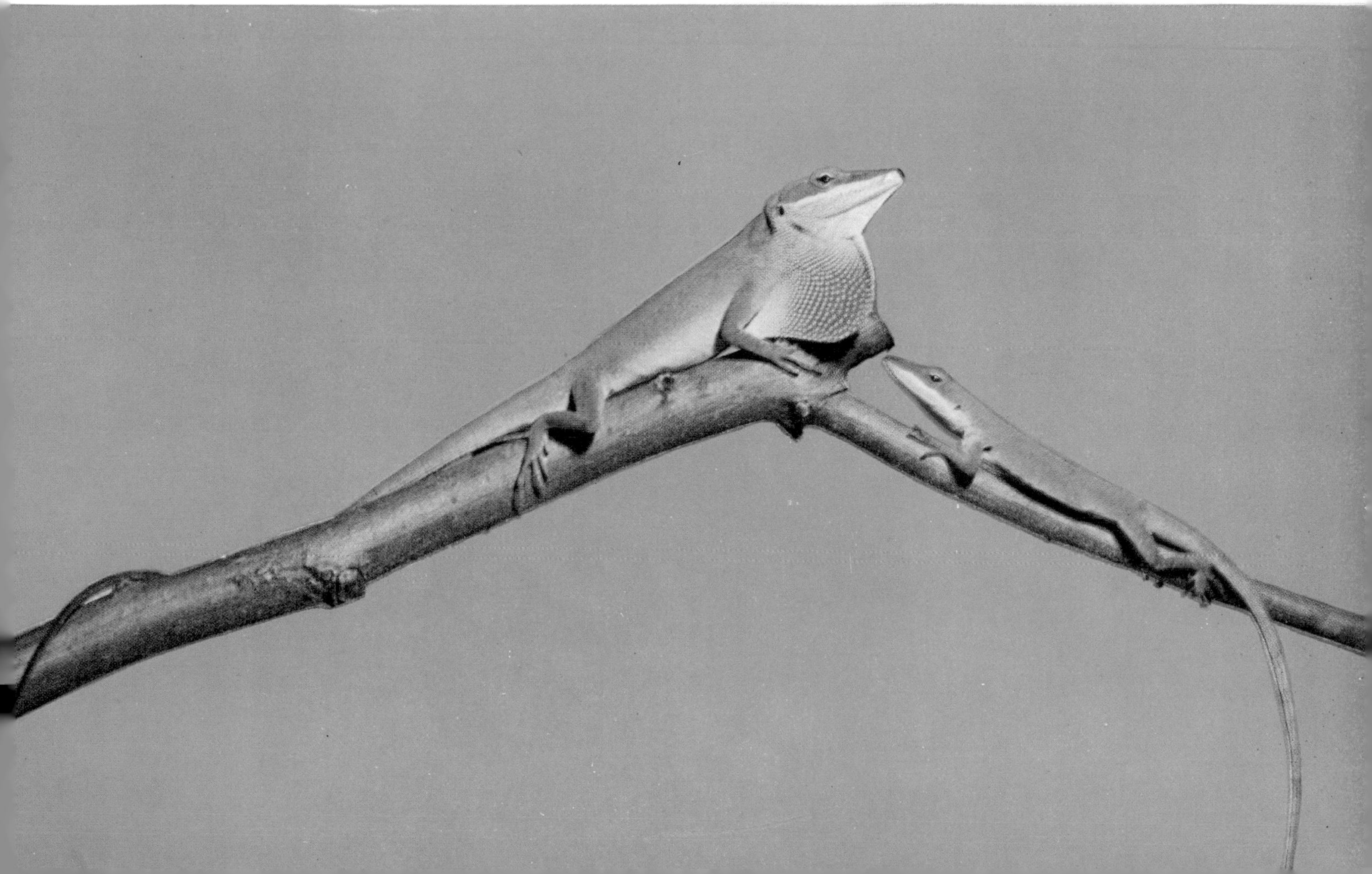

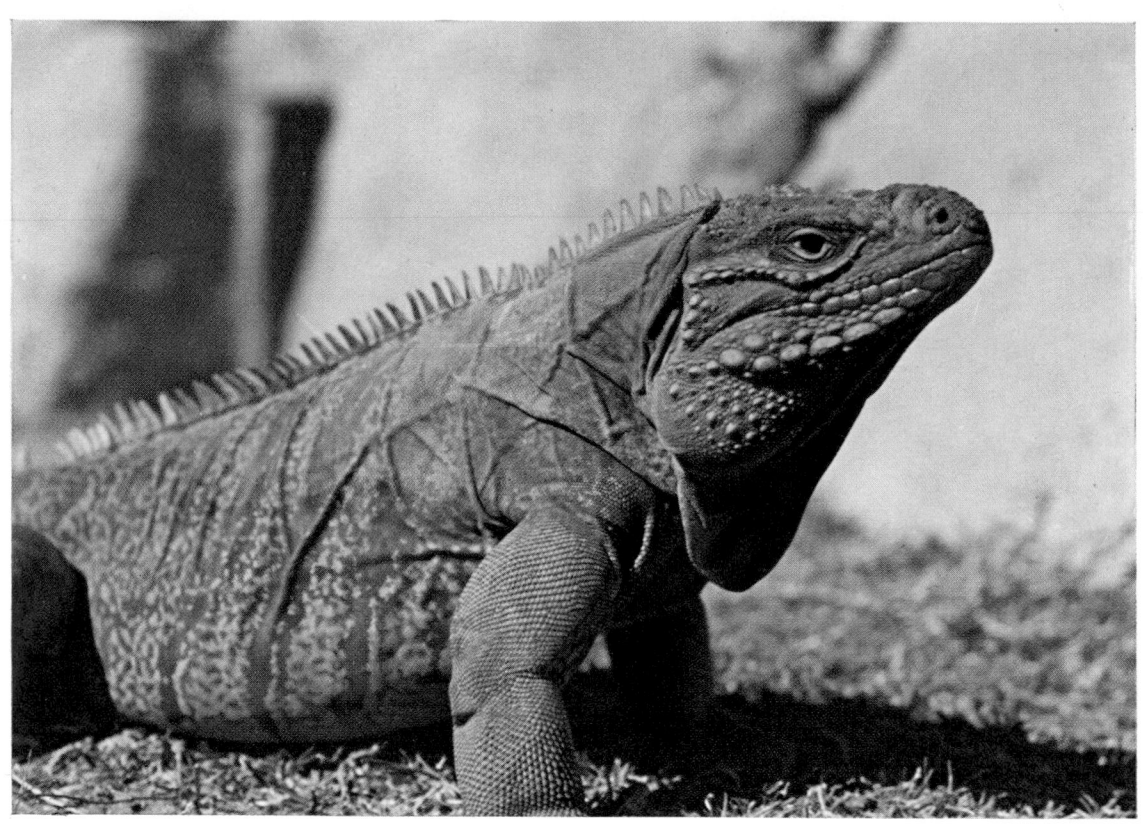

33. Cuban Ground Iguana (*Cyclura macleayi*)

[CY LA TOUR AND SAN DIEGO ZOO]

34. Cuban Ground Iguana

[CY LA TOUR AND SAN DIEGO ZOO]

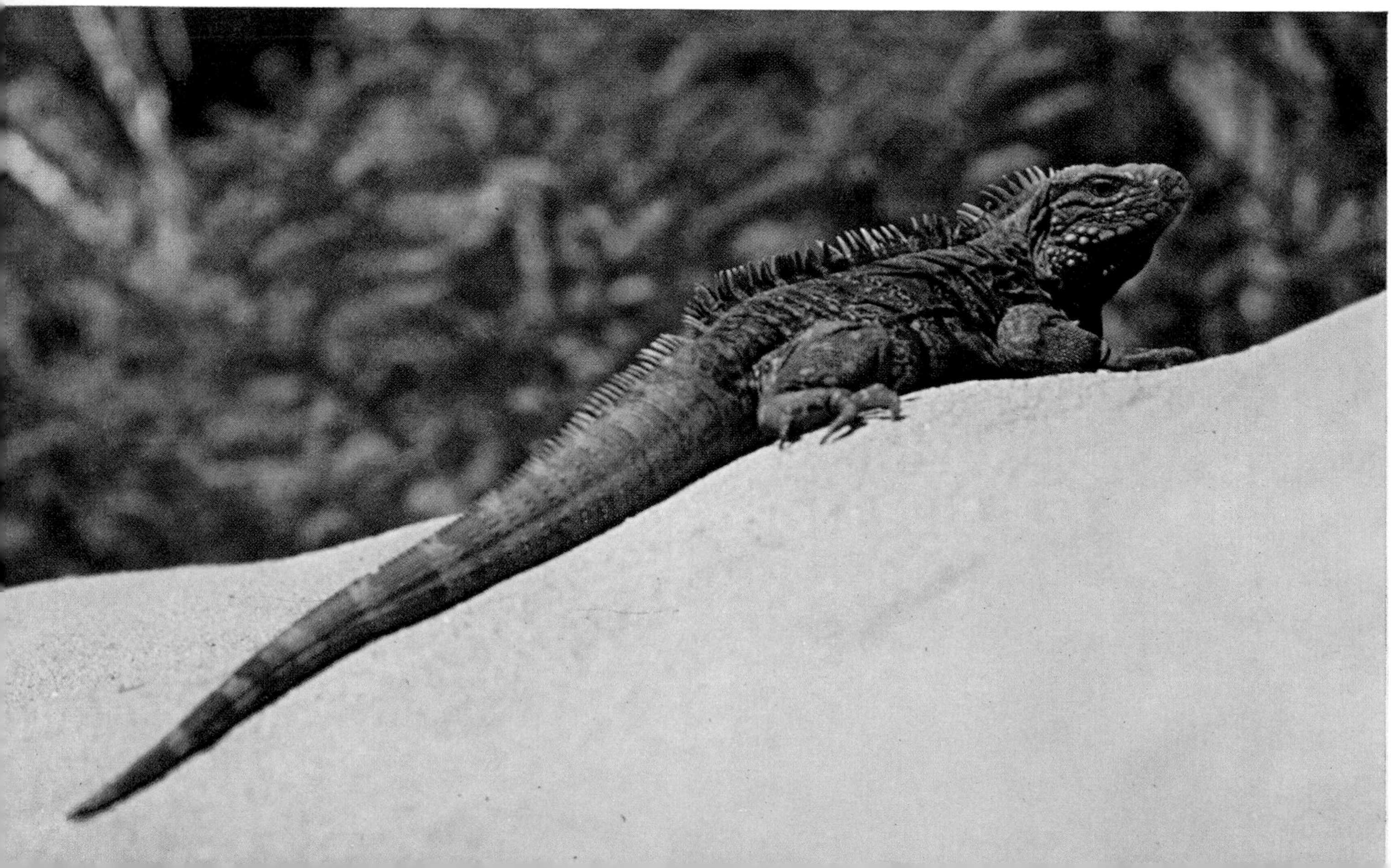

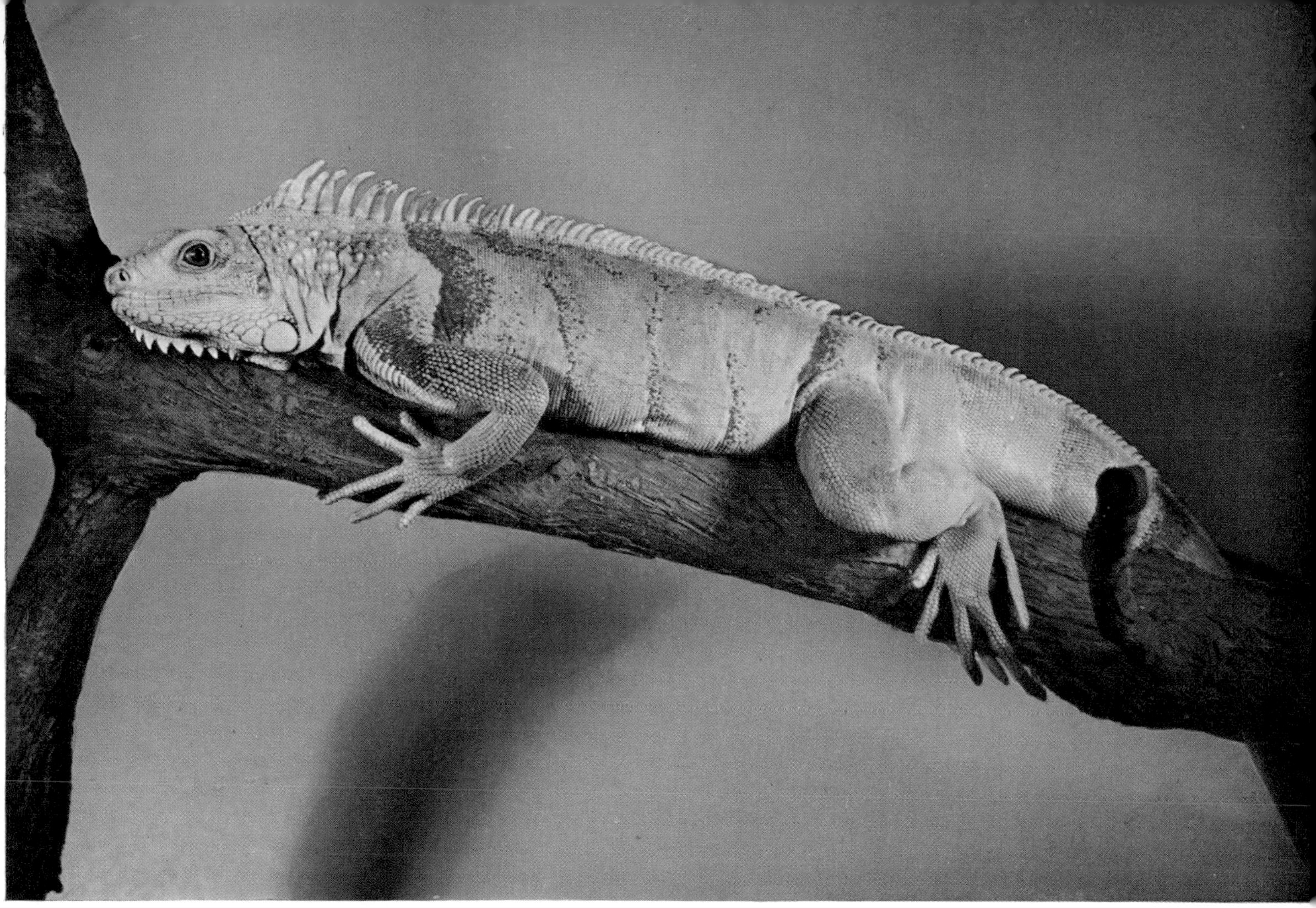

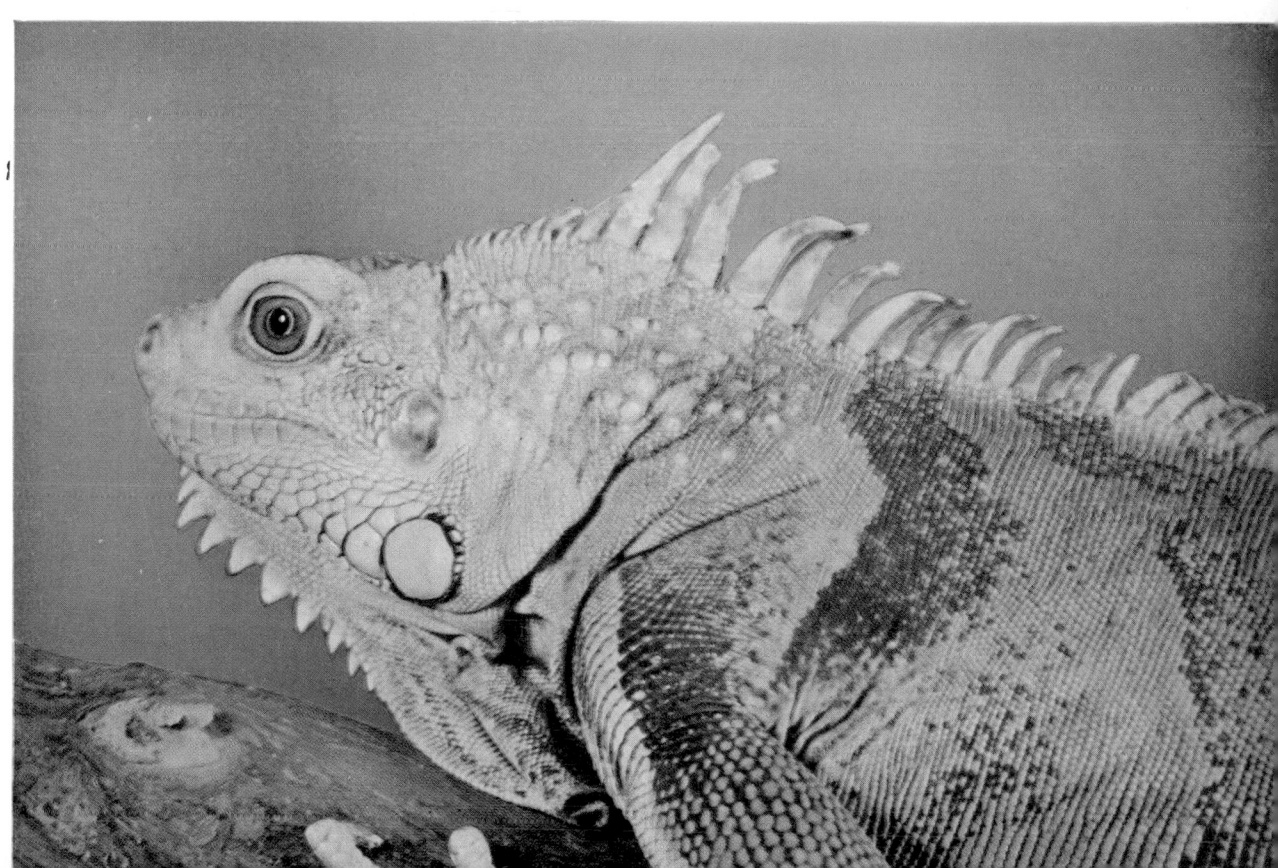

35. Common Iguana (*Iguana iguana*)

[CY LA TOUR AND BROOKFIELD ZOO]

36. Common Iguana

[CY LA TOUR AND BROOKFIELD ZOO]

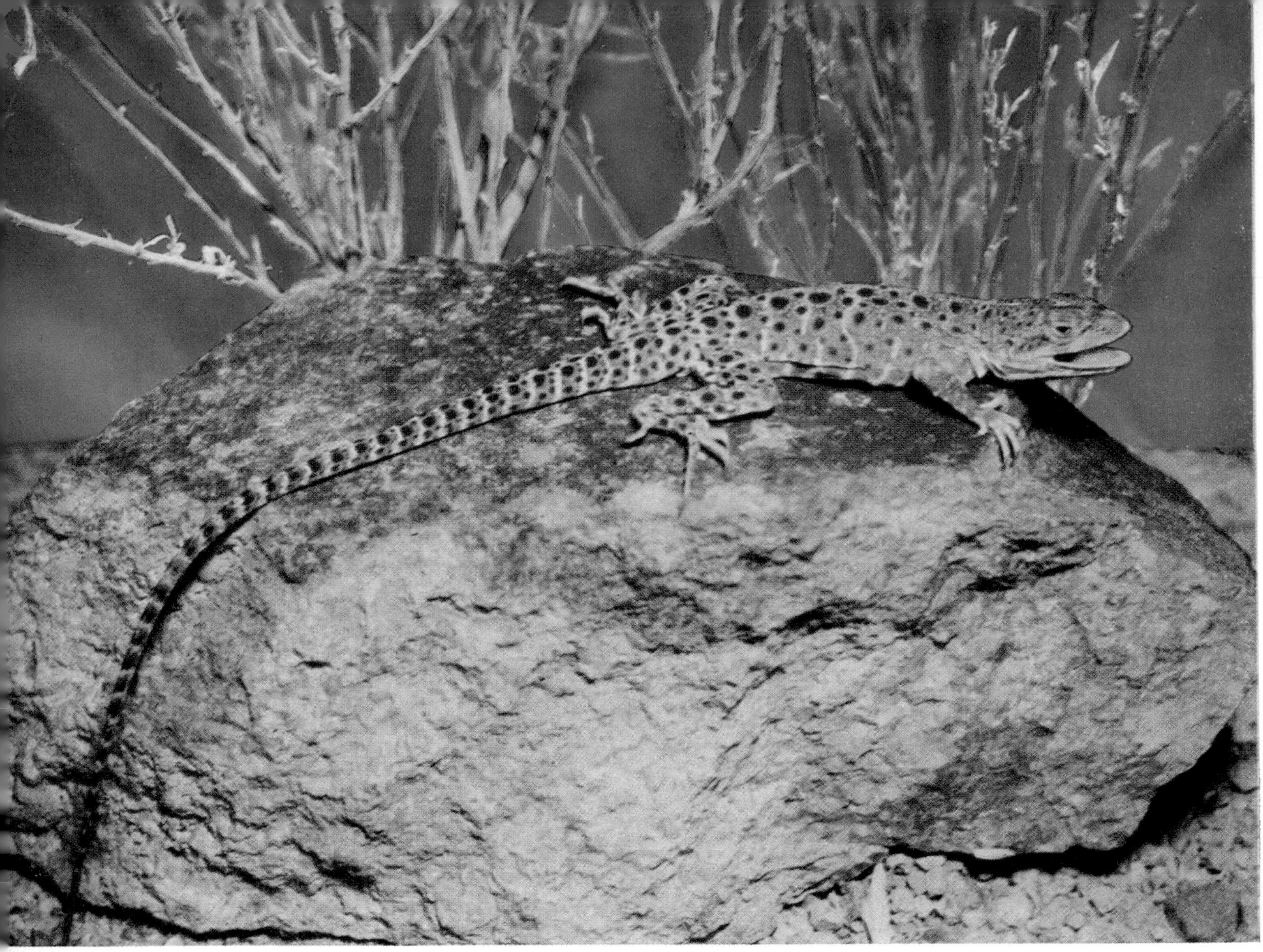

37. Leopard Lizard (*Crotaphytus wislizeni*)

[HAL H. HARRISON : NATIONAL AUDUBON]

38. Gridiron-tailed Lizard (*Callisaurus draconoides*)

[HAL H. HARRISON : NATIONAL AUDUBON]

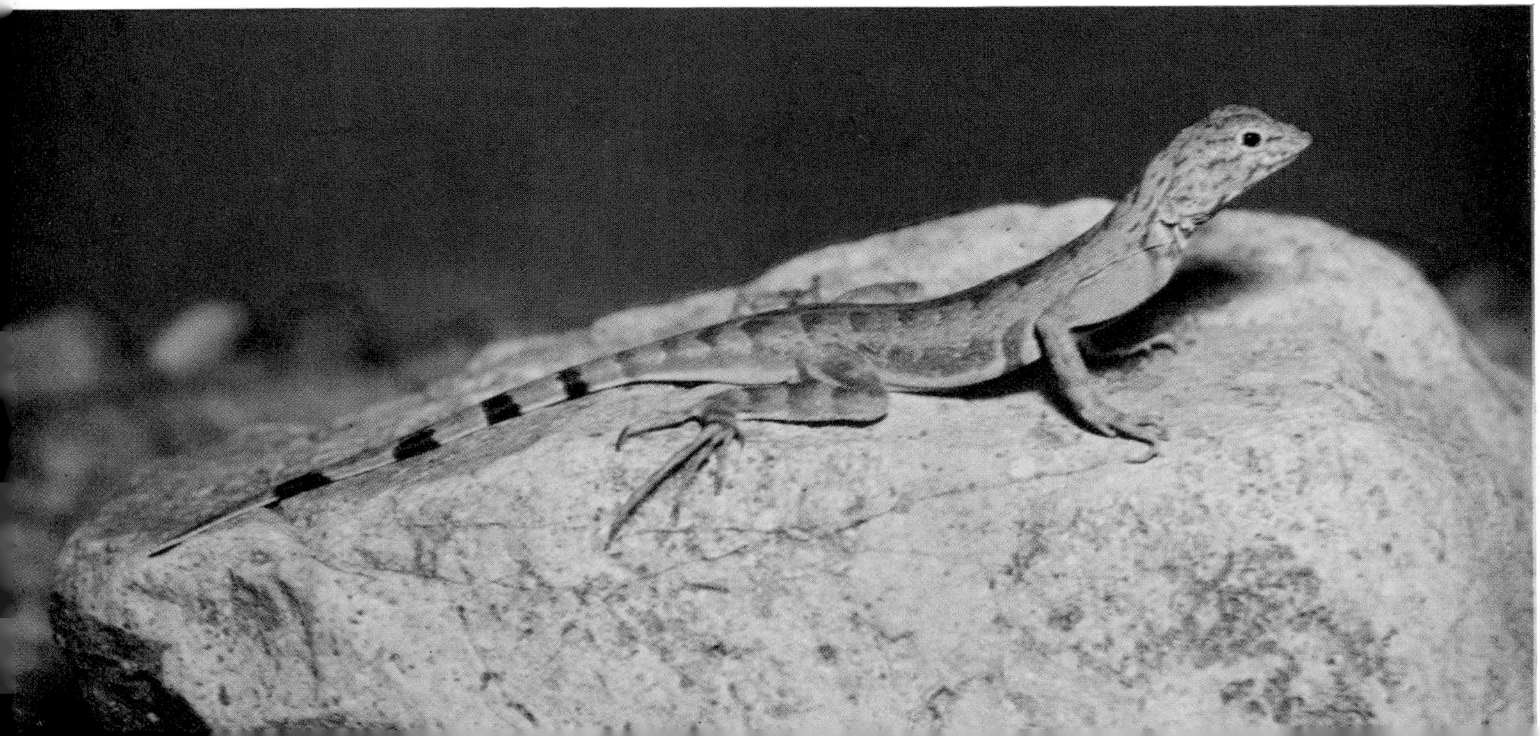

39. Side-blotched Lizard (*Uta stansburiana*)

40. Lesser Earless Lizard
(*Holbrookia
maculata*)

41. Fence Lizard
(*Sceloporus
undulatus*)

42. Fringe-toed Iguanid (*Uma notata*)

43. Coast Horned
Toad
(*Phrynosoma
coronatum*)

⟶

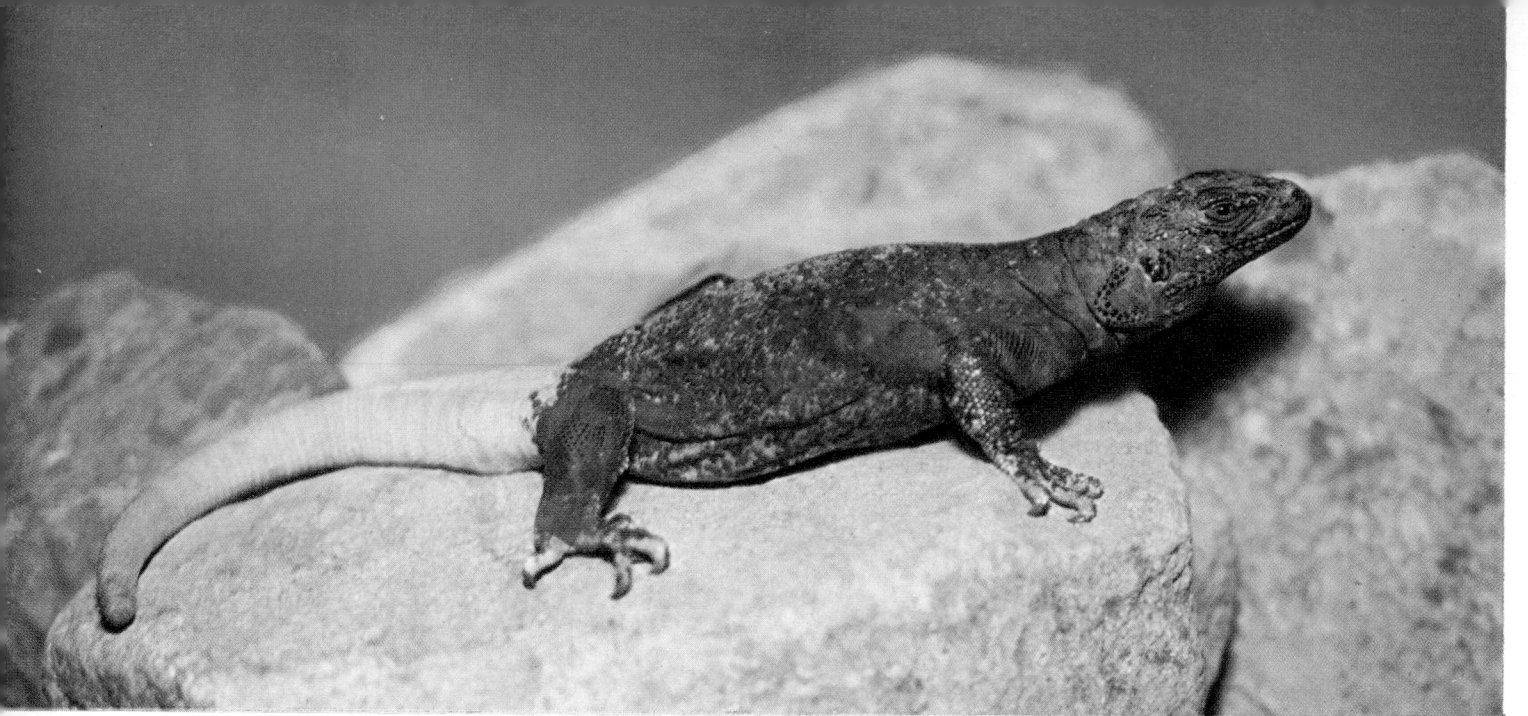

44. Chuckwalla (*Sauromalus obesus*)

[HAL H. HARRISON : NATIONAL AUDUBON]

45. Desert Spiny Lizard (*Sceloporus magister*)

[HAL H. HARRISON : NATIONAL AUDUBON]

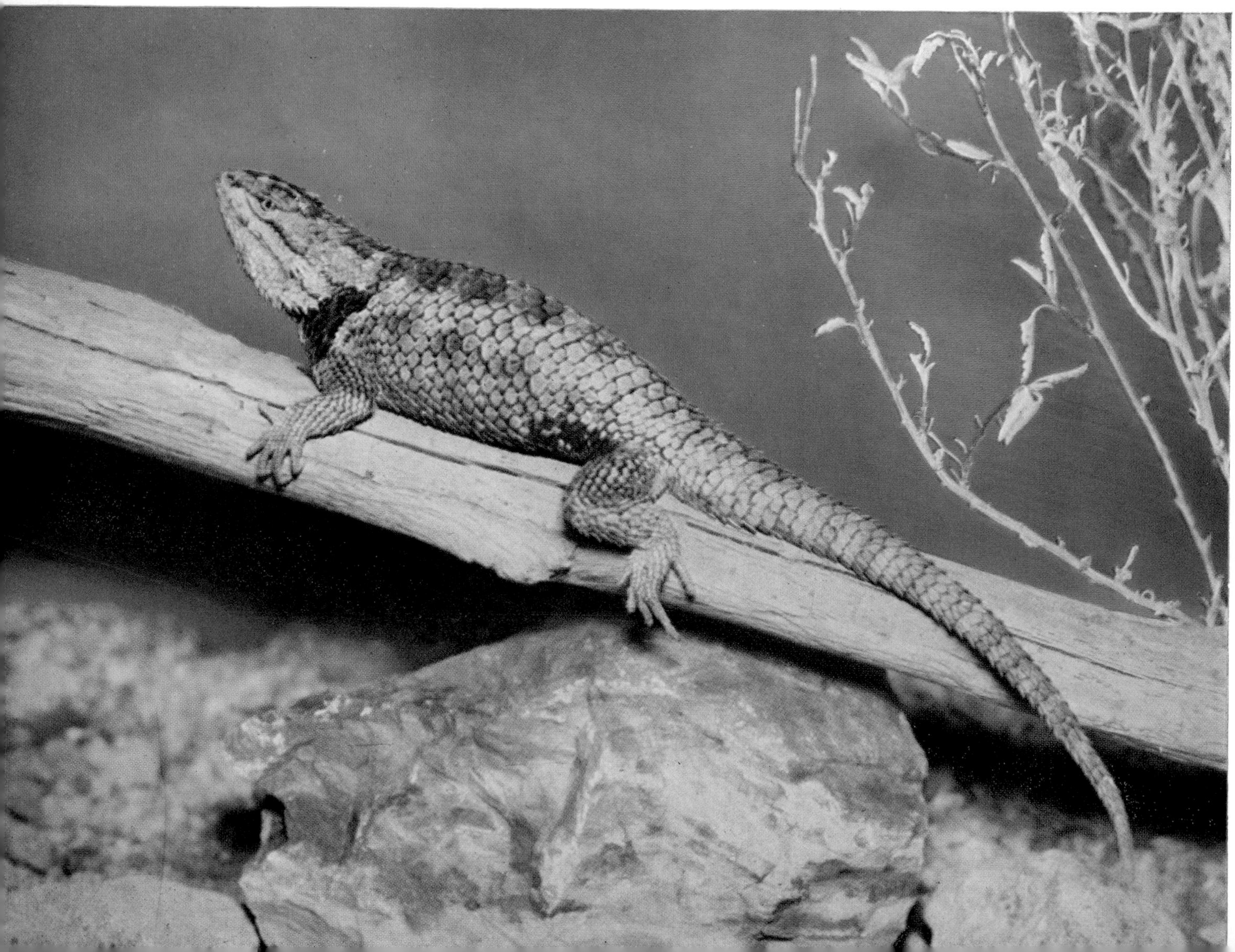

46. Clark's Spiny Lizard
(*Sceloporus clarki*)

[ROY PINNEY]

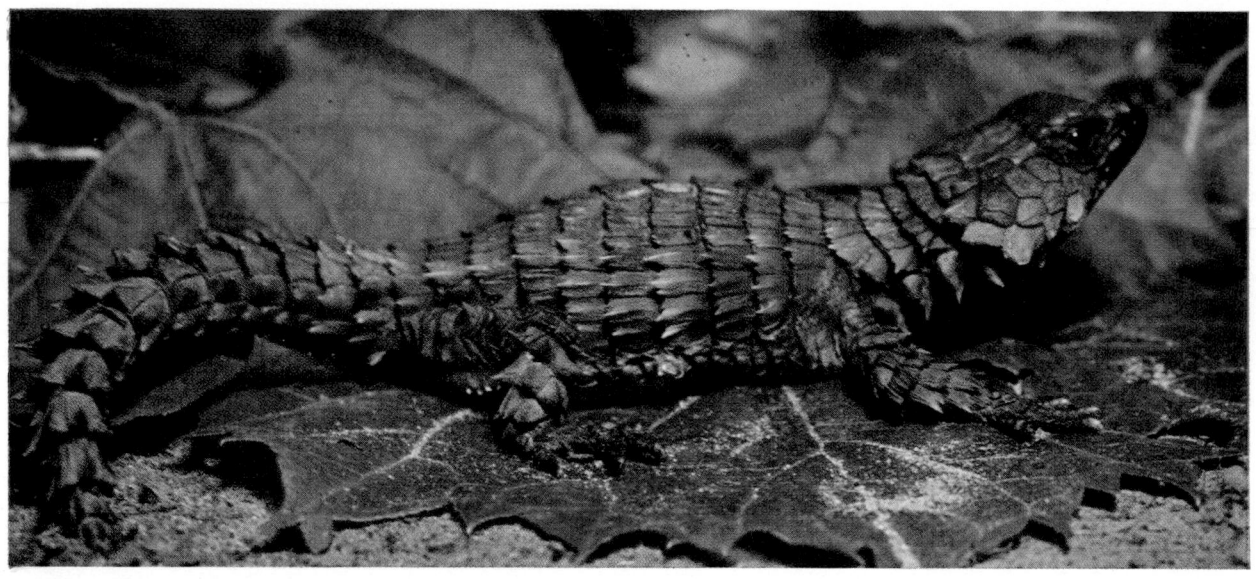

47. Armadillo Lizard (*Cordylus cataphractus*)

[CY LA TOUR AND DETROIT ZOO]

48. Western Collared Lizard (*Crotaphytus collaris baileyi*)

[WILLIS PETERSON]

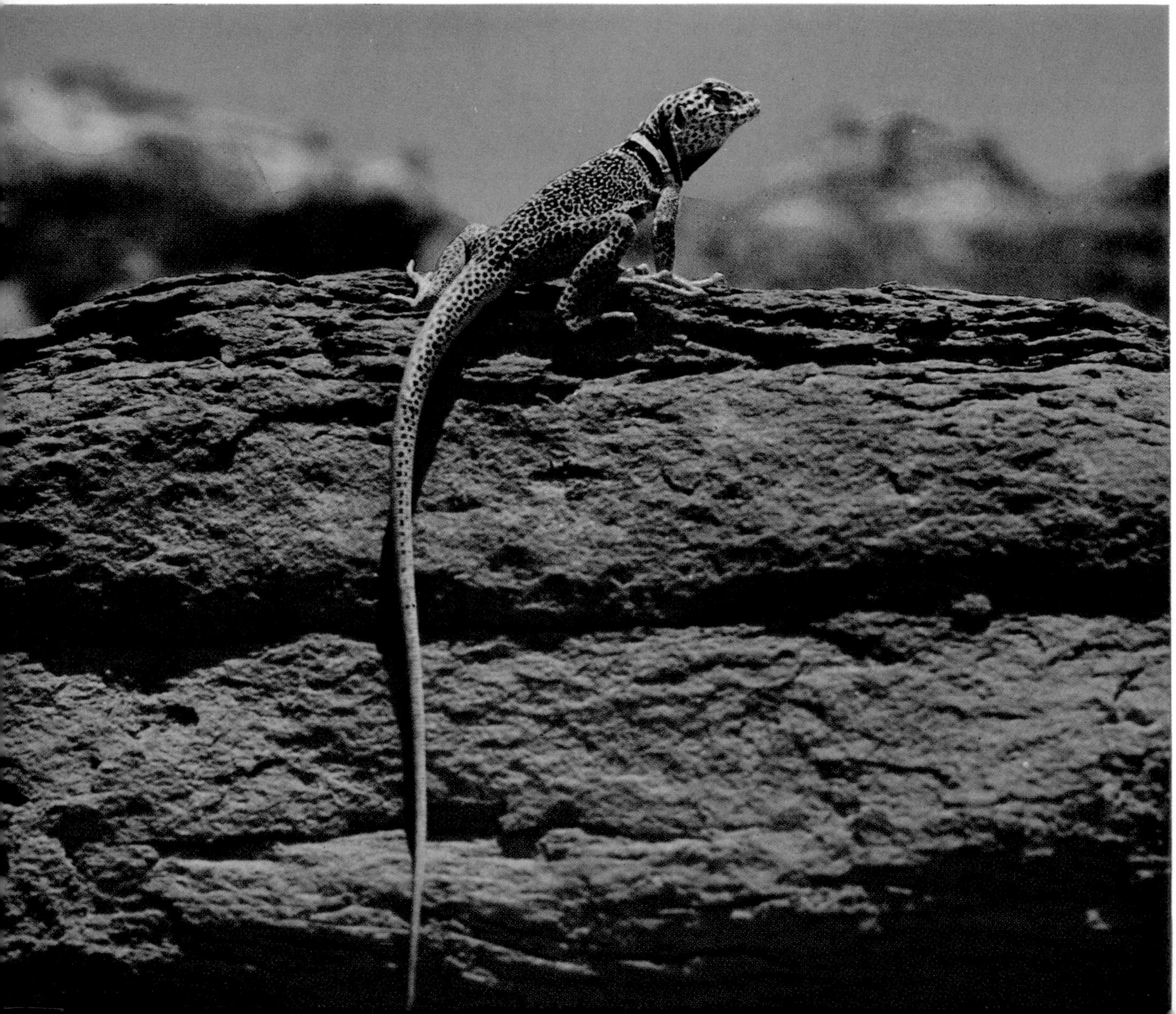

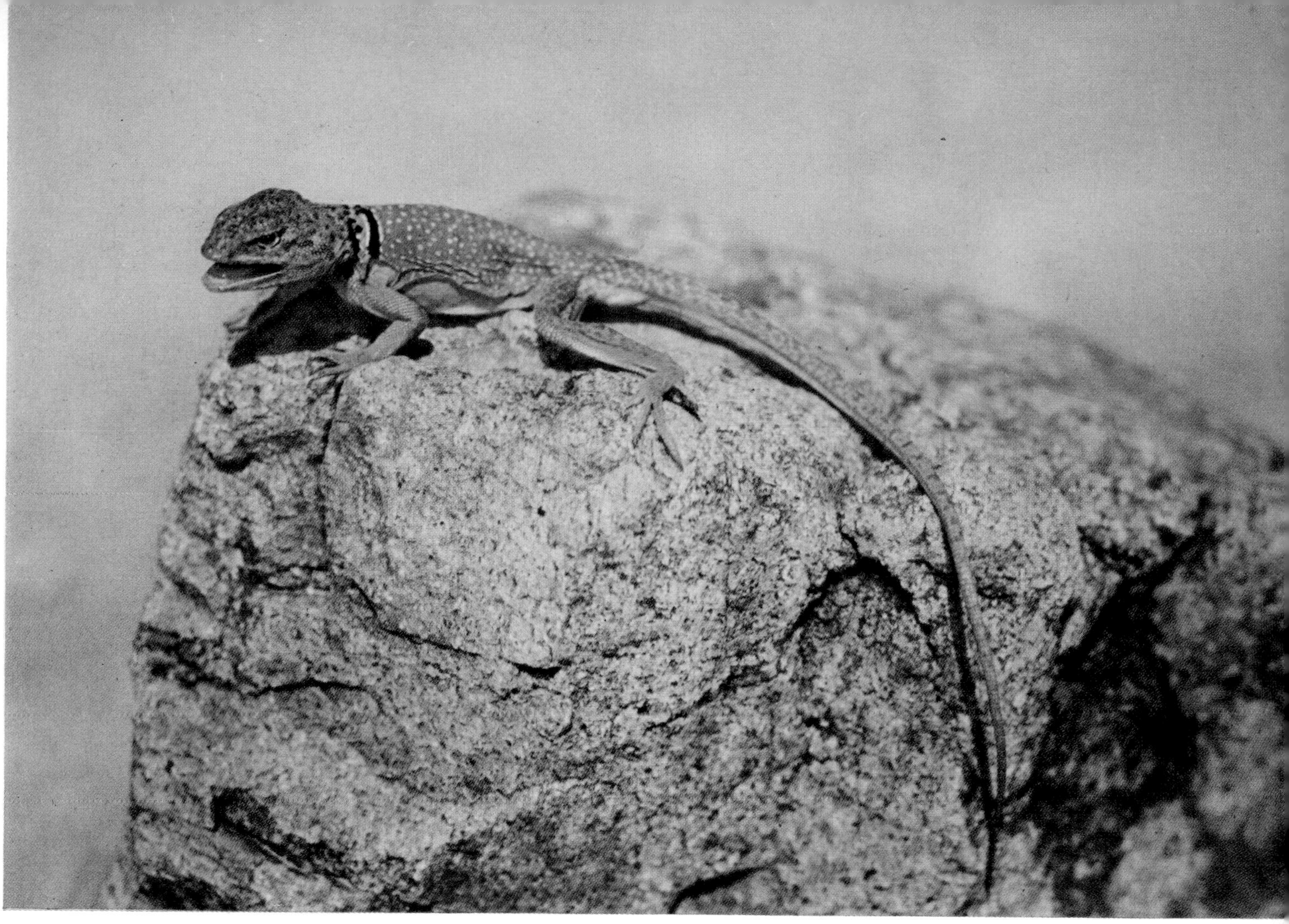

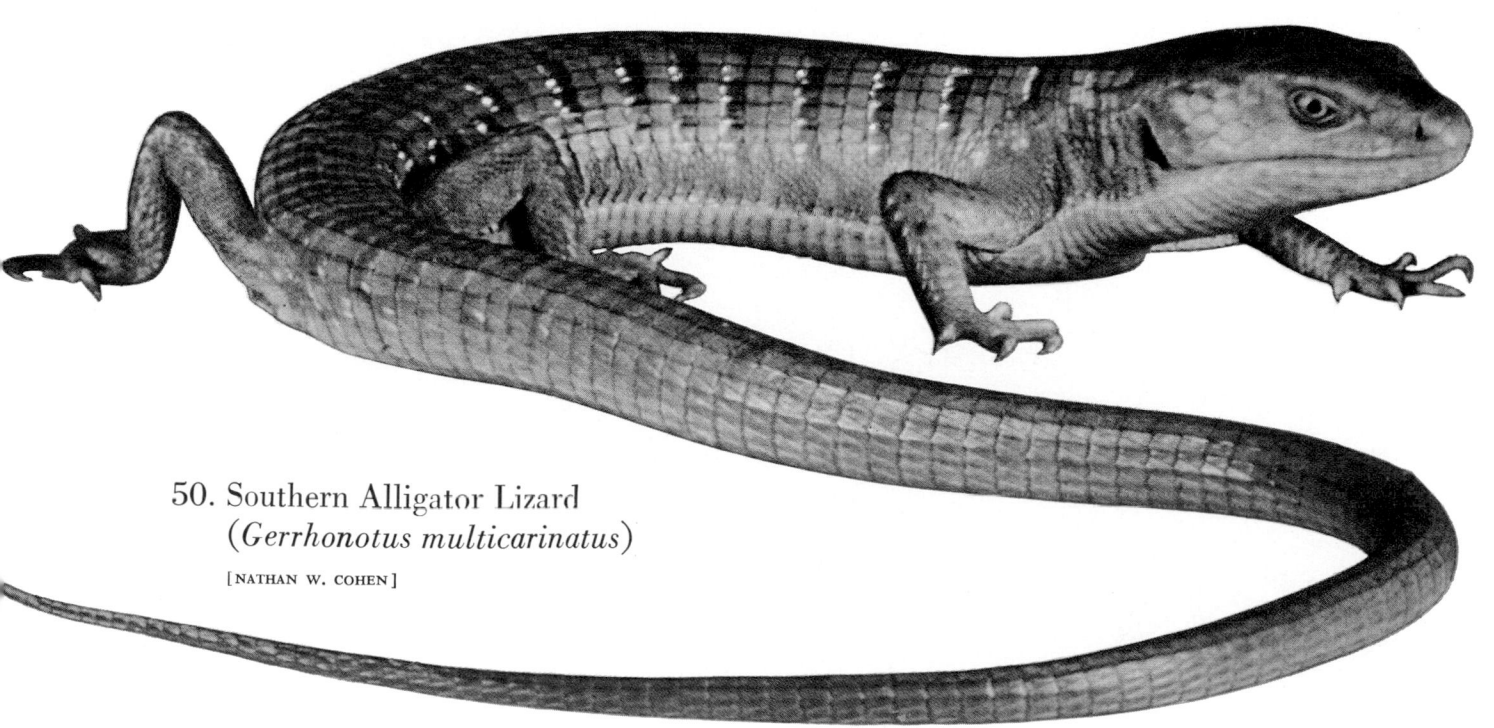

49. Eastern Collared Lizard
(*Crotaphytus collaris collaris*)

[HAL H. HARRISON : NATIONAL AUDUBON]

50. Southern Alligator Lizard
(*Gerrhonotus multicarinatus*)

[NATHAN W. COHEN]

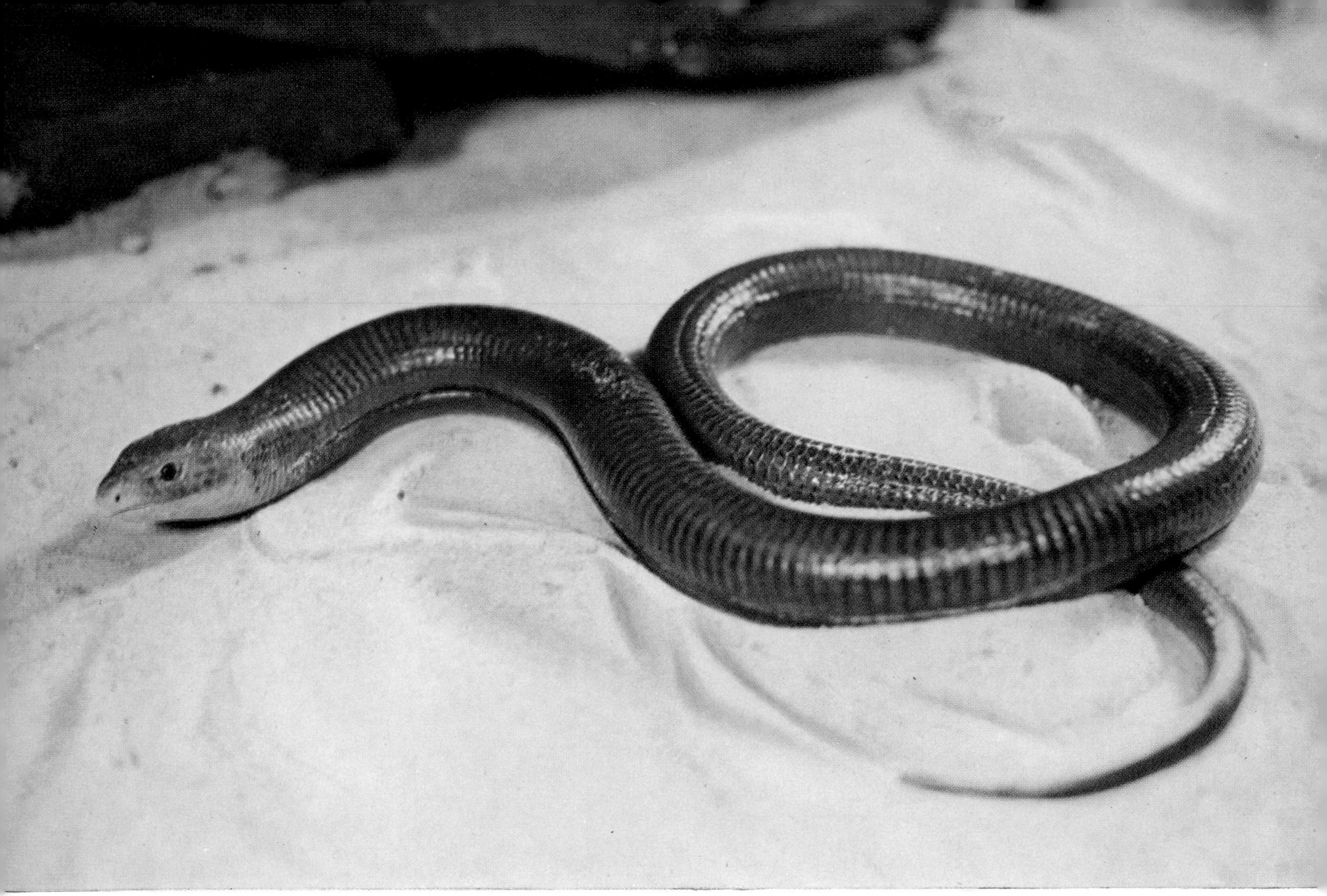

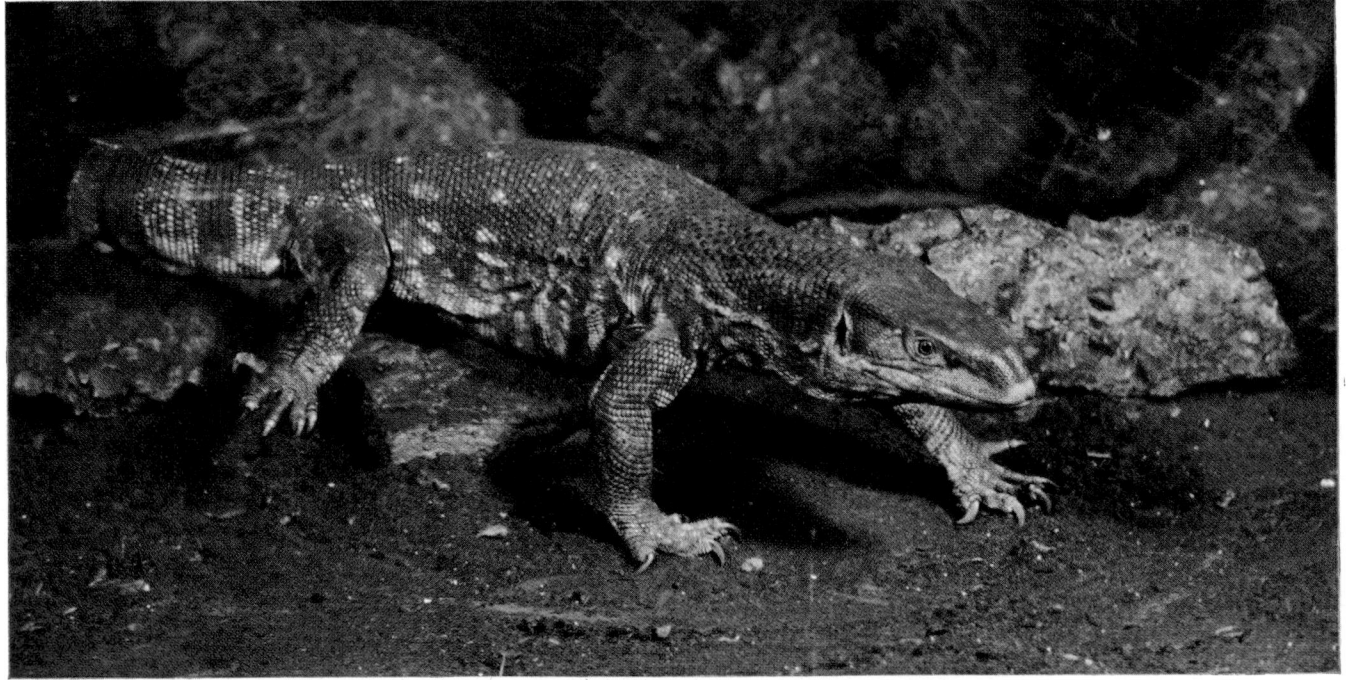

51. Scheltopusik (*Ophisaurus apodus*)

[ROY PINNEY AND PHILADELPHIA ZOO]

52. African Savanna Monitor (*Varanus exanthematicus*)

[JOHN MARKHAM]

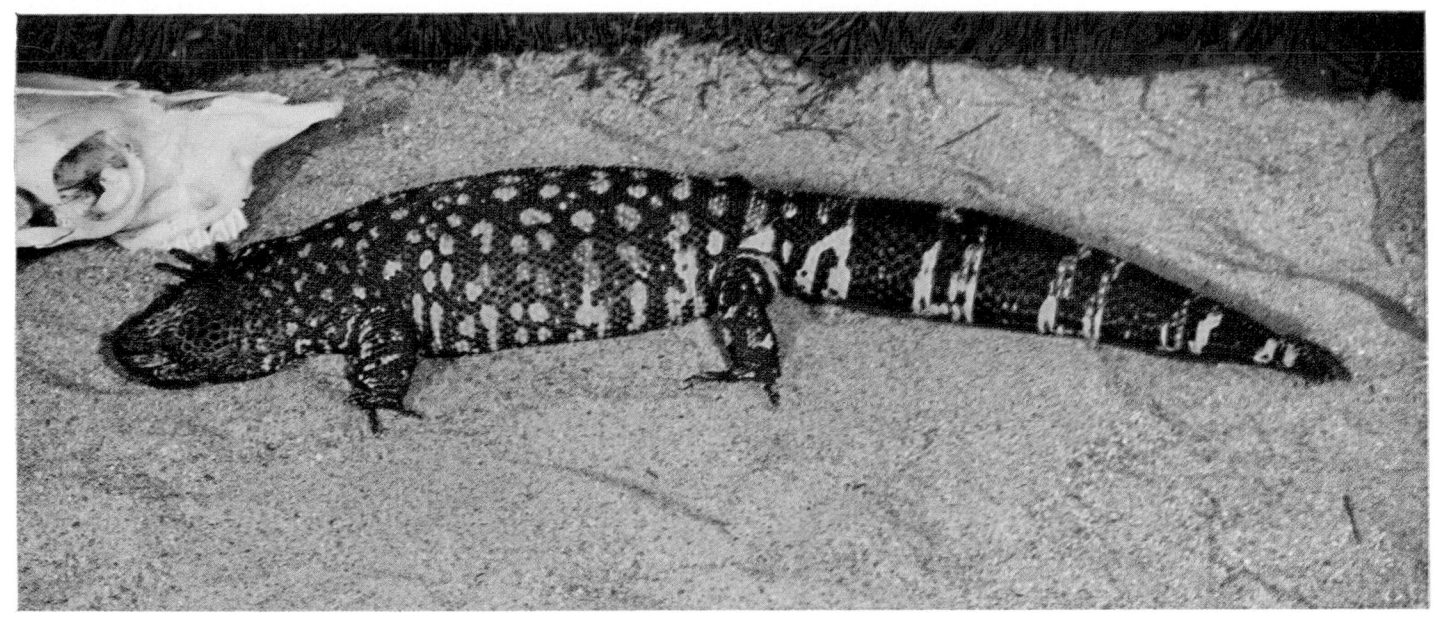

53. Beaded Lizard (*Heloderma horridum*)
[VAN NOSTRAND]

54. Gila Monster (*Heloderma suspectum*)
[ROY PINNEY]

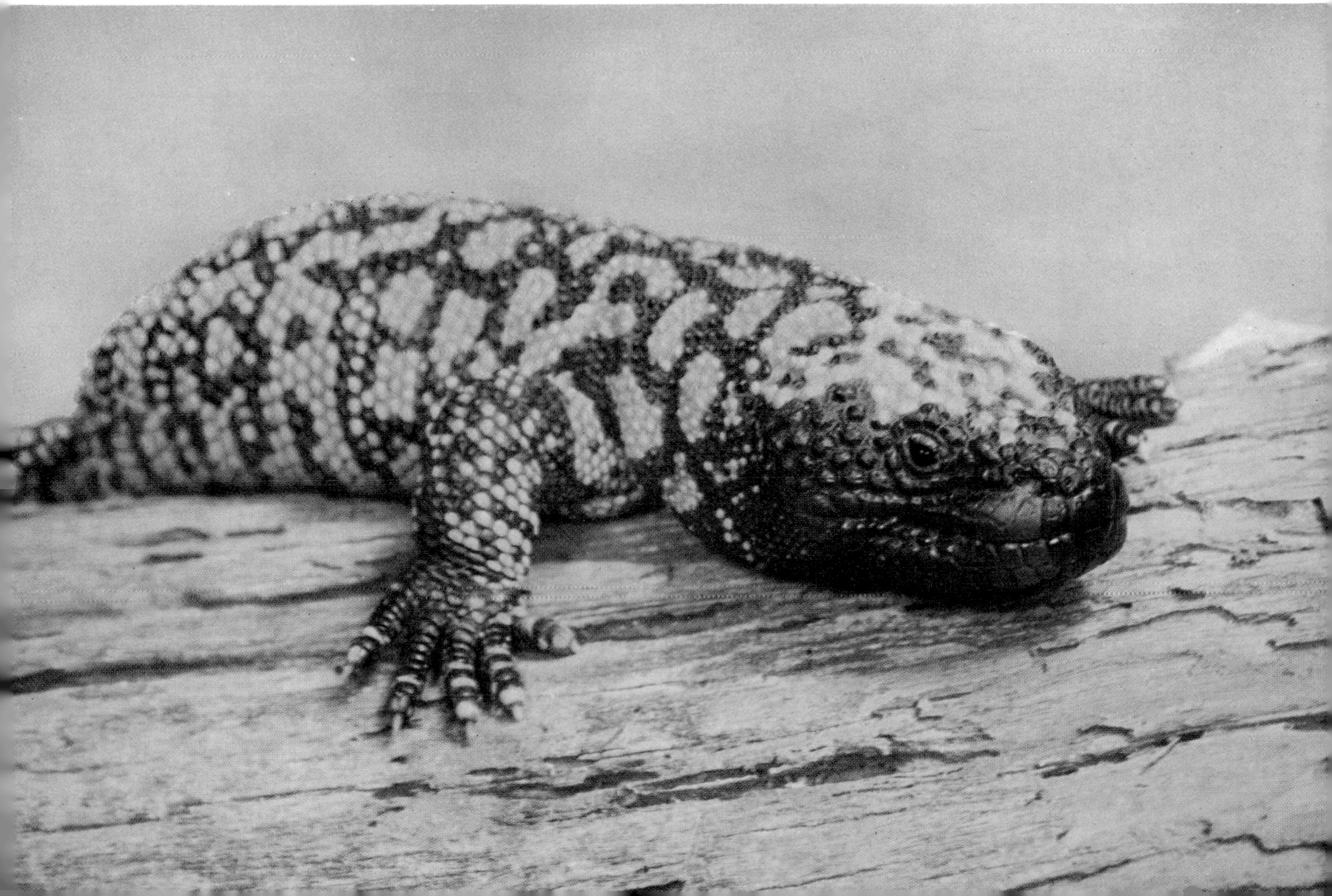

55. Tegu
(*Tupinambis
teguixin*)

[JOHN MARKHAM]

56. Jeweled Lacerta
(*Lacerta lepida*)

[CY LA TOUR AND BROOKFIELD ZOO]

57. Red Worm
Lizard
(*Amphis-*
baena alba)

[JOHN MARKHAM]

58. Viviparous Lacerta
(*Lacerta vivipara*)

[JOHN MARKHAM]

59. Sudan Plated
Lizard
(*Gerrhosaurus
major*)

[ROY PINNEY AND
NATIONAL ZOO,
WASHINGTON, D.C.]

[continued from page 96]

lizards (genus *Holbrookia*) of the Southwest and the smooth-throated lizards (genus *Liolaemus*) of Chile. Not all the partly flattened iguanids are restricted to ground level. Some—for instance the utas (genus *Uta,* Plate 39) of the Southwest—often climb bushes and low trees. Nevertheless, the extreme case of flattening is found in a strictly terrestrial group, the horned toads (*Phrynosoma*).

Iguanid tails are usually longer than head and trunk, but there are exceptions. The horned toads, for instance, have much shorter tails. On the other hand, a common iguana, *Iguana iguana,* is mostly tail; an iguana of four and a half feet has a head and trunk length of about one and a half feet. Although the common tail form is long and tapering, many variations are found. The tail may be cylindrical as in the collared lizard (*Crotaphytus*), or flattened on the sides as in the iguana, or provided with a high crest as in the basilisk, *Basiliscus basiliscus.*

Tails with rings of spiny scales are found in several groups, for example the spiny-tailed iguanids (*Urocentron*) mentioned earlier, and the narrow-tailed iguanids (genus *Stenocercus*), both of South America. In North America the horned toads have spiny tails; but, unlike those of the two South American groups, which have relatively smooth bodies, the tail spines of the horned toads are merely a continuation of the spinosity of the body.

The Iguanidae use their tails in a number of ways in locomotion and defense. The common iguana is an accomplished swimmer and obtains its power in water from sidewise beats of its long tail. The basilisk, the collared lizard, and other iguanids capable of running with their forequarters off the ground use their tails as counterbalances to the front ends of their bodies. The arboreal long-legged (*Polychrus*) and helmeted (*Corythophanes*) iguanids also employ the tail as a counterweight to the front part of the body, but in bipedal leaping instead of running. In the process of jumping, these arboreal iguanids perch clasping a small branch with the hind feet, while the forequarters and tail are free in space and counterbalance each other. Still other arboreal iguanids, such as the sword-tailed iguanid of Jamaica (*Xiphocercus*), have prehensile tails, of obvious advantage to their modes of life.

The common iguana takes advantage of the power in its tail to use it as a whiplash against small enemies. This three-foot whip is aimed with considerable accuracy, and, when it smacks a small dog in the head, it earns respect and life. We have had our boots lashed by a cornered iguana in Guatemala, and we can attest to both the accuracy and force of the weapon.

Iguanids with spiny tails apparently used these appendages defensively, like the spiny-tailed agamids (*Uromastix*). One iguanid, whose scientific name, *Hoplocercus spinosus,* means "spiny weapon-tail," turns its body sideways and arches its wicked-looking tail when confronted by an enemy.

Probably because of the many uses for their tails, the iguanids do not break off their tails as easily as, for instance, geckos, but the latter group uses the tail almost exclusively for a last-ditch defensive effort. The Iguanidae resemble the Agamidae in this characteristic.

Adaptations in body form and structure have permitted the iguanids to occupy many kinds of habitats and to assume many kinds of habits. Since

Banded Basilisk (*Basiliscus vittatus*)

Double-crested Basilisk (*Basiliscus plumbifrons*)

no iguanid has degenerate limbs, they all have five clawed digits on each limb. These sharp claws enable every genus to climb bushes or trees. But some, such as the horned toads, are only rarely, if ever, seen in vegetation above ground. Others, the tree lizard, *Uta ornata,* of our Southwest, for example, though spending much time in bushes and low trees, seems to have little special modification for such an existence except the all-important behavior characteristics—a sort of arboreal psychology. But one little item probably helps the southwestern tree lizard: its tail is covered with pointed scales that act as numerous gripping devices when pressed against bark.

Still other iguanids are even more arboreal and have more obvious adaptations to this habit. For example, the anoles (genus *Anolis*), which include our so-called American chameleon, *Anolis carolinensis,* have the next-to-the-last joint of each digit expanded and equipped below with transversely broadened scales. Just as in the geckos, these scales are covered with a great many tiny hooks that, again as in the geckos, enable the anoles to cling to vertical surfaces. The false anoles (genus *Phenacosaurus*) of northern South America go the true

anoles one better by adding a prehensile tail to the clinging toe pads.

A different approach to arboreal life is taken by the long-legged iguanids (*Polychrus*). These South American forest-dwellers, in addition to the side-to-side-flattened body so typical of tree lizards, have the habit of moving slowly, which makes them very difficult to locate. This method of hiding from enemies and stalking insect food has been adopted by several groups of lizards but is most highly developed in the chameleon family. As a supplement to their slow motion, the long-legged iguanids have the ability to spring from branch to branch. This is where the long hind legs come into play, for, by bending and suddenly straightening them, these lizards leap almost like frogs.

Many iguanids of a number of genera are primarily ground-dwellers. These include many of our native lizards such as the collared lizard (*Crotaphytus*), some of the spiny lizards (genus *Sceloporus*), and the zebra-tailed lizard, *Callisaurus draconoides.* In tropical America the casque-headed lizards (genus *Laemanctus*), the narrow-tailed iguanids (*Stenocercus*), and, in temperate South America, the smooth-throated lizards (*Liolaemus*)

Short-horned Horned Toad (*Phrynosoma douglassi*)

W. BYRON MILLER : FISH AND WILDLIFE SERVICE

among others are terrestrial. Besides the cylindrical or somewhat flattened body, these lizards have no specializations in common. But the group does contain the fastest members of the family. Bipedal running is restricted to the largest terrestrial iguanids. The collared lizard, its southwestern neighbor the desert iguana, *Dipsosaurus dorsalis,* and the basilisks of Central America all run in this fashion when pursued, and travel at a fast clip while doing so. However, the zebra-tailed lizard (*Callisaurus*) apparently is the fastest of all, being able to travel between fifteen and eighteen miles per hour.

A number of ground-dwelling iguanids burrow to a limited extent. Our desert iguana and the Brazilian spiny-tailed iguanid, *Hoplocercus spinosus,* use their claws to dig tunnel-like retreats that are rarely more than twice the length of the owner. Some iguanids, instead of digging their own holes, take refuge in rock crevices. This habit may not fall properly under the heading of burrowing, but the tendency to retreat into dark places may be a first step in the development of true burrowing. At any rate, a southwestern lizard, *Sceloporus poinsetti,* related to the fence lizard, habitually hides in rock crevices. Another southwestern iguanid, the chuckwalla, *Sauromalus obesus,* which also takes shelter in rock crevices, inflates its body with air and thus wedges itself tightly when attempts are made to pull it out from between two boulders.

The unlovely horned toads (genus *Phrynosoma*) take advantage of their excessively flattened bodies to bury themselves in sand by sidewise movements. One edge of the body, tilted slightly downward, pushes sand on the back. Then the other side is tilted and shoved into the sand, throwing a little more on the back. By a rapid series of such movements, the horned toad goes straight down into the sand, belly first. On some occasions the horned toads dig their way into sand head first. With the neck slightly bent, the sharp, steeply sloping head is plunged into the sand and, by strong lateral movements of body and hind legs, pushed farther in. But then the neck is arched upward, so that additional pushing by the hind legs, although covering more and more of the body, sends the lizard forward just below the surface until only the tail is left exposed. A few sidewise flicks of the tail buries it. And then the head pops up. In this position these lizards are almost invisible, while at the same time they have a clear view of their small world.

Digging in sand has been carried to a fine point by another group of southwestern iguanids (genus *Uma*). These lizards, which live only in areas of loose sand, dive into the sand at the slightest hint of danger and disappear from sight. Their movements through sand are so rapid that most people describe their subsurface locomotion as "swimming." And many parts of these lizards are adjusted to this strange mode of life. In the first place, the body is flattened but, unlike that of the ungainly horned toad, still elongate, enabling the lizard to knife its way through the sand yet leave it enough length to employ "swimming" undulations. The tip of the snout is sharpened to an edge by having the lower jaw shorter than the upper and actually countersunk into the upper. The push given by the hind legs in sand swimming is multiplied by the development of a fringe of scales on the toes. As the feet are drawn forward the fringing scales collapse; as the feet are kicked back the scales stick out, thus increasing the surface area brought to bear against the sand. The fringes act like snowshoes when *Uma* runs on the loose surface of dunes. Finally, the nostrils and ear openings are protected from sand grains by valves and the eyes by fringed eyelids.

Despite their sand-burrowing abilities, neither the horned toad nor *Uma* leads a truly subterranean life. In fact no iguanid does, and this constitutes another point of similarity with the agamids. Development of an underground existence, found only in other lizard families (for examples, the flap-footed lizards and the worm lizards), is accompanied by reduction or loss of limbs. The failure of the Iguanidae and the Agamidae to even shorten the limbs appreciably is a measure of their failure to develop subterranean offshoots.

Some iguanids, like agamids, are capable of changing color. The rapidity with which this is done by our southeastern green anole, *Anolis carolinensis,* has given it the misnomer of "chameleon," a name that should be reserved for the true Old World chameleons. It is commonly supposed that the anole changes color in order to match its background, turning brown if placed on the ground and green if placed on a leaf. But so far we have no good evidence that this is true.

On the other hand, many observations and experiments have shown that the anole changes color in response to temperature and light. If the lizard is cold, say in a room at 50 degrees, it assumes its brown coloration. If the temperature is raised to 70 degrees, the anole turns green *but* only if it is in the dark or in very dim light. In bright light it remains brown. The same relationships hold true at 85 degrees. Now, if we raise the temperature to 105 degrees, the anole becomes a pale grayish green and stays that color regardless of the amount of light. Fortunately for curious herpetologists, an anole takes from three to ten minutes to change color, so that by flipping on a light it is possible to see what particular color the lizard has assumed in the darkness.

Other iguanids become lighter or darker in response to temperature and light. The collared lizard (*Crotaphytus*), the horned toads (*Phrynosoma*), and the spiny lizards (*Sceloporus*) become dark at low temperatures and light at high ones; in darkness these lizards become pale, but darken in bright light. Certain cells of the skin of these lizards contain microscopic grains of black pigment. When these pigment grains are spread out in the cells, the animal appears dark. Conversely, the animal appears pallid when the pigment is concentrated at the centers of the cells.

The anole and some of the other iguanids change color according to their emotional state, just as we saw in the agamids. Iguanids are as quarrelsome as agamids and usually, among those capable of color change, take on a particular shade when they win a fight and another shade when they lose. The male anole, for instance, turns green if he wins an encounter and brown if he loses.

Most of the battles between male iguanids take place regardless of the presence or absence of females. Each male establishes a home territory and tries to keep other males out. In nature these territories include the feeding ranges of several females, and undoubtedly the bluffing and fighting of the males has its origin in competition for mates— the eternal triangle. A male usually attempts to bluff other males from a distance, so that, if successful, the territory is kept free of undesirable strangers. In order to do this, though, a male must be able to draw attention to himself from a distance, and this is accomplished most often by color display and posturing. A male anole, perched on a bush in his territory, spreads out his throat dewlap or fan, which exposes the scarlet skin between the scales. This brilliant flash of red is conspicuous and can be seen at a distance.

In some iguanids the males develop patches of color on their sides, and often on their throats as they mature. Males of our southwestern zebra-tailed lizard, *Callisaurus draconoides*, have blue or blue-green areas crossed by black bars at the juncture of belly and sides. Males of the Peruvian smooth-headed iguanid, *Leiocephalus guentheri*, have rosy areas on the throat and sides of the belly. Such conspicuous patches of color are shown off by several types of postures. Male fence lizards, *Sceloporus undulatus*, of the eastern United States bob up and down, thus exposing the blue patches of the throat and belly. A male West Indian smooth-headed iguanid, *Leiocephalus schreibersi*,

challenges other males from a distance by flattening the body from side to side, while forelegs and hind legs raise the body high and so display the blue and pink bars of its sides.

Occasionally this long-distance flashing of colors fails to work, and a male moves in on another's territory. Then bluffing begins at closer range and may give way to a real fight. Certain behavioral traits—such as bobbing, flattening of the body, elevation of crests if present, and puffing out of the throat—are so ingrained in lizards that they appear in these encounters regardless of what species is involved.

Two male anoles, for example, approach one another, flattening the body from side to side and turning sidewise. At the same time the throat is puffed out, though the dewlap is not usually extended at such close range, and a low fleshy ridge rises on the nape, adding to the apparent increase in body size. The two anoles circle, always keeping broadside to one another, and threaten with open jaws. If one is not completely overawed by this time, they may bite, interlocking jaws and shaking vigorously until one or both fall from the branch. The fall may not end the fight, for these pugnacious little lizards may climb back to the arena and go at it again. On rare occasions these bouts may last over an hour and a half.

The male of the terrestrial West Indian species, *Leiocephalus schreibersi*, also puffs out its throat and raises a ridge that, in this case, extends down the length of the back. It also tries to bob, but can only rock back and forth because its exaggerated flattening of the body keeps the belly in contact with the ground.

As in the agamids, some of these motions or slight modifications of them are used in courtship. The males of most iguanids, whether anole, fence lizard, or marine iguana, *Amblyrhynchus cristatus*, bob and puff out their throats as they advance toward females. But there is usually a subtle difference between fighting and courting bobs. The fence lizard lifts his entire body off the ground when challenging another male, but when courting he keeps his hind quarters on the ground and bobs only with his head and forequarters. The male anole flattens his body and raises his nape during his fighting bob, but not when courting.

Sometimes the female will have nothing to do with an amorous male. She may indicate her reluctance merely by running away, and at such times is rarely pursued far. The females of a few species (for example, the fence lizard and collared lizard) show their unwillingness by raising the body high on all four legs, arching the back, and hopping up and down stiff-legged. Faced with this response, the courting male turns his attentions elsewhere.

Should the female be willing to mate, she either stands her ground or moves only a short distance. Some females give a more positive sign of their mood; the female anole turns her head to one side in a gesture we can only describe as coy. Encouraged, the male iguanid approaches, but always from the side and slightly to the rear. When close enough, he grips the female's neck with his jaws, clasps the top of her far hind leg with his foot, and slips his tail under hers. He inserts his hemipenis as soon as his vent comes opposite hers. Once the male grips the female's neck, she becomes passive and remains so for the duration of the mating, which lasts three to ten minutes.

Almost without exception, female iguanids lay eggs, and even the most arboreal of them, like the anole, lay their eggs in the ground. The female digs a hole with her snout, and sometimes with her fore-feet. Then she places her vent over the opening, and the eggs are forced out. If the egg does not fall in the nest, it is shoved in. Finally, the female pushes soil into the hole and packs it down. That is the last she sees of it.

The female green anole lays only one or two eggs at a time, and the hole she digs is correspondingly small. Females that lay more eggs, such as an eastern fence lizard (four to seventeen eggs) or a basilisk (about eighteen eggs), usually dig deeper nests, although sometimes the eggs are merely placed under a rotting log. The eggs of most North American iguanids take one and a half to two and a half months to hatch.

The few species of iguanids that give birth to young instead of laying eggs usually live in cool climates. The bunch grass lizard, *Sceloporus scalaris*, strictly a mountain-dweller, carries its ten or so eggs until they hatch inside the body of the female. The same is true of certain species of smooth-throated iguanids (genus *Liolaemus*) living in the Andes Mountains of southern South America. Presumably, by retaining the developing eggs, the females of these live-bearers will keep the eggs warmer than they might otherwise be, simply because the females must themselves seek out warm situations. In their habitats it would be difficult for these lizards to lay their eggs in a place that would be sufficiently exposed to be warm by day but not so exposed as to become dangerously cold at night.

Like most lizards the iguanids feed primarily on insects, spiders, and other small invertebrates. One or two medium-sized species feed extensively on vegetation. Our desert iguana, *Dipsosaurus dorsalis*, eats buds, flowers, and leaves of desert plants as well as insects; a specimen in our laboratory is addicted to dandelion flowers. The common iguana, *Iguana iguana*, and the black iguanas of Central America (genus *Ctenosaura*) are strict vegetarians. Another plant-feeder, the crested iguana of the Galapagos Islands (*Conolophuis*), eats cactus, spines and all, and thrives.

Despite the fact that forty species of iguanids live in the United States, only one is found exclusively in our country. Lizards, like all animals, do not recognize political boundaries, but are limited in their distributions by natural divisions such as climate, vegetational types, and so forth. Therefore, since the vegetation and climate are the same in adjacent areas on both sides of our Mexican border, it is not surprising that thirty-seven of our iguanid species are also found in Mexico. Only the little Florida scrub lizard, *Sceloporus woodi*, and two species of anoles fail to enter Mexico. The Florida scrub lizard is the only iguanid confined to the United States. The two anoles also occur in Cuba.

These three lizards and the eastern fence lizard, *Sceloporus undulatus* (Plate 41), are the only members of the family living east of the Mississippi River. Sagra's anole, *Anolis sagrei*, just barely enters the country, living on Key West and a few places in peninsular Florida. The green anole, *Anolis carolinensis*, is a southern species not occurring north of a line running from North Carolina to eastern Texas. This little iguanid, which reaches a maximum length of seven inches, makes a charming addition to the southern landscape as it scampers around in trees and bushes flashing its scarlet dewlap. Thousands of them are sold as pets every year under the name "chameleon"; most of them starve to death in a few weeks because of improper care.

The eastern fence lizard has a much more extensive range than the green anole. It lives from the Atlantic coast to Arizona and Utah, and from the Gulf coast and central Mexico north to an arc from Pennsylvania through central Indiana to northern Nebraska. The blue throat and belly patches of the male, which is brown and black above like the female, show as it scampers over the ground and climbs in bushes and low trees in search of its food. In the East its habit of sunning on rail fences gave it its common name.

Many more species and genera of iguanids are met with in the drier country west of the states bordering the Mississippi River. The collared lizard, *Crotaphytus collaris* (Plates 48 and 49), the earless lizards (genus *Holbrookia*), and the horned toads (genus *Phrynosoma*) are found in the plains. The collared lizard, so named because of the black rings around its neck, is a medium-sized iguanid about twelve inches long, most of which is a thin, tapering tail. Although often running bipedally to escape danger, the collared lizard will turn if cornered and face its enemy with determined and strong jaws. Its equally handsome relative, the leopard lizard, *Crotaphytus wislizeni* (Plate 37), is confined to more westerly states.

The earless lizards (*Holbrookia,* Plate 40), as their common name suggests, have no external eardrum or ear opening. How well they can hear, and even whether they can hear at all, are still unanswered questions. These small lizards are five to seven inches long and usually lay between five and seven eggs. They are strictly ground-dwellers in plains or semidesert areas. The Texas earless lizard, *Holbrookia texana,* has black bars under its white tail and at times curls this conspicuously marked appendage and waves it slowly, an activity that is still not understood.

The "horns" of the horned toads (genus *Phrynosoma,* Plate 43) consist of six to ten spines of varying length growing out from the rear of the head. In the flat-tailed horned toad, *Phrynosoma m'calli,* the horns are almost as long as the head, whereas in *Phrynosoma douglassi,* sometimes called the "short-horned horned toad," the spines are scarcely as long as the diameter of the eye. Despite such differences and slight variations in the size and number of spiny scales on the back and sides, the fifteen species of horned toads are a rather uniform lot. Short, stubby heads, fat but flattened bodies, and short tails characterize them all. Their methods of digging have been described already.

Though food and reproduction are quite ordinary in this genus, the defensive behavior is most strange. When frightened, these lizards sometimes squirt a few drops of blood from their eyes. The blood is said to be irritating to the eyes of small mammals, but information on this subject is still fragmentary and uncertain. It is not easy to understand how squirting out a little blood can protect these lizards from any predator.

Farther west, in the Great Basin and in the Arizona and Mohave deserts, we come to the home of additional iguanid groups. The desert iguana (*Dipsosaurus*) and the chuckwalla (*Sauromalus,* Plate 44) climb creosote bushes to eat leaves and flowers. Both of these lizards retreat underground to avoid the cold desert night, but the chuckwalla normally spends the night deep in a rock crevice, while the desert iguana usually goes down an abandoned rodent burrow. The desert iguana depends on rodents for food, too, since it eats large quantities of rodent droppings in the spring.

In appearance the desert iguana is one of the most pleasing in aspect of the North American iguanids. Its short head and rounded body, together about five inches long, are covered with fine, smooth scales except for a row of keeled scales forming a low ridge or crest down the middle of the back. The rounded, tapering tail, from eight to ten inches long, is ringed with keeled scales. The entire lizard is grayish brown with a network of a warmer reddish brown.

The speedy gridiron-tailed lizard, *Callisaurus draconoides* (Plate 38), so called because of the black-and-white barring under the tail, is also an inhabitant of the arid Southwest, living in sandy and gravelly areas and in desert flats. When traveling at high speed, it runs semi-erect on its hind legs and can change direction abruptly. At rest, it curls and wags its conspicuously marked tail just as does the Texas earless lizard.

Close relatives of the gridiron-tailed lizard, the fringe-toed iguanids (genus *Uma,* Plate 42), live only in areas of fine, wind-blown sand in California, Arizona, and Sonora, Mexico. The special adaptations of these sand-swimming lizards, which are from seven to nine inches long, have been described. Their diet consists mostly of insects, but small amounts of buds and leaves are also eaten.

A zoologist dropped down in northern Mexico could not distinguish the country from southern Arizona or New Mexico if he had to depend on the iguanid lizards. In Sonora, for example, he would find the familiar desert iguana, chuckwalla, Texas earless lizard, collared lizard, fringed-toed lizard, and some of the same spiny lizards.

The spiny lizards (genus *Sceloporus,* Plates 45 and 46), incidentally, have their headquarters in Mexico. This genus, which contains fifty-four species, is represented in Mexico by fifty-two. Fourteen of the fifty-two also live in the United States. Their blunt, triangular heads, round and somewhat stocky bodies, cylindrical, tapering tails, and coarse, pointed scales, to which the common name refers, are generally reminiscent of the true agamas (genus *Agama*) of the Old World. And just like the agamas, the spiny lizards are typical ground-dwellers, although many of them occasionally climb shrubs and low trees, and a few are rock-crevice forms. Most of them are brown or brownish green above, with indistinct markings except for the black collar found in a number of species. Males of all species have large blue areas on the throat and belly. With the exception of several mountain species, they all lay eggs, averaging about ten per clutch. The diet consists of insects and other small invertebrates, although the larger species (up to ten inches) may eat small lizards from time to time.

Casque-headed Lizard (*Laemanctus serratus*)

Farther south in Mexico the groups found in the United States drop out, and tropical Central American genera take their places. The rather large black iguanas (genus *Ctenosaura*) have their headquarters in this narrow strip of land. Several of the iguanid genera native to Central America have crested heads. In the casque-headed iguanids (genus *Laemanctus*), the flattened top of the head projects backward over the neck in a broad shelf. The helmeted iguanids (genus *Corythophanes*) have a long bony process projecting out over the neck and connected with the latter by skin. Some of the basilisks (genus *Basiliscus*) have crests on the rear of the head, too, but in this genus only the males bear the ornamentation.

The helmeted iguanids (*Corythophanes*) utilize their crests for defense on the same principle as the frilled agamid: if an animal can increase its size, a number of potential enemies will take their hunger elsewhere. When confronted by a snake, for instance, a helmeted iguanid will bend its head down, thus raising the tip of the long bony process at the rear still higher and fanning out the skin between the process and the neck, and at the same time expand its throat dewlap. The result is that the apparent depth of the head is tremendously increased. An enemy looking at one of these lizards head on would not be aware of any increase in size; it would be the same as looking at a broad knife edgewise. But the lizard orients its body broadside to the enemy to take full advantage of the display. We had several of these iguanids alive in our laboratories, and they gave this defensive reaction to live snakes,

always keeping the side of the head broadside to the snake and tilting the head slightly if the snake were held a little higher or a little lower.

Central America is also the home of many anoles (genus *Anolis*, Plate 32). To the herpetologist, discouraged by his failures to identify species of this genus, it sometimes seems that all iguanids are anoles. About 25 per cent of the roughly seven hundred species of Iguanidae are members of the genus *Anolis*. They range from North Carolina (the green anole) through Central America to southern Brazil and are well represented in the West Indies. Guatemala alone has twenty-one species.

With 165 species in the genus, we expect the anoles to show a great variety of body form. They do and they don't. They show more variety than most genera of iguanids, but not the kind of variation that marks the difference, say, between the spiny lizards (*Sceloporus*) and the fringe-toed lizards (*Uma*). The heads of anoles are usually triangular and sloping downward to the snout. One Brazilian species, the leaf-nosed anole, *Anolis phyllorhinus*, has a sidewise-flattened, scaly structure that projects forward from the tip of the snout beyond the mouth for a distance equal to the rest of the head.

Some anoles have flattened, crested tails and others cylindrical tails. They also vary in the presence of skin folds at the throat and in the form of scales. The majority of the anoles are five to nine inches long, about one-fourth are smaller, and about one-fourth exceed ten inches. The biggest species, the knight anole, *Anolis equestris* (Plates 29, 30, and 31), of Cuba, sometimes reaches a length of eighteen inches, but, since the tail forms two-thirds of that, it is still just a small lizard. There is a corresponding type of large anole on each of the other larger islands of the West Indies—Jamaica, Hispaniola, and Puerto Rico.

The expanded fingers and toes of anoles mark them as climbers, and most species are usually seen in bushes and trees. Though many species are found in gardens and around houses, we think of anoles as being typically forest animals. Two Cuban species are often seen in the twilight zone of caves. Animals that live in caves either never leave them or venture out only at dusk or night. Bats are good examples of this. But these cave anoles run out into the sunlight occasionally, and apparently protect their eyes from the bright light at those times by closing their eyes and peering through clear areas in the lower lid.

In addition to the anoles, other arboreal lizards live in the great tropical forests of South America. The common iguana, *Iguana iguana* (Plates 35 and 36), and the basilisks (genus *Basiliscus*) are found

Brazilian Iguanid (*Enyalius catenatus*)

Patagonian Iguanid (*Diplolaemus darwini*)

along streams. The iguana is a special target for man because its flesh and its eggs are highly esteemed as food.

The long-legged iguanids (genus *Polychrus*) are also at home in these forests. Besides being able to leap from branch to branch, the long-legged iguanids are adapted to life in trees by a particular type of camouflage, composed of color, form, and behavior. In the first place, these lizards ordinarily move slowly, which habit of itself helps to hide them from both their insect food and their enemies. But, when one of them stands stock-still on a branch with tail stuck out stiffly behind, the oval body flattened from side to side looks remarkably like a leaf. Adding to the illusion are a greenish ground color and diagonal bars on the sides suggesting veins of a leaf. Some of

Haitian Anole (*Anolis chlorocyanus*)

WILHELM HOPPE

the same elements of disguise crop up in other arboreal lizards (see chameleons).

In the open grasslands and in rocky, mountainous parts of South America, the arboreal forest groups give way to other iguanid genera that are, naturally, ground-dwellers. The weapon-tail (*Hoplocercus*) mentioned above digs its short tunnels and hunts its insect prey in the tree-dotted grasslands of southern Brazil. In the dry and high country south of Brazil, the dominant members of the family are the smooth-throated iguanids (genus *Liolaemus*). Herpetologists are far from agreed on the number of species in this genus, but there are at least thirty and possibly as many as fifty. In many ways the smooth-throated iguanids recall the spiny lizards (genus *Sceloporus*) of southwestern United States and Mexico. The short heads, the almost cylindrical bodies, the keeled scales, the preference for semiarid habitats, and the large number of species are all like *Sceloporus*.

Up north again in the West Indies, the most common iguanids are the anoles. Roughly fifty species are scattered between Cuba on the west and the Windward Islands on the east. Another common West Indian iguanid genus, *Leiocephalus*, also occurs on the mainland of South America. But the distinctive, native groups of West Indian iguanids are more interesting in this geographical survey. Five of these native genera are closely related to the anoles and as a group are restricted to Cuba, Jamaica, and Hispaniola. Two of these anolelike lizards, the false chameleon (*Chamaeleolis*) and the sword-tailed iguanids (*Xiphocercus*), have prehensile tails. Another, the Cuban water anole (*Deiroptyx*), lives along streams and at times of danger dives into the water and hides under stones. *Chamaelinorops* has sharply angulate ridges along the back. It is found only on Hispaniola and Navassa Island.

The common iguana, *Iguana iguana,* is apparently a recent immigrant to the southern Lesser Antilles and the Virgin Islands from northern South America, and has driven out the native ground iguana (genus *Cyclura,* Plates 33 and 34) from these islands. The ground iguana, which reaches a length of four feet, has been found as a fossil in caves of Saint Thomas, Virgin Islands, where the common iguana is part of the living fauna.

The ground iguanas (*Cyclura*) are among the most primitive members of the family Iguanidae. Their closest living relatives are also confined to islands, but in widely separated parts of the globe. Two of them live in the Galapagos Islands, seven hundred miles off the coast of Ecuador. The shores of these isolated bits of land once swarmed with the marine iguana, *Amblyrhynchus cristatus*. Dogs and cats, originally released by sailors, have greatly reduced the numbers of these large (up to five feet in length) lizards on several of the islands. But they are still abundant on other islands. On a visit to the Galapagos in 1929, we counted seventy-five marine iguanas, some of them piled three deep, in a space thirty feet square on Narborough Island. Though other species of lizards occasionally enter the ocean, the marine iguanas are the only modern lizards that utilize the sea for a habitat. Like all of the really large iguanids, they are herbivorous, feeding exclusively on seaweed, which they obtain by diving, and they take refuge in the water when alarmed.

Inland, the marine iguanas are replaced by the Galapagos land iguana, which is slightly smaller (up to four feet long). It is also herbivorous, and feeds on many plants including cactus, the spines of which seem to cause it no discomfort.

The other living relative of the West Indian ground iguanas is found across the Pacific in the Fiji Islands. The Fijian iguanid (*Brachylophus*) has a low crest on its neck and small scales, and, like the ground iguanas, is moderately large for a lizard,

Rhinoceros Iguana (*Cyclura cornuta*)

False Chameleon
(*Chamaeleolis chamaleontides*)

reaching a length of about three feet. Its extremely long fingers and toes are equipped with sharp claws that are of importance to its arboreal existence. Aside from the fact that it feeds on leaves, we know little about the habits of this isolated lizard that is apparently nearing extinction.

The last group of iguanids occurs off the eastern coast of Africa, on Madagascar and some of the small adjacent islands. The seven species fall into two genera—one, *Hoplurus*, with very strongly keeled scales around its tapering tail and the other, *Chalarodon*, with smooth scales. These lizards, which range in size up to fifteen inches, are bush-climbers and ground-dwellers.

The Night Lizards
(*Family Xantusidae*)

A crowbar may not appear to be a useful tool in hunting six-inch lizards, but it is just that in certain parts of California. For areas of flaking massive rocks are the favorite haunts of the granite night lizard, *Xantusia henshawi,* one of an exclusively American lizard family. Typical of the family, this lizard has small scales on its back and sides contrasting with the large ones on its belly, and a rather ordinary lizard shape: bluntly pointed head, legs with five digits, and a tail slightly longer than the head and trunk. The thing that is not ordinary about the granite night lizard and all of its family is the absence of movable eyelids. Like the geckos, these lizards have on each eye a permanent "spectacle," a clear scale derived from the lower eyelid and covering the eye.

By day this particular species remains hidden in rock crevices and in the cracks between rock layers in arid parts of southern California. To lift the great flakes of rock in order to catch it then requires a good crowbar. At night, however, this yellowish, black-spotted lizard crawls over the rock in search of its food, which includes ants, bees, crickets, beetles, spiders, and even scorpions and centipedes.

Many of the same habits are displayed by the Arizona night lizard, *Xantusia arizonae,* which also lives on large rock masses and feeds on insects and other small invertebrates. This grayish five- or five-and-a-half-inch creature gives birth to one or two young at a time, a pattern repeated in all four members of the genus *Xantusia.* Another species, the yucca night lizard, *Xantusia vigilis,* gets its common name from its choice of habitat—rotting yucca logs and branches. Until that habitat was discovered, the yucca night lizard was considered a rare species. Now it is recognized to be one of the commonest lizards in adjoining parts of California, Nevada, Utah, and Arizona. The fourth member of the genus, the island night lizard, *Xantusia riversiana,* occurs only on three islands off the coast of California.

There are only seven additional species in the family, and they are found in Mexico and Central America and (one species only) in Cuba. The three genera into which these species fall differ from *Xantusia* only in minor details of scalation. Each genus seems to have a particular kind of habitat. *Xantusia* sticks to arid regions, *Gaigeia* to the pine belt in high mountains of southern Mexico, and *Lepidophyma* to moist tropical lowlands. The Cuban night lizard, *Cricosaura typica,* has been collected only in areas of loose limestone rocks.

The Skinks
(*Family Scincidae*)

In large areas of the world skinks are the most abundant lizards. This is true, for instance, in the great forests of Africa and the East Indies. In the United States, only the iguanids are more numerous. Yet skinks are not seen often because they are retiring, living amidst the leaf litter in woods, or in decaying logs, or under stones. Many species, especially in the Old World tropics, spend much of their lives underground.

In general skinks have conical heads, cylindrical bodies, and tapering tails. Their legs are short, or in many cases nonexistent. They are covered by overlapping scales that, for the most part, are smooth and shiny. To be sure, some have heavy, blunt heads; others have bodies that are a little flattened from above; the tails may be short or long; and the scales are sometimes keeled. As a family, however, they are elongate, cylindrical, smooth, shiny lizards. The Solomon Islands giant skink, *Corucia zebrata,* is the largest member of the family, and it barely exceeds two feet. The vast majority are less than a foot long, and most are shorter than eight inches.

This is one of the two largest families of lizards, having over six hundred species, and yet it shows much less variety of body form than either the iguanids or agamids. No skinks have the flattened body shape of the horned toads (*Phrynosoma*) or the toad-headed agamids (*Phrynocephalus*), or the leaf-shaped body of the helmeted iguanid (*Corythophanes*) or certain of the agamids (e.g., *Calotes*).

In choice of habitat, too, the skinks are less versatile than the other large families. As we said above, skinks are mostly ground-dwellers and burrowers. Many can and do climb in bushes and trees, but only one shows any specilization for arboreal life. The exception is the Solomon Islands giant skink, *Corucia zebrata,* which has a prehensile tail. None, for instance, is able to leap from branch to branch like the arboreal long-legged iguanid (Polychrus), and none can glide like the flying agamids (*Draco*). A few, such as the keeled skinks (genus *Tropidophorus*), live along the edges of streams, but none is truly aquatic like the marine iguana, *Amblyrhynchus cristatus,* or as aquatic as the common iguana, *Iguana iguana.* Even on the ground, where they are really at home, the skinks have a relatively uniform crawling or scampering mode of life. There are no accomplished runners among them, none that, like many of the iguanids (e.g., the collared lizard, the basilisks, etc.) or agamids (e.g., the frilled lizard), can raise the body and run on the hind legs. When it comes to burrowing, however, the skinks stand out. They have tried almost every approach to burrowing made by lizards. But even here the iguanids and agamids have a method impossible for skinks to use, and that is the sidewise burrowing of the horned toads and the toad-headed agamids.

The relative uniformity of the skinks in body form and their relatively limited modes of life are merely two sides of the same coin. Apparently the heredity of the family is such that, practically speaking, they have been unable to adapt along the lines necessary for successful arboreal specialization, which calls for modified body form or special gripping devices other then claws, or for bipedal running, which calls for long hind legs. And, being unable to change body form and structure in these directions, they have been unable to exploit these modes of life the way iguanids, agamids, and geckos have.

Instead, the family heredity of skinks has predisposed them for burrowing and a subterranean life. This predisposition is shown by the modification of a number of structures. For example, the openings of the sense organs tend to become protected or closed off. The lower eyelid is the movable one in lizards, and typically it is opaque and scaly; but in many skinks a large transparent plate occupies most of the area of the lid. This "window" enables the skink to protect its eyes against particles of soil or ground debris and still see, though somewhat imperfectly.

Many stages of the development of the "window" can be seen in a variety of skinks. Among the mabuyas (genus *Mabuya*), a very large group of ground-dwelling skinks found all around the world in the tropics, the lower eyelid is covered with small scales in most species, but in a few a transparent disk takes up the center of the lid. The little brown skink, *Lygosoma laterale,* of southeastern United States also has a small "window." In certain Oriental relatives of the little brown skink, for example the Travancore skink, *Lygosoma travancoricum,* the transparent plate occupies more than half of the lower lid.

The ultimate in this development is seen in the lidless skinks (genus *Ablepharus*), in which the transparent plate covers the entire area of the lower lid and is in place over the eye at all times. The scientific name of the genus, which means "without eyelids," is clearly a misnomer. The "window" or "spectacle," as it is usually called in this final stage, greatly reduces the mobility of the lower lid. A lid covered with many small scales, which is characteristic of lizards in general, is very flexible, being able to bend slightly at the edge of every scale. An eyelid of this sort could almost be rolled up like a window shade. But as the transparent plate becomes larger, the flexibility of the lid decreases, until finally, when the plate covers the entire eyelid, the lid is no longer capable of being lowered. This is precisely the situation in the lidless skinks.

In a number of burrowing skinks the eyes have become quite small. This development crops up in the snake skinks (genus *Ophioscincus*) of Southeast Asia, in the dart skinks (genus *Acontias*) of Africa

Little Brown Skink (*Lygosoma laterale*)

and Madagascar, in the sand skink, *Neoseps reynoldsi,* of Florida, and in many others. Some of these burrowers have "windows" in the lower eyelid; others do not. It is common for the eyelid to be thickened and relatively immovable in these burrowers, which really should be called subterranean since they spend practically their entire lives underground.

In lizards with well-developed external ears, the eardrum either lies right at the surface or is more or less deeply sunken so that a short tube leads down to it from an opening behind the head. Many agamids, e.g., Sita's lizard, some flying lizards, and the Indian bloodsucker, and a few skinks, such as the keeled skinks (genus *Tropidophorus*), have superficial eardrums. But the great majority of skinks have sunken eardrums. The openings leading to these deep eardrums are very small or completely closed in many burrowing or subterranean skinks, thus preventing soil particles from tearing the relatively delicate membrane.

Both the ear and the eye are protected in subterranean lizards like the Philippine short-legged skinks (genus *Brachymeles*) and the dart skinks of Africa. But there is an important difference in the fates of these two sense organs. Despite the clearing of the center of the eyelid, the amount of light entering the eye is reduced, as is always the case when light passes through a filter. Furthermore, a smaller eye usually is less sensitive than a larger one. Therefore, the alteration of the eyes of subterranean skinks has led to an impairment of vision. But this is small loss to an animal living in almost perpetual darkness.

Similarly, the loss of the external ear, which is designed to detect air-borne vibrations that are reduced if not absent in the subterranean world, is no handicap to burrowers like the Florida sand skink (*Neoseps*) or the blind skinks (*Typhlosaurus*) of South Africa. But the underground world is not devoid of sound, for all burrowing insects, such as scarab beetles and immature cicadas, make noises as they scratch their way through the soil. These vibrations, which are transmitted by the semisolid earth, naturally are important to insect-eating lizards. External ears with eardrums at the end of a tube are not as effective listening devices for such sound waves as the whole outside of the head. It is likely that even the few burrowing skinks having external ear openings hear with the surfaces of the head. The subterranean skinks thus listen to the crawling noises of their insect prey in much the same manner as a person gets the tone from a tuning fork by putting it against his teeth or temple.

The other structures that show obvious modifications for burrowing are the limbs and the head. The tendency among lizards to lose the limbs is best shown by the skinks. Approximately two-thirds of skink genera have degenerate legs. A number of skinks have somewhat shortened limbs, but these are not included in our estimate. Nevertheless, slight shortening is the beginning of limb degeneration, followed closely by loss of some of the digits.

The genus *Scelotes* of Africa and Madagascar offers a fine example of what has happened many times in the family Scincidae. Bojer's skink, *Scelotes bojeri,* from Mauritius Island, has reasonably well-developed limbs. If the foreleg is laid back against the side and the hind leg stretched forward, the two meet. Both legs have five digits. Several others in this genus, for example the black-sided skink, *Scelotes melanopleura,* of Madagascar, still have five fingers and toes, but the legs are ridiculously short. If the forelimbs and hind limbs are pressed against the side, they come nowhere near meeting; the gap is several times the length of a leg. Still other members of this genus (for example, *Scelotes bipes*) have tiny hind limbs, each of which has two toes, but no forelimbs. Finally, we come to species such as the South African plain skink, *Scelotes inornatus,* that have no legs at all.

Some skink genera have not carried this process so far. The lidless skinks (genus *Ablepharus*), for example, have lost some of the fingers and toes and shortened the legs, but none has lost either pair of limbs. Beginning with five fingers and toes, the lidless skinks run through species with four fingers and five toes, four fingers and four toes, three fingers and three toes, and down to two fingers and three toes.

Notice that the forelegs never have more digits than the hind. It seems to be a general pattern in skinks that the front legs degenerate slightly faster than the rear ones. In the genus *Scelotes,* we found species having small hind limbs and no forelimbs, but none with the reverse combination. As another illustration, our sand skink (*Neoseps*) has only one digit on its front leg but two on the rear; furthermore, its hind leg is twice the size of the front one.

Along with the degeneration of the limbs, something happens to the tail. Skinks that, like the mabuyas (genus *Mabuya*), have well-developed legs typically have moderately long, tapering tails. The African five-lined skink, *Mabuya quinquetaeniata,* and the East Indian brown-sided skink, *Mabuya multifasciata,* have long legs for this family, and their tails are correspondingly long (a little longer than the head and trunk) and begin to taper close to the base. Many of the slender skinks (genus *Lygosoma*) have degenerate legs, and these always have tails that remain approximately the same thickness as the body for quite a distance.

Now, a lizard without legs has lost the organs that most lizards use for propulsion. Yet locomotion is an essential function, and the limbless, snakelike skinks use a serpentine type of locomotion, throwing the body into horizontal curves and pushing against lumps of soil, stones, and any uneven surface. The tail assists the trunk in this process. And this is where the importance of the thickness of the tail enters. A slender, fragile tail could lash around rapidly but could supply little or no power. On the other hand, a thick, muscular tail can exert enough force to be an effective partner of the body. Here is a nice illustration of the response of the body to the forces of natural selection.

A burrowing animal without strong legs is left with one one digging tool—its head. The head must be pushed through the soil by a muscular body. The pressures exerted in these movements are too great for the ordinary lizard head, although the conical snout of skinks is a better shape to start with than most. But apparently further improvements of the form can make subterranean life still easier, even for skinks. Many, though not all, burrowing skinks have the snout drawn out into a pointed cone, as in the case of the Ceylon skinks of the genus *Nessia*. Further refinement leads to the countersinking of the lower jaw, so that it does not protrude from the outlines of the skull. This extreme condition is found in a number of limbless or nearly limbless skinks—the African blind dart skinks (genus *Typhlacontias*), the Asian sand skinks (genus *Ophiomorus*), and the Florida sand skink (*Neoseps*), to name but three.

Yet another mechanical problem faces a limbless burrowing skink. Like all lizards, skinks have somewhat flexible skulls, a disadvantageous characteristic for an instrument that must be pushed through a resisting medium. This difficulty has been partially overcome by modifying the scales that cover a skink's head. These scales are arranged in a definite number and pattern that varies only slightly among the terrestrial skinks. The head scales can be considered to form a sheath around the skull, a sheath that is capable of slight bending at the junctures between scales. The sheath can reduce the flexibility of the skull, especially if the sheath itself is made more rigid. And this is what many subterranean skinks have accomplished through fusion of scales and elimination of scale junctures. Besides the groups mentioned in the preceding paragraph, burrowers without countersunk jaws, such as the Asian snake-skinks (genus *Ophioscincus*), have eliminated a number of head scales.

Like most lizards, skinks feed primarily upon small invertebrate animals. Insects, being most numerous, naturally contribute heavily to the diet. The largest skinks, like the largest iguanids and agamids, are vegetarians. The prehensile-tailed skink, *Corucia zebrata,* of the Solomon Islands, the largest of all, eats nothing but vegetation, as does the foot-long Cape Verde skink, *Macroscincus coctaei.* The other large skinks, the Australian genera *Egernia* and *Tiliqua,* which reach lengths of one to almost two feet, are at least partly herbivorous, feeding on fruits, leaves, and mushrooms. The teeth of these vegetarians tend to be blunter than those of insectivorous skinks, and several have broad-crowned grinding teeth.

The teeth of the insectivorous skinks, a category including all of the North American species, are much more pointed and may be simple cones or set with two to three small, sharp cusps. Collecting their food is a relatively simple matter—they grab a caterpillar or grasshopper or beetle with their jaws, crush it between their teeth, and swallow it. If the prey is small enough, it may be lapped up with the tongue. Skinks have thick, oval tongues covered with flattened, overlapping, pimplelike projections. Since the tongue is coated with sticky mucous and the projections overlap toward the throat, small ants and spiders do not slide off the tongue once it touches them.

A group of Ceylon skinks (genus *Nessia*) feeds chiefly on earthworms. Earthworms present some mechanical problems to would-be predators that can grasp them only with jaws. While trying to swallow this long, slippery object, these lizards, which have either very tiny, useless legs or none at all, must prevent the earthworm from backing out of their jaws. The problem is solved by the shape of the teeth, which are pointed and curve backward, forming a strictly one-way passage into the throat.

For protection from enemies, skinks rely mainly on their retiring habits. In addition they lean on the old lizard trick of snapping off part of their tails and escape during the moment the predator's attention is distracted by the violent wriggling of the disconnected piece. Occasionally a herpetologist will collect a snake that has nothing in its stomach but a freshly caught skink tail.

Some idea of the importance of this safety device to the skink is given by an excellent study of the Great Plains skink, *Eumeces obsoletus.* It was found that the older the skink, the less likely it was to have an intact tail; about three-fourths of nine-month-old skinks had complete tails, and the proportion dropped to one-third in one-year-olds and to one-fifth in three-year-olds. If they had been unable to break their tails, only one-fifth as many would have reached their third birthday.

The efficiency of the tail in this job is enhanced in some skinks by conspicuous coloration. The Polynesian blue-tailed skink, *Lygosoma cyanurum,* as its name implies, has a bright blue tail that contrasts sharply with its black or brown body. When this five- or six-inch lizard sacrifices its tail in an emergency, the twitching bright object becomes the most conspicuous thing in sight. The bird or would-be collector gets the booby prize, and the skink disappears. The tails of some of our skinks, for example the Pecos skink, *Eumeces taylori,* and the five-lined skink, *Eumeces fasciatus,* are bright blue only when the animals are young and when the hazards of life are greatest.

The color patterns found in this family of lizards run the gamut from stripes, crossbars, and spots to a uniform color without markings. Stripes are probably the commonest form of marking, and they may be broad or narrow, and on the side or on the back. Our little brown skink, *Lygosoma laterale,* has a broad streak on each side, the Polynesian blue-tailed skink narrow ones on its back; and other species, including the American western skink, *Eumeces skiltonianus,* have both types. Browns, olives, and the somber tones generally predominate, although, as we noted in the preceding paragraph, bright colors also appear.

Unlike the iguanids, agamids, and true chameleons, skinks lack the ability to change color rapidly. But changes do take place in many species either as they age or as the seasons change. We have already mentioned two American skinks that have bright blue tails only as juveniles. Besides losing the blue of the tail, large adults of the five-lined skink also lose the dark and light stripes characteristic of the young. The Great Plains skink, *Eumeces obsoletus,* has light head markings that disappear as the animal approaches maturity.

During the breeding season the males of certain species acquire reddish or orange hues. Males of the five-lined skink, *Eumeces fasciatus,* develop red heads, whereas males of the Oriental brown-sided skink, *Mabuya multifasciata,* have large orange or red patches on the sides behind the arms at this time of year.

As they mature, male skinks often develop broad, muscular heads. Although we know almost nothing about the courtship of skinks, probably because of their secretive habits, it is evident that the males use these strong heads in fighting. Here again we run into a profound difference between the skinks on the one hand and the iguanids and agamids on the other. Whereas in the last two bluff is an important element of "fights" between males, it apparently has at most a minor role in the skinks. Excellent field observations of our five-lined skink reveal that when two males see each other during the breeding period, the red heads must have the same effect on them as a red scarf is supposed to have on a fighting bull. They rush at one another with open jaws and bite hard. Pieces of skin and flesh may be torn off, and undoubtedly some males die as a result. There is no puffing out of a throat dewlap or inflation of the body or any other ritualistic motion such as is seen in iguanids and agamids. These skinks mean business, and they get right to it.

Since no skink has a throat fan, this element of display is lacking in their courtship. In fact there is very little diplay of any sort, or even much of a courtship. A male in the breeding season follows the track of a female by scent until he sees her. Then he pursues her. If she is not in breeding condition, she scurries off and hides. If she is, the male has no trouble in catching her. In the case of the five-lined skink, the male's first action when he gets close is to touch her with his tongue. Next he grips the center of her back near the shoulders with his jaws and places one hind leg over the base of her tail. He then slips his tail underneath hers, bringing their vents close together, and inserts a hemipenis.

Most families of lizards seem to be committed to one mode of reproduction or another. The geckos, for example, lay eggs almost without exception. So do the iguanids. But the skinks are about evenly divided between those that lay eggs and those that are viviparous and give birth to young ready to leave the embryonic egg membranes. Even some genera seem undecided, a case in point being the genus *Mabuya,* which includes live-bearers and egg-layers.

A clutch may contain anywhere from two to twenty-three white eggs, roughly one-half or two-thirds of an inch long in females seven to ten inches long (the American five-lined skink and the keeled Indian mabuya, *Mabuya carinata,* respectively). As the embryos develop, the eggs grow slightly. For example, eggs of the Great Plains skink, *Eumeces obsoletus,* in a natural nest increased in length about 20 per cent in the six weeks they were kept under observation.

The female deposits the eggs in a small hole she has dug, or lays them in a rotting log or under a rock. One group of species, the genus *Eumeces,* which includes our five-lined and Great Plains skinks, guards the incubating eggs. The female coils her body around the eggs or lies among them. This habit was originally referred to as "brooding," but, because we have no clear-cut evidence that the female warms the eggs, it would be better to avoid that term. The female does not stay with the eggs constantly, leaving the nest at intervals to feed. On her return she usually touches several of the eggs with her tongue.

"Guarding" is also a questionable term for the female's function, since she often scurries off at any sign of danger. Nevertheless, she probably does keep away small animals incapable of harming her but quite able to eat the eggs. Much of the female's time in the nest is spent turning the eggs. One suggestion as to the value of this activity is that the turning prevents one part of an egg from remaining in contact with the damp soil and thus rotting at that point. At any rate, during the month or six weeks of incubation, the female puts a high polish on the soil by her continuous movements within the nest.

As a general rule, the live-bearers have smaller broods. The large blue-tongued skink, *Tiliqua scincoides* (Plate 66), of Australia normally has around ten young at a time, although it may have as many as fifteen. The smaller mabuyas have smaller broods, the East Indian brown-sided skink, *Mabuya multifasciata,* giving birth to about six young. Differences in the size of the species will not account completely for differences in brood size. The foot-long stumptailed skink, *Tiliqua rugosa* (Plate 65), which has a body length about twice that of the mabuya, has only two offspring per brood. And no wonder, for each baby is half the length of the mother. There just is no room inside the female for any more.

Skinks are found in all continents except Antarctica, where no animal with a choice in the matter would live anyhow. Southeast Asia and the East Indies are the headquarters of the family, with half or more of the species found there. By contrast, the Western Hemisphere has only a handful of skinks. Each major region of the Old World has its own characteristic groups of skinks, just as we have seen in other families of lizards. But this family, to a greater extent than any other, includes a number of genera that overlap not only continents, but hemispheres.

For example, in the principal genus of the United States, *Eumeces,* about one-half of the species live in the United States and Central America. The remainder occur in the Far East (China and Japan mainly), southwestern Asia, and North Africa. Except for one species living in northeastern Indo-China, this genus is not found in the tropics of southeastern Asia, Africa, or South America. In short, these egg-layers are native to the North Temperate Zone outside of Europe, except for a minor occurrence into the tropics.

The genus *Mabuya,* to which we have referred many times, is another group straddling both hemispheres. But, unlike *Eumeces,* it is primarily tropical. For instance, many species occur in Southeast Asia, the East Indies, and tropical Africa. It is not restricted to the tropics, however, since several species live in North Africa and Southwest Asia, both of which are temperate. In the Western Hemisphere its distribution is confined to tropical Central and South America. Why it should not appear in the United States is a mystery.

Then there are the small lidless skinks (genus *Ablepharus*) found around the globe in the tropical belt—Australia, the East Indies, tropical Africa, South America, and the islands of the South Pacific. Several of the approximately twenty-five species live in the North Temperate Zone, in southeastern Europe, North Africa, and Southwest Asia. A single species, Bouton's skink, *Ablepharus boutoni,* has spread throughout the island world of the tropical Pacific and now occurs on the coasts of Peru and Chile as well as on Australia, Madagascar, and the coast of East Africa.

The other widely distributed skinks are the slender skinks (*Lygosoma*). This genus, the largest reptile genus in number of species, contains no less than three hundred species. With such a fantastic swarm, it is not in the least surprising that the slender skinks occur on several continents. They are numerous in Australia, less so in Africa, and more so in Southeast Asia and the East Indies. In fact most of the three hundred live in the Oriental tropics. Despite the great number of species, less than a dozen live outside of the tropics. And, even more remarkable, only one species reaches the Americas—the little brown skink, *Lygosoma laterale,* of southeastern United States.

But there are signs of another attempt at invasion. The Polynesian blue-tailed skink, *Lygosoma cyanurum,* known from New Guinea in the west to the Hawaiian Islands in the east, has now turned up on Clipperton Island, an isolated atoll only eighteen hundred miles west of Panama.

The major types of skinks in the United States have been mentioned: the little brown skink, the Florida sand skink (*Neoseps*), and the fifteen species of the genus *Eumeces.* The five-lined skink, *Eumeces fasciatus* (Plate 67), is the common species of the eastern half of the country, occurring in every state east of a line from Minnesota to Texas, excepting only Vermont, New Hampshire, and Maine. Its favorite habitat is a rocky woodland open enough to have patches of sunlight on the ground. As noted earlier, the juvenile color pattern—five milky white or yellowish stripes on a black or dark brown base finished off with a bright blue tail—gradually changes as the animal grows older. The

[129]

tail acquires the black or brownish tone of the body, the light stripes become dull or disappear entirely, and the head turns distinctly reddish in breeding males, which have a head and trunk length of about three inches and a tail twice as long. As is true of all its relatives, the five-lined skink feeds almost exclusively on insects and other small invertebrates. Spiders, crickets, grasshoppers, beetles, and even land snails seem to be the most important items. If the prey is large enough to offer some resistance, the skink, while grasping the unfortunate creature with its jaws, bangs it against the ground until it is dead or incapable of effective movement.

The little brown skink, *Lygosoma laterale,* which reaches a maximum length of four and three-fourths inches, is found south and east of an arc connecting southern New Jersey, Pennsylvania, Indiana, Missouri, and eastern Texas. Its pale brown back and dark brown sides are not especially colorful, but this lizard is interesting to us partly because it is the only skink in the United States with a cleared "window" in its lower eyelid. Its one to five eggs are laid in June or July in humus, or in or under rotting logs, and hatch in about two months. By the following spring the hatchlings reach sexual maturity.

The Florida sand skink, *Neoseps reynoldsi,* alone among American skinks shows the family propensity for extreme modification for subterranean life. As stated above, the sand skink has undergone degeneration of the limbs to the point where it now has one digit on the front leg and two on the rear. Furthermore, it no longer has an external ear opening, and its eyes are very small. By means of horizontal undulations, the sand skink "swims" through the sand in which it lives, an activity considerably eased by the fact that the lower jaw is countersunk into the upper. And this is about all we know of this rarely seen American lizard.

All of the species west of the range of the little brown skink are members of the genus *Eumeces.* The largest is the Great Plains skink, a robust, ashy gray animal with black-edged scales that reaches a length of about a foot. It is found in the southern half of the plains as far southwest as central Arizona in rocky areas. Up to twenty-one eggs are laid in June or July. In addition to the usual skink fare of insects and spiders, this large species also eats small lizards.

The other western and the fifteen Mexican and Central American species of this genus have much the same mode of life. Some live at high elevations and some in drier situations, but essentially they are all ground-dwellers and are commonly found under rocks, logs, etc. All species guard their eggs.

In the southern part of Mexico the mabuyas (genus *Mabuya*) make their appearance. The dozen or so American species range southward down to northern Chile and central Argentina. All of the mabuyas have well-developed legs, a somewhat flattened yet nonetheless cylindrical body, and a long, tapering tail. They are not burrowers but instead are ground-dwellers that often climb into bushes, part way up tree trunks, or over rocks. The common mabuya, *Mabuya mabouya,* a dark-sided brown skink found from Mexico to Brazil and Bolivia, has adapted itself to life around houses in small towns and villages and so become one of the lizards most often seen in Latin America.

Except for the four- or five-inch lidless skink, *Ablepharus boutoni,* which has recently invaded a few coastal areas, the mabuyas are the only representatives of the family in South America. The skinks, consequently, are the only large family of lizards having more species and genera in North America than in South America.

Compared to other parts of the world the Americas have an impoverished skink fauna. In Africa the family begins to flourish, and many types are found, including a number of subterranean genera. Still, south of the Sahara the mabuyas are the most conspicuous. The African five-lined skink, *Mabuya quinquetaeniata,* occurring almost throughout this vast region and down the Nile Valley, seems to be the most abundant, probably because it lives around houses and may be seen all day scampering in the sun over mud huts and on the trunks of palms. This eight- to ten-inch lizard starts life with a blue-striped black body and a blue tail. As the females mature the black of the body becomes brown, the stripes golden, and the tail brown. The males usually lose the juvenile pattern and colors completely, and end up as brown lizards having a yellow lip and a black throat. The white, oblong eggs are laid under stones or logs, and, although the usual number is probably around ten, as many as forty have been found under a single log in different stages of development.

Fernand's lizard, *Lygosoma fernandi,* which, at fourteen inches, is probably the largest skink in Africa, has a mode of life very different from that of the five-lined skink. It is never found outside of the equatorial rain forest, and therefore is not one of the sun-loving skinks. The bright red sides barred with black seem out of place in a lizard that is at least as active at night as during the day. Using its blunt head and thick neck, it digs a simple burrow leading to an enlarged chamber. The constant rubbing of this hard-skinned animal gives its burrow a characteristic smoothness. As is often the case, the people of the forest think this retiring lizard is a bad omen, and if they see one abandon any plans made for the day.

South of the equatorial belt the skink fauna includes many groups with degenerate limbs. The genus *Scelotes,* which has already been discussed in this connection, has the largest number of species (nineteen) and shows all stages of limb degeneration down to complete absence of legs. Usually, the more degenerate the limbs, the more subterranean the habits. Those with forelimbs and hind limbs still present live in leaf mold and under rocks and logs. All species of *Scelotes* give birth to from two to six young, the eggs undergoing their entire incubation within the body of the female.

The dart skinks (genus *Acontias*) and the blind skinks (genus *Typhlosaurus*) of South Africa are completely limbless. Their scales are especially hard and smooth, which should make wriggling through the soil easier. If caught and placed on top of the ground, they move surprisingly fast, using snakelike horizontal undulations. Both genera have the consolidated head scales typical of specialized burrowers, and the blind skinks even have their eyes covered by scales.

Several genera of African skinks—the mabuyas (genus *Mabuya*), the dart skinks (genus *Acontias*),

and *Scelotes*—have representatives on the neighboring island of Madagascar. But one mabuya and the ubiquitous Bouton's lidless skink are the only species common to Madagascar and the adjacent coast of Africa. The other forty-three species are found only on Madagascar and the small islands around it. And about one-third of that number are subterranean types having very degenerate limbs or none at all.

North of the Sahara the skinks, with one exception (the African five-lined skink, *Mabuya quinquetaeniata*), belong to groups different from those found south of the desert. In fact, just looking at the skinks, we gain the impression that North Africa is not part of the rest of the continent. The relationships of this northern fauna are obviously with arid and semiarid southwestern Asia as far east as West Pakistan. We have seen evidences of the same relationship in the distribution of the spiny-tailed agamids.

From Asia Minor these skinks have invaded southeastern Europe, and one of the lidless skinks, *Ablepharus pannonicus,* has reached as far as Hungary and Rumania. Two additional species of different genera are now found in Greece. From North Africa several species of cylindrical skinks (genus *Chalcides*) have moved across the Mediterranean at

Cylindrical Skink (*Chalcides chalcides*)

narrow points into southern Europe, one entering Italy, using Sicily as a steppingstone, and two entering Spain via Morocco and the Straits of Gibraltar.

With such close ties between North Africa and Southwest Asia, their skink faunas must be considered as a unit. Three groups we have met before. Five species of the tropical genus *Mabuya,* eight species to the egg-guarding *Eumeces,* and several species of lidless skinks (genus *Ablepharus*) live in this temperate region. The other three genera are rather specialized, each in its own way.

The cylindrical skinks, (genus *Chalcides*), which are marked by very short or degenerate legs and thick tails, crawl in a serpentine fashion over the ground or on old stone walls in situations as diverse as desert oases and the French countryside. Apparently all of these insectivorous lizards give birth to active young.

Although they can and do burrow, the cylindrical skinks are not nearly as specialized along these lines as the Asian sand skinks (genus *Ophiomorus*). These small skinks, none of which exceeds seven or eight inches, live in sandy areas from Greece through Asia Minor to West Pakistan. The conical head with its countersunk lower jaw is a burrowing adaptation we have noted before. Two of the six species have no legs at all, and the others have shallow grooves into which their ridiculously small legs fit. One of these lizards, Blanford's sand skink, *Ophiomorus blanfordi,* kept alive in our laboratory for several months, remained buried in loose sand the whole time. Since the sand was less than an inch deep, we could see how rapidly this skink could "swim."

The other specialized skinks in this arid, temperate region are also sand skinks but of a different

sort. Their ability to swim through sand has earned them the name of "sand fish" (genus *Scincus*). The eight species have countersunk lower jaws like the previous genus but have rather broad snouts that sharpen to an edge. Unlike the Asian sand skinks (genus *Ophiomorus*) and a great many other pronounced burrowers, the sand fish retain well-developed legs. The digits are flattened and have fringes of projecting scales reminiscent of the American sand-dwelling umas and apparently enabling them to move over the surface of the loose sand. Nevertheless, the sand fish spend most of their time under the surface searching for insects in the sandy deserts from Algeria to West Pakistan.

Just a little farther east and south in Asia the skinks change radically. Animals adapted to dry, temperate-zone climates, lizards like the sand skinks (*Ophiomorus*) and *Eumeces,* are out of place and poorly equipped for life in the warm, humid Oriental tropics. Instead they are replaced by mabuyas (genus *Mabuya*), hordes of slender skinks (genus *Lygosoma*), and a number of groups peculiar to Southeast Asia.

The dozen or so mabuyas of India and the Indo-Chinese region closely resemble their relatives in Africa and South America—they have robust cylindrical bodies, tapering tails, and well-developed legs. They are always the most conspicuous skinks, abundant around houses, active by day, and making scratching, rustling sounds as they pursue insects and each other. Some species give birth to from three to seven young; others lay up to twenty-five eggs.

Much less is known about the cat skinks (genus *Ristella*) of India. All four of these small (up to five inches long) lizards have retractile claws, a feature rarely found in lizards. How these claws

Sandfish (*Scincus philbyi*)

STANDARD OIL COMPANY

are used is still a mystery. We assume they are a refinement for an arboreal life, but, since we are not even sure that the cat skinks live in trees, this is an unconfirmed guess. We do know that these species live only in the hills of southern India, a region of forests and therefore a likely place for arboreal skinks. Their breeding habits are unknown.

The other skinks peculiar to southeast Asia are subterranean forms with degenerate limbs (the genus *Nessia* of Ceylon) or none at all (*Barkudia insularis* and *Sepsophis punctatus,* both of India). All have the very small eyes and consolidated head shields we have come to expect. Because of their borrowing habits they are rarely seen, and little is known of them except their body form and the fact that the Ceylon skinks (genus *Nessia*) lay two eggs.

The keeled skinks (genus *Tropidophorus*), one of the very few groups of aquatic skinks, are also found in Southeast Asia, ranging from Siam and Indo-China southward and eastward in the Malay Peninsula, Borneo, Celebes, and the Philippines. These six- to ten-inch lizards have slightly flattened tails, their only obvious modification for life in water. Actually, they are not as aquatic or as accomplished swimmers as the common iguana, and spend most of the time on the banks of small streams, feeding on insects and small crabs. Catching them is quite another matter, as we can attest, because they dart into tangles of brush that accumulate along every creek or dive into the water and hide under rocks. The keeled skinks are viviparous and have up to nine young at a time.

Despite the fact that the East Indies have about a hundred species of skinks, only one genus is confined to this vast area. The great majority of East Indian skinks are members of genera we have met in the Americas, Africa, and Asia, and will meet in the Australian region. The genus of slender skinks (*Lygosoma*), for instance, has seventy-five species in the East Indies. A number of them spill over into Southeast Asia and New Guinea (which on zoological grounds we group with Australia). But for the most part they are limited to one or several of the East Indian islands, as for example the striped slender skink, *Lygosoma vittatum,* which is found only on Borneo. This lizard is arboreal but often moves out of the forest into small clearings and lives on the short pilings that support most houses in Borneo. Black on the head and fore part of the trunk, and with five yellow-green stripes that fade into the olive color of the rear of the body, this six-inch skink makes an attractive splash of color as it hurries after its insect food.

In the still larger clearings of villages and towns throughout most of the East Indies, the most con-

ARAMCO

Sandfish

spicuous skink is the brown-sided mabuya, *Mabuya multifasciata,* a member of another widespread genus. Though it too is sometimes seen climbing house pilings, it is much more common on the ground than is the striped slender skink.

The short-legged skinks (genus *Brachymeles*) of the Philippine Islands constitute the only uniquely East Indian genus. These ground-dwelling burrowing skinks have elongate bodies and thick tails, and move in serpentine fashion to make up for the uselessness of their feeble limbs.

Farther south, in the Australian region, the skink fauna is still dominated by the slender skinks (genus *Lygosoma*), but, as was true among the geckos and agamids, several of the genera are found nowhere else. The casque-headed skinks (genus *Tribolonotus*), occurring on New Guinea, have a bony head with six long points projecting from its rear margin. Unlike the iguanids and agamids, which have evolved all manner of head adornments, the casque-headed skinks represent this family's only achievement along these lines.

The Australian region is also the home of several groups of very large skinks. The twenty-four-inch Solomon Islands giant skink, *Corucia zebrata,* has been mentioned already. Some of the blue-tongued skinks (genus *Tiliqua*) of this area approach the Solomon Islands giant in size, but, whereas the Solomons skink has a prehensile tail and climbs, the blue-tongued skinks have neither such a useful tail nor the ability that goes with it. They are strictly ground-dwellers.

The other genus (*Egernia*) of large Australian skinks rarely exceeds twelve inches. Unlike the smooth blue-tongued skinks, this genus runs to spiny scales that become excessively sharp on the tail in

Cunningham's Spiny-tailed Skink (*Egernia cunninghami*)

certain species. One of them, the spiny-tailed skink, *Egernia stokesi,* lives in rocky places and uses these spines to advantage. Once it crawls into a crevice between two rocks, the long, spiny scales catch on the surface and prevent its being pulled out.

Skink Relatives

(*Families Anelytropsidae and Dibamidae*)

Three genera of blind, earless, and essentially limbless burrowing lizards are included in this section. The genus *Dibamus,* with three species ranging from southern Indo-China and the Philippines south to New Guinea, has always been treated as a distinct family, though recognizably closely related to skinks. Its conical head has one very large scale covering the muzzle and four smaller scales, two of which cover the eyes. These small (less than a foot long), short-tailed lizards have often been taken from rotting logs. One rather hard-shelled egg of *Dibamus* has been found in a decayed log.

In one characteristic the dibamids differ from all other limbless or near-limbless lizards, namely, the males have flaplike hind legs whereas the females have none. The male's legs have several limb bones but are not divided externally into digits.

The two remaining genera, which are limbless in both sexes, have sometimes been divided into two families. *Feylinia,* from equatorial Africa, has four species. Usually they are discovered under decayed logs, where their food, almost exclusively termites, is abundant. The only defense of these foot-long lizards is feigning death, although why that should prevent many potential predators from eating them is far from clear. Like many other reptiles, *Feylinia* is surrounded by superstitions, one of the myths being that it can enter the human body at will and cause death when it leaves.

The other genus, *Anelytropsis,* lives in central eastern Mexico. The single species reaches a length of about eight inches. For some unknown reason it has been collected only three or four times, and is therefore counted among the rarest lizards in the world. Once it was found under a rotten log next to an ant nest, which may be a clue to its food, and once under a rock on a bushy slope.

The Girdle-tailed Lizards

(*Family Cordylidae*)

We tend to think of continents as separate units despite the narrow connections, such as Panama or the Sinai Peninsula, between some of them. But, if we look at the world from a biological point of view, the continents are not units. In fact, the major divisions of animal and plant distribution usually coincide with climatic zones and may cut across several continents, as for example the desert life zone embracing the Sahara, the Arabian peninsula, Persia, and northern India. Other life zones cover only part of a continent, such as the grasslands and savannas of Africa, stretching southward from the Sahara to the Cape of Good Hope.

Through the eastern and southern parts of this grass country, the girdle-tailed or cordylid lizards make their homes, especially where rock formations crop out. This small family includes only twenty-three species, and just one of those, the common girdle-tail, *Cordylus cordylus,* is found in Ethiopia and Kenya at the northern limit of the range. In fact, this one species almost covers the entire family range, living as far south as Cape Province, South Africa. The bulk of the family, however, lives in South Africa, and Cape Province alone has fourteen species as well as all the four genera into which the species are grouped.

The common name "girdle-tail" refers to whorls of large, keeled scales encircling the tail in all members of the family. In two of the genera, the club-tailed cordylids (genus *Cordylus*) and the false club-tails (genus *Pseudocordylus*), the keels of the scales on the tail are long and usually curled outward at the tip, converting the tail into a very spiny appendage and recalling similar tails in the Iguanidae and Agamidae. And there is a good reason for calling them club-tails. When they are cornered by certain enemies, especially snakes, the heavy, armored tail may be swung vigorously from side to side and with good effect. In fact one club-tail that was headed down the gullet of a puff adder, one of the large African vipers, suddenly began to flail the snake, which thereupon released the front end of the lizard and looked for a meal elsewhere.

At the other end these lizards usually have a broad triangular head swollen at the temples, with a moderately thick body and well-developed legs. (Four of the species, those forming the genus *Chamaesaura*, the South African snake lizards, differ radically from this description, but we will re-turn to them later.) The scales covering the head are large and arranged in a fixed, symmetrical pattern, but those of the back show much more variation and may be large or small. In several genera the scales are important in defense, and most thoroughly so in the club-tailed cordylids (*Cordylus*).

When trouble looms, the girdle-tailed lizards, like almost all lizards and indeed most other animals, seek to defend themselves first by escaping. The cordylids, which as we mentioned before are most abundant in rocky areas, head for shelter in rock crevasses. And their bodies are well adapted for escape in such narrow spaces. For one thing the club-tails (*Cordylus*), the false club-tails (*Pseudocordylus*), and the flat lizards (*Platysaurus*) all look as though they had been passed through a wringer; their heads, bodies, limbs, and tails are flattened, enabling them to squeeze into tight places.

If the enemy attempts to extract them, it is presented first with a tail that, in the club-tails and false club-tails, is spiny and therefore not only is unpleasant to grab firmly but also catches on the rock surfaces, thus clamping the lizard in place. When in an equally threatening situation, most lizards of other families usually fracture the tail voluntarily, but not the cordylids—although, given a sufficient tug, their tails will break.

Despite the absence of long spines, the tails of the flat lizards (*Platysaurus*) do obtain some purchase with the keels on the scales. On their shoulders and necks the flat lizards have folds of skin bearing spiny scales that may also catch on rock surfaces. The club-tails, however, are more specialized in this area, too, for most of them have strong, spiny scales projecting from the rear of the head.

These head spines, which call to mind those of the horned toads, function not only in the cramped quarters of rock shelters but also out in the open. One species in particular, the armadillo lizard, *Cordylus cataphractus* (Plate 47), which is only about ten inches long, uses these spines as part of a remarkable defensive posture. When caught away from a rock shelter, the armadillo lizard rolls on its back and grasps its spiny tail with its mouth. Thus the tightly curled lizard protects its soft belly and presents a spiny head and tail to its enemy. But this defense would have a great gap except for one thing: all the scales of the head, back, and limbs have a bony central layer that makes the entire exposed surface as hard as rock. Only after all sign of danger has passed will the lizard uncoil and right itself.

A related species, the sungazer, *Cordylus giganteus,* which at fifteen inches is the largest member of the family in terms of bulk, has a slightly different defensive posture that is based on the same principles. Instead of coiling its body, the sungazer lies flat on its belly and stretches its limbs back along the sides. This leaves only its hard, spiny surfaces exposed to the enemy, and the sungazer resists vigorously all attempts to turn it over on its back. The important thing, just as in the case of the armadillo lizard, is to protect the soft belly. Incidentally, the common name "sungazer" is based on the lizard's habit of basking.

Earlier we referred to four members of the family Cordylidae that differ radically in appearance from the other species. These four, the snake lizards (genus *Chamaesaura*), are, as their name implies, slender, drawn-out creatures. Though not as bulky as other members of the family, they are certainly the longest, three of them reaching a total length of two feet, of which three-fourths is tail. Their snakelike appearance is enhanced by the degeneration of their legs. Only one species, the Transvaal snake lizard, *Chamaesaura aenea,* has five digits, all clawed, on each limb. All the others have at most two toes per leg, and one species, the large-scaled snake lizard, *Chamaesaura macrolepis,* of South Africa, has no front limbs at all.

Like the glass snake, the snake lizards have good eyes and are not in the least inclined to the burrowing habits of, say, the limbless skinks. Instead, the snake lizards are active inhabitants of grasslands, moving rapidly through the vegetation with serpentine undulations and often with the head and forelimbs raised off the ground.

In other habits the snake lizards do not differ from the other girdle-tailed lizards. All feed primarily on insects, spiders, earthworms, and other invertebrates, and so have typical lizard diets. But another feature of this family is not usual; every species is a live-bearer, which is true of few other lizard families. The developing eggs, customarily two to four in number, are retained in the body of the female until ready to hatch.

The Gerrhosaurids

(*Family Gerrhosauridae*)

Like the cordylids, this family of lizards has its headquarters in Africa south of the Sahara. But unlike the cordylids, the gerrhosaurids have reached Madagascar, and two of the six genera and twelve of the twenty-five species now live there exclusively. Although lizards in general and, in fact, all reptile groups are creatures of warm, humid cli-

mates, the gerrhosaurids do not enter the great rain forest of Central Africa despite the fact that they range right up to its borders. This is a puzzling matter and one of the most interesting types of evolutionary problems: why have certain animals failed to enter adjacent habitats that seem so suitable for their modes of life? In this case as in so many others the answers are still unknown.

Be that as it may, the gerrhosaurids are ground-dwelling lizards that are intermediate between the skinks and lacertids. These long-tailed lizards have, like the lacertids, head shields that are fused to the skull and, like the skinks, bony cores in the body scales. These scales are arranged in longitudinal and cross rows and, because of their bony centers, encase the gerrhosaurids in a hard shell. Running low on each side of a typical gerrhosaurid is a long groove or fold that may act as an accordion pleat to permit expansion of the otherwise hard case when the female's body is full of eggs.

The yellow-throated plated lizard, *Gerrhosaurus flavigularis,* is a foot-and-a-half-long (over two-thirds of which is tail), olive or brownish lizard with a narrow yellow stripe on each side. It occurs from the Sudan and Ethiopia southward through East Africa to the Cape of Good Hope, and therefore occupies most of the geographic range of the family. Within this vast grass and scrub country, it hunts insects by day, but despite its length it is rarely seen. It scampers through the dry grass rapidly and disappears into its burrow, which is usually under a bush, at the least sign of danger. The female lays from four to six inch-long eggs in a shallow hole. Egg-laying is evidently characteristic of the entire family.

Although the five-toed limbs of the plated lizards have no obvious digging specializations they are clearly able to do the work well, and in the sun-baked soil of that semiarid country that may not be easy for even the most highly adapted burrower. It has been suggested that they do the tunneling during the rainy season when the ground becomes soft. Even so, they do a thorough job, for the Sudan plated lizard, *Gerrhosaurus major* (Plate 59), a yellow-spotted black lizard about eighteen inches long, digs tunnels that are several feet long and end in a chamber roughly twelve inches below the ground. If one of these lizards is cornered in a passageway, it resists being pulled out by clutching the soil with its claws and by inflating its body.

As do so many lizard families, the gerrhosaurids have an evolutionary tendency to lose their legs. This is best illustrated by the South African whip lizards (genus *Tetradactylus*), whose scientific name, meaning "four digits," is a true misnomer. One species has five digits on each leg, another four, a third three on the front limbs and two on the hind, and a fourth one on each limb; and, finally, one species has no front legs at all. Even the five-toed whip lizard, *Tetradactylus seps,* sometimes acts as though its legs were relatively unimportant. When moving slowly, its legs do most of the work, but when it moves rapidly most of the propulsion is provided by snakelike undulations of the two-inch body and five-inch tail.

Representatives of this family in Madagascar resemble the plated lizards (*Gerrhosaurus*) in having strong limbs, each with five digits, and no indication of serpentine adaptations. The girdled lizards (genus *Zonosaurus*) are large, robust ground-dwelling creatures. One of them, *Zonosaurus maximus,* a drab, dark brown lizard seen most often on the banks of forest streams, shares the title of largest species in the family with the rock plated lizard, *Gerrhosaurus validus,* of southeastern Africa; both attain lengths slightly in excess of two feet.

A casual comparison of the girdled lizards with the plated lizards does not reveal any striking differences between the two groups. However, the second Madagascan genus, the keeled gerrhosaurids (*Tracheloptychus*), not only is the only group in the family with sharply keeled scales, but also has a very short lateral fold. Whereas other gerrhosaurids have this pleat extending from the neck to the hind leg, in the keeled gerrhosaurids it is limited to the neck. Another odd feature of these eight- to ten-inch lizards is the presence of a large movable scale in front of the ear opening. Now these lizards have been caught on riverbanks, and, while we have no information to confirm the suggestion, it is possible that they are aquatic and that the movable scale is a valve used to close off the ear opening just as in the case of the crocodiles.

The Teiid Lizards

(*Family Teiidae*)

The teiid (pronounced "tee-id") lizards, along with the iguanids, are the lizards most characteristic of the New World. Probably the teiids' claim to the title is better than the iguanids', since no teiids occur outside of the Western Hemisphere, whereas seven iguanids live in Madagascar. In addition to the general similarity in geographic distribution, each of these American families has a counterpart in an Old World lizard family: the Agamidae (Asia and Africa) and the Iguanidae form a pair, and the Lacertidae (Eurasia and Africa) and the Teiidae form another.

The typical or nonspecialized teiid is very similar to the average lacertid in body form, development of the limbs, and scalation. Probably the average reader confronted with one of the lacertas of the Mediterranean and one of the ameivas, a teiid from tropical America, would see no family differences. As a matter of fact, without knowing their country of origin, a herpetologist might have difficulty in deciding which lizard belonged to which family unless he examined the teeth or the skull. The Teiidae do not have teeth with hollow bases; the Lacertidae do. The head shields of teiids are separated from the bones of the skull; those of the lacertids are not.

Both families exhibit considerable variation in scalation, and each has independently arrived at similar combinations. For example, the jeweled lacerta, *Lacerta lepida,* of the Western Mediterranean and the teiid genus *Ameiva* have small granular scales covering the back and sides and large scales on the belly. The scales on the front part of the backs of both the Peruvian teiid *Dicrodon heterolepis* and the Egyptian lacertid *Acanthodactylus boskianus* are rather small and keeled but become larger toward the tails; the belly scutes are larger still, and the tails have rings or whorls of scales. Even more striking is the example of the grass lacertid, *Takydromus sexlineatus,* and the South American teiid *Kentropyx striatus,* both of which have large keeled scales on the back, a band of small granular ones on the sides, and large keeled scales on the belly.

Although the teiids are distributed from Maryland and southern Wisconsin in the United States to Chile, the bulk of the approximately two hundred species live in the tropics. But, within this relatively restricted area, the Teiidae have undergone a remarkable evolution and developed into one of the most highly varied families of lizards. Consider just the matter of scalation. For instance, despite the fact that the skinks form one of the largest lizard families, they are a rather uniform lot when it comes to their scaly covering. The iguanids and the agamids have several types of scalation and the lacertids still more. But the teiids surpass them all. The descriptions given in the preceding paragraph do not begin to cover the possibilities in this family.

All of the body scales may be the same size, as in the Colombian genus *Calliscincopus.* Or they may be sharply divided into different size groups as in the ameivas (genus *Ameiva*) and racerunners (genus *Cnemidophorus*) with their small back and side scales and large belly shields. In some genera the back has one scale size, the sides another, and the belly a third. The back scales may be round, oblong, or hexagonal; smooth or keeled; or arranged in longitudinal and diagonal rows or in transverse rings. Then there is the caiman lizard (*Dracaena*), a teiid with scales that look for all in the world like those of a caiman or alligator.

Teeth, too, show a great range of variation. Those at the front of the jaws are always conical, but the side teeth may be conical or equipped with two or three cusps. Some species have flattened molarlike teeth and others large flat crushers. The two-cusped teeth are flattened either from side to side or from front to rear. Though most teiids have strong, well-developed legs, certain genera have only the tiniest, most useless, rudimentary ones. And, of course, the change in development of limbs is part of a change from the robust typical lizard shape to a wormlike or snakelike form. In size, teiids run from the caiman lizard's four-foot length down to the three or four inches of the smallest species.

This family seems to be a case of "you name it, we have it." The classification within the family reflects the abundance of types. Between thirty-five and forty genera are recognized. These genera have moved into a variety of habitats, so that the family now lives in forests and in deserts, on seashores and high in the Andes, in water and on land. Several genera, e.g. the worm teiids (*Scolecosaurus*) and the snake teiids (*Ophiognomon*), have adopted secretive burrowing habits in leaf mold, but very few have left the ground and become arboreal.

In truth, relatively little is known of the habits of the great majority of teiids. For instance, we have no information on the breeding habits of most genera, although it is assumed that most if not all lay eggs. Those teiids whose breeding activities have been observed are oviparous. The mating behavior of the six-lined racerunner, *Cnemidophorus sexlineatus,* of the southeastern third of the United States is probably the best known. A sexually active male attempts to straddle a female, and, if she is responsive, he rubs his hip region against her back while nipping at her neck. Then the male slips his tail under hers and, with his body arched over her back, grips her opposite side in his jaws, at the same time inserting a hemipenis into her vent. Early in summer the female lays four to six white eggs, three-fourths of an inch long and with flexible shells, in shallow depressions or under rocks. The young hatch in eight to ten weeks.

The eggs of two of the giants of the family, the three-foot tegu, *Tupinambis nigropunctatus,* of Brazil and the four-foot caiman lizard, *Dracaena guianensis,* are naturally rather large. Those of the tegu average two inches in length and those of the caiman lizard about three.

The only members of this family occurring in the United States are the racerunners and whiptails (genus *Cnemidophorus*), which live in all but the northeastern and extreme northern states. All nine species have rather long, pointed heads covered above with large shields; strong legs; a long tail; large belly scales; and small, granular back scales. The smallest, the little striped whiptail, *Cnemidophorus inornatus,* of the Southwest, reaches a maximum total length of slightly more than eight inches, and the largest, the Arizona whiptail, *Cnemidophorus stictogrammus,* a maximum of about seventeen inches.

These active, diurnal lizards are striped or spotted or both, the ground color usually being brownish or blackish and the stripes and spots yellowish. Unlike the females, which are usually whitish below, the males tend to have brilliant coloring on the throat, chest, or belly. Males of the spotted whiptail, *C. sacki,* for instance, have orange or pink throats and black or purplish blue on the belly. The undersides of male six-lined racerunners are pale bluish. The assumption by males of bright patches of color is a common phenomenon, and, as in other families of lizards, notably the agamids, iguanids, and lacertids, male racerunners posture and flash these colors at other males as part of a bluffing or warning behavior.

In the southeastern United States the six-lined racerunner is a common inhabitant of fields, roads, and other open areas, especially where the soil is sandy. Like all members of the genus, it is a terrestrial lizard noted for its very fast dashes between points of cover. Capturing these speedsters is sometimes complicated by the sudden stops they make, for our eyes tend to continue moving when an object being followed stops so abruptly. Racerunners usually occur in colonies, and many interesting hours can be spent watching these active lizards hunting their insect food, chasing rival males, and courting females.

From the United States the racerunners extend southward through Central America and across northern South America down to northern Argentina. In Mexico they are joined by two other genera, the ameivas (*Ameiva*) and the spectacled teiids (*Gymnophthalmus*). The latter, which are found from Mexico all the way to Argentina, are small, secretive lizards less than six inches long (only two of which are taken up by head and trunk), with short legs and only four fingers. Many of the teiids have a transparent disk in the otherwise scaly lower eyelid, and, as in the case of some lacertids and skinks, the disk in the spectacles has come to occupy so much of the eyelid that the latter is no longer movable.

The other Mexican genus, the ameivas, are much more like the racerunners, having long whiplike tails, granular back scales, strong limbs, the same patterns of light stripes and spots on a dark ground color, and the same active, terrestrial habits, but are on the average somewhat larger. In fact, the only fixed difference between the two genera lies in the structure of the tongue, which can be retracted into a sheath at its base in *Ameiva*. The fifteen to twenty species of *Ameiva* range from Mexico and the West Indies to Bolivia and Uruguay.

The number of teiid genera, and consequently the variety of modes of life they adopt, increase rapidly southward in Central America until a maximum is reached in the rich tropical regions of northern South America. Colombia alone has eighteen genera and Brazil twenty-three. Both of these countries have the big tegu, *Tupinambis nigropunctatus,* which because of its fondness for chicks and eggs is called "poulterer's wolf" or "egg thief" in some areas. Despite its husky body and strong jaws, this yellow-spotted, yard-long lizard takes advantage of its speed and dashes off at the slightest alarm like any chicken thief, four-footed or otherwise. But the tegu does not usually compete with man for food. The bulk of its diet consists of frogs, lizards, insects, and other small creatures. Even leaves and soft fruits are eaten.

One aspect of the tegu's life is rather puzzling, and that is its predilection for laying its eggs in a most improbable place for a terrestrial lizard. Certain termites in northern South America build large spherical nests in trees, nests so hard that they must be hacked or sawed in order to be broken. At least eight clutches of tegu eggs have been recovered from such nests, some of them as high as twelve feet above ground. The female tegu must have tremendous power in its legs and claws to rip open these hard nests. But, once the eggs are deposited, they are given the best of protection by the termites, which quickly repair the damage to their nest and in the process seal in the eggs. Of course, the newly hatched tegu must work just as hard to get out of the nest, but, judging by published reports of encounters with baby tegus, they are strong enough for the job.

Northern South America is also the home of the large caiman lizard, *Dracaena guianensis,* probably the best known of the few amphibious teiids. Its flattened tail, which has a double crest just like the tail of a caiman or alligator, is the principal swimming aid of this olive-brown reptile as it hunts through the coastal swamps for its favorite food of snails. These hard creatures pose no mechanical problems for the caiman lizard; it merely maneuvers them between its large, flat teeth, crushes them, then carefully spits out the shell fragments before swallowing. The much smaller brown water teiid, *Neusticurus rudis,* a six- to eight-inch neighbor of *Dracaena,* feeds on tadpoles, small fishes, and aquatic insects.

The great majority of tropical teiids spend their lives crawling over the ground. As a slight modification of this general habit, the wormlike or snakelike teiids usually tunnel through the loose debris that litters the great rain forest, and this secretive behavior naturally has prevented our learning very much about them. However, enough has been seen of one, the Guiana earless teiid, *Bachia cophius,* to indicate that, despite its diminutive legs which are only one-fiftieth of the lizard's length, it still uses these tiny three-toed appendages when it is moving slowly. If for some reason the lizard is in a hurry, it resorts to a serpentine type of locomotion, throwing the body and tail into lateral undulations while the legs are held against the sides or dangle uselessly. But in extreme emergencies this four- or five-inch reptile flings itself forward and into the air by a springlike flick of its tail. Such a leap carries it forward almost a foot and into the air about ten inches.

Discussion of the tropical teiids would be incomplete without mention of the defensive behavior of the little rough teiids (genus *Echinosaura*). These four- to six-inch dark brown inhabitants of the rain forests of Panama and Colombia have long, pointed heads and slender bodies with intersecting arcs of large scales scattered over the back. All in all their dark colors and rough, slender outlines give them the appearance of rough-barked twigs. On the forest floor against the dark, mottled background of debris they are practically invisible, and their slow movements help conceal them. However, should one be touched, it becomes absolutely rigid, heightening its protective resemblance to a twig or piece of wood.

Outside of the truly tropical parts of South America, whether the direction followed leads to the coastal deserts of Peru, to the cool climate of Chile, or to the mild climate of Argentina, the variety of teiids diminishes rapidly. In general the small, highly modified types disappear and the medium-sized, long-legged forms are left. Argentina, for instance, has several species of racerunners (*Cnemidophorus*), one ameiva, a tegu (*Tupinambis*), and the teyu, *Teius teyou.* The last is about the size of a racerunner or ameiva (roughly one foot over all) and looks remarkably like those two widespread teiids, even down to the fine scalation of the back and the striped and spotted pattern. But the teyu, unlike the others, has only four toes on each hind foot. The loss of a toe by this active lizard is not an indication of degeneration of the limbs, which are just as long and just as functional as those of the racerunners.

Similarly, the significance of a difference in the ways the teeth are oriented is unknown. Teyu, racerunner, and ameiva all have two-cusped teeth, but the teyu's teeth are flattened from front to rear so that the cusps are arranged across the jawbone, whereas those of the racerunner and ameiva are arranged in line with the jaw. Now logic would seem to indicate that this difference might be tied up with diet. But the logic of biology is not that simple, for all three feed mostly on insects. To make the matter even more complicated, the characteristic teiids of arid coastal Peru, the genus *Dicrodon,* have teeth exactly like those of *Teius.* However, one species, the coarse-scaled *Dicrodon (D. hetero-lepis),* feeds primarily on insects, whereas a second, the fine-scaled *Dicrodon (D. guttulatum),* is almost an exclusive herbivore.

The same Peruvian deserts are also inhabited by the three-foot false monitor, *Tejovaranus flavipunctatus,* a predaceous teiid that probably feeds on *Dicrodon.* When it is seriously intent on covering ground, this big yellow-spotted blackish lizard runs on its hind legs with its forefeet and tail raised off the ground in the manner of certain iguanids and agamids. The same bipedal gait has been observed in the strand racerunner, *Cnemidoporus lemniscatus.*

Finally, at the end of the family range, in Chile, only one species of teiid occurs. Most teiids, even those of the United States, are warmth-requiring reptiles. The cool climate of central Chile, therefore, obliges the fifteen-inch Chilean teiid, *Callopistes maculatus,* to remain under cover most of the day. But during the hours of maximum solar intensity, this spotted reptile is extremely active, searching for enough food, which consists of insects and small lizards, to keep it going another day.

The Lacertids

(*Family Lacertidae*)

These lizards are considered to be typical of the whole group, even though they are found only in the Old World. In view of the fact that the whole idea of animal classification grew up in Europe, it is understandable that the European biologists selected the most abundant of their lizards to symbolize the type. And they made a good choice when they picked the lacertids as *the* common lizards.

For lacertids have scaly bodies, conical heads, movable eyelids (with rare exceptions), and well-developed legs and tails. More than that, they have cylindrical, slightly elongate bodies, giving them a generalized "lizard" appearance. We do not find in the lacertids the specialized body forms of the iguanids and agamids; the degenerate limbs of the skinks, worm lizards, and other families; or the modified climbing devices of the geckos. In short, the lacertids are close to the average of all the diverging adaptations evolved by lizards in the course of geologic time.

A description of the European fence lizard, *Lacerta agilis,* which lives in the area north of the Alps from England to Central Asia, will convey a more definite image of a lacertid. Its conical head and blunt snout bear large scales. The neck and cylindrical body are covered above by small, hexagonal keeled scales on the back and larger and smoother scales low on the sides. Below, the trunk has six long rows of smooth, rectangular scales that are much larger than those of the sides and back. The long, cylindrical, tapering tail is circled by rings of oblong scales, keeled above and becoming smaller toward the tip. The lower eyelid is freely movable and covered with many small scales. Behind the head is the large oval opening of the external ear; it is a short tube leading to the eardrum, which is readily visible. Each of the well-developed limbs has five clawed digits.

Almost all of the 150 species of lacertids fit that description. They scarcely vary at all in body form. A few, like the Oriental grass lizards (genus *Takydromus*), have longer and flatter snouts than the common lacertas (genus *Lacerta*). Some genera have large, keeled scales in longitudinal rows on the back separated from the equally large belly scales by a band of small scales on each side.

Two African species of common lacertas, *Lacerta echinata* and *Lacerta langi,* have a broad ring of very spiny scales around their tails. This ring of scales, which are not as spiny as, say, those of the spiny-tailed agamids (genus *Uromastix*), though still unique in the family Lacertidae, is confined to the basal portion of the tail. The function of this odd tail is not obvious, but it may have something to do with the considerable climbing ability of these forest lizards.

Another African forest lacertid, the fringe-tailed lacertid, *Holaspis guentheri,* as its common name implies, has an unusual tail on each side of which scales project outward, downward, and backward. This climbing lizard keeps its tail pressed against the tree, apparently so that the projecting scales catch in the bark and act as gripping devices. A similar adaptation is found in one of our native iguanids, the Texas tree lizard, *Uta ornata.*

The lacertids also show some slight variation in the scalation of the lower eyelid. Just as we saw in the skinks, some of the lacertids have developed a large transparent disk in the center of the eyelid. In the snake-eyed lacertids (genus *Ophisops*) of North Africa and Southwest Asia, the central disk has become so large that the eyelid is no longer movable.

The lacertids are small or medium-sized lizards. The jeweled lacerta, *Lacerta lepida,* of southwestern Europe and northwestern Africa is the giant of the family and reaches a length of only two and one-half feet. Half a dozen species grow to eighteen inches, but most species never exceed a foot. Indeed lacertids give the impression of being even smaller, because anywhere from two-thirds to four-fifths of the length is made up of a slender tail, which is often hidden from view by stones or vegetation.

Unlike iguanids, agamids, and true chameleons, lacertids are incapable of rapid color change. However, a number of species change color with age. Cantor's fringe-toed lacertid, *Acanthodactylus cantoris,* of Southwest Asia is brightly marked when young with black and white streaks, which tend to disappear as it grows older. The green lacerta, *Lacerta viridis,* of Europe starts out in life as a brown lizard with one or two rows of yellowish white spots but gradually becomes bright green.

Commonly male lacertids differ from the females in coloration. The male green lacerta, for instance, is a gold-green, the female grass green. A more pronounced difference between the sexes is found in the European fence lizard, *Lacerta agilis,* in which the male is green and the female brown. The bright desert lacertid, *Eremias nitida,* of central Africa has a black body with six light lines and, in mature males only, a row of blue-edged light spots low on the side.

The great Charles Darwin thought that the brighter color of male animals generally was a device for attracting females. Whatever the story in other vertebrates, the more gaudy coloration of male lacertids (and other lizards) has little to do with the female and is a means of recognition between males. Lacertids hunt, find mates, and recognize enemies largely by sight. If a male fence lizard, *Lacerta agilis,* sees one of his kind that has green sides, he scoots away if the other male is much larger, or he attacks it if they are approximately the same size. Males of the bright desert lacertid, *Eremias nitida,* probably rely on the row of blue-edged spots to distinguish one sex from another.

Combats between male lacertids lack some of the elements of iguanid battles. The lacertids in general are not able to change their body form. They have no crests to raise, no throat fans to flash, and no means of flattening the body noticeably. Consequently the males do not habitually turn broadside to one another as do iguanids or agamids. Instead, when squaring off, two lacertid males face each other with body raised on stiffened legs, back arched, head held low, and throat slightly puffed. Then they charge, bite, and tear, usually rolling over and over in the process. Skin is torn and blood drawn often in these contests. As soon as it becomes evident that one is the stronger, the weaker dashes off at the first opportunity. And, since they are incapable of emotionally induced color change, the aftermath of the fight does not include "victory" and "defeat" colorations such as follow iguanid or agamid battles.

Courtship also is simpler among lacertids than among iguanids. In the early weeks of spring, a male lacerta approaches a female and, if she does not immediately dash off, comes close enough to grip her tail with his jaws. Usually she moves, but at a much slower pace and for a much shorter distance than a nonreceptive female. On his part, the male does not bite as hard as he does in a fight, for he never tears the female's skin. If another male appears on the scene, the rival must be driven off. Then the male approaches the female again, finally gripping the rear of her back with his jaws. As she raises the base of her tail, the male places one hind leg across her back, while retaining his mouth grip on her back, slips the base of his tail under hers, and inserts a hemipenis into her vent.

The same male and female will mate several times during one breeding season, though not necessarily always with each other. After separating following copulation, each goes his own way to hunt food, and it is a matter of chance whether they encounter each other when next they are ready to mate.

Apparently with just one exception, all lacertids lay eggs. In the case of the European fence lizard, *Lacerta agilis,* the six to thirteen eggs, each about one half-inch long, are usually laid in a shallow hole dug by the female in June or July. Breeding takes place in May or June, so that, by the time the eggs are laid, the embryos have already begun to develop. Incubation outside the mother's body takes from seven to twelve weeks, depending on the temperature prevailing in that particular place and season.

The exception to the egg-laying habits of the family is the well-named viviparous lacerta, *Lacerta vivipara* (Plate 58). This live-bearer occurs across

Bosc's Fringe-toed Lacertid (*Acanthodactylus boskianus*)

the middle and northern parts of the Eurasian land mass and is the only lizard living within the Arctic Circle. At this high latitude the lizard has at most three months in which it can be active. If eggs were laid in this cool summer climate, they probably never would hatch. On the other hand, the female, by constantly moving about so as to remain in the sunlight of the long northern summer day, maintains a relatively constant high body temperature. Therefore retention of the eggs within the female's body results in their incubation at a higher average temperature than can be found elsewhere in that unfavorable climate and insures rapid development of the embryos. Even in Central Europe, where the summer season is longer, the viviparous lacerta lives mostly in mountains, so that it still faces the problems imposed by a cool summer. This example of adaptation to cool climates is made more interesting by the fact that the viviparous lacerta becomes an egg-layer in the southernmost part of its range,

the Pyrenees Mountains of northern Spain, where the summer season is presumably long enough for the eggs to hatch.

In general appearance and in many anatomical details, the lacertids resemble the teiid lizards. The two families differ only in certain features of head anatomy. Of more general interest is the fact that these two lizard families form a related pair with complementary geographic distributions. This has already been discussed in the section on teiids.

The lacertids are found throughout Europe and Asia. Only one species lives in the East Indies and none in Australia. They are especially abundant in Africa, fully half of the twenty-two genera in the family occurring south of the Sahara.

The distribution of the African genera is associated almost diagrammatically with the type of vegetation. South Africa, eastern Central Africa, and North Africa naturally have lacertids that are adapted to life in open country. On the other hand, the great forests of West and Central Africa have several specialized arboreal forms. For example, the fringe-tailed lacertid, *Holaspis guentheri,* is found only in the forest belt. In addition to its non-skid tail described earlier, this small (three and one-half inches) lizard has a row of padlike scales under the foot and a series of short, projecting scales along the bases of the toes, both of which structures may help the lizard cling to smooth-barked trees. This forest lizard, orange below and boldly striped with yellow and black on its back, lays two eggs at a time.

The African rain forest is also the home of two large common lacertas, the spiny lacerta, *Lacerta echinata,* and Lang's lacerta, *Lacerta langi,* both of which have a broad ring of spiny scales around the base of the tail. These bright green animals, which are about a foot long, live in trees, clinging with their strong claws. Perhaps the pointed scales on the tail may help, but we have no observations to confirm this suggestion.

Each of the areas of open country has some of its own native forms. South Africa, for example, has several genera that occur nowhere else. Among them the five species of blunt-headed lacertids (genus *Nucras*) live in grasslands or semiarid scrub veld from sea level to high mountain slopes. These striped or spotted lizards, usually ten to twelve inches long as adults, have small, smooth scales covering their backs and large ones on the belly.

One of the blunt-headed lacertids, Delalande's lacertid, *Nucras delalandi,* a rather sluggish lizard, has a peculiar way of protecting itself from snakes, one of its principal enemies. If a snake grabs it by any part of the body other than the head, the lizard bends its body and grasps one of its hind legs with its jaws. The snake works its own jaws around to the lizard's head in order to begin swallowing the unfortunate animal in the accustomed manner. But there is no end, only a circle. Even if the snake tries the tail, it is very soon blocked by the closed circle.

From north to south in the dry parts of Africa, the desert lacertids (genus *Eremias*) are probably the commonest representatives of the family. Not confined to sandy wastes, these seven- or eight-inch lizards also live in semiarid scrub grassland and in rocky desert. Their color pattern, usually consisting of light stripes or light spots arranged in longitudinal rows, makes them very difficult for the human eye to follow, especially as they often scamper about during the hottest time of day when the glaring sun creates heat waves all around. The ancient Egyptians preserved specimens of the desert lacertids as mummies to be carried as charms in small boxes.

A rather specialized group, the fringe-toed lacertids (genus *Acanthodactylus*), also ekes out a living in the inhospitable wastes of the Sahara and Arabian Deserts. The dozen species are small to moderate in size (five to nine inches), striped or spotted, and quite ordinary except for their fingers and toes. As the common name implies, the digits have a series of scales that project along the sides and form a comblike fringe. In general appearance and function this modification of the digits is just like that found in the fringe-toed iguanids (genus *Uma*), another desert-living group. By increasing the surface area of the fingers and toes, the fringes help these lizards move across loose sand.

But the fringe-toed lacertids are not restricted to areas of loose sand as are their iguanid counterparts. These lacertids are equally at home in rocky deserts and even occur along the grassy banks of the Suez Canal. Nevertheless, the desert is their true home, and their short dashes, each ending with the head and forequarters held high as if to get a better view of the landscape, are a characteristic sight in this arid region.

Since the lacertids are the only family of lizards well represented in Europe, this is the first opportunity we have had to mention the close relationship between the faunas of Europe and the Mediterranean coast of North Africa. This relationship is shown clearly by the plated lacertids (genus *Psammodromus*), a group of four species that are four to eight inches long and have large, keeled scales covering back and sides. They are found from the Mediterranean coast of France southward through Spain, and along the coast of northwestern Africa only as far east as Tunisia. Although the

Plated Lacertid (*Psammodromus algirus*)

region in which they live is hot during the summer day, the nights are cool, so that these ordinarily fast lizards are sluggish in the morning and must bask in the early sun to "get up steam."

The western Mediterranean area is also the home of many common lacertas, including the jeweled lacerta, *Lacerta lepida,* not only the largest but also one of the most handsome members of the family. This Spanish two-footer, justly a favorite of zoo-keepers and European terrarium enthusiasts, is generally brownish above, this color giving way on the sides to a bright yellowish green that covers the belly. The back is liberally sprinkled with small greenish or yellowish wormlike markings, while the sides have three or four rows of large black-edged blue spots. The large head, which in old males becomes deeply wrinkled above, is green. Unlike the great majority of its relatives, which live on a strict

Green Lacerta (*Lacerta viridis*)

ERICH SOCHUREK

Wall Lizard (*Lacerta muralis albanica*)

ERICH SOCHUREK

diet of insects and other small invertebrates, the big jeweled lacerta hunts and feeds on lizards, small snakes, and even young mice. Once its prey is spotted, it keeps its eyes glued on the unfortunate animal and, in a very short while, charges down on it with great speed. The mouse or snake is shaken and beaten against the ground while half-crushed in the lizard's jaws. When its prey is thoroughly subdued or, more likely, dead, the lacerta swallows it, finishing off the job by cleaning the sides of its jaws with its long tongue like a cat that has had its milk.

North of Spain the characteristic lacertas of Central Europe make their appearance: the viviparous lacerta, the European fence lizard, the green lacerta, *Lacerta viridis,* and the wall lizard, *Lacerta muralis.* The green lacerta, the largest of the four, reaching a total length of sixteen inches, apparently requires warmer temperatures than the others and spends more time basking in the sun, a reflection of its generally more southern distribution. Its large size enables it to feed not only on large insects but also upon young lizards.

The wall lizard, a black-spotted grayish or reddish brown animal growing to eight inches, got its common name from its habit of living on and in the stone walls separating fields. It is one of the many animals that, like our robin, follow man's culture and may even be called "weed" species. In southwestern Germany the females begin to lay eggs late in April. A clutch varies from two to eight eggs, and two or three clutches may be laid in one season.

Southeastern Europe also has its share of common lacertas—sixteen species occur in the Balkan Peninsula and southern Russia. But in addition, this area, which is on the fringe of the arid region formed by North Africa and Southwest Asia, has several representatives of this dry-country fauna, two desert lacertids (genus *Eremias*) and one snake-eyed lacertid (genus *Ophisops*). The latter genus, consisting of five species four to eight inches long, each with transparent, immovable lower eyelids, is common in semideserts from Turkey across Iran and the northern half of India. Besides the desert lacertids (*Eremias*), another genus typical of the deserts of North Africa, the fringe-toed lacertids (*Acanthodactylus*), inhabits the sandy wastes of Iran and West Pakistan.

This predilection for dry areas may account for the feeble development of the Lacertidae in peninsular India and Southeast Asia. This humid region with large forests, although it is the home of a great variety of agamids, geckos, and skinks, harbors only two genera and four species of lacertids.

[continued on page 161]

60. Chameleon

[FRITZ GORO]

61. Jackson's Chameleon (*Chamaeleo jacksoni*)
[ROY PINNEY]

62. Meller's Chameleon
(*Chamaeleo melleri*)
[JOHN MARKHAM]

←

63. Flap-necked
Chameleon
(*Chamaeleo
dilepis*)
[JOHN MARKHAM]

→

64. Eyed Chalcides (*Chalcides ocellatus*)

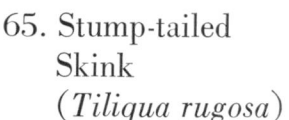

65. Stump-tailed
Skink
(*Tiliqua rugosa*)

66. Blue-tongued Skink (*Tiliqua scincoides*)

67. Five-lined
Skink (*Eumeces
fasciatus*)

[HAL H. HARRISON:
NATIONAL AUDUBON]

68. Annulated Boa
(*Boa annulata*)
[WALKER VAN RIPER]

69. Cook's Tree Boa
(*Boa cooki*)
[JOHN MARKHAM]

70. Eme   Tree Boa (*Boa canina*)

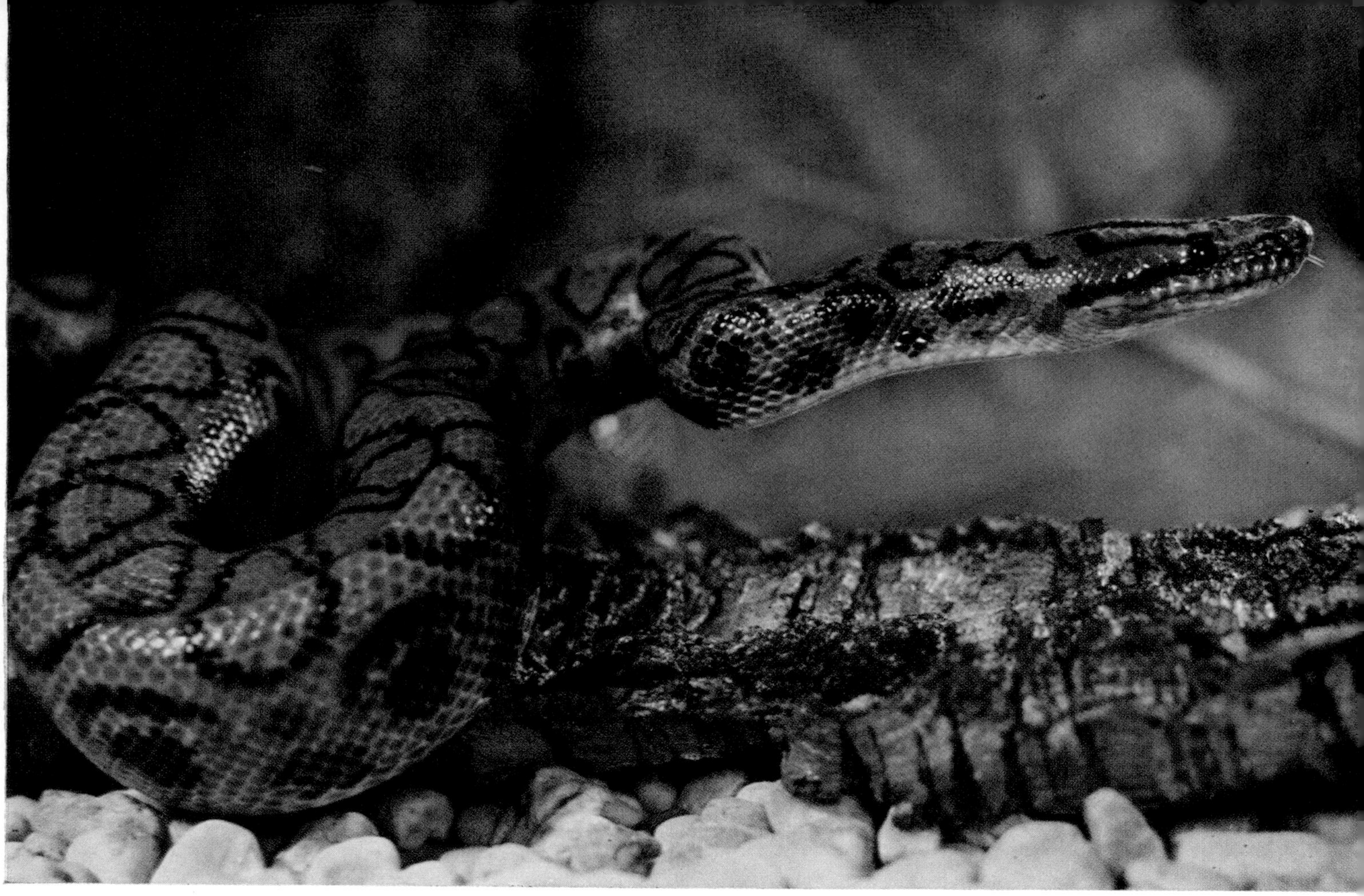

71. Rainbow Boa (*Epicrates cenchris*)

[ROY PINNEY AND PHILADELPHIA ZOO]

72. Rosy Boa (*Lichanura trivirgata*)

[HAL H. HARRISON : NATIONAL AUDUBON]

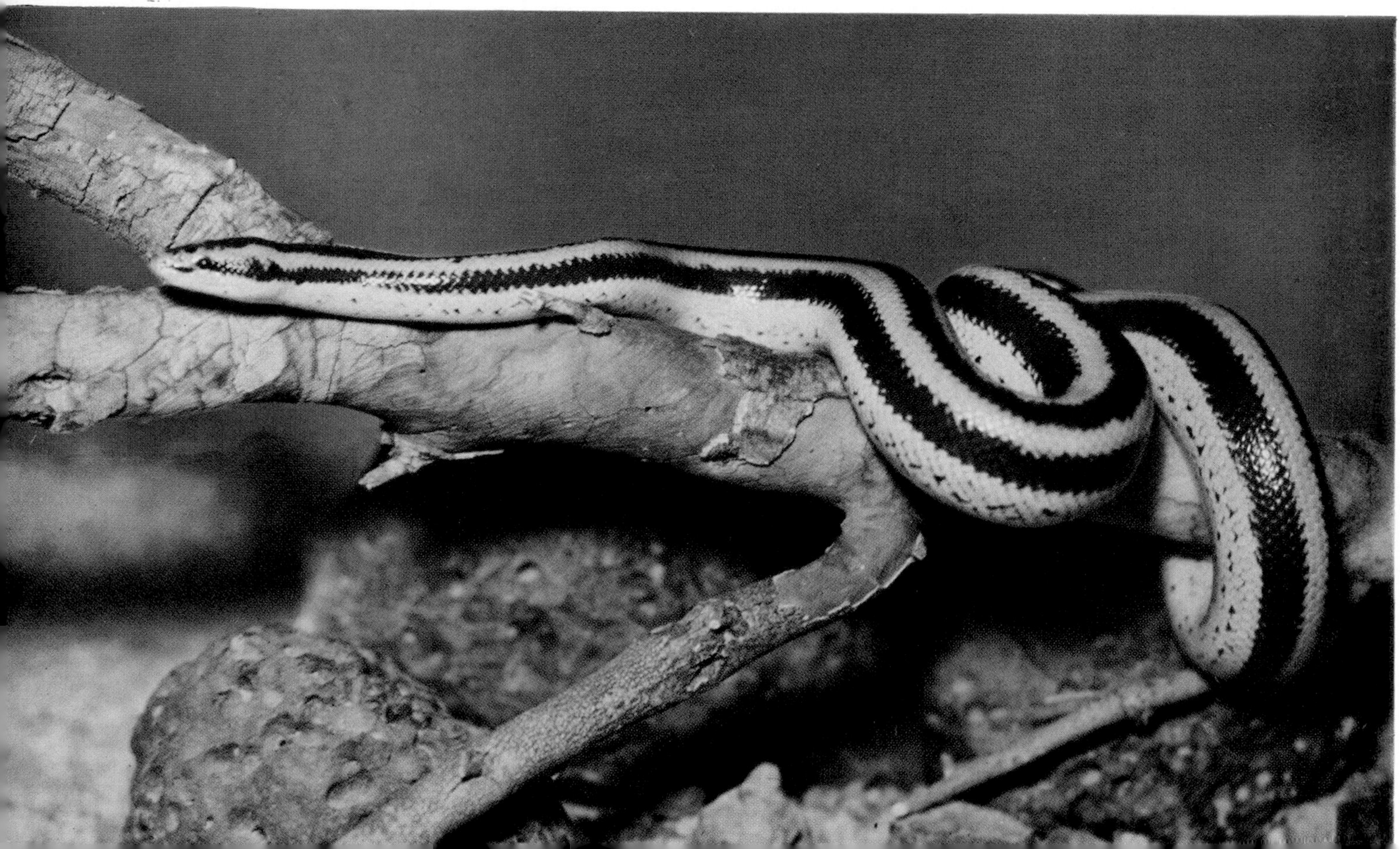

73. Boa Constrictor (*Constrictor constrictor*)

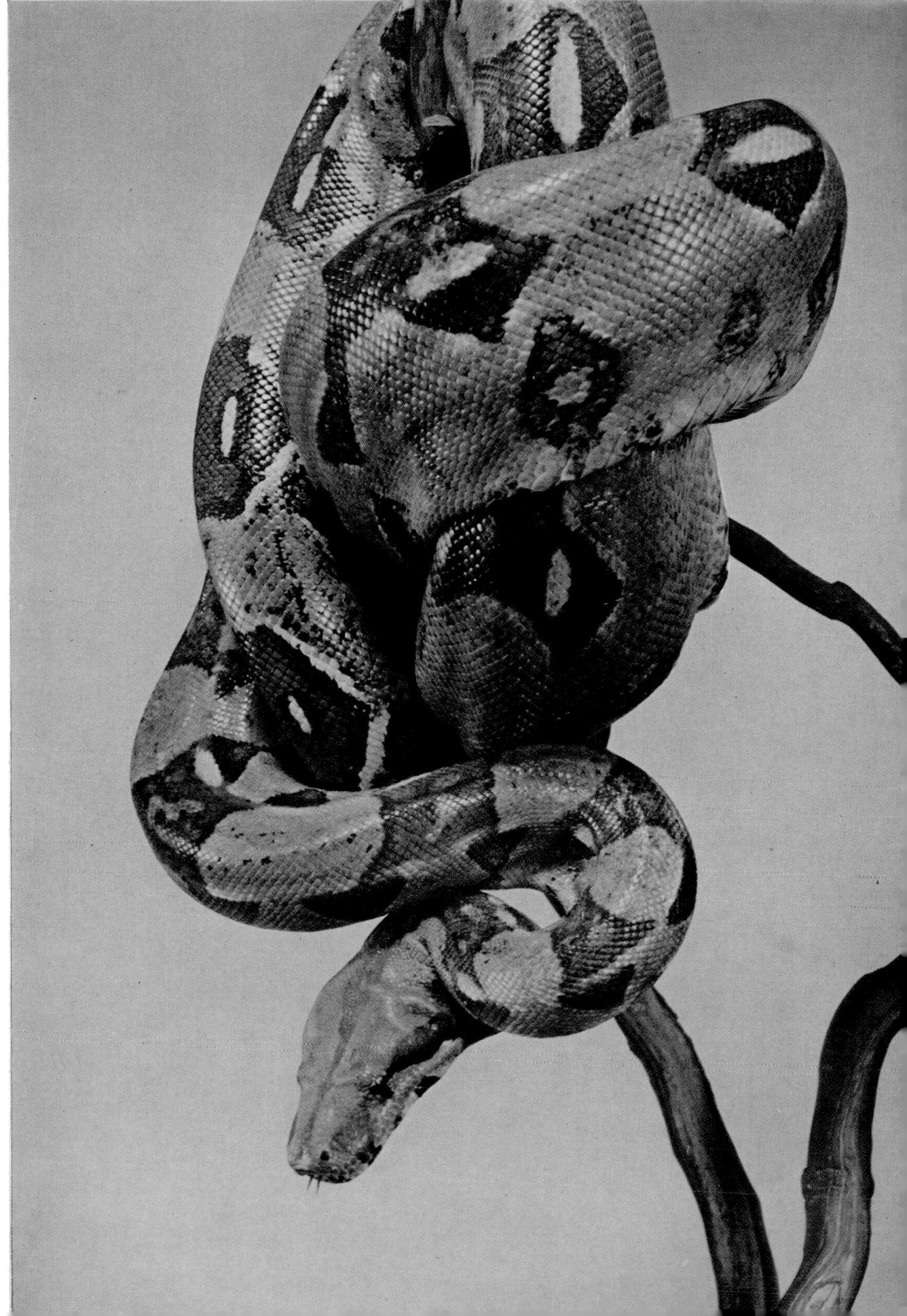

74. Anaconda (*Eunectes murinus*)

75. Garden Tree Boa (*Boa hortulana*)

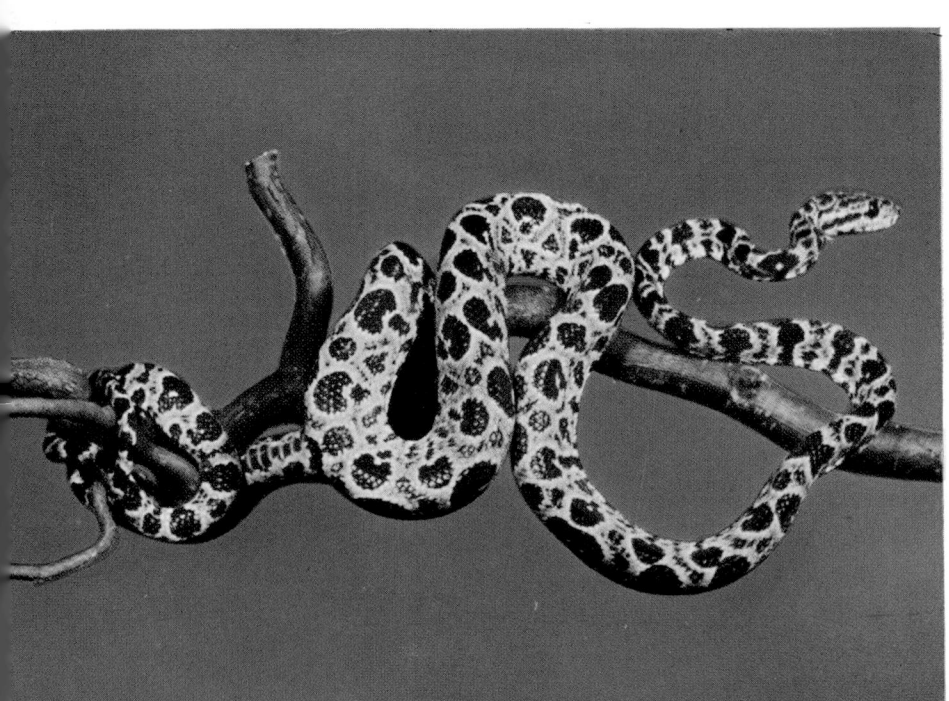

76. Indian Python (*Python molurus*)

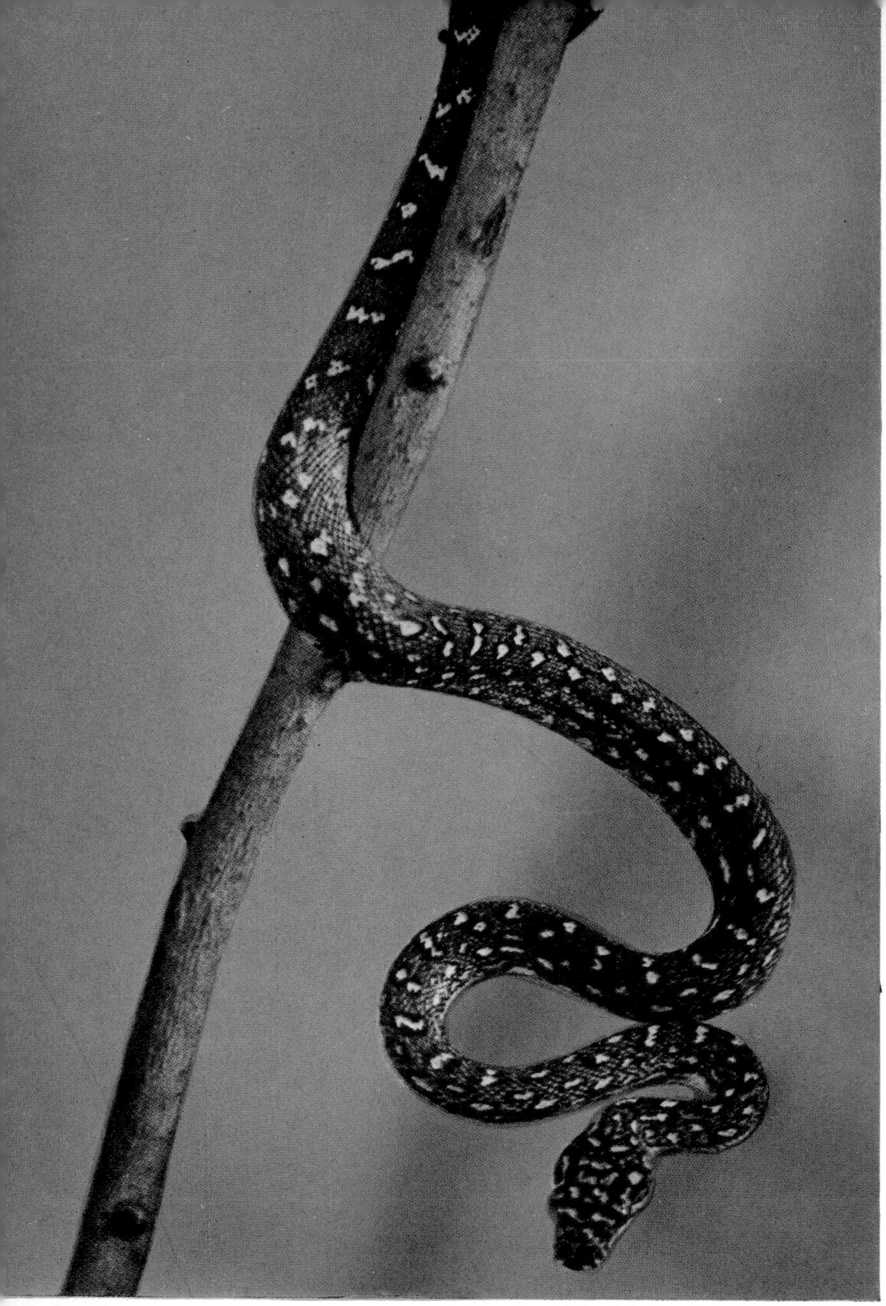

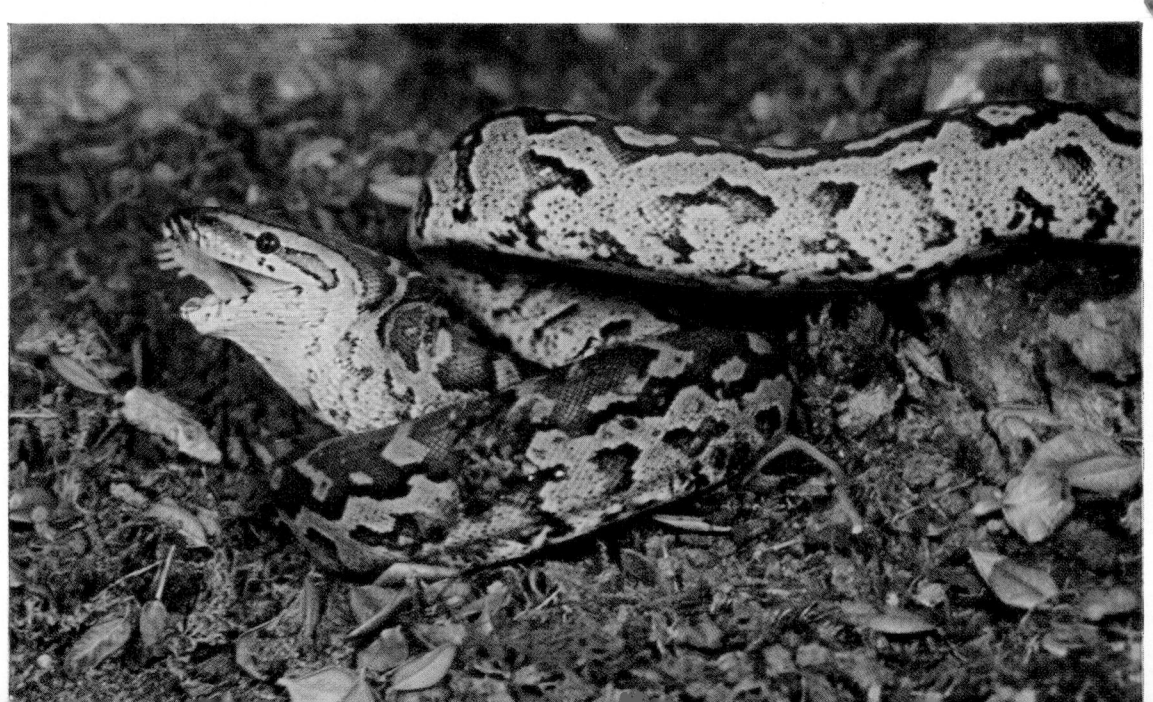

77. Diamond Snake
(*Morelia argus*)

[CY LA TOUR AND BROOKFIELD ZOO]

78. African Python
(*Python sebae*)

[JOHN MARKHAM]

79. Ball Python (*Python regius*)

[JOHN MARKHAM]

80. Mangrove
Water Snake
(*Natrix sipedon
compressicauda*)

[HAL H. HARRISON:
NATIONAL AUDUBON]

81. Common European Water Snake (*Natrix natrix*)
[JOHN MARKHAM]

82. Red-bellied Water Snake (*Natrix erythrogaster*)
[ROY PINNEY AND NATIONAL ZOO, WASHINGTON, D.C.]

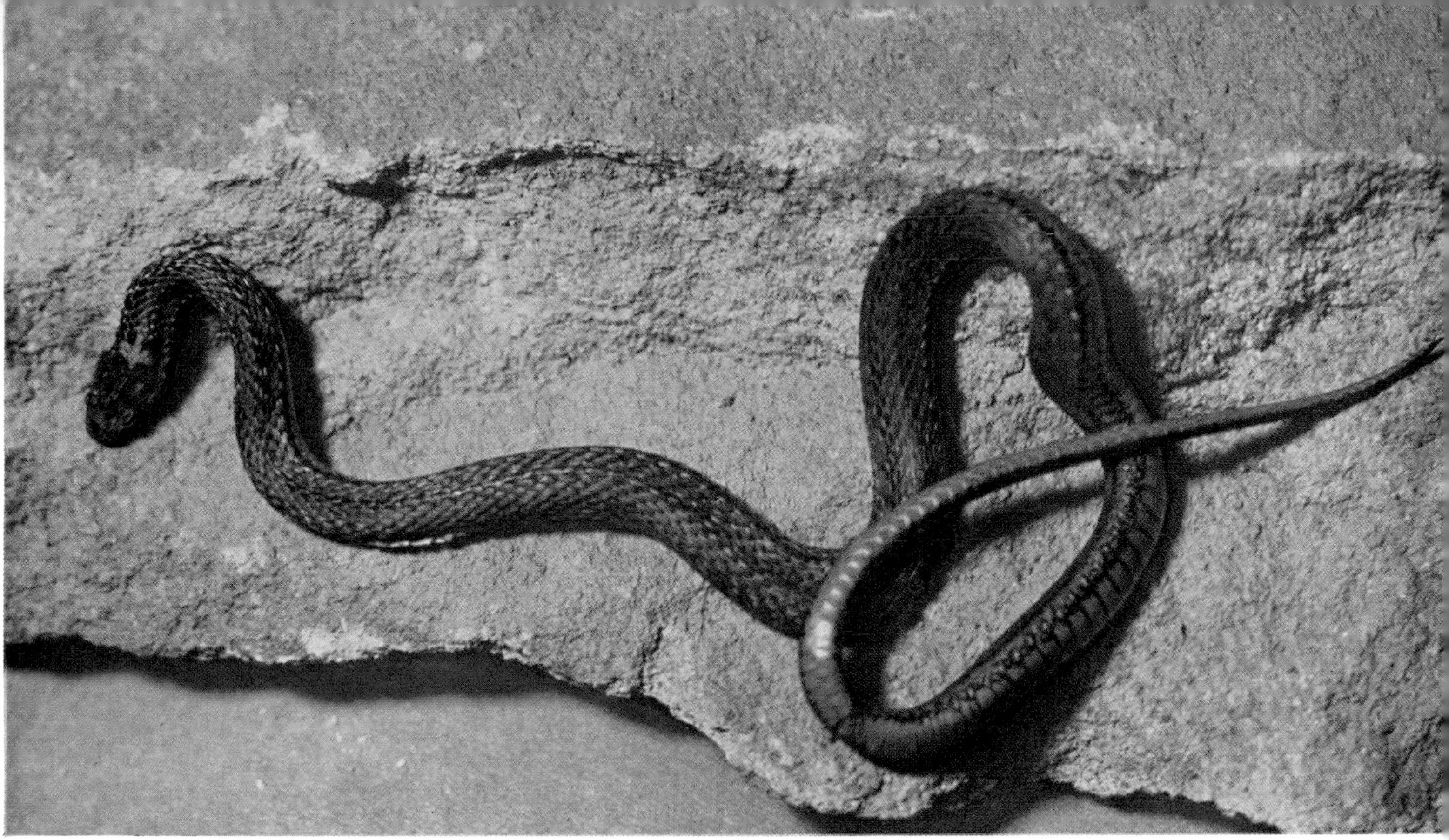

83. Red-bellied Snake (*Storeria occipitomaculata*)

[HAL H. HARRISON : NATIONAL AUDUBON]

84. Brown Water Snake (*Natrix taxispilota*)

[ROY PINNEY]

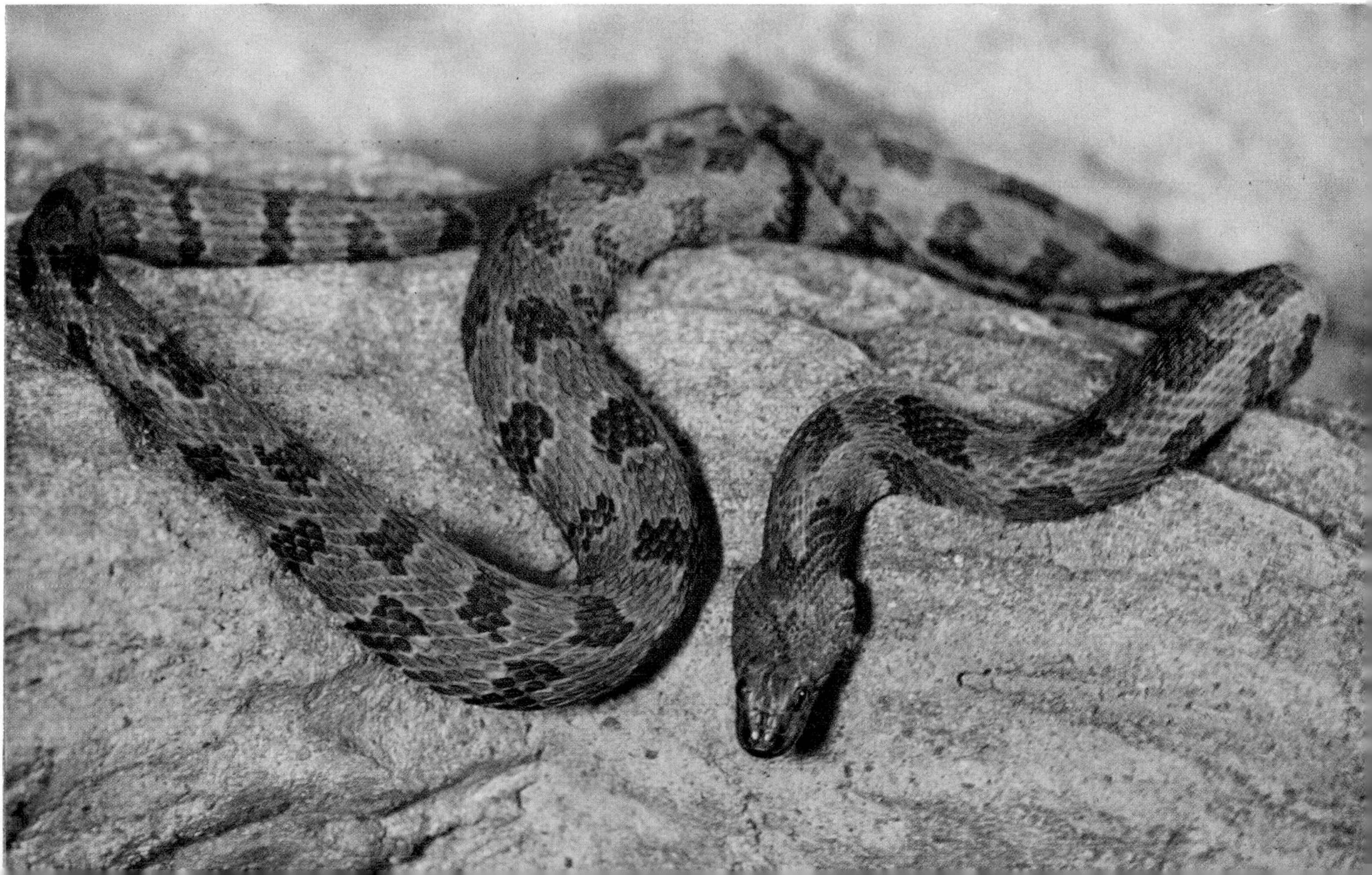

85. (above) Hog-nosed Snake (*Heterodon*)   86. (below) Hog-nosed Snake playing dead

[continued from page 144]

One genus, the Indian lacertids (genus *Cabrita*), is found only in dry forests of this subcontinent. Similar to the snake-eyed lacertids, the two species of *Cabrita* have large transparent disks in the center of the lower eyelids, which, however, remain movable. These six-inch striped lacertids lay about six eggs.

The other two lacertids of Southeast Asia, members of the long-tailed grass lacertids (genus *Takydromus*), shun the forests. As their common name indicates, they are at home in grassy country and have developed a "grass-swimming" kind of locomotion. The lizard clutches the tops of tall grass stems so that its body is held well above the ground and makes short jumps from stem to stem, often turning so sharply that its course is difficult to follow. The tail is very important in preventing the grass from collapsing under the lizard's weight. A grass lizard with a head and trunk length of two or two and a half inches has a tail twelve to fourteen inches long, and thus is able to distribute its weight over a number of grass stems.

One of these green lizards, the six-lined grass lacertid, *Takydromus sexlineatus,* is the only lacertid to penetrate the East Indies, living on Java, Borneo, and Sumatra. This genus, in effect, inhabits the edge of the lacertid world. Certain species are found at some point along the entire eastern flank of Asia from the Malay Peninsula and Indo-China northward to Manchuria. Islands such as Japan, Formosa, and Okinawa, which are close to the mainland, have been successfully invaded by the grass lacertids. But the family has not been able to jump the great water gap to the oceanic islands the way skinks and geckos have.

The Worm Lizards

(*Family Amphisbaenidae*)

Perhaps a book intended for general readers is not the place to display how great are the gaps in biological knowledge. However, one of the services we can render is to indicate that man still has much to learn about the world he lives in. This is a book about reptiles, and this is the section on lizards, yet under these headings we are including a group of animals we are not positive are reptiles, let alone lizards. Nevertheless, herpetologists for years have called these creatures "worm lizards" and considered them as reptiles, so we will follow that tradition with the understanding that this is a tentative arrangement.

But why all the indecision? Surely an animal either is a lizard or it isn't. Well, part of the trouble lies in the difficulty of defining an animal group so that all of its members are included by the definition and all nonmembers are excluded. We can say that lizards are scaly reptiles having limbs, movable eyelids, and an external ear among other things. But we have already described lizards that have no visible external ears and no movable eyelids, and many lizards have no limbs.

At a quick, superficial glance, worm lizards do resemble earthworms. They have long cylindrical bodies ringed with shallow grooves, usually blunt heads and tails, no hind limbs and with three exceptions no forelimbs, no signs of external ears, and no readily visible eyes. To all intents and purposes they are completely subterranean, and most of the peculiarities just mentioned are adaptations to that type of life and crop up in other subterranean lizards (see the discussion of burrowing skinks, pages 125–127). But other features of the worm lizards are quite distinct. For example, a captive worm lizard placed on the ground moves in a straight line, without the horizontal serpentine undulations characteristic of every other elongate lizard. In fact the worm lizard may even throw its body into vertical undulations. Also, the worm lizards have only a single functional lung, as do certain long-bodied burrowers of other families, but the worm lizards are the only ones in which the right lung (instead of the left) has disappeared.

Worm lizards or amphisbaenids, because of the single, basic adaptation to a burrowing life, are a uniform-appearing lot—much more so than any other large lizard family. Except to become longer or shorter, thicker or more slender, the amphisbaenids hardly vary in body form. Most of the species are about one foot long, and the giant of the family, one of the Central African single-shield worm lizards (genus *Monopeltis*), measures only twenty-seven inches. Both tails and heads are short in this family, the former rarely exceeding one-tenth of the total length. In general, the tails are blunt, just like the commonest head form, and this similarity has earned the amphisbaenids the name of "two-headed snake" in some regions.

More variation is seen in head shapes, which fall into three types, the commonest, as we have just said, being the blunt, rounded kind. Many amphisbaenids, including our only native species, the Florida worm lizard, *Rhineura floridana,* have a sharp, horizontal, keel-like edge to the snout that presumably serves as a spade. Oddly, the horizontal keel may be in a plane midway between the top and bottom of the animal, or level with the top of the head, or level with the bottom. The keel of the Florida worm lizard has the last position, and the entire head slopes downward toward the keel. The third type of head shape is flattened from side to side, so that a sharp vertical keel is formed at the snout.

Differences in head shape may reflect differences in digging efficiency. Perhaps the species with sharp snouts are better at burrowing in hard soil. At any rate, head shape seems to have little to do with feeding habits, since all apparently feed on small invertebrate animals, especially ants and termites. Since many species of amphisbaenids have been found in ant and termite nests, the gathering of that kind of food presents no problems. Fortunately for the worm lizards, they are immune to the bites and stings of soldier termites and ants, and are even known to resist the attack of army ants, those scourges of tropical rain forests.

The underground nests of termites and ants are utilized as incubators as well as pantries. Most if not all of the amphisbaenid eggs discovered so far have come from such nests. Exactly what proportion of the species in this family are oviparous is not certain, but evidently this is the common mode of reproduction. Only one amphisbaenid, the North African *Trogonophis,* is known to be viviparous, the newborn being about one-third or one-fourth the length of the adult.

The geographic distribution of worm lizards, though mainly tropical, is not exclusively so. Approximately half of the species are found in the New World and the remainder in Africa, with one

Arabian Worm Lizard (*Diplometopon zarudnyi*)

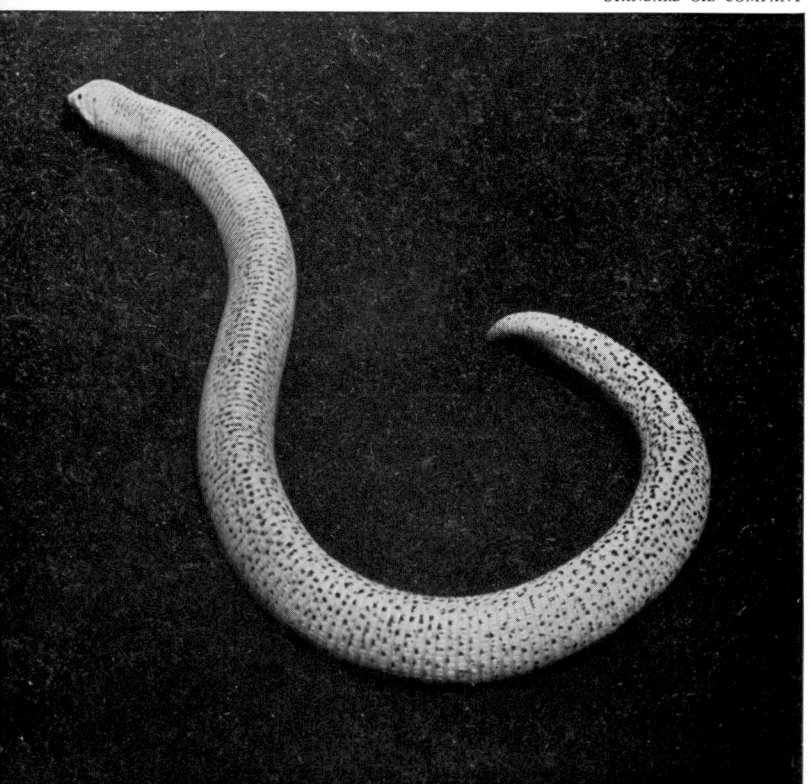

species in Spain and three others in southwestern Asia. As indicated before, the Florida worm lizard, *Rhineura floridana,* is the only species occurring in the United States, and it burrows in the soil and leaf mold of peninsular Florida. When discovered under logs, this foot-long, pinkish creature retreats down its hole tail first, although sometimes its very coarse and tough tail is used to stopper its burrow. At the other edge of the continent, in Lower California and along the Pacific coast of Mexico, live the remaining three worm lizards of North America. All members of one genus (*Bipes*), they are remarkable for one feature: the possession of short but stout front legs. Though small (less than one-twentieth of the total length), these limbs have distinct digits, and in one species all five are sufficiently developed to bear claws.

Far to the south, in extreme eastern Panama, the amphisbaenids reappear. The roughly sixty species of South America, now placed in five genera, range down into Argentina and Paraguay. The most widespread and as a consequence the best known South American species are the common red worm lizard, *Amphisbaena alba* (Plate 57), and the spotted worm lizard, *Amphisbaena fuliginosa.* Both have been found frequently in ant nests and are sometimes called "ant-king" or "mother ant" (the sex is apparently obscure) by the natives, who believe that they are reared and fed by the ants. Of course there is more than a grain of truth in that belief, because the worm lizards do eat their hosts and so in a sense are fed by the ants. Both of these foot-and-a-half-long species are occasionally discovered crawling over the forest floor after rains. If the red worm lizard is touched at such times, its body becomes rigid, and both head and tail are raised off the ground. In a moment the animal relaxes and begins to feel about with its tail just as a snake would do with its head. Judging by other people's experience, this behavior thoroughly confuses the issue of which stumpy end is head and which tail.

On the other side of the world, there are slightly fewer species but almost twice as many genera. Just three genera occur outside of Africa. One of these, *Blanus,* has three species in Turkey and adjacent parts of Asia Minor and a fourth along the coasts of Algeria and Morocco and in Spain. Another North African amphisbaenid, the sharp-tailed worm lizard, *Trogonophis wiegmanni,* is thought erroneously by the natives to be the very poisonous young of the horned viper, *Cerastes cornutus.*

The main center of Old World amphisbaenids is south of the Sahara. Though it is most abundant in the central rain forests, the family extends southward almost to the Cape of Good Hope.

The Anguid Lizards
(*Family Anguidae*)

The difficulties caused by the lack of common names have been mentioned several times already in this book, and here we have another example. Some of the genera of the Anguidae have widely used common names, for example, glass snake for *Ophisaurus,* alligator lizard for *Gerrhonotus,* and slowworm for *Anguis.* But there is no all-inclusive popular name for the family, and so we revert to the standard modification of the scientific name.

Probably no general common name exists partly because of the different body forms exhibited by the anguids. The alligator lizards of the western United States and the galliwasps (genus *Diploglossus*) of Central America, for instance, resemble typical lizards except for somewhat elongate bodies. On the other hand, the glass snakes of America and Asia and the equally limbless slowworm of Europe look more like snakes. Of course the resemblance to snakes of these last two lizards is very superficial, and is completely destroyed as soon as one sees them blink their eyes. Actually they are no more snakelike than other limbless lizards we have already mentioned—the flap-footed lizards, the snake lizards, and some of the skinks. And, like all these limbless lizards, the glass snakes and the slowworm have the distinctive lizard ability to break off the tail voluntarily, a capacity not possessed by any snake.

In fact the glass snakes may almost be said to shatter their tails, for they are often broken into several pieces. Since the tail of the slender glass snake, *Ophisaurus attenuatus,* is twice the length of head and trunk, the lizard sometimes appears to be breaking in the middle of its body. The old story that the glass snakes can rejoin the pieces of tail is, of course, absolutely false. They can, however, grow a new tail, but the regenerated tail never reaches the length of the original. It must be very effective for lizards to sacrifice the tail to a predator, for during the course of evolution lizards have developed special fracture planes in the centers of vertebrae. As soon as the tail snaps, muscle bundles swell instantly at the break and prevent any loss of blood.

The anguids as a whole are completely scaled, have rather blunt heads, and have many internal anatomical features in common. However, they are readily divisible into three groups or subfamilies. Although this division is based on various parts of the anatomy, a tendency toward loss of limbs appears in each subfamily and is reminiscent of the skinks, in which the same trend crops up again and again. In two of the subfamilies the trend goes all the way, as represented by most glass snakes and the slowworm, in which all external trace of limbs is lost although the internal bony girdles associated with legs persist.

In the third subfamily, the galliwasps, a complete sequence from the five-toed condition through four-, two-, and one-toed limbs is formed by living species. The limit is reached by one South American genus (*Ophiodes*), in which the front limbs are absent but the hind limbs are present as single-toed little flaps. One of these lizards, *Ophiodes striatus,* has the peculiar habit of resting with its ridiculously tiny hind legs spread out.

One of the characteristics of the anguids is the presence of bony centers in the scales, a feature already noted in a few other lizard families. These scales, called "osteoderms," are especially hard and smooth in the galliwasp subfamily and make it very difficult to maintain a grip on these animals when they squirm. In this respect they recall the skinks, to which they were once considered related. However, the structure of the skull and the way the teeth are replaced show their true relationships to the anguids.

The skull and the blunt teeth of the galliwasps, and of the subfamily formed by the alligator lizards and the glass snakes, are fitted for crushing their prey, which consists primarily of insects and spiders, although some of our glass snakes and alligator lizards also eat small lizards. In stalking an insect, the Oregon alligator lizard, *Gerrhonotus multicarinatus scincicauda,* creeps slowly forward, turning its head from side to side in order to look at the insect with each eye. When it reaches striking distance, the lizard slowly puts both hind limbs forward and then, utilizing the leverage so obtained, suddenly thrusts its body forward and snaps its jaws over the unfortunate prey.

Obviously the glass snakes and slowworm cannot use this technique. But the speed and agility of the glass snakes make up for the deficiency of limbs. On the other hand, the slowworm, *Anguis fragilis,* has no need of speed because it feeds to a large extent on slugs. These slimy creatures require special mechanics of eating. A crushing apparatus, such as the other anguids have, would be relatively ineffective in handling this slippery prey. Everyone has mashed flies or other insects with his fingers, but some time try doing the same with a slug. It is not as easy. The slowworm, however, does not use the nutcracker technique; it could not. Its teeth are pointed and fanglike, totally unsuited for crushing but certainly capable of penetrating a slug's mucous coating and holding the slippery animal fast.

A hunting slowworm glides up to a slug, arches its head above the prey, then deliberately seizes the slug in the middle. Occasionally it chews the slug from end to end before swallowing, but at other times it merely holds the slug a few seconds.

Now, the different feeding adaptations of the slowworm and glass snakes do not force totally different diets on them. On the contrary, both anguid types feed on spiders, insects and their larvae, and snails, but the primary food and the mechanics of feeding are different. The slowworm, whose dentition is not effective in crushing, prefers soft-bodied prey, whereas the glass snakes, which have good crushing teeth, tend to avoid slippery items. A glass snake eating a snail will grab the shell and either swallow the snail whole or, if it is too large, crack it between the jaws before swallowing. But a slowworm has its own technique. It seizes the snail's body with its sharp teeth and then, working its jaws around to the snail's head, begins to swallow, gradually pulling or sucking the snail out of its shell.

No such basic differences exist in the defensive behavior of the anguids. All of them rely on the common lizard device of a broken, squirming tail to decoy an enemy while the lizard makes a frantic dash to safety. One experimenter placed an alligator lizard in a cage with several magpies, which immediately attacked the lizard but were distracted by the gyrating tail left behind as the lizard headed for shelter. And of course the fragmented tail of a hard-pressed glass snake leaves an enemy with several squirming decoys, while the lizard escapes.

Another defensive technique of the anguids, relatively common in snakes but not among lizards, is the use of odoriferous anal excretions. When caught, some of the alligator lizards, the glass snakes, and the slowworm exude a foul-smelling material and attempt to smear it on their enemy. This behavior has been observed mainly as a reaction to one kind of enemy—herpetologists.

An additional distinctive defensive mechanism has been attributed to the southern alligator lizard, *Gerrhonotus multicarinatus*. On several occasions a newly captured lizard has grasped one hind foot in its jaws and maintained the grip for some time. It has been suggested that snakes, which form one of the principal types of enemies of these lizards, would be unable to swallow an alligator lizard in this position because they could find no end to start down the throat.

Reproductive habits are varied within the family, some species being viviparous and others oviparous.

Live-bearing occurs in certain of the galliwasps (for example, *Celestus plei* of Puerto Rico and *C. montanus* of Honduras), in at least one of the alligator lizards (*Gerrhonotus coeruleus*), and in the slowworm. Egg-laying is the rule in other alligator lizards and in all the glass snakes. At the time of mating the males become pugnacious, and true fights—not the shams common in iguanids, for instance—have been observed in a number of species. In fact males of the scheltopusik, the glass snake of the Balkan region and Asia Minor, *Ophisaurus apodus,* snap at any moving thing during the breeding period.

For a small family of lizards, the anguids have an extensive geographic distribution. Although the great majority of sixty or so species are limited to the New World, a few live in Eurasia. Perhaps the most outstanding aspect of the anguids' distribution is that they are the only Old World lizards not occurring in the tropics of Asia or Africa.

The only genus found in both hemispheres is *Ophisaurus,* the glass snakes. The glass snake of southern China, *Ophisaurus harti,* a moderate-sized species with a head and trunk length of about ten inches and a fifteen-inch tail, is pale olive on the back and marked with bright blue on the sides. The young are almost white above and black on the sides. Typical of the glass snakes, the female lays five to seven one-inch eggs in shallow depressions under rocks, logs, or decaying vegetation. She guards them, though not with too much courage. Incubation requires at least one month, and at hatching the young are about five inches long.

Another species, *Ophisaurus gracilis,* lives in extreme northeastern India and in northern Burma. Having a body length of about five inches and a tail roughly twice as long, the Indian glass snake is one of the smaller members of the genus. The giant of the genus, and indeed of the whole family, is the scheltopusik, *Ophisaurus apodus* (Plate 51), an inhabitant of southwestern Asia and southeastern Europe, a glass snake with a total length of almost four feet. A mere statement of length does not give an adequate idea of the scheltopusik's size, for, contrary to the great majority of snakelike lizards, it is thick-bodied, with about the thickness of a man's wrist. It would take too many spiders and insects to fill the stomach of a creature this size, and so the scheltopusik eats lizards, mice (which it crushes with one snap of its jaws), and other small vertebrates that abound in the rocky, broken country it inhabits.

The remaining Old World glass snake is a species living in extreme northwestern Africa. Beyond the fact that it occurs in Morocco, it is almost unknown.

However, a great deal is known about the other Old World anguid, the slowworm, *Anguis fragilis*. Because it occurs over the whole of Europe, from England to the Caucasus and as far north as southern Sweden, European naturalists have had many opportunities to watch it in the wild and study it in captivity. As a matter of fact, naturalists have been able to study individual slowworms for prolonged periods, since it is the longest-lived lizard known. At least half a dozen of these lizards have lived over twenty-five years in captivity. The record, however, is held by a specimen that lived fifty-four years in the Zoological Museum in Copenhagen. Its crowning glory was the fact that at age forty-five it mated successfully—with a female that had been kept in captivity twenty years.

Slowworms are viviparous, and an adult female of about eighteen inches has between six and twelve young in a litter. At birth the young, pale gold and black, are about three inches long. This length is doubled during the first year, and by the third year, when the males become sexually mature, the lizards are approximately ten inches long.

In England the slowworm lives in pastures, gardens, and open woodland. Generally it is active at night, when the slugs and earthworms that form the staple items of its diet are most easily found. Only during the coolness of early spring, and during the late summer when the pregnant females bask, are slowworms commonly seen in daylight.

These habits are very similar to those of our glass lizards, which are most active at dusk or at night, although they are occasionally seen basking in the spring. Until recently it was thought that only one species of glass snake lived in the United States, but now three species are recognized. The

Slowworm (*Anguis fragilis*)

eastern glass snake, *Ophisaurus ventralis,* a native of the Atlantic and Gulf coastal plains, is the best known. This brown striped or checkered animal is the longest lizard in the United States, reaching a total length of slightly more than three feet, of which two-thirds is tail. It sometimes burrows and is turned up by plows. In general it seems to prefer moist woods and damp grassy fields. The eastern glass snake is one of the most satisfactory American reptiles to keep as a pet. It thrives on a variety of insects and earthworms and will even take food from the hand. Its only disadvantage is the ease with which the tail is broken if the lizard is handled roughly.

Like all members of the genus, the eastern glass snake lays eggs, from four to seventeen in a clutch. The eggs are about three-fourths of an inch long when laid and slowly increase to approximately one inch during the two-month incubation period.

The distribution of American glass snakes ends in western Texas just about where the distribution of the alligator lizards (genus *Gerrhonotus*) begins. Five species occur in the United States, the largest, the Texas alligator lizard, *Gerrhonotus liocephalus,*

Texas Alligator Lizard (*Gerrhonotus liocephalus*)

reaching a total length of twenty inches, and the smallest, the northern alligator lizard, *Gerrhonotus coeruleus principis,* less than ten inches. In general the alligator lizards have relatively short legs and long bodies, with the result that they have a sinuous type of locomotion. Most of them are terrestrial, but the southern alligator lizard *Gerrhonotus multicarinatus* (Plate 50), is a good climber and has a prehensile tail.

Only two species are at all well known and both, the southern (*multicarinatus*) and the northern (*coeruleus*) alligator lizards, occur along the Pacific coast. Although their ranges have almost the same north-south extent (despite the common names), and although both seem to prefer wooded country, the northern alligator lizard usually lives in cooler and more humid habitats. The two species also differ in reproductive habits, the northern being viviparous (two to fifteen young in a litter, and averaging six or seven) and the southern oviparous (six to twenty eggs in a clutch). Here again, as in the chameleons, lacertids, and certain iguanids, we see the parallel between cool habitat and viviparity.

The alligator lizard subfamily ranges down Central America as far as Panama. The last subfamily, the galliwasps, is strictly a New World group, its members living in the West Indies and on the continents from southern Mexico to northern Argentina. As a whole, the galliwasps are another unknown among the reptiles. Practically no information concerning habits and habitats is available.

The Legless Lizards

(*Family Anniellidae*)

The anguid lizards have close relatives in the family Anniellidae, the legless lizards of California and Lower California. These small burrowing lizards, of which there are only two species, have no trace of external limbs and lack ear openings, but do have movable eyelids. Most of their specializations are adaptations for subterranean existence. Loss of limbs, absence of external ears, and smallness of eye all reduce obstacles to movement through soil. Smooth scales, a very compact skull, and a countersunk lower jaw improve the efficiency of a burrower that must use its head.

In coastal California south from the San Francisco Bay area, the California legless lizard, *Anniella pulchra,* a silvery or black animal, lives in sand or sandy loam through which it can tunnel with ease. Apparently compact, hard soils are avoided for mechanical reasons. The lizard spends most of its life underground, usually within four inches of the surface, and is able to detect its insect prey while beneath the surface by means of the senses of smell and touch. Like many of the anguids, the California legless lizard is viviparous, with litters of one to four born in autumn. At birth the legless lizards are two and a half to three inches long, of which less than a third is tail. By the time they have reached maturity, at three years of age, they are about eight to ten inches long.

The second species, the Geronimo legless lizard, *Anniella geronimensis,* is found along the west coast of Lower California and on adjacent Geronimo Island.

The Xenosaurids and Shinisaurids

(*Family Xenosauridae*)

The relationships of certain lizards, including the four species grouped under this family heading, are still obscure. Until very recently the Chinese lizard *Shinisaurus crocodilurus* was always placed in a family by itself, and we may yet have to revert to that arrangement. The other three species, all in the genus *Xenosaurus,* live in central Mexico and Guatemala. Moderate in size (ten to fifteen inches), all four have strong legs and robust bodies. Most of their body scales are small and granulelike, but scattered among them are larger scales arranged in chevrons across the body. These large scales run out on the top of the tail of *Shinisaurus* in two rows and have suggested the scientific name, *crocodilurus,* which means "crocodile tail."

More is known about the habits of the Chinese *Shinisaurus* than about the Mexican species. *Shinisaurus* lives along streams and feeds partly on tadpoles and fishes. It is also given to basking on branches overhanging the water, into which it presumably dives when danger appears.

The Gila Monsters

(*Family Helodermatidae*)

Although in every part of the world lizards are accused of being venomous, the Gila monster, *Heloderma suspectum* (Plate 54) of southwestern United States and adjacent Mexico, and its relative,

the beaded lizard, *Heloderma horridum* (Plate 53), of western Mexico, are the only truly venomous lizards. These two species are the sole remaining members of the family Helodermatidae, which is also known from a thirty- to forty-million-year-old fossil discovered in Colorado. Every well-equipped zoo has its Gila monsters, and often its beaded lizards, which make good zoo animals both because of the interest of the public in venomous reptiles and because these lizards live well in captivity.

The appearance of the rather sluggish helodermatids befits their slow movements. A large blunt head, furnished with small, beady eyes, is followed by a somewhat elongate and stout body and an unusually thick tail. The short legs end in powerful digits equipped with remarkably strong claws. Like most other lizards, the Gila monster is covered with scales, but unlike the majority of this group of reptiles, its scales do not overlap in shingle fashion. Instead, the scales merely abut one another, forming rows in both crosswise and diagonal directions on the back and sides. The form and arrangement of the scales are responsible for the name "beaded" lizard. "Gila," of course, refers to the basin in the part of Arizona where the Gila monster is relatively abundant.

Both species are black or brown, irregularly marked with light areas that vary from yellowish white to pink. Young individuals generally have more extensive light areas than do old lizards. Though very similar, the two species differ considerably in color. For example, the mainly pink and yellow Gila monster, *H. suspectum,* has four or five bands on the tail, whereas the largely black beaded lizard, *H. horridum,* has six or seven. Other conspicuous differences between the two are found in the relative lengths of the tail and in size. The maximum recorded length for the beaded lizard is thirty-two inches; the largest known Gila monster is only twenty inches long.

Large lizards may be herbivorous (iguanas) or carnivorous (monitors), and the latter type usually rely on quick movement to catch their prey. Contrasting with these, the Gila monster and the beaded lizard, which are also carnivorous, do not depend on rapid motion to catch their prey. They merely walk up on their food, which consists primarily of animals that cannot run—nestling birds and baby mammals—and the eggs of birds and reptiles.

The helodermatids hunt almost exclusively by means of their chemical senses: taste and smell. In a recent experiment an egg was moved along the ground in a tortuous route, beginning at the snout of a captive Gila monster and ending about a yard from the lizard. The lizard began to follow the trail, lost it several times, rediscovered it, and continued hunting along the trail, despite the fact that the egg lay in plain view and at one stage was only five inches away. Now, unlike dogs and other mammals, lizards and snakes do not pick up odors solely with their nostrils. When a Gila monster follows a scent, it flicks its tongue out at frequent intervals almost as though it were tasting the soil. Actually the tongue carries scented particles to a pair of pits in the roof of the mouth. These pits form the surface layer of an organ, named after its discoverer Jacobson, that is sensitive to chemicals, and in effect is an organ of taste. This especially reptilian organ is most highly developed in the snakes.

As a hungry Gila monster or beaded lizard wanders slowly over the ground in its arid native haunts, it sniffs the air and tastes the soil. Should it pick up the odor from the nest of a ground-nesting bird (such as a quail or dove), it will follow the scent and make a meal of the eggs or helpless young. Or it might come to a burrow opening and, first testing with its nostrils and Jacobson's organ, crawl down the hole to feed on young rodents.

Like other animals living in the deserts and near-deserts of the Southwest and Mexico, the helodermatids must be able to withstand long periods in which food is not available. Repeated observations on captive Gila monsters demonstrate that these lizards can survive without food for months. Of course, a Gila monster loses considerable weight during a long fast and may become emaciated. The most interesting changes in appearance take place in the tail. This ordinarily very plump appendage can shrink as much as 20 per cent in girth in slightly over one month. One Gila monster, caught in an extremely emaciated condition in a part of Arizona that had suffered from drought for three years, fed well in captivity, and in six months its tail almost doubled in bulk. Food not required for the immediate activities of these lizards is converted into fat and stored in the tail. Indeed, in a well-fed captive Gila monster, the muscles, tendons, and bones form only a small proportion of the plump tail's volume.

Despite the great interest attached to these large lizards, we know very little about their way of life. Probably part of our ignorance is explained by the rather short intervals in which the helodermatids are active. Ordinarily they move about only during the rainy seasons, which means that the Gila monster, for example, may forage actively only in June, July, and August in parts of Arizona. And if, as frequently happens in these arid regions, there is a prolonged drought, the Gila monster apparently remains in its burrow underground. Although both the Gila monster and the beaded lizard are sometimes seen during the day, they usually emerge from their burrows at night.

Both members of this family lay eggs, the clutch size ranging from three to fifteen. Like all reptile eggs, those of the helodermatids vary in size as much as chicken eggs. The usual dimensions, however, are approximately one and a half inches in diameter and two and a half inches long. The Gila monster apparently mates in July and lays its eggs near the end of that month or in early August. The beaded lizard deposits its eggs in late fall, but, since this information is based entirely on captive lizards, we cannot be sure that it is true in nature. The Gila monster apparently buries its eggs in moist sand, and the young hatch in about thirty days. Unfortunately so few observations on breeding habits have been made that some of the preceding statements may have to be changed materially.

The venom apparatus of all poisonous reptiles is basically the same, and consists of a salivary gland modified to produce the venom and grooved teeth that conduct the venom into the wound of the animal bitten. But the apparatus of the helodermatids differs substantially from that of snakes. For one thing, the venom glands are in the lower jaw of the Gila monster and the beaded lizard but above the upper jaw in all venomous snakes. Furthermore, in snakes the grooved teeth are confined to the upper jaw, while in the helodermatids teeth of both upper and lower jaws are grooved. In general, the venom apparatus of these lizards is rather diffuse compared to that of snakes.

Between eight and ten upper teeth and six and eleven lower ones are grooved, always on the front and often on the rear edges. The poison gland has many ducts which, instead of ending at the bases of the fangs, open at some distance from the teeth, so that the venom must flow along a mucous fold between lip and lower jaw before reaching the grooves.

This rather inefficient arrangement prevents the Gila monster and beaded lizard from utilizing the stabbing or biting stroke of the vipers and cobras. Instead these lizards must grip an enemy tightly with both jaws and hang on, giving time for the venom to flow into the wounds. With their very strong jaws, the helodermatids are well equipped to hang on and have the grip of the proverbial bulldog. In fact one of the main problems in treating Gila monster bites is to disengage the jaws; in extreme cases pliers may be needed.

Persons bitten by Gila monsters invariably experience great pain in the area of the bite. But since the venom, like that of cobras, acts on the central nervous system, the real danger lies in paralysis of the respiratory organs. Treatment of Gila monster bites should follow that for snake bite. The basic steps are removal of as much venom as possible and prevention of its spread away from the wound. Fang punctures should be enlarged by incisions with a razor blade or sharp knife, and a loose tourniquet applied above the wound. The victim should be kept as quiet as possible. Because so few people are bitten by these lizards, Gila monster antivenin is not now available, nor is it likely to be in the future. Cobra antivenin, which is an antineurotoxin, has some effect on Gila monster venom, but not enough to warrant its use.

The history of exploration is full of exaggeration, especially when the early explorers discussed ferocious or poisonous animals. Consequently, it is remarkable that one of the first accounts of the helodermatids, written by the Spaniard Francisco Hernández in 1577, should stand today as one of the most accurate estimations of these venomous lizards. Hernández wrote (as translated by C. M. Bogert), "The bite of this animal though harmful is not mortal, for which reason it is more dreaded for its appearance than for its bite, and it never tends to harm anyone unless offended or provoked."

In the nearly four hundred years following Hernández, we have accumulated almost as much misinformation as information about these two venomous lizards. Fortunately, all that is known or reputed to be known about the Gila monster and the beaded lizard has been analyzed and summarized in a recent exhaustive study. After checking every instance of a human bitten by a Gila monster, whether reported in newspapers, magazine articles, or letters, authors of that study conclude that only eight victims are known to have died. But even that number does not give us a fair estimate of the virulence of helodermatid venom, because several of the victims were either alcoholics or definitely under the influence of alcohol when bitten. Nevertheless Gila monsters and beaded lizards should be treated with the caution and respect due venomous reptiles. Since most of the reported bites have been received from captive animals, the helodermatids cannot reasonably be considered a menace to vacationers. But they should not be kept as pets.

Komodo Dragon Lizard
(*Varanus komodoensis*)

The Monitor Lizards
(*Family Varanidae*)

Monitor lizards might well serve as the prototype of dragons. A long head and neck, followed by a relatively heavy body and a long thick tail, all supported by strong legs furnished with cruel-looking claws—what could be more dragonlike? The resemblance is enhanced by a slender forked tongue that can be extruded far beyond the mouth. To this add aggressiveness and large size, and we have our mythological fire-breathing monster—all except the fire.

In fact, the largest of these essentially tropical lizards is called the Komodo dragon lizard, *Varanus komodoensis*. The giant among the lizards of today, the Komodo dragon reaches a length of ten feet and a weight of three hundred pounds. Oddly enough, this gigantic resident of the East Indies lives only on the small island of Komodo, which is just twenty miles long and twelve miles wide, on two adjacent islets that are even smaller, and on a small area of the larger island of Flores.

At the other end of the scale is the short-tailed monitor of western Australia, *Varanus brevicauda,* which just reaches a length of eight inches. Of the remaining monitors, seven species never grow longer than two and a half feet, another ten are three to five feet long, and four become six-footers.

Despite their great range in size, monitors present an almost uniform appearance. The brief description given in the first paragraph applies to all, and only minor differences distinguish the various species. Some have tails circular in cross section, others

tails flattened from side to side. Certain species have longer snouts, and others have slightly enlarged scales on the nape of the neck. But the kind of radical variation in body form and scalation seen in some lizard families, such as the Iguanidae and Agamidae, is not met with in the Varanidae. The uniformity of the monitors is expressed by the classification—there is only one living genus, *Varanus,* in the family.

Most animals have become adapted to one particular mode of life and are specialized for, let us say, a life in trees, or a life in streams and lakes, or a burrowing existence, etc. But there are some exceptions, animals that are not so narrowly specialized, and consequently are at home in many situations and capable of many activities. Among the lizards, the best examples of the "generalist" (as opposed to the specialist) are the monitor lizards. To be sure, certain kinds of monitors, like the small Gillen's monitor, *Varanus gilleni,* from Australia, apparently spend all of their lives in trees, while others, like the African savanna monitor, *V. exanthematicus* (Plate 52), seem never to climb trees or to go in water. But to the Malayan monitor, *V. salvator,* and the Nile monitor, *V. niloticus,* it makes no difference if the business of living obliges them to climb tall trees, swim deep rivers, run over the ground, or dig a burrow. They are physically and psychologically equipped to do any of these things and to do it well.

Traveling by native dugout on the muddy rivers of the Malay Peninsula, Sumatra, and Borneo, one is impressed by the number of Malayan monitors seen along the banks. Beginning around eight o'clock in the morning, these dark, almost black, reptiles emerge from their retreats to bask in the sun. At the first sign of danger, perhaps the knock of a paddle against a gunwale, the monitor dives into the river. The movement may be an awkward and noisy "belly flop" or a silent crocodilelike disappearance beneath the surface.

Once in the water this monitor is completely at home. Many times we have watched monitors dive and have waited five or ten minutes while the three or four men in our party looked up and down the river in vain for the reappearance of the animal. Exactly how long the Malayan monitor can remain submerged is not known. But its counterpart in Africa, the Nile monitor, can stay under water for an hour. The swimming movements of the Malayan monitor are very similar to those of a crocodile: the limbs are laid back along the body while the main propulsive force comes from sidewise beats of the flattened tail.

But not all escape movements of this lizard lead into the water. We have seen a few heavy five-footers heave themselves up the bank and go crashing into the jungle. Every monitor track on these riverbanks shows deep claw marks, and it is doubtful that, without these daggerlike structures, the monitor could mount the banks. For that matter, without these claws the monitor could not dig its burrows or climb trees or defend itself so well at close quarters.

As soon as the morning sun has warmed the Malayan monitor, it begins the search for food. Almost any animal matter will do. Fish, crabs, frogs, birds, eggs, rats, even decaying meat—all are eaten. We once baited a fish trap with pig intestines but caught no fish because a monitor stole the bait. Occasionally a large monitor will rob a chicken coop, and in some places the Malays claim that, of every seven chickens lost to vermin, four are taken by biawaks (as monitors are called in Malay), two by civet cats, and one by pythons. This seems only fair, since, at least in Borneo, the monitor is often eaten by people and is supposed to taste like chicken. We have eaten them and must say that the resemblance is to very old and tough roosters.

The diet of the Malayan monitor is typical of the whole family. The larger the monitor, the larger the prey it can handle. The Komodo dragon lizard, for example, will tackle small deer and pigs. On the other hand, the smallest species feeds mostly on insects and small invertebrates. Even large monitors, however, seem unable to resist eggs. The Australian lace monitor, *V. varius,* which grows to five or six feet, makes a specialty of robbing birds' nests. Occasionally it comes a cropper when trying to pull this trick on cockatoos, for these parrot-family birds defend their nests vigorously, and their extremely strong beaks usually force the lizard to break all manner of cross-country speed records.

When devouring the large prey, monitors tear the flesh with teeth and claws. They do not normally chew or crush their food, as do iguanids and other lizards, but swallow their prey whole or in large chunks. As an example, there is a large Malayan monitor, now a museum specimen, that swallowed a six-inch turtle.

In this regard monitors resemble snakes, and here we come to the matter that herpetologists find most interesting about these lizards. For the Varanidae are closely related to the lizards that were the ancestors of the snakes, and certain habits and structures of monitors seem to foreshadow the conditions in snakes. The habit of swallowing large objects is a case in point, since it is one of the monitor's unique features among lizards and is

Desert Monitor (*Varanus griseus*)

characteristic of all snakes. Animals with this habit must protect the brain case from the pressure the food object will exert against the roof of the mouth. Like the snakes, the monitors have developed an almost continuous, solid bony sheath around the brain and thus differ from the great majority of lizard families.

Other snakelike features of the monitors include the long forked tongue and its use in conjunction with Jacobson's organ (see page 168). Monitors apparently rely entirely on Jacobson's organ for their chemical trailing of prey, just as do snakes. Other lizards also use Jacobson's organ and the tongue for this purpose, but their tongues are not very protrusible and therefore not as specialized as those of monitors for this function.

One of the hallmarks of the entire lizard group is the ability voluntarily to snap off the tail and then to regenerate the missing portion. The monitors, like the snakes again, have lost these capacities. Of course an enemy may succeed in biting off the end of a monitor's tail, but it is not a voluntary act on the part of the monitor. Afterward the wound heals at the cut surface, and the monitor has a permanently shortened tail.

Enemies of monitors are not as numerous as are those of other lizards because, in general, the monitors are relatively large. Everywhere man is the monitors' most dangerous enemy, not only because monitors are large enough to make a reasonable meal but also because monitors feed on chickens. Aside from man, the larger carnivorous mammals, birds of prey, and crocodiles are the monitor's principal enemies.

When confronted by danger, a monitor's first concern is escape. The Malayan monitor and the Nile monitor almost invariably head for water. Other species run to their resting retreats, which in the case of the Indian monitor, *Varanus bengalensis,* is often a tree hollow and in the desert monitor, *V. griseus,* a hole in the ground. Forest species, such as the Bornean rough-necked monitor, *V. rudicollis,* usually scamper up trees.

Another forest species from Borneo and Sumatra, Duméril's monitor, *V. dumerili,* though it may retreat up trees, frequently dashes to a burrow in a muddy stream bank. Five days in succession we stalked a Duméril's monitor, and five days we heard it crash through the vegetation on its way into a hole in a creek bank. We never succeeded in locating the entrance to the burrow, which was undoubtedly hidden by a tangle of dead branches, but by approaching the small stream from opposite directions, we and our Dyak hunter were certain that the lizard lived somewhere under the steep bank. On the sixth day the Dyak caught it.

But, if escape is impossible, monitors will defend themselves, and a big Malayan or Nile monitor can put up a fine defensive show. The body is inflated, and the animal hisses with its mouth open while the strong tail is lashed from side to side. Just how effective the tail is against most predators is unknown. Restricting our consideration to the observations of the most careful field naturalists—and this is especially important when dealing with the usually exaggerated accounts of animal ferocity—we come out with the conclusion that, while small predators might be deterred by the blows of a big monitor's tail, a man will not. The monitor's best defense, outside of escape, rests with its strong jaws and dagger-sharp claws. And it is not reluctant to use them. A five-foot monitor can be a formidable object.

All species of monitors lay eggs that have a leathery shell. Naturally, the Komodo dragon lizard has the largest eggs (two and a half inches by four inches) and the smaller species eggs proportional to their size (generally smaller than hen eggs). The clutch, varying from seven to thirty-five, is usually deposited in holes in the ground, but in arboreal species it is placed in hollow trees.

Gould's Monitor emerging from burrow (*Varanus gouldi*)

In South Africa the Nile monitor, *V. niloticus,* often lays its eggs in large, moundlike termite nests. These earthen nests have very hard walls except during the rainy season, which coincides with the monitor's egg-laying period. The monitor tears a hole in the rain-softened wall, lays her eggs, and departs. Then the frenzied termites repair the nest, thereby enclosing the eggs. Although the termites pay no attention to the eggs, the colony provides them with fresh air, which is always circulating through the channels and chambers of the nest, and protection from some predators as soon as the repaired wall hardens in the sun.

The eggs, which require months of incubation, are eaten by natives wherever monitors occur. By all accounts one monitor egg tastes like another, and our opinion, based on eating eggs of a Bornean forest monitor, *Varanus dumerili,* is that they will never take the place of hens' eggs.

Strictly an Old World family today, the monitors once inhabited North America and are known from Wyoming fossil beds that are about sixty million years old. Now they live in Africa, in southern Asia, in the East Indies, and in Australia.

One species even occurs on certain of the Polynesian islands. This, the Pacific monitor, *Varanus indicus,* ranges from Celebes and Timor in the eastern part of the East Indies to the Marshall Islands in the mid-Pacific. Evidently this monitor, which reaches a maximum length of about four and a half feet, was carried from the East Indies by the Polynesians and deliberately planted on the small Pacific islands in order to provide a meat supply. Except for birds, these monitors were the only large land vertebrates on these islands. Now the Pacific monitor is not as abundant as it once was. Presumably many of them have died as a result of attempting to eat the big South American toad, *Bufo marinus,* which was introduced into the islands shortly before World War II in order to control insects in the coconut groves.

Farther to the west, in Australia, we come to the true home of the monitors. Approximately half of the living species are found there, and that half includes the smallest species, the short-tailed monitor, *V. brevicauda,* and two of the largest, the lace monitor, *V. varius,* and the perentie, *V. giganteus,* both of which grow into six-footers.

The East Indies have almost as many species of monitors as Australia, but despite the proximity of the down-under continent to parts of the Indies, only one species, the Timor monitor, *V. timorensis,* occurs in both areas. Undoubtedly the most spectacular of the East Indian monitors is the giant Komodo dragon lizard. Yet except for its great size, the Komodo lizard is no more interesting than the much better known and more widely distributed Malayan monitor, *V. salvator*.

Because of its wide distribution, the Malayan monitor lives in territory inhabited by a number of its relatives. In Borneo, Sumatra, and the Malay Peninsula, it shares space with Duméril's, *V. dumerili*, and the rough-necked monitor, *V. rudicollis*. In Burma and adjoining eastern India it shares the country with the Indian monitor, *V. bengalensis*.

Despite its vast size the Indian subcontinent has only three monitors, and just one of them, the Indian monitor, lives in the south. In the arid northwest of Pakistan, the desert monitor, *V. griseus*, is the common species. Like other lizards we have mentioned, the desert monitor ranges all the way across this dry country that stretches from northwestern Pakistan to the western Saharan provinces of Africa. This monitor is said to dislike water, but this statement seems just a bit unnecessary to us. Where is it likely to find water in that arid land?

Most lizards are active only at moderately warm temperatures. Extremes of either hot or cold usually prevent normal activities. The desert monitor, because of the great daily temperature range characteristic of deserts, can be active only by day and even so must retreat to its burrow to avoid the hottest hours at midday. The winters in southwestern Asia are sufficiently cold to compel the desert monitor to hibernate for several months.

South of the Sahara the Nile monitor, *V. niloticus*, makes its appearance and is found all the way to the Cape of Good Hope, and from east to west across the whole of Africa in both forested and open country. Its predilection for riverbanks keeps it out of the desert but has enabled it to move up the Nile into southern Egypt. Like its relative, the Malayan monitor of the Far East, the Nile monitor is disliked heartily by farmers because of its fondness for chicken.

The Nile monitor is also an enemy of the crocodiles in Africa, tearing open the crocodiles' nests and eating the eggs. This may be an ancient habit, dating back to the earliest monitors, which may have fed on eggs of those long since extinct relatives of the crocodiles, the dinosaurs.

The Earless Monitor

(*Family Lanthanotidae*)

It may seem odd that, after two hundred years of intensive zoological exploration of all corners of the world, numerous species of animals are still represented in museum collections by less than half a dozen specimens. In fact some species are known from only a single individual. Naturally, we cannot truthfully say that we know much about such animals, and it is unlikely that we shall until more observations on both living and preserved specimens are made. Therefore a certain interest and urgency are attached to these "rare" species that common species do not arouse.

But few of the many rare reptiles have been surrounded with the romantic aura of the foot-long Bornean lizard, the earless monitor, *Lanthanotus borneensis*. The first specimen was announced to the herpetological world in 1878, and since that time probably no more than six have been collected. All have come from the central portion of the colony of Sarawak, which lies along the northwest coast of Borneo. Why more specimens of this lizard have not been caught is a mystery. We are somewhat embarrassed to have to admit that on two separate expeditions to Borneo, we have failed to collect it or even to meet a native who had seen it. But at least we can claim the distinction of having seen all but two of the known preserved specimens.

Whatever the causes for the scarcity of earless monitors in museum collections, the reasons for the attention herpetologists have given it are clear. In the first place, about twenty years after the discovery of *Lanthanotus*, a truly great herpetologist decided that the earless monitor belonged in the Gila monster family Helodermatidae. This opinion, if it stood, meant that the Gila monster family had a very peculiar geographic distribution, with two species in southwestern North America and one across the Pacific in Borneo, and that there was probably another poisonous lizard in the world. To herpetologists, no less than to the general public, venomous reptiles have a fascination all their own.

But there was more to the scientific interest than that. For the earless monitor, whether a member of the Helodermatidae or not, was certainly a member of the group of lizard families (including the Gila monsters and the true monitors) from which snakes arose. And if we are to understand the evolution of the snakes, we must first know something about their ancestors.

During the first half of this century, herpetological opinion had the earless monitor in and out the Gila monster family too many times to count. This kind of indecision was a clear indication of how little was known, and much of the ignorance resulted from lack of sufficient preserved specimens. Finally, in 1954 two American herpetologists published the conclusions of an exhaustive study and decided that the earless monitor belonged in a family of its own, the Lanthanotidae. It is at least as closely related to the true monitors (family Varanidae) as to the Gila monsters, and even more closely related to several extinct families of lizards.

A nonherpetologist would probably be unimpressed by *Lanthanotus,* for the earless monitor is rather undistinguished in appearance. It is moderate in size (about sixteen inches over all), and it has no bizarre crests or flaps of skin or obvious peculiarities of limbs or tail. In short, it looks like a very ordinary sort of lizard. Its body is rather long compared to its legs and head, but not excessively so. The neck is as thick as the rear of the head, which is a little flattened and covered with small scales. Though the scales covering the body are peculiar, only the specialist would give them a second thought. Most of the scales are small, but enlarged ones are arranged in six longitudinal rows on the back, and the two central rows run out on the tail.

The shape of the head and body and the short legs do recall the Gila monsters. Special resemblance to our venomous lizards, however, ends there. As for the matter of poison, the earless monitor must be considered nonvenomous since it has no grooved teeth or any other indications of a poison apparatus.

Turning now to the snakelike features of the earless monitor, several have already been mentioned in the section on the true monitors: a highly protrusible and retractile tongue, a solid bony brain case, and a loss of the common lizard ability to regenerate the tail. The difference between the true monitors and the earless monitor in these snakelike characteristics is that, except for the inability to snap off and regenerate the tail, the earless monitor is more like a snake. For example, the brain case is more solidly encased in *Lanthanotus* than in the true monitors.

In this area, too, the search for knowledge is held back by a dearth of specimens, for, if living earless monitors were available, it would be possible to watch the action of the tongue and jaws and to discover what and how it eats. These things have direct bearing on the problem of the evolution of snakes, and until live specimens can be observed progress in this field will be limited.

One additional characteristic of the earless monitor foreshadows the present condition of snakes. The lower eyelid has a clear, transparent scale or "window" that probably is the antecedent of the "spectacle" covering the eye in all snakes. Although a clear window in the lower lid is common to many lizards—for example, certain skinks and lacertids —it is found only in the earless monitor among the lizard families that must have given rise to snakes.

Having come as close as we can to snakes among the lizards, it is time now to take a look at the snakes themselves.

The Snakes

(Order Serpentes)

THE NAME Serpentes is a happy choice for the snake group, since in popular language serpent conveys the same meaning as snake. The term "Ophidia" is almost equally well known, but "Ophidia" and the adjective "ophidian" are best relegated to literary and strictly popular usage.

Many of the most distinctive features of the order Serpentes are associated with the elongation of the body, which seems to be the result of the adoption of the "lateral undulatory" mode of locomotion by the ancestral lizard group. Correlated with the elongate body form are loss of limbs, lengthening of the internal organs, and loss of one lung.

The fact that in snakes the food is swallowed whole has governed the loosening of the jaw apparatus and the multiplication of hinge joints in the lower jaw, so that the mouth can be expanded to be drawn over prey that is much greater in diameter than the snake's body. The expansibility of the body is equally essential, and this may well be correlated with the original loss of the front limbs and shoulder girdle. We are inclined to think that the rapid evolution of the typical snakes of medium size in the Tertiary Era was coincident with the great evolution of the rodent group among mammals, prey and predator keeping pace in their evolution, so that both fit into the natural environment supplied by the seed plants.

Giant Constricting Snakes

(Family Boidae)

There is a great fascination for most people in the giants of the snake group, the boas and pythons. Along with the venomous snakes, these are always the principal attractions in the reptile house in any zoological garden, and no circus side show is complete unless it has a boa or python with a snake charmer, or preferably a snake charmeress. Quite obvious parallels to the snake charmers of the Orient, with their exhibitions of both harmless and venomous snakes, are now springing up along the main highways of the United States in the form of so-called snake farms. Some of these vie with each other in the claims on their garish billboards as to which has the most gigantic of the giant snakes.

The giant snakes fall into two distinct series, distinguished in common language as the boas and pythons, and in scientific terms as the families Boidae and Pythonidae. So far as bony structure goes, the boas are distinguished from the pythons by only a single conspicuous feature, the absence of the supraorbital bone in the roof of the skull. It has been argued that this bone might easily have been lost independently at different times during the evolution of the snakes, and that the distinction between two groups of snakes that have numerous important features in common is unnecessary. There is, however, a profound difference between the pythons and boas—the various kinds of pythons all lay eggs, and the equally numerous types of boas all normally bear living young. There are also some striking differences in the geographic distribution of these two families that support their recognition as natural groups.

Some of the characteristics common to both families are striking evidence that they are the most primitive of living snakes. Pythons and boas have as much interest for the zoologist as for the general public in having such features as the vestiges of the pelvis and of hind limbs, and well-developed paired lungs; the higher snakes have lost all trace of the limb and pelvic vestiges, and have the left lung entirely suppressed, with the right elongated to fit more perfectly the elongate form of the snake body. The hind-limb remnants consist usually of the three elements of the pelvis, widely separated from those of the opposite side, and the femur; externally there is only a claw, and this is so small in females that it may easily be overlooked. In the males, however, the external horny claw is conspicuous.

Both types of giant snake, like many kinds among more familiar and more modern families of snakes, kill their prey by constriction. The prey animal is usually struck by the open, strongly toothed jaws of the snake, and in the same extremely swift movement, coils of the body are thrown forward and envelop the small mammal or bird that is the victim. Two or three coils are then so tightened as to prevent breathing and probably to stop the action of the heart. When all motion of the prey ceases, the snake releases its coils and proceeds to swallow it in just the same way as do snakes in general.

The family of the boas includes about a dozen generic groups. The kind best known by common name is the boa constrictor, *Constrictor constrictor* (Plate 73), of the American tropics, which is found from the coasts of Mexico through tropical South America to Paraguay and the northern Argentine. "Boa constrictor" is in fact, to most people, almost a synonym for "gigantic snake." There are, however, several kinds of pythons, and the anaconda among the true boas, that are very much larger than the snake most properly known as the boa constrictor, which rarely exceeds ten feet in length, and whose greatest reported length is fourteen feet. The ordinary specimens of the boa constrictor encountered in the forests and along streams are usually from six to nine feet long.

Small boa constrictors have long been widely known in the United States because they were formerly brought in by the banana trade. When the bunches of bananas were shipped entire, the space beneath the several "hands" afforded a fine place of concealment to a snake or lizard or spider, and even to the small arboreal mouse opossum. A great variety of tropical arrivals thus reached the United States as "stowaways." Young boa constrictors were the most abundant of these visitors to reach the retail grocery stores, and the finding of so brilliantly colored a snake coiled within the overlapping hands of bananas would be a newsworthy event in any small town in the country. In larger cities, many of these small boas were taken to the local museum or zoological garden. An annulated boa, *Boa annulata,* that arrived in the United States from Ecuador in this fashion is shown in Plate 68.

The giant anaconda, *Eunectes murinus* (Plate 74), of northern South America is much the largest member of the boa family. This creature ranges (not without some geographical variation) from the Orinoco Basin through the Amazon and the Guianas. It is reported to reach a length of twenty-nine feet, but this is a much-greater-than-average length, and it is difficult to find an authentic record of more than twenty-five feet. From time to time, adventurous groups attempt the capture of some of the giant creatures reported from the Orinoco and Amazon drainages in eastern Colombia, in the hope of claiming the long-standing prize of $5000 offered by the

Cuban Boa (*Epicrates angulifer*)

New York Zoological Society for a thirty-foot specimen. For a zoo, such a price would scarcely be excessive for so popular an attraction. It is an extremely persistent item of folklore in South America that anacondas reach vastly greater lengths and diameters than those that scientists accept. Reports of forty feet are commonplace in travel literature, and even eighty feet is claimed. No fragment of skeleton or skull or skin that would substantiate such a claim has found its way to any museum or zoo in the world. Further discussion of the size reached by giant snakes will be found in connection with the reticulated python. The difficulties in the way of collecting and preserving such large creatures are great, and for this reason there is still uncertainty as to how many forms of the large anaconda there may be. It has been suggested that the forms in the Amazon, the Orinoco, and the Guiana region may even be separate species. A much smaller species of *Eunectes,* known as the Paraguay anaconda, occurs in the rivers of southern South America.

Like other boas, the anaconda bears living young; and a litter of thirty-four from a mother seventeen feet long has been reported. The newborn young measured about twenty-seven inches in length.

The anaconda is a creature of the rivers, but feeds primarily on the mammals and birds that frequent the riverbanks. In northern South America it is also known to overpower and eat the small caimans of that region; these are crocodilians, close relatives of the alligator.

Boas and pythons are remarkable for their pleasing colors and color patterns, and in many forms for striking iridescence of the skin, especially of the new skin when the old skin has recently been shed. This feature gives its name to the rainbow boa of South and Central America, *Epicrates cenchris* (Plate 71), a member of an otherwise West Indian genus. Another remarkably colored boa is the brilliant green emerald boa, *Boa canina* (Plate 70), which has white or yellow crossbands on the middle of the back, a coloration that is surely an effective aid to the snake's concealment as it lies in wait in the treetops for its prey of birds or lizards. In other ways than its coloration the emerald boa exhibits the stamp of adaptation to life in the treetops. Since it feeds largely on birds, it needs its long and strong front teeth to make certain of their capture at the first stroke. To give it secure anchorage in moving about high above ground it has a prehensile tail, much more specifically prehensile than that of the only partly arboreal boas. The emerald boa comes to rest on a branch by balancing the half-coils of one side against those of the other, with the branch firmly held by the tail beneath the coils.

ERICH SOCHUREK

Sand Boa (*Eryx johni*)

Boas such as *Boa hortulana* (Plate 75) and its relative, Cook's tree boa, *Boa cooki* (Plate 69), occasionally climb using a technique called the "concertina method." The snake wraps the front part of its body around a slender tree trunk, pulls up the rear of the body, which is then coiled around the pole, and reaches upward with the front end to get a new and higher grip.

Other boas have left life in the treetops or in the rivers to take up an almost completely subterranean life, living and moving about beneath the surface of the soil, especially in sandy regions. They fairly swim through the sand, feeding on the equally subterranean lizards. The sand boas of the genus *Eryx* range from North and East Africa to India and to Central Asia. They are found in Europe in extreme southeastern Russia. The body form in the sand boas is quite as characteristically adjusted to burrowing as is that of the tree snakes to arboreal life. The head is shortened and strengthened, and is not wider than the cylindrical body. The tail is noticeably short and is so blunt as to resemble the head.

The West Indies have a remarkable series of snakes of the boa family. One group of quite small boas (*Tropidophis*) ranges through the larger islands and the Bahamas and has a considerable variety of forms on Cuba and Hispaniola. These little boas have a relative in far-off Brazil and Paraguay, and others in Central America (*Ungaliophis*) and Ecuador (*Trachyboa*). The rainbow boa has a series of relatives in the West Indies, including at least one on each of the larger islands of the Greater Antilles. The Cuban species, *Epicrates angulifer,* is much the largest of these, sometimes reaching a length of fourteen feet.

Other than the sand boas of North Africa and southwestern Asia, and certain viperlike forms (*Enygrus*) in the South Sea islands, the only boas found in the Old World are the two distinct kinds in Madagascar and two in the Mascarene Islands. The species in Madagascar are close relatives of the American boa constrictor and emerald tree boa and are usually listed as belonging to the same genera, *Constrictor* and *Boa*. The remarkable geographic relations are not altered if the Madagascan species of *Constrictor* is given the generic name *Acrantophis* and the species of *Boa* is referred to as *Sanzinia*. How snakes of the opposite sides of the world can be thus related is a long story, a part of which has already been told in our discussion of iguanas, a family of lizards that likewise mainly inhabits the Americas but has representatives in Madagascar.

It is surprising to find boas in some of the South Sea islands. They belong to the New Guinean group *Enygrus,* and one of them, *Enygrus asper schmidti,* is named for the senior author. We remember especially how one of the specimens on which this description was based was captured, for it defended itself most actively and struck like a viper; in addition, its angular head and vertical pupils gave it a viperlike mien, and its stocky body made it look still more like a viper. The group has a remarkable distribution on the periphery of that of the pythons; the species of *Enygrus* range eastward from New Guinea to the Fiji Islands and Samoa. In our experience these snakes are terrestrial rather than arboreal. Almost nothing seems to be known about their habits.

There was a curious report of the presence of snakes on the remote Marquesas Islands, based on the occurrence of a word for "snake" in the Marquesan language. No land snake has ever been found in the Marquesas; and in compiling his Tahitian dictionary, Dr. Edmund Andrews subsequently discovered that the word for "snake" had been invented by those who translated the Bible into the language of the South Sea islanders.

The two species of small boas found in southwestern North America form a most distinctive element in the fauna of the United States, just as the sand boa does in that of Europe. One of these, the rosy boa, *Lichanura roseofusca,* has two races in California, one on the western side of the Coast Range, one to the east; the eastern one ranges into western Arizona, and both forms occur farther south in Mexico, but do not extend to the tropical zone. The rosy boa is a small creature, reaching a length of a little more than three feet, its head well set off from the neck, its tail short but tapering. Its normal habitat is the chaparral of the Coast Range foot-

hills, and it does not seem to go above the altitude of 4500 feet. These little boas are slow-moving snakes that never attempt to bite. They are most active in evening and at night, but they may be found abroad during the day. The food consists largely of small rodents and probably of nestling birds. Like all of the boas, the rosy boa bears living young. There is a record of six young, each about a foot long, born to a captive mother snake. A second species, *Lichanura trivirgata* (Plate 72), occurs in Lower California.

The other kind of boa in the United States is the rubber boa, *Charina*. It takes its name from its peculiar rubbery appearance. Its body form is that of the typical burrower, with head little wider than the body and with a very short tail in which the vertebrae are consolidated into a single bony mass. The rubber boa is not a desert creature, nor confined to sand like its European counterpart, the sand boa. It is found mainly in humid regions from central California through the Rocky Mountain region as far north as Montana. The rubber boa is a peculiarly inoffensive snake that never tries to defend itself by biting. Like the rosy boa, it is likely, if annoyed, to roll into a compact ball with its head inside and its stubby tail waving about as though it were the head. This snake does not grow much longer than two feet. The newborn young are six to nine inches long, and usually only three or four in number. The food seems to consist mainly of small rodents and lizards.

The most distinct of the snakes related to the boas are now placed in a separate subfamily, the Bolyerinae. The genus *Bolyeria* occurs, together with *Casarea,* which is related but entirely distinct, on Round Islet, near Mauritius. On the main island they were exterminated by the feral pigs that also destroyed the famous dodo and the rest of the remarkable Mauritian fauna.

Bolyeria and *Casarea* (they have no vernacular names) are distinguished from the other boid snakes by the presence of spines on the underside of the posterior vertebrae and by a most peculiar additional joint in the maxillary bone, which is divided into front and rear sections. This is a feature found in no other snakes whatever. A negative characteristic distinguishes *Bolyeria* and *Casarea* from all other types of the families Boidae and Pythonidae, namely, the total absence of vestiges of the hind limbs. Thus it is mainly the presence of the coronoid bone in the lower jaw that marks the subfamily Bolyerinae as primitive and as related to the boas.

The Python Family

(*Family Pythonidae*)

The pythons of the Old World are the counterparts of the boas in the New. They equal the boa family in their variety of habits and habitats, in the boldness of their color patterns, and in the iridescence of the scales of the new skin shortly after the old one has been shed. Like the boas, the pythons have a pair of well-developed external claws at the sides of the anal cleft. These mark the internal vestiges of the hind limbs. These two families of snakes are plainly the closest living relatives of the ancestral snake type. The pythons differ from the boas in laying eggs, which, in most forms at least, are incubated by the mother.

The python family includes seven quite distinct types, only a few of which are familiar in European or American zoological gardens. In number of species, the largest of the groups in which the individuals of several kinds grow to very large size is the genus *Python*. Its various forms are found from West Africa throughout the continent south of the Sahara, and then again (with a gap in southwestern Asia) from India to South China and throughout the East Indies to the easterly island of Timor. Instead of the true pythons, in New Guinea and Australia we find a variety of other python types, mostly much smaller forms. The larger pythons bring prices up to several hundred dollars in the live-animal trade.

Several kinds of true pythons, and especially the largest species, are familiar in zoological gardens and circuses. We may list them, roughly in geographic arrangement from west to east, as follows:

The ball python (*Python regius*)—West Africa
The African python (*Python sebae*)—Africa south of the Sahara
The Angolan python (*Python anchietae*)—Angola, West Africa
The Indian python (*Python molurus*)—India, Ceylon, the East Indies
The short-tailed python (*Python curtus*)—Malay Peninsula, Sumatra, Borneo
The reticulated python (*Python reticulatus*)—Southeastern Asia, the East Indies, the Philippines
The Timor python (*Python timorensis*)—Flores and Timor Islands in the East Indies

All of the pythons, so far as known, lay eggs and incubate them by pushing them together into a heap, around which the mother snake coils herself, with her head laid on top. There is a true incubation by the snake, for the temperature within the snake's coils is as much as 12 degrees Fahrenheit above that of the surrounding atmosphere. The temperature of a male snake, measured in the same cage as that in which the female was brooding her eggs, as reported by the Paris Zoo, was only a little above air temperature. The mother snake remains coiled around the mass of eggs until the young begin to hatch, though she may leave her station briefly to drink. The time from egg-laying to hatching may be as much as eighty days. The number of eggs may exceed a hundred.

The largest of the species of true pythons is the well-named reticulate python, *Python reticulatus,* the common name and the Latin name being for once in agreement.

The reticulate python is usually to be seen in any large zoological garden. The species is found from southern Burma through southeastern Asia and in all of the larger East Indian islands, and reaches the southern Philippine Islands. Its easternmost limits in the Lesser Sunda Islands (the chain extending from Java eastward to the Moluccas) are the islands of Timor and Ceram.

This gigantic snake is notably inoffensive when encountered in the wild. The largest one we have stumbled across in jungle measured eleven feet. Though it merely lay across the path, we decided not to risk the possibility of being bitten by its approximately one hundred long teeth, and so we shot it. On another occasion we climbed a small tree to capture a three-and-a-half-foot python, which made no attempt to bite, despite the fact that young snakes tend to defend themselves more vigorously than adults.

Most accounts of its attacks on man are pure inventions. There is, however, an authentic case of a Malay boy of fourteen being attacked and swallowed on the island of Salebabu (Talaud Islands). This species inhabits the densest forests but is extraordinarily prone to invade cities. Major Stanley Flower, a naturalist resident in the Far East for many years, wrote in 1899 that it was very numerous in the city and suburbs of Bangkok and that in almost every compound he knew of, one or more pythons had been found within the preceding few years. "Strange to say," he wrote, "it is not in quiet jungle forest that the python prefers to live, but in the busiest spots along the Menam, where steamers and junks are loading and unloading, steam-launches whistling, steam-saws buzzing, rice-mill chimneys filling the air with smoke, and hundreds of noisy coolies passing to and fro; here he selects some hole, or crevice in a building, timber stack, or bank to spend the day in, and at night makes an easy living, devouring fowls, ducks, cats, dogs, and, it is said, pigs. A python was found in 1897 in the King's palace."

This secondary habitat along the riverbanks of cities accounts for the frequent stories of accidental transport in the cargo holds of ships. A specimen reached London in this way, and was safely turned over to the Zoo. This species swims freely, even out to sea, and was one of the first reptiles to reach Krakatoa from Java or Sumatra after the great eruption of 1888 destroyed all life on the island. It is thus found even on smaller Malayan islands.

The newly hatched young measure from two to two and a half feet, and weigh four to six ounces. Growth is rapid during early life, averaging two feet or more per annum; after four or five years, the rate slows to about one foot. It is commonly stated that the reticulate python reaches a length of more than thirty feet, and without question this length is closely approached. The longest reasonably authentic measurement in the literature is twenty-eight feet, for a specimen that weighed 250 pounds.

A large *Python reticulatus* with its eighty-two eggs was collected in Sumatra by Philip Chancellor and Norton Stuart for the Chicago Natural History Museum. A celluloid model of the snake coiled around its conical pile of eggs is shown in the museum's Hall of Reptiles. The snake was reported by Mr. Stuart to be twenty-six feet long; but this measurement proves to have been based on the skin, and it is best to estimate the actual length in life and in the flesh as twenty-two feet. The eggs, which adhered in a firm mass, measured about four inches by three. The greatest age on record for the reticulate python is twenty-one years.

The Indian python, *Python molurus* (Plate 76), is perhaps the most familiar of the larger kinds of pythons, and is usually to be seen in zoological gardens and the menageries of circuses. Like the reticulate python and the African python, it has a bold pattern of broad dark brown markings on a light brown ground color, these markings edged with yellow. It seems possible to confirm a length of twenty feet for the Indian species, but most specimens are much smaller. A nineteen-foot specimen weighed 200 pounds, which indicates a much more stockily constructed body than does the twenty-eight feet and 250 pounds of the reticulate python.

The food of the Indian python consists of mammals, birds, and reptiles of suitable size, and even large frogs may be eaten. Large specimens take mammals of considerable size, but not, as is often reported, full-grown deer, horns and all. The great power with which the prey is constricted is shown by the finding of the remains of a leopard in the stomach of a python eighteen feet long; the leopard had been able to inflict only insignificant wounds on its attacker. Young specimens feed on mammals as large as a house rat. Older specimens commonly take fowls, pheasants, ducks, even peacocks; by far the most common food consists of mammals of all kinds and of any size up to that of pigs and the smaller deer.

The period of development of the eggs from mating to egg-laying is three to four months. The number of eggs varies greatly, from 8 to 107. Eggs from a twenty-foot specimen measure about four and a half by two and three-fourths inches. They doubtless increase in size after laying. The time required for hatching is about eight weeks.

The greatest age on record for the Indian python is seventeen years.

The Indian python falls into two quite distinct geographical races, a smaller, paler, typical subspecies, *Python molurus molurus* of India and Ceylon, and the larger and darker *Python molurus bivittatus* of Burma and the East Indies. The darker form, which may be referred to as the Burmese python, ranges through the area inhabited by the reticulate python as far eastward as Celebes; it does not occur in the Philippines.

The Indian python is as much a part of the stock in trade of the snake charmers of India and southeastern Asia as are the cobras. Its sluggish disposition and bright and handsome color pattern afford it an effective display, though it is scarcely much of a performer. The darker Burmese subspecies is said to be much more irritable and prone to bite.

The common African python is *Python sebae* (Plate 78), named for Albert Seba, whose great four-volume description of a personal collection, published in 1734, served Linnaeus and other early naturalists as a source book for their descriptions of animals. The African python is found over most of Africa south of the Sahara Desert, and though mainly a creature of open plains and savannas, it freely enters the forested areas. This species is often termed the "rock python," but we have applied this name to an Australian group of pythonid snakes, and the African species is not at all confined to rocky terrain.

It was the African python that appeared to have been known to the ancient Greeks, but only from travelers' tales. By Roman times both the Indian and African pythons were known, though they do not seem to have been common in the Roman Circus. A gigantic snake, brought from the upper Nile, is reported from the processions in honor of Dionysus in Alexandria in the time of the Ptolemies. There can be little question that Virgil had seen a python before writing his vivid description of the snake that coiled about Anchises' tomb: "Scarce had he said, when from the shrined base a slippery snake trailed huge seven coils, in each seven folds; and circling tranquilly the tomb, slid o'er the altar; dark blue streaks its back lit up, its scales a sheen of spotted gold as (when the sun shines opposite) the bow darts from the clouds a thousand varied hues." This describes very well the size and slow movements and brilliant iridescence of a python that has recently shed its skin.

The African python is one of the larger forms, less heavy-bodied than the Indian python, but perhaps with a greater maximum length, exceeding twenty feet. It feeds on large rodents, ground birds, small antelopes, and pigs. A wild-caught thirteen-foot specimen contained a sixty-pound water antelope. The African python feeds well in captivity and usually becomes quite docile. Like the other large pythons, if surprised in the wild, its first move is to escape, which it can do with astonishing speed. Frequently, especially if it has just killed an animal, the African python will strike with mouth wide open and inflict a terrible wound. There is at least one authentic record of a woman being attacked and killed while washing clothes along a river; the python in this case measured fourteen and a half feet.

Young individuals grow at about the same rate as the Indian and reticulate pythons. Large specimens vary considerably in weight, depending on the time since the previous meal. One fourteen-and-a-half-foot snake weighed 128 pounds, but another, fifteen and a half feet long, weighed only 60 pounds. The greatest age reported for the African python is fifteen years.

In some parts of Africa this species is eaten by the natives. Herbert Lang's field notes * describe the techniques of catching it. "They are often caught by means of traps set at their holes. The pythons hereabouts [in the Belgian Congo] have the habit of taking refuge in holes, often large excavations, in former termite hills, simply to sleep. During the rainy season the natives follow their tracks, and if they find the retreat a noose is at once set in front of the hole. The snake is usually caught behind the neck. The natives also spear them."

The smaller true pythons are interesting, but of course for things other than size. The ball python, *Python regius* (Plate 79), of West Africa (Nigeria to Liberia) has the peculiarity of coiling into a tight ball, with the head inside, when it is molested. The

* Published in the senior author's paper on the snakes of the Belgian Congo, *Bulletin of the American Museum of Natural History,* Vol. 49, p. 55, 1923.

ball is so uniformly round that it rolls easily on a flat surface. As this habit indicates, the species is especially inoffensive and agreeable to handle. Unfortunately from the point of view of zoo display, captive specimens become too tame to ball. The species reaches a length of about five feet.

The short-tailed python, *Python curtus,* found in the Malay Peninsula, Sumatra, and Borneo, has an exceptionally short tail, as its name implies, and a very thick body. Its brick-red color has given it a second common name, the blood python. Maximum size is about nine feet. Captive individuals feed well on rats. It is apparently confined to watercourses more than the other pythons and in that habitat should be able to catch rats, which are abundant along streams in the jungle. The only clutch known included just ten eggs. The Timor python seems to be the rarest species of true python. The largest known specimen is ten feet in length.

The Australian python, long known as *Python spilotes,* is now distinguished as a closely related but separate genus *Morelia,* with the species name *argus,* which refers to the bright yellow spots, one on each scale, though these are not especially eyelike. At intervals there are groups of larger yellow diamond-shaped markings on the bluish black ground color, and these give rise to the name "diamond snake" (Plate 77). This is a relatively abundant snake in Australia and New Guinea, and another color phase occurs in addition to the yellow-spotted one. In this variety the pattern of dark brown markings on a light brown ground color is much more like that of the true pythons; it receives still another name, "carpet snake" or "carpet python."

The diamond python or carpet python has a long and quite prehensile tail and climbs freely, but is equally at home on the plains and in the water. It feeds mainly on small mammals and on birds. It is sometimes kept in barns or granaries to control the numbers of rats and mice. The larger specimens feed on the abundant introduced rabbits of Australia. It reaches a length of about twelve feet. In captivity it is known to reach an age of only a little more than four years, though the other larger pythons have a life expectancy of at least twenty years.

Several species of a distinct group of the python family, the rock pythons (*Liasis*), are found in the Australasian region. One of these, the amethystine rock python, *Liasis amethystinus,* reaches a length of twenty feet, and thus compares in size with the larger true pythons. It lives in mangrove trees along the northeast coast of Australia and feeds mainly on opossum. The five species of rock pythons range from Timor and the southern Philippines through the Moluccas, New Guinea, and northern Austra-

Carpet Python
(*Morelia argus*)

lia, as far eastward as the Bismarck Archipelago. All have larger and more regular head shields than the true pythons, and they tend to a uniform olive color above, more yellowish below, without any of the bold patterns of the familiar pythons.

Another small group of pythonids (*Aspidites*) is strictly Australian; the native Australian name for them is "woma." These snakes reach a maximum length of eight feet. Like the rock pythons, the womas are characterized by large symmetrical head shields. But unlike other pythons, the womas eat snakes, including the deadly venomous black and tiger snakes.

One of the smallest of the pythons, *Nardoana,* is found in New Guinea and the Bismarck Archipelago. Its vertical pupil marks it as nocturnal, and it is familiar to the European residents of those remote islands because it enters houses and chicken coops in search of mice. It reaches a length of only about four feet. Its coloration, though variable, is usually brown with black spots or rings; the newly hatched young are bright orange with sharply defined black rings.

The two remaining types of pythonids to be discussed are of great interest because they are so completely adjusted to quite different modes of life, arboreal and subterranean, and especially because in these respects they quite startlingly parallel equally distinctive types of boas.

The first of these is the green tree python, *Chondropython viridis,* of New Guinea. Like the green tree boa, this form is mainly a pure leaf green, and it carries the color resemblance to the extent of having white spots along the back. The needs of life in the treetops are met by the greatly enlarged front teeth, for grasping fugitive food, and by the extreme prehensility of the tail. This beautiful snake is rare in museum collections and seldom reaches an American zoological garden.

The subterranean type is the burrowing python of West Africa, *Calabaria reinhardti,* which is distributed from Liberia throughout the Congo rain forest. Like the ball python, *Calabaria* rolls into a tight ball when handled. Its cylindrical body, very small and compact head with reduced head shields, smooth scales, narrow ventral plates, and very short tail, all mark this form as a burrower, and in fact as a burrower in loose soil and leaf mold rather than in sand.

The burrowing python grows to a length of little more than three feet. Herbert Lang, the great zoological explorer, writes * about the series collected by himself in the upper Congo region:

* Op. cit., p. 58.

The general color is dark brown with irregular lighter markings. These become yellowish pink on the sides, and the venter is brown, marked with pink. Tip of head and tail nearly black. Some specimens have a milky white band around the tail about 20 mm. from the tip, still further increasing its superficial resemblance to the head. Iris brown, pupil vertically elongate. One had swallowed a mouse, which was disgorged before injection. Specimens were taken crawling about in the forest among the moist dead leaves. This snake nearly always holds its head vertically downward, as if trying to burrow; the tip of the tail is often held away from the ground, and, in contrast to the immovable head, is slightly moved to and fro. When seriously annoyed it rolls itself into a compact ball, the head in the center, which it is very difficult to straighten out. It never tries to bite. The natives believe that it has two heads, and are much afraid of it.

Blind Burrowing Snakes

(*Families Typhlopidae and Leptotyphlopidae*)

Two families of snakes, the blind snakes (Typhlopidae) and the slender blind snakes (Leptotyphlopidae), are so much alike in outward appearance, and even in details of scale characters, that they seem at first sight to be evidently and even closely related. Study of their skeletons and skulls shows that they are not really related at all, and that there are not only ample reasons for distinguishing them as separate families, but even evidence that the typhlopid snakes, at least, may be blind burrowing lizards instead of blind burrowing snakes. The anatomy of these creatures is certainly one of the exciting subjects for study in the field of herpetology.

The characteristics that make these two families of snakes look so much alike are all associated with their burrowing habits. They are smooth and cylindrical, usually with blunt, rounded heads and always with very short tails, which are rounded like the heads. There are no broadened ventral plates, the scales of the belly being just like those of the sides and back, small and very smooth and shiny. The head shields are so much modified and reduced that it is difficult to compare them with those of ordinary snakes. The eyes in both types are small and are concealed beneath large scales, through which the vestiges of the eyes may be discerned. As to the internal anatomy, both families prove to have vestiges of the hind limbs and much shortened and consolidated skulls. When the limb vestiges are examined, however, it is found that in the typhlopids they are reduced to a single pair of cartilages, whereas in the leptotyphlopids the pelvis is quite well developed and the thigh bone is present and may even bear an external spur beside the vent.

The skulls of the two families of blind snakes differ even more. In the absence of functional limbs, burrowing snakes must dig with their heads, and this puts severe mechanical strain on the skull. The common or unmodified snake skull is a rather loose and flexible structure and therefore not especially adapted for digging. Like the skulls of all specialized burrowing snakes, those of the two families concerned here have undergone fusion of bones and strengthening of the skull architecture. But these processes have taken place in quite different ways in the typhlopids and leptotyphlopids.

One of the differences in the skulls involves the dentition. In the typhlopids the upper jaw is fixed and is set, in a fashion very unlike that of a snake, crosswise of the skull. There are no teeth in the lower jaw, except for the single tooth on each side in the primitive genus *Anomalepis*. The Leptotyphlopidae, on the other hand, have relatively large teeth in the lower jaw but no teeth in the upper jaw, which, however, has the usual orientation and is in line with the long axis of the skull.

The few typhlopids that do not belong to the genus *Typhlops* are all found in tropical America. They form an interesting series, with *Anomalepis, Helminthophis,* and *Liotyphlops* making up one group, in which the head shields are large and more or less like those of the more familiar snakes; *Typhlops,* with greatly modified but still large head shields, forms the second stage; *Typhlophis,* with only very small scales on the head, stands last. Even the rostral shield, which is enormously enlarged and covers the whole front of the head in the other genera, is only a very small scale in *Typhlophis.*

The genus *Typhlops* includes nearly two hundred species and is represented in Africa and Madagascar, in southeastern Asia and the East Indies, in the Australian Region, and in tropical America. A single small species is found in southwestern Asia, and this form is the only one that ranges as far to the north as Greece. In the Americas, the relatively few species are confined to the tropics, specifically from southern Mexico to Paraguay.

Relatively little is known about the habits of the typhlopid blind snakes. Both large and small forms are known to feed on ants and termites. Even the larger species are found in termite nests. The Asia Minor blind snake, *Typhlops vermicularis,* lives well in captivity on a diet of ants and ant pupae. In its mating, first described in 1955, the smaller male winds several tight coils around the posterior part of the body of the female, with his head extending away from hers.

The tail of most blind snakes has a short but sharp spine on the terminal scale. When held in the hand, the typhlopid makes regular exploring movements with the tail, and the spine pricks the skin, though not sufficiently to draw blood, even in the largest kinds. This behavior has given rise to the belief that these harmless creatures have a venomous sting in the tail. It is also possible that the spine is used as an aid in locomotion. By fixing the tip in the ground, the snake can either push its body forward or pull it backward.

One very small species of blind snake, *Typhlops braminus,* less than five inches long, is often referred to as the "flowerpot snake," for it has often been found in the earth in flowerpots when these have been set outdoors on the ground. Entering flowerpots is only an extension of the usual habitat of this snake among the roots of plants, where it probably feeds on minute insect larvae and other soil-dwelling animals rather than on termites. This habit of living in cultivated plants has led to the accidental transportation of the flowerpot snake all over the world. It has only recently entered Hawaii, but it has been in southern Mexico long enough to be well established. In the Old World it is found in Madagascar, in southeastern Asia and the East Indies, and in very many of the Pacific islands.

Though the largest of the typhlopid snakes reach a length of thirty inches, the majority never exceed a length of eight inches. Most of the species are believed to lay eggs, but a few species have been found to be live-bearing. Diard's blind snake, *Typhlops diardi,* of southeastern Asia, an eighteen-inch species, bears three to eight young at a time.

The other family of blind snakes, the Leptotyphlopidae, includes about forty species. Their distribution is surprisingly different from that of the Typhlopidae, for they are found abundantly in Africa, with somewhat fewer species in tropical America, and two species that range as far north as the southwestern United States. None occurs in the Oriental or Australian Regions.

These snakes do not attain anything like the large size of the typhlopids, the largest being probably *Leptotyphlops macrolepis* of Venezuela, which perhaps reaches a foot in length. Most species measure six or seven inches as adults, the smaller forms being little more than four inches long. The two species found in the United States are *Leptotyphlops dulcis,* the Texas blind snake, and *L. humilis,* the western blind snake. These creatures burrow in the soil and are most frequently exposed to view when one turns over a stone or log. It has been found, however, that they do come to the surface of the ground in early evening, disappearing again after dark, for specimens are rather frequently found "dead on road," where they have been killed by automobiles. They lay about four very elongate eggs, and their food consists of small insect larvae and especially ants and termites.

In the tropics, the ubiquitous termites supply food for these blind snakes, and their nests afford secure egg-laying places. *Leptotyphlops septemstriata*, described from a specimen whose origin was unknown in 1801, was rediscovered in British Guiana in 1920 in the course of studies by Dr. Alfred E. Emerson on termites and their nests.

More Burrowing Snakes

(*Families Anilidae, Uropeltidae, and Xenopeltidae*)

Three families of primitive nonpoisonous snakes remain to be discussed before we come to the principal more advanced families, both harmless and poisonous. All three of these remaining primitive families are burrowers and have cylindrical bodies, smooth scales, small heads, and short tails.

The first of these types of snakes, the family Anilidae, is represented by only three genera, and these by very few species. Vestiges of the hind limbs and of the pelvic girdle are present internally, with a small external claw at each side of the anal cleft. There are teeth on the premaxillary bone, and the coronoid bone is present in the lower jaw, both features being those of the more primitive snakes. The head shields and the bones of the skull are less reduced and less consolidated than in the Typhlopidae and Leptotyphlopidae. The eye is very small. The ventral plates are much reduced but are distinct, in sharp contrast with those of the typhlopids and leptotyphlopids.

Of the three genera, *Anilius,* the false coral snake, is South American, whereas *Cylindrophis* and *Anomochilus* are found in southeastern Asia. This curiously disjunct distribution is found in many other groups of animals. Its explanation is one of the main subjects of the science of the geographic distribution of animals.

The false coral snake, *Anilius scytale,* owes its name to its rings of brilliant red, set off by alternate black rings; there are no alternating yellow rings set between the black and the red, which is the usual character of the venomous coral snakes of the family Elapidae in South America. *Anilius scytale* reaches a length of about thirty inches. It is livebearing. Its food consists mainly of other snakes and small lizards.

The Oriental relative of *Anilius* is the pipe snake, *Cylindrophis,* of Ceylon, southeastern Asia (where it is a common inhabitant of the swampy rice fields), and the East Indies. In all seven species the body is cylindrical and the ventrals are only slightly widened. The color is black above, often with a reddish crossbar on the neck, and black and white beneath, with brilliant red on the underside of the tail. When this snake is molested, the tail is rolled up and raised, as it is in so many snakes (see *Diadophis,* Plate 90), while the head is concealed. The food of *Cylindrophis* appears to be other small snakes and eels, but it does not boggle at a meal even longer than itself. Two to ten living young are produced at a time, each about eight inches long.

The remaining genus, *Anomochilus,* is found only in Sumatra and Malaya. This dark brown, whitespotted snake is still more strictly a burrower, with a very small eye, and without the mental groove (a longitudinal furrow) on the chin, which is so much a characteristic of the normal snake type, and which is associated with wide-spreading jaws.

The second family of these primitive burrowers, the shield-tailed snakes, Uropeltidae, is entirely confined to the Indian Peninsula and Ceylon. These snakes are distinguished, as the common name suggests, by the presence of modified scales at the tip of the short tail. In its simplest form, the last scale on the tail is flattened from side to side. Following one evolutionary direction, the next stage, seen in the genus *Plectrurus,* consists of a flattened scale having two superimposed sharp points. In a different direction, the terminal scale develops two ridges, as in the genus *Melanophidium.* Then the entire end of the tail becomes flattened and sloping, many scales acquiring coarse keels, as is seen in the genus *Uropeltis.* The final result of this evolutionary trend is an enormous roughened shield that occupies half of the tail in the ten species of *Rhinophis.* How these snakes use their peculiar tails is still not clear. It has been suggested that the species of *Rhinophis* plug the entrances to their burrows with the large, coarse shields. Possibly the tails are used in locomotion in the way *Typhlops* employs its spiny tail.

This family is the first thus far mentioned in which there are no vestiges of the hind limbs. The skull is much consolidated, as is characteristic of burrowing snakes, with several of the bones of the typical pythonid or boid skull absent. There are no teeth on the premaxilla, which lies at the front tip of the skull, evidently in association with the very pointed snout. All of the species are small, few reaching a length of as much as a foot.

These snakes burrow expertly in soft earth, apparently by thrusting the snout forward and then turning it from side to side, for the body muscles are greatly strengthened in the neck region, which may be distinctly thicker than the rest of the body. Preserved specimens often exhibit a peculiar sidewise crook of the neck. All of the species bear living young, numbering three to eight at a birth. The food consists mainly of earthworms and insect larvae. These small snakes, none of which is as much as two feet long, are especially inoffensive. When caught, they do not try to escape, but twine around the fingers or around a stick, and may be carried in that position for a long time. One of the genera, *Melanophidium,* has a mental groove on the chin, and thus resembles the normal snakes more closely than do the remaining six genera, which have no such groove. The genera are distinguished by the degree of prolongation of the snout, the degree of concealment of the eye beneath the covering scale, and the varied development of the tail shield. Many are brightly colored, with red, orange, black, or yellow in various striking combinations. The black forms are brilliantly iridescent. Forty-three species of this family have been described.

The remaining family of burrowing snakes, still marked as a primitive type in having teeth on the premaxillary bone, is also Oriental and tropical American. The family Xenopeltidae is represented in southeastern Asia by the genus *Xenopeltis,* with the single species *Xenopeltis unicolor.* This is a brownish snake with highly iridescent scales. Its iridescence has given it the book names of "sunbeam snake" and "iridescent earth snake." It reaches a length of about forty inches. The body form is cylindrical, the head is little wider than the neck, and the tail is short. The only defensive behavior of this snake when it is molested is an extremely rapid vibration of the tail, a reaction extremely widespread among the colubrid snakes, foreshadowing the development of the rattle of the rattlesnakes.

Xenopeltis has a remarkable dentition, in which the teeth are numerous and those of the lower jaw are set on a loosely hinged dentary bone. One might expect to find so odd an arrangement of the jaws and teeth associated with peculiar food habits, but this does not seem to be the case. The food of *Xenopeltis* consists of other snakes, frogs, small rodents, and even birds, though it may be suspected that

birds are probably taken only when found dead on the ground.

Evidence has recently been brought forward for classifying the West Mexican snake *Loxocemus* with the Xenopeltidae. *Loxocemus,* on the basis of skull characters and vestigial hind limbs, has been thought to belong with the pythons, which are otherwise unknown in the Western Hemisphere. In having limb vestiges *Loxocemus* is much more primitive than *Xenopeltis,* and it thus may indicate relations of the family Xenopeltidae with the whole series of primitive snake types. It must be added that the reference of *Loxocemus* to relationship with *Xenopeltis* raises as many problems as it solves, so that this classification is no more than tentative. Almost nothing is known of the habits of *Loxocemus* except that it is a burrower, probably in leaf mold or loose soil.

The Oriental Water Snakes
(*Family Acrochordidae*)

The name "water snake" is so appropriate for almost any snake that swims freely and feeds on fishes that it has been applied to a great variety of distinct kinds of snakes. Next to the venomous sea snakes, the genera *Acrochordus* and *Chersydrus* are the snakes most completely adjusted to aquatic life. They are placed in the distant family Acrochordidae, which ranges from the coasts of India through the East Indies to the Solomon Islands.

We refer to these snakes specifically as water snakes because they are so exclusively aquatic, living in the estuaries of Oriental rivers and freely entering the sea. They are even more helpless on land than are the more primitive sea snakes. "Water snake" for these snakes is more than a book name, for it is their skins that make the snakeskin leather used for women's shoes; thus it is not only a trade name, but is known to the users of these snakeskins as well. These snakes have juxtaposed scales, i.e., scales with nonoverlapping edges, like the most highly modified of the sea snakes of the family Hydrophidae. It is this feature, plus the large size of *Acrochordus,* that makes their skins especially suitable for leather. The irregular mottled pattern on this leather contributes to its popularity.

These snakes are entirely without ventral plates, which would not be useful in swimming. They are live-bearing, so that they need not come ashore for egg-laying, and about thirty young are produced at a time. The scales of the head are astonishingly modified, with no enlarged plates except the labial scales along the lips. The nostrils are on the upper side of the snout, an adjustment to breathing without raising the head out of the water; and a tight, valvelike closure of mouth and nostrils is also an adjustment to life in the water. Certain features in the skull indicate their relationship with the xenodermine snakes of the family Colubridae, which do not appear to be aquatic.

The larger species, *Acrochordus javanicus*, reaches a length of six feet in the large and heavy-bodied females, which are much larger than the males. The Siamese refer to this snake as the "elephant's trunk snake," and the name "Java wart snake" may be found in books; but in ladies' shoes and handbags it is "water snake."

The other genus and species of the family, *Chersydrus granulatus*, is perhaps a little more specifically adjusted to swimming by the raised keel on the mid-ventral line. It ranges farther to both east and west than *Acrochordus*, reaching India and Ceylon, and the Solomon Islands in the western Pacific. It is only about half as large as *Acrochordus*.

The family Acrochordidae has usually been regarded as no more than a subfamily of the Colubridae; but it is so extremely specialized for aquatic life that it is best given the rank of a separate family.

The Colubrid Snakes

(*Family Colubridae*)

The great majority of the living types of snakes are harmless or only slightly venomous. They compose the family Colubridae, within which the specialized subfamilies are of unusual interest—one has developed into an extreme dependence on birds' eggs for food, one lives mainly on snails, one lives on brackish or marine tide flats and feeds on crabs; and there are two additional groups, little understood, that also stand outside of the main mass of colubrid snakes. The two main groups, from which the specialized types have been derived, are the Colubrinae, which do not have grooved teeth for venom conduction, and the Boiginae, in which some of the teeth at the rear of the upper jaw are enlarged and provided with a groove along the front edges. Within this great complex of about 250 genera, plus the 20 genera of the specialized subfamilies, all of the principal ecological types of snakes are to be found—little modified terrestrial forms; cylindrical burrowing snakes with blunt heads and short tails; arboreal forms with elongate heads, elongate bodies, and elongate tails; and aquatic types that are little modified in form but fully adjusted to life in the water in their behavior.

A small group of snakes in the East Indies and southeastern Asia is the Xenoderminae, most peculiar in having labial scales with upturned edges at the rear, expanded bony plates on the spines of the vertebrae in most of the genera, and other features. *Xenodermus javanicus* is unique among snakes in having scales like some lizards, that is, without overlapping edges and with rows of enlarged and keeled scales separating the small dorsal scales, which are gradually enlarged on the sides. This peculiar-looking snake lives in moist soft earth, and has been found most often in wet cultivated areas and on the dikes between rice fields in Java. In such situations it can easily secure its preferred diet of frogs.

Although all of the remaining genera in this subfamily are interesting in one way or another, not much is known about their modes of life. *Stoliczkaia*, named for one of the pioneer zoological explorers of Asia, is represented by one species in the mountains of Borneo and one in the hills of Assam, northeastern India. *Achalinus*, an earthworm feeder, is found from Japan to Indo-China. *Fimbrios* of Indo-China represents the extreme modification of the labials, which gives it a look of having a fringe of soft projections around the snout. The function of this apparatus is wholly unknown. Most remarkable of all, there are two genera in northwestern South America and Central America that have the vertebral spines expanded like those of *Xenodermus*, and these perhaps belong to this subfamily. These are *Xenopholis*, of Colombia, and *Nothopsis*, of southwestern Central America, Colombia, and Ecuador.

Another unusual subfamily of snakes, the Sibynophinae, has the unusual lower jaw of *Xenopeltis*, namely, a long dentary bone bearing very small teeth and loosely hinged to the rest of the jaw. It is not at all understood how this type of jaw apparatus works. The species in Madagascar, southeastern Asia, and Central America were all formerly regarded as belonging to the genus *Sibynophis*. The Central American forms are now distinguished under the generic name *Scaphiodontophis*, the name referring to the slightly widened tips of the maxillary teeth. In these forms the color pattern is very striking, consisting of alternating partial rings or crossbands of red, black, and yellow on the front part of the body, with a lengthwise striping of rows of black dots on the rear. Ivan T. Sanderson, who found a specimen in British Honduras, was greatly impressed by this anomalous coloration, and figured it (in his book, *Living Treasure*) as a "double snake." The Oriental species of *Sibynophis* are oviparous and lay two to four eggs at a time. The Madagascar species are distinguished as composing the genus *Parasibynophis*.

Next we come to the principal subdivisions of the family Colubridae, the Colubrinae or colubrines, which are so numerous that only a few types can be mentioned. In general, our discussion will be along ecological lines and will follow the colubrines into their various modes of life.

Terrestrial colubrid snakes represent the normal, familiar snake. They are in general alert and active and have well-developed eyes, broad ventral plates, and moderately long tails. They show the least amount of modification of body form, scale characters, and head shields. Characteristically the body tapers into a moderately slender tail, and also tapers slightly from the thickest part at mid-body forward to the neck. The head is distinctly wider than the neck but usually not much wider. Tapering of the body is accompanied by loss of scale rows as well as by reduction in their size, and the mode of dropping out scale rows may be characteristic in different genera. For example, in certain of the European whip snakes (genus *Coluber*), the first rows lost are low on the side, the next (proceeding along the body) are high on the side, then low, and so on. In several kinds of snakes the mid-dorsal row drops out. In most colubrids, however, the scale rows dropped are those below the middle of the side.

The head shields of terrestrial colubrids are extremely uniform; and, since their modifications are so much used in describing the specialized nonterrestrial types, we list them for future reference. Their names are among the first details a student of snakes must learn, from the *rostral,* at the tip of the snout and bordering the mouth, to the *parietals,* the largest of the head scales at the back of the head. Behind the rostral, on the top of the head, are a pair of *internasals,* and behind these a pair of *prefrontals.* Then come three scales across, a *supraocular* over each eye and an angular, more or less five-sided scale between them, the *frontal,* with its posterior angle wedged between the pair of *parietals.* On the sides of the head, a row of *labials* borders the mouth, and above them, beginning at the rostral again, the *nasal* (with the nostril), the *loreal,* one or more *preoculars* (just in front of the eye), the lidless eye, and then one or more *postoculars,* followed by the *temporals* wedged between the parietals and the last labials. The *mental* at the front of the chin, the two series of *lower labials,* and the two pairs of *chin shields* between them complete the list of head shields.

Typical of the central, unmodified terrestrial co-lubrids is the smooth snake of Europe, *Coronella austriaca.* As its common name implies, this species has smooth (instead of keeled) scales and thus exhibits one of the traits of many terrestrial colubrids. The smooth snake, which rarely exceeds two feet, is one of the three snakes found in the British Isles, where it is confined to a limited area in the south of England and where it is associated with the sand lizard, *Lacerta agilis,* on which it preys. It occasionally eats small mammals, and, like its American relatives, the king snakes, sometimes eats small snakes. The males have been observed to engage in fighting, with the fore part of the body raised, as is to be seen in vipers, rattlesnakes, and many other types. Mating takes place in both spring and fall, after the females are four years old and about twenty inches long. The young are born alive in late August or early September, the broods numbering from four to fifteen young. The smooth snake ranges far to the north on the continent, to latitude 63 degrees in the Scandinavian peninsula, and is found as far south as the Balkans and Greece. It is one of the commonest snakes of central Europe; it is replaced in Spain by a related form.

The principal directions of modification among the terrestrial colubrines are in manner of locomotion or activity and in diet. The smooth snake (*Coronella*) is rather slow-moving, and so are its close relatives in the United States, the king snakes (genus *Lampropeltis*). Like *Coronella,* the king snakes have smooth scales and typical, unaltered head shields. These moderate-sized snakes, which usually average between three and four feet as adults, are oviparous and lay about ten eggs in a clutch.

The king-snake genus *Lampropeltis* (Plates 111, 112) includes also the somewhat smaller milk snakes, *Lampropeltis doliata* (Plate 107), and some of the red-, yellow-, and black-ringed species are sometimes referred to as "false coral snakes." They have really as much claim to being called "coral snakes" as have the venomous species, and "harmless coral snakes" would be the better term. The milk snake of the northeastern United States has brown blotches on a grayish ground color when adult, though it is quite bright red, black, and yellow when very young. It is to this snake that the familiar fable of a snake sucking milk from cows in the pasture is most usually applied in the United States, though many other snakes are also so blamed, and the story is essentially world-wide. It is somewhat surprising to be able to trace the transition from the northern milk snake through more than one line of relationship to brightly ringed forms, in which the alternating yellow and black and red colors encircle the body.

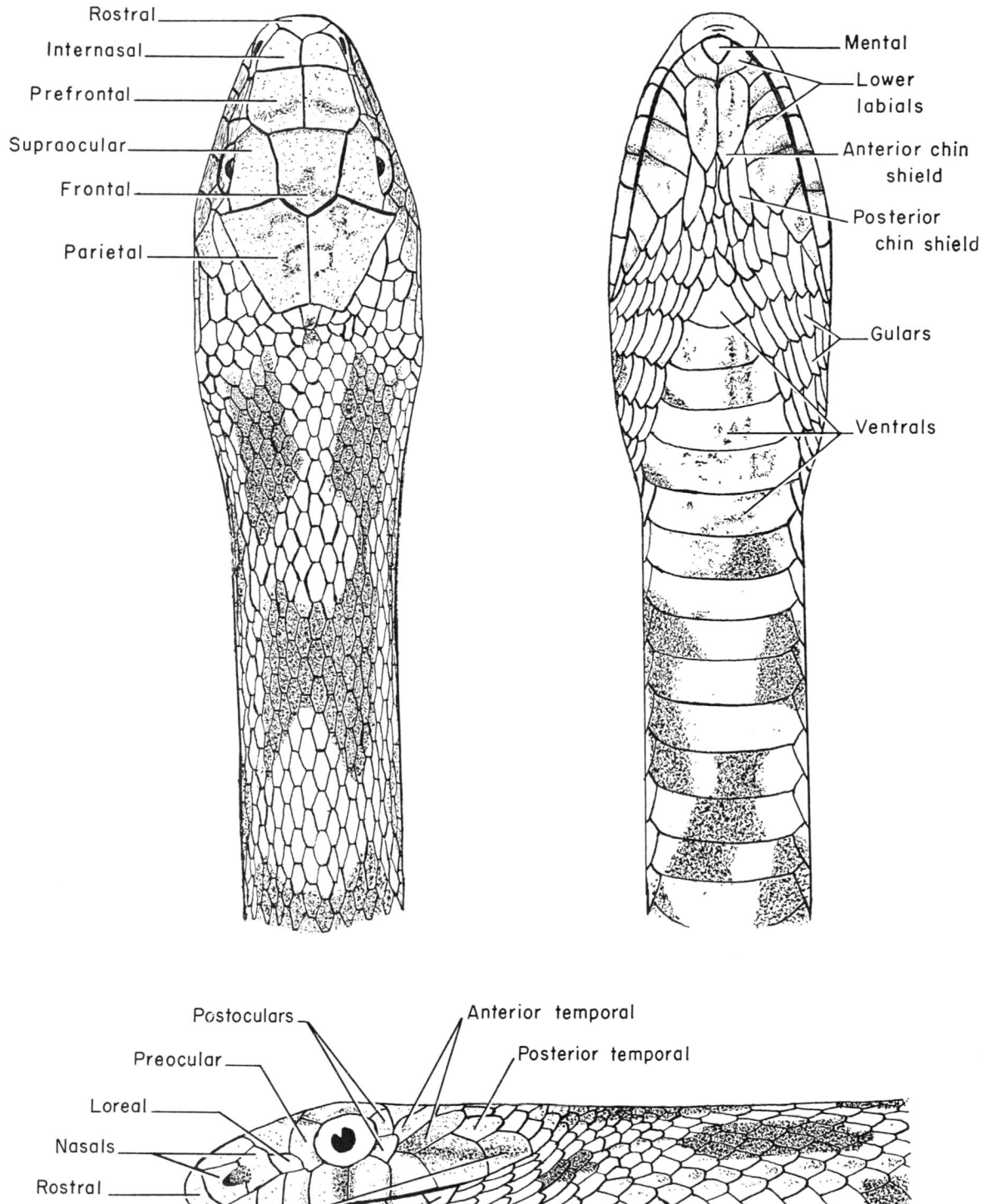

Rostral
Internasal
Prefrontal
Supraocular
Frontal
Parietal

Mental
Lower labials
Anterior chin shield
Posterior chin shield
Gulars
Ventrals

Postoculars
Preocular
Loreal
Nasals
Rostral
Upper labials
Lower labials
Anterior temporal
Posterior temporal

Nomenclature of head shields of a colubrid snake (a fox snake, *Elaphe vulpina*)

California King Snake (ringed phase) (*Lampropeltis getulus californiae*)

California King Snake (striped phase)

The common king snake, *Lampropeltis getulus,* is distributed across the North American continent from Virginia to California and is represented in different parts of its range by quite distinct color forms. Along the east coast, for instance, it has a chainlike pattern of yellow on black (*L. getulus getulus*). In the Mississippi Valley the color pattern consists of a whitish or yellowish speckling on the greenish ground color (*L. getulus holbrooki,* Plate 113), while in California (*L. getulus californiae*) two color patterns appear, one of yellow rings and one of yellow stripes on a black or brown ground color.

The king snakes also represent one of the types of dietary specialization, feeding to a large extent on other snakes, though also eating rodents and other mammals, lizards, and frogs. It is to these snake-eating habits that this genus owes its common name. Although the European smooth snake has a similar diet, it does not constrict its prey in the way king snakes do. Almost in one motion, a king snake strikes its prey, say a hog-nosed snake (*Heterodon*), and twines itself around the prey's body, killing by suffocation in exactly the same manner as the giant constricting boids and pythons.

King snakes attack and eat venomous snakes, but it is not true that they have any special preference for them. On the other hand, rattlesnakes show definite signs of adaptation to the attack of this age-old enemy. When confronted by a king snake, the rattler does not assume its usual defensive coil with head and neck held poised to strike. Nor does it rattle. Instead it keeps its head and neck, the parts the king snake attempts to grasp with its jaws, on the ground and raises a loop of the body high in the air and strikes clumsily at its enemy with this loop. Only as a last resort, and usually when the one-sided battle is all but over, will the rattler bite.

But it is a futile gesture, for the king snakes are immune to rattlesnake venom, and indeed to the venom of our other poisonous snakes. Immunity to snake venom is characteristic of all snake-eating snakes, which, incidentally, appear on all continents. The extent of this immunity and the fearlessness of the snake-eaters was brought home to us in Guatemala. We had seen no venomous snakes and had assumed that these were relatively scarce in that particular district. Then one day we saw and shot a six-and-a-half-foot musurana, *Clelia clelia,* a smooth-scaled, terrestrial colubrine snake. It was so swollen that we opened it to count the eggs that we thought must account for its girth. But instead of eggs it was crammed full with a six-foot fer-de-lance.

The most ubiquitous of the terrestrial snakes in North America are the lengthwise-striped garter snakes (*Thamnophis,* Plate 104); in the northern

Two-headed California King Snake

Green Water Snake (*Natrix cyclopion*)

Common North American Water Snake (*Natrix sipedon*)

United States and Canada these may be the only familiar snakes, for it is this group that extends farthest north of all snakes in the Western Hemisphere. Many of the garter snakes depend mainly on earthworms for food, but in general they take any animal of suitable size that they encounter. The more elongate garter snakes are distinguished as ribbon snakes, and tend to live along streams and to feed especially upon frogs. All of the garter snakes are live-bearing.

The garter snakes as a group lead away from the strictly terrestrial colubrines to aquatic genera. In fact, several species of western garter snakes are as aquatic as the related genus of true water snakes (genus *Natrix*). The water-snake genus is one of the most successful, most widespread, and most abundant groups of nonvenomous snakes in the world; there are no less than seventy-five species. Considering that nine species occur in eastern North America, it is surprising that only one *Natrix* is found in the Pacific region, and that one is confined to Lower California and the Pacific coast of Mexico. None occurs in Central or South America. Most of the species live in the Old World, the East Indies, and India, each of these areas having about

twenty-five. North Africa has only two, and both are also found in Europe, which has altogether three species. In general, the water snakes have strongly keeled scales and rather somber coloration, although some have brighter hues. This is especially true of the young of the common water snake of North America, *Natrix sipedon*, with its reddish brown bands, and of the triangular water snake of Malaya, *Natrix trianguligera*, with its bright red triangles.

Wherever they are found, the water snakes have the habit of defending themselves by means of a foul-smelling anal secretion. First, however, they attempt to escape from enemies by diving or swimming away. But, if cornered, the common European water snake, *Natrix natrix*, and the brown water snake of the United States, *Natrix taxispilota* (Plate 84), and many others inflate their bodies, flatten their heads, and strike viciously. The bites are just mildly painful and are dangerous only in the event of secondary infection. As a last resort, and usually after they have been grasped, they twine around the enemy and emit the musky anal secretion.

[continued on page 209]

87. Corn Snake (*Elaphe guttata*)

88. San Francisco
Garter Snake
(*Thamnophis sirtalis
tetrataenia*)

[NATHAN W. COHEN]

89. Striped Whipsnake (*Coluber taeniatus*)

[HAL H. HARRISON : NATIONAL AUDUBON]

90. Western Ring-
   necked Snake in
   defensive attitude
   (*Diadophis amabilis*)
   [NATHAN W. COHEN]

91. Striped Racer (*Coluber lateralis*)
[ROY PINNEY]

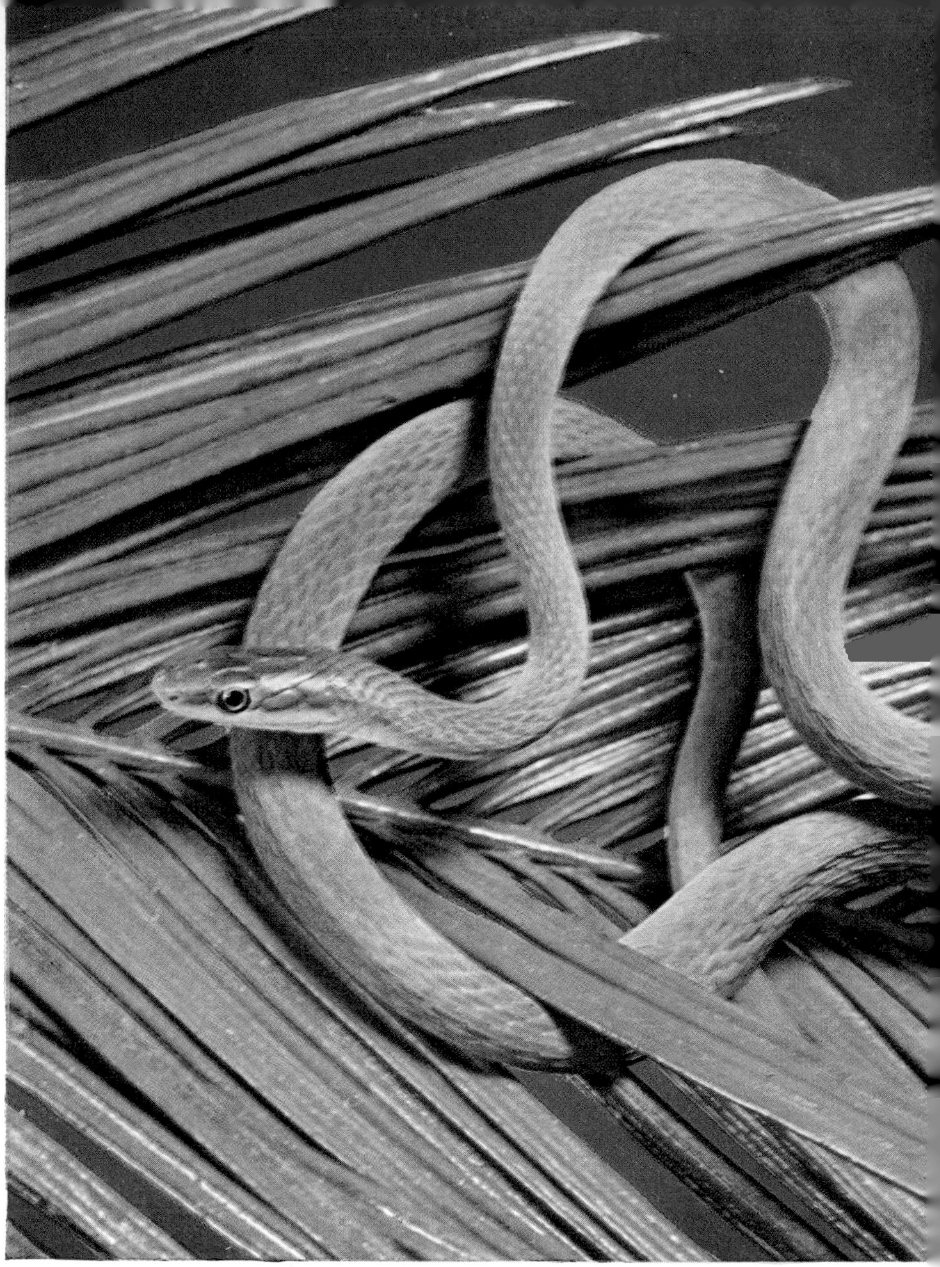

92. Sonoran Racer
(*Coluber bilineatus*)

[HAL H. HARRISON:
NATIONAL AUDUBON]

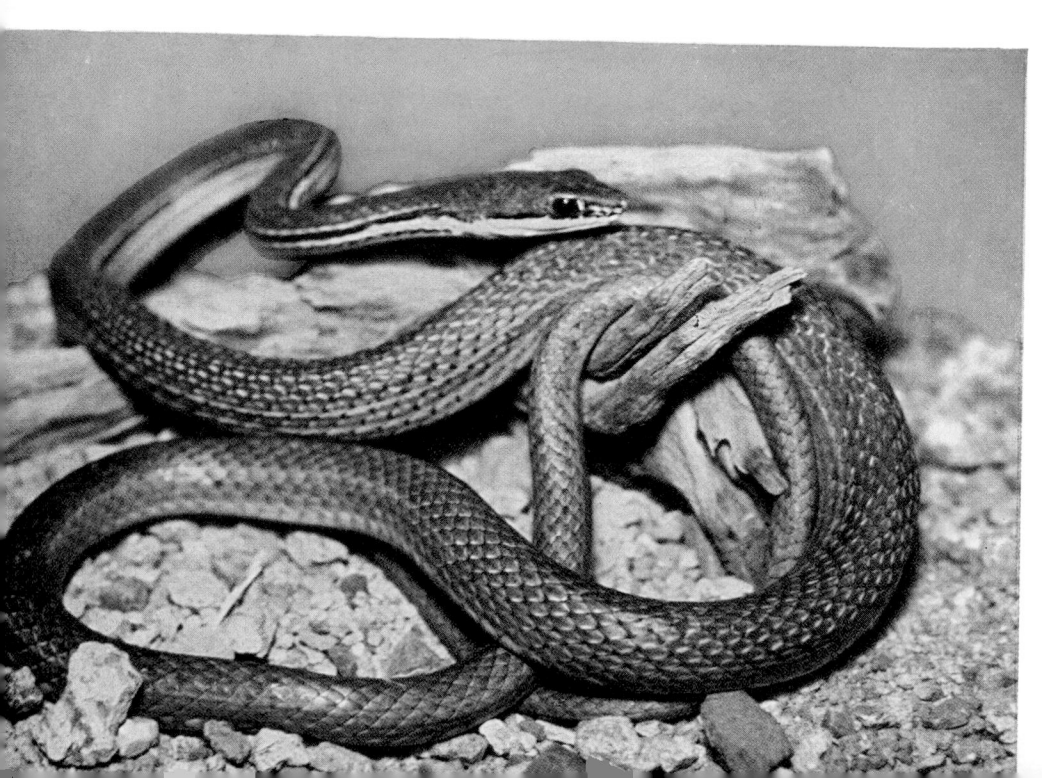

93. Rough Green Snake
(*Opheodrys aestivus*)
[ROY PINNEY]

94. Red Racer
(*Coluber
flagellum
piceus*)

[ROY PINNEY AND
PHILADELPHIA ZOO]

95. Smooth Green Snake (*Opheodrys vernalis*)

[ROY PINNEY]

96. Aesculapian Snake (*Elaphe longissima*)

[JOHN MARKHAM]

97. Yellow
Rat Snake
(*Elaphe
obsoleta
quadri-
vittata*)

[ROY PINNEY]

→

98. Yellow Rat Snake swallowing egg

[CHARLES HACKENBROCK AND STATEN ISLAND ZOO]

99. Yellow Rat Snake swallowing egg

[CHARLES HACKENBROCK AND STATEN ISLAND ZOO]

100. Black Rat Snakes hatching
(*Elaphe obsoleta obsoleta*)

[HAL H. HARRISON : NATIONAL AUDUBON]

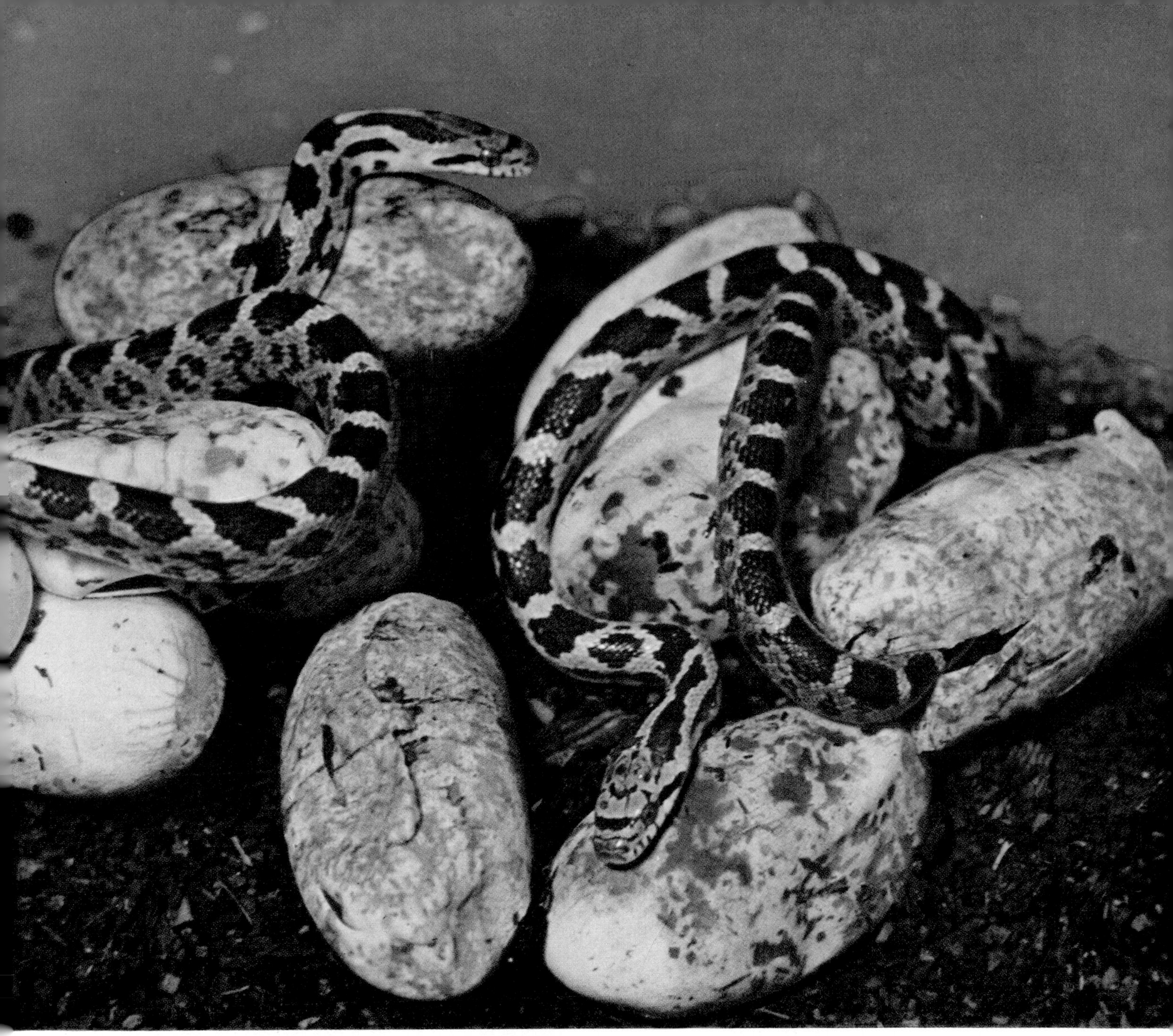

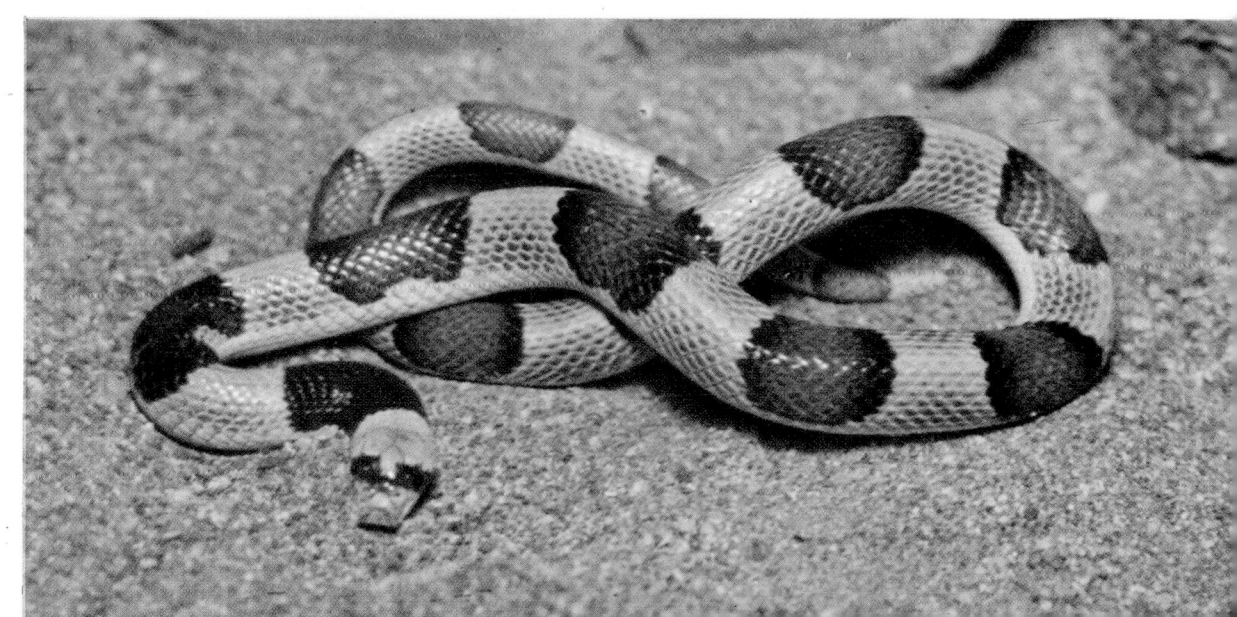

101. Pima Leaf-nosed Snake (*Phyllorhynchus browni browni*)

[HAL H. HARRISON: NATIONAL AUDUBON]

102. Indigo Snake (*Drymarchon corais*)

103. Indigo Snake
laying egg

104. Black-necked
Garter Snake
(*Thamnophis
cyrtopsis*)

105. Plains Garter
Snake
(*Thamnophis
radix*)

106. Long-nosed
Snake
(*Rhinocheilus
lecontei*)

[HAL H. HARRISON:
NATIONAL AUDUBON]

107. Milk Snake
(*Lampropeltis
doliata*)

[JOHN MARKHAM]

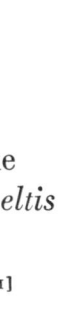

108. Sonora Gopher Snake
(*Pituophis catenifer affinis*)

[CY LA TOUR]

109. Bull Snake with eggs
(*Pituophis catenifer sayi*)

[H. A. THORNHILL: NATIONAL AUDUBON]

110. Glossy Snake (*Arizona elegans*)

[ROY PINNEY]

111. King Snake (*Lampropeltis getulus*)

[ROY PINNEY]

112. King Snake swallowing Water Snake

[CHARLES HACKENBROCK AND STATEN ISLAND ZOO]

113. Speckled
King Snake
(*Lampropeltis
getulus
holbrooki*)
[JOHN MARKHAM]

114. Arizona Mountain King Snake (*Lampropeltis pyromelana*)
[ROY PINNEY]

115. Bull Snake (*Pituophis catenifer*)

[continued from page 192]

Though similar in defensive behavior, the North American species differ radically from those of the Eastern Hemisphere in reproductive habits. All the American species are viviparous and give birth to from six to fifty-eight young at a time. The European and the Asiatic species, on the other hand, are oviparous, the common European water snake laying up to seventy-three eggs. Fish, frogs, crayfish, and even earthworms are the main items of diet, the proportions of each varying from species to species.

Not all of the terrestrial colubrines are as slow-moving as the king snakes and European smooth snake. In fact one of the main adaptations of this group is toward speed. A concomitant of speed in snakes is elongation. This is perhaps best exemplified by the racers and whip snakes of the genus *Coluber,* an oviparous group occurring across the United States and Mexico, in Europe, in North Africa, and in Asia. All are slender, long-tailed, large-eyed, aggressive snakes, feeding on rodents, birds, frogs, lizards, and snakes. They do not constrict their prey but pin it to the ground with part of the body while working their jaws to the prey's head preparatory to swallowing.

Speed in snakes is a difficult thing to assess. The racers and whip snakes are among the swiftest of snakes, and yet the fastest reliably measured speeds are slightly over three and one-half miles per hour, a mark that the average man, walking, can exceed without any difficulty—at least on a road. Yet a European whip snake, *Coluber gemonensis,* or the American midwestern blue racer, *Coluber constrictor flaviventris,* on a wooded, rocky slope can disappear with lightning speed, and the western coachwhip, *Coluber flagellum flavigularis,* of the United States is difficult to run down among the rocks and mesquite of its habitat. What makes these snakes even more troublesome to catch is that they can move through the branches of bushes as fast as they can on earth, and are as likely to disappear into a rodent burrow or into a stream as they are to remain on the ground.

Throughout the world the largest of the nonvenomous snakes, other than the boas and pythons, seem to be terrestrial forms. In North America the indigo snake, *Drymarchon corais couperi* (Plates 102, 103), reaches a length of nearly eight feet. Close relatives of this snake, but brown instead of indigo

Blue Racer (*Coluber constrictor flaviventris*)

FRITZ GORO : *Life* MAGAZINE

Blue Racers hatching

black, are found throughout tropical America. This length is reached also by the partly arboreal black rat snake, *Elaphe obsoleta*. In Asia the rat snakes of the genus *Ptyas* reach the same dimensions, and the related *Zaocys* of Burma and the Malayan region may have individuals twelve feet long. These are truly gigantic snakes. In Borneo we came face to face with a keeled rat snake, *Zaocys carinatus,* lying extended on a limb, and so close that we thought we might obtain a perfect specimen by shooting it in the neck with the fine shot of a .22 caliber pistol. We fired, and the forest seemed to explode as the gigantic snake thrashed about in a cloud of twigs and leaves before making off, evidently uninjured.

The close relations of the European, East Asian, and North American snake faunas, illustrated so well by the water snakes (*Natrix*), are also evident in the distribution of the numerous snakes of the genus *Elaphe*. These egg-laying snakes, which collectively are known as rat snakes or chicken snakes, form a transition between terrestrial and arboreal colubrines.

One of the structural modifications characteristic of arboreal snakes is a change in the shape of the ventral plates. It is possible to arrange living arboreal snakes into a series, including first the flat type of ventral plate; next a bent but curved, U-shaped ventral plate; then a ventral with a weak keel at the bend; and finally a ventral with a sharp keel and notch. The chicken snakes are in the stage having weakly keeled ventral plates. At least one function of the keel is to provide a sharp corner or

[210]

projection that the snake can press against bark and thus obtain better purchase. This is such an effective mechanical device that the southeastern North American corn snake, *Elaphe guttata* (Plate 87), and our Eastern black rat snake, *Elaphe obsoleta* (Plate 100), can climb up the trunk of a large tree by wedging their bodies between the ridges of bark and hitching upward at least partly by means of the keeled ventrals. Of course an important ingredient that is not visible is something we might call the "arboreal psychology."

Both of the collective names "rat snake" and "chicken snake" refer to favorite food items, although the only chickens they can swallow are very young ones. Nestling birds and eggs are obtained in trees, and rodents and other small mammals in their burrows. The mammalian and avian prey are killed by constriction, and these food habits apply equally to American and Eurasian species. The fact that a corn snake—whose warm browns, reds, and yellows make it one of the most beautiful snakes— that was kept in our laboratory for sixteen years ate thirteen mice at one feeding gives some idea of the potential economic importance of this genus.

A European representative of this genus is the Aesculapian snake, *Elaphe longissima* (Plate 96). Widespread in southeastern Europe and Asia Minor, this species is at any rate the snake most plausibly identified with the snake symbol of Aesculapius, the Greek god of medicine. It is a curious commentary on the somewhat disgracefully widespread fear of harmless snakes in America that in Europe a large snake should for so long have been the symbol of health, protected from molestation, and widely introduced by the Romans during their occupation of western Europe. They generally introduced it at the baths, which were often replaced by modern health resorts, and this accounts for the curiously isolated populations of the Aesculapian snake in Switzerland and Germany.

In addition to the keeling of the ventral plates, arboreal colubrines show evolutionary trends toward green coloration and elongate bodies, as illustrated by the chicken snakes of southeastern Asia, *Elaphe prasina.* In the United States only the rough green snake, *Opheodrys aestivus,* has these characteristics. This two- to three-foot snake lives in shrubs and low trees and is almost invisible unless it is moving. The primitive genus *Uromacer* of the West Indies has two green species, one green all over and one green with a white-and-yellow line along the sides, a pattern that appears repeatedly among tree-dwelling forms. Green tree snakes are especially characteristic of the tropical forest regions, and

Corn Snake
(*Elaphe guttata*)

Africa has a genus, the African green snakes (*Chlorophis*), in which an all-green coloration is combined with a slender, elongate form and keeled ventral and caudal plates.

After examining elongate tree snakes that have strikingly lengthened heads, it is disconcerting to find that this form is not repeated in the evolution of all tree snakes. Another whole series of tree-dwellers, including some with the most elongated bodies of all snakes, have disproportionately wide and short heads, which are made the more conspicuous when the neck is extremely slender just back of the head. The colubrine genera *Tropidodipsas* and *Sibon* are examples of this form, which appears also in the rear-fanged boigines, notably in the snail- and slug-eaters of the genus *Dipsas* in South America, and reaches an extreme in *Imantodes* of Central and South America. In the boigine

Imantodes, whose elongate body and tail have a remarkably high number of ventral and caudal plates (four hundred) the several species form an evolutionary series of progressive modification. The less modified forms have the ordinary dorsal scales of most colubrid snakes, whereas in the species *cenchoa* the scales of the mid-line of the back are wider than long. When the snake is observed in action, climbing about in a bush, the long and slender neck is extended outward to bridge the space between one branch and the next; the slender body is strongly compressed by muscular action. This, of course, is the application of the mechanical relations in a vertical beam; the direct mechanical relation is made still more conspicuous when the flattening of the body is so extreme that the wide ventral and dorsal scales produce a flange at top and bottom wider than the flat body, thus simulating

Black Rat Snake (*Elaphe obsoleta*)

MASLOWSKI AND GOODPASTER : NATIONAL AUDUBON

an I beam. The same body form and enlarged mid-dorsal scales, and the same behavior, are equally evident in some of the species of *Dipsas*.

The colubrines have also taken to burrowing, and have done so in two quite distinct ways. In the first, the head is used as an auger and twisted in order to loosen the soil. The rostral shield, the scale at the tip of the snout, is the scale that cuts into the soil, and it is usually altered from the normal rounded colubrine shape. Few of the burrowing colubrines of this sort lead truly subterranean lives; they dig mainly in search for food, and have evolved few of the extreme modifications of the subterranean colubrines.

The hog-nosed snakes (genus *Heterodon;* Plates 85, 86) of eastern North America, so called from the sharply keeled and upturned rostral scale, are examples of this type of burrowing colubrine. These snakes have short and thick bodies, feed mainly upon toads, and are egg-layers. There are three species, the common and very widespread northern and eastern one, a southeastern one with an even more sharply upturned rostral scale, and the species of the western plains in which the development of the rostral for digging reaches an extreme. All three species have unusual reactions when approached by a larger animal. They face an aggressor boldly, inflate the front half of the body to twice its normal diameter, and spread the head and neck. The flattened neck recalls that of the cobra, and the bright colors of the skin between the scales display a conspicuous checkered pattern. This is accompanied by vigorous striking and loud hissing and blowing of the air from the lungs. The common names "spreading adder," "blow snake," and "puff adder" attest to the impression made by this behavior. If the snake is then actually molested, all the aggressive actions are abandoned, it goes through an apparent convulsion, and plays dead, lying perfectly limp on the ground, belly up. So fixed is the pattern of playing dead with the belly up that if the snake is righted, it will instantly turn wrong side up again, as if to demonstrate that it is indeed dead. If not further molested, the hog-nose presently raises its head and surveys the situation; and if all is quiet, it turns right side up and crawls away. The South American harmless snake *Lystrophis,* perhaps quite directly related to *Heterodon,* has the same habits of aggressive behavior combined with playing dead.

Another North American example of the augur-like burrowing colubrid is the genus *Pituophis* (Plates 108, 109, 115), the bull snakes. These oviparous snakes, which have the rostral shield enlarged, elongated, and curved upward onto the top of the head, are able to produce an exceptionally

Hognosed Snake moulting (*Heterodon platyrhinos*)

Blunt-headed Tree Snake (*Imantodes cenchoa*)

loud hiss by expelling air past a small appendage of the epiglottis. All the species are constrictors and often go into rodent burrows in search of the inhabitants. A five-foot bull snake killed in Utah contained thirty-five small mice. One we captured in Nebraska contained a clutch of four eggs of a ground-nesting sparrow, four newly hatched young birds, four half-grown birds, and four fledglings almost ready to leave the nest. The predation of snakes on the populations of ground birds, which is matched by their feeding on wild mice and other rodents, is evidently an effective part of the over-all "balance of nature."

In colubrid snakes the dividing line between secretive habits of life under logs or in leaf mold and true subterranean existence is not sharp. The second principal burrowing type, characterized by fusion or loss of certain head scales, has evolved a number of times in this subfamily of snakes, and prob-

ably many of these cases have passed through a "secretive" stage before becoming more or less completely subterranean. The rough earth snake, *Haldea striatula,* a ten-inch, viviparous species ranging from Virginia to Texas, is an American example of the secretive stage. It feeds on insects, earthworms, and other invertebrates, which it finds under bark and logs. Another, the worm snake, *Carphophis amoena,* of the eastern half of the United States, a nine-inch oviparous species, is usually found under stones, logs, or bark, and feeds mainly on earthworms. This is a common mode of life among the colubrids, and examples are found in all parts of the world. The egg-laying Oriental worm snakes (*Trachischium*) of northeastern India, like our worm snakes, are gentle, inoffensive creatures living under stones and rocks, and again feeding on earthworms.

The truly subterranean colubrines have had to solve a number of mechanical problems in the course of their several evolutionary histories. Originally the colubrid snake had a very flexible skull, probably the basic modification of the snakes as a whole and representing an adaptation to swallowing relatively large prey. This flexible skull covered with a rather large number of scales is a very poor device for boring into soil, and strengthening it has been the most important evolutionary problem of burrowing colubrids. Strength and rigidity can be achieved by consolidation of the bones of the skull and also by reduction in the number of head shields, since there is a tendency toward bending at the juncture between scales.

A serpentine body has a tremendous amount of surface area, and the friction it causes underground adds to the work load of the snake. This problem has been partly met in the subterranean snakes by the development of extremely smooth scales and cylindrical bodies. The cylindrical body has developed in association with a low number of scale rows. Whereas most terrestrial colubrines have anywhere from nineteen to thirty-five scale rows and a change in number along the body, the secretive and subterranean forms usually have less than nineteen rows, and often as few as thirteen, without any variation in number from neck to end of body.

Whiplike motions of the tail, though functional in locomotion on the surface, are practically useless underground, and natural selection has tended to favor tail reduction in burrowers, especially since this would also reduce surface area and friction. Subterranean snakes have gone a step farther and developed short, thick, and pointed tails that probably help them through the ground.

These modifications of head and body have not

developed in the augerlike burrowers, such as the hog-nosed snakes (*Heterodon*) and long-nosed snake (*Rhinocheilus*) of southwestern United States. Mud does not offer the same resistance as ordinary dry soil, and burrowing snakes of that habitat, for instance the mud snake, *Farancia abacura,* of southeastern United States, are not as modified as other subterranean forms. However, the mud snake, a four-foot oviparous species, has smooth, shiny scales, a short, pointed tail, and fused internasal shields on the head, and has lost the preocular scale. But the mud snake's skull is not appreciably changed from the typical flexible colubrid construction. Often some head scales are lost or fused in the secretive colubrines, which usually burrow to a certain extent. The rough earth snake, *Haldea striatula,* for example, has fused internasal shields and no preocular.

Complete specialization for subterranean life is found in colubrines from many parts of the world. The short-tailed snake, *Stilosoma extenuatum,* of Florida, a smooth-scaled, short-tailed, cylindrical snake, has often been turned up by plows. Its internasals are normally fused with the prefrontal scales on top of the snout, and the loreal scale on the side of the head is absent. In the numerous species of the subterranean South American spindle snakes (genus *Atractus*), the skull has lost much of its usual flexibility, and some of the head scales have been lost. The reed snakes (genus *Calamaria*) of the Orient have lost at least eight of the normal head scales, and the skull has become even more compact and rigid than in *Atractus.*

There are many transitions between the complete absence of posion and poison-conducting apparatus in the snakes thus far considered, and the primitive types of venom and venom-conducting teeth of the rear-fanged snakes, the Opisthoglypha, which are gathered together, somewhat artificially perhaps, in the subfamily Boiginae. In them, one to three of the teeth at the rear of the upper jaw are enlarged and provided with deep grooves (on the front edges) for the conduction of a weak venom from the modified salivary glands into the struggling prey.

Only one of the rear-fanged snakes, the notorious boomslang, *Dispholidus typus* (Plate 121), of Africa, is potentially dangerous to man. This green or brown five-foot bush-dweller is an inhabitant of the open country and not of the forest regions. Ordinarily it is a mild-tempered snake and takes considerable abuse before puffing out its neck in a threatening posture. It should be treated with respect, however, for several human fatalities have been attributed to the boomslang's bite.

The subfamily takes its name from the genus

M. W. F. TWEEDIE

Paradise Tree Snake (*Chrysopelea paradisi*)

Boiga, of which the brilliant black-and-yellow mangrove snake, *Boiga dendrophila* (Plate 120), is typical. The mangrove snake has a broad and short head, a rather widespread type among the rear-fanged snakes, even when they are slender-bodied and arboreal. On the other hand, tree-dwelling snakes of the boigine type have repeatedly evolved the extreme of elongation of head exemplified especially in the long-nosed tree snake, *Dryophis*

[215]

nasuta, of Malaya and the East Indies and the African vine snake, *Thelotornis kirtlandi.* In snakes with greatly elongated heads the pupil of the large eye may be horizontal, as it is in the long-nosed tree snake, and thus in line with the form and markings of the head. Snakes with extremely elongate heads are well represented in the American tropics by the genus *Oxybelis,* in which the several alternative colorations of tree snakes are exhibited in the very distinct species—green with a white lateral stripe in *fulgidus,* brown (i.e., bark-colored and vinelike) in *aeneus.*

The African sand snakes, *Psammophis,* are typical terrestrial forms, modified for swift locomotion by their elongate bodies and tails. They have a group of enlarged teeth at the middle of the upper jaw, in addition to the greatly enlarged poison fangs at the rear. There are a number of species of sand snakes in the various parts of Africa. One, in Angola, has only eleven rows of dorsal scales on its slender body.

Discussion of this subfamily would be incomplete without mention of that most remarkable object, the flying snake. Members of a group of slender tree snakes (*Chrysopelea;* Plate 124) common in the forests of Malaya and the East Indies are reputed to launch themselves from high branches and fly, or more properly glide, for some distance to a lower branch or shrub. The more reliable of these reports note that the belly in gliding is concave, the ventrals being pulled inward between their sharp keels. But a few of the published accounts are somewhat embellished with fanciful descriptions of the snake dipping, turning, and slowly settling down on a bush in the manner of a bird. We carried out some experiments in Borneo with a barred tree snake, *Chrysopelea pelias,* in order to test its flying abilities. Although our snake refused to cooperate to the extent of gliding, it very clearly launched itself into space by a sudden straightening of the looped tail.

A small group of rear-fanged snakes has taken to aquatic habits, usually in fresh-water habitats, but its members are almost equally at home in the brackish water of the tropical coasts of Asia and eastward to northern Australia. All of these snakes, which are grouped together as the subfamily Homalopsinae, within the Colubridae, bring forth living young and are adjusted to life in the water in having the nostrils on the upper side of the snout, in the valvular closure of the mouth, and in other respects. It is noteworthy that they are able to swallow their food (usually fishes) under water. The most diversified genus is *Enhydris,* with about sixteen species. The largest of these, *Enhydris bocourti,* reaches a length of more than three feet. The most remarkable of these snakes in appearance is *Herpeton,* of the coasts of Siam and Indo-China, which has a pair of scaly appendages on the snout. The snakes of the genera *Fordonia* and *Cerberus* live in great numbers on the muddy tidal flats of the north coast of Java, taking refuge in crab holes when approached. *Fordonia* lives mainly on crabs, and experiments have shown that crabs are strongly affected by its venom, whereas it has little or no effect on either frogs or mammals. The other snake, *Cerberus,* appears to be a fish-eater. Its venom appears to be effective not only on fishes but also on crustaceans. Crab-eating is somewhat remarkable among snakes, but it may be remembered that certain harmless American water snakes eat crayfishes. The largest and most thick-bodied of the homalopsine snakes is *Homalopsis buccata.* The species is widely distributed along the coasts of southeastern Asia and of the East Indian islands, living much on land but never far from water and not much above tide limits.

Snail-eating is widespread among the smaller harmless sakes, the little red-bellied snake, *Storeria occipitomaculata,* of North America being known to feed freely on slugs (the snails without shells). Feeding on snails *with* shells is less common, but a whole group of snakes has become adjusted to this diet, or to a combination of slugs and other snails. These snakes are exemplified by the genus *Dipsas* in tropical America and *Pareas* and *Haplopeltura* in southeastern Asia and the East Indies, the three forming the subfamily Dipsadinae. They have strong modifications of the jaw apparatus, and are remarkably different from all normal terrestrial snakes in the absence of the mental groove on the chin. The plates on the chin are set crosswise, and interlock to make it relatively rigid. The lower jaws of *Dipsas,* it now appears, can be inserted into a snail's shell and twisted sharply outward to hook the elongate front teeth into the snail's body. It is then easy to pull the snail's body out of the shell and eat it, with the net saving that the digestive system of the snake is not burdened with the shell. The American snakes of the genus *Sibon* have a mental groove and unmodified jaw apparatus, but feed on snails and are otherwise very similar to *Dipsas. Sibon* forms a neat link between the subfamily Dipsadinae and the Colubrinae.

The dipsadine snakes are not the only ones with a special arrangement for rejecting unwanted food containers. An even more elaborate device is that of the subfamily Dasypeltinae, the true egg-eaters. Many of the larger snakes eat eggs, as has been noted above, but such snakes as the chicken snake and bull snake, which only occasionally take eggs,

Egg-eating Snake (*Dasypeltis scaber*)

either digest shell and all or by contorting the body manage to break the egg after it is swallowed. The snakes of the genus *Dasypeltis,* the African egg-eating snakes, have carried egg-eating to an extreme of specialization. The mouth and neck are astonishingly distensible, and a surprisingly large egg may be swallowed as far as the neck. The amount of skin on the neck is so much increased that when it is distended by an egg the small scales stand far apart on the stretched skin. The ventral projections on the snake's neck vertebrae are elongate and sharp, and their tips pierce the dorsal wall of the gullet, so that the row of six or eight points forms a veritable saw, against which swallowing motions are brought into play and a cut made in the eggshell. This at once collapses from the pressure of the distended neck skin, and the contents of the egg are forced into the stomach. The pellet of eggshell and egg membranes is then rejected. *Dasypeltis* has the teeth of both jaws much reduced. The Indian egg-eater, *Elachistodon westermanni,* seems to be much less modified than *Dasypeltis,* but it bears the same efficient "egg saw" in its neck. In *Elachistodon,* also with the dentition much reduced, there are grooved teeth at the rear of the upper jaw; it seems reasonable to conclude that the grooved teeth might have been lost in the African form, and that the remarkable egg saw of both types does indicate that they have a common ancestor. *Dasypeltis* measures from two feet to thirty inches in length. *Elachistodon* reaches about the same over-all length.

Considering now the geographic distribution of the Colubridae, the relationship that holds true for all living reptile groups applies to this family of snakes, namely, the greater diversity of types is in the tropics. In fact, only one subfamily, the Colubrinae, has really made a successful invasion of the Temperate Zone. The rear-fanged Boiginae, the only other sizable subfamily, is predominantly tropical.

Some conception of the differences in the distributions of these two subfamilies can be obtained from a comparison of the faunas of several large areas. Approximately thirty-six genera of colubrids occur in the United States; only six of them are rear-fanged snakes, and just one of the six, the black-headed snakes (genus *Tantilla*), ranges north of the extreme southwestern states. By contrast, Colombia in tropical South America has forty-eight colubrid genera, of which fully one-third are rear-fanged. Similarly, the small area of the tropical Malay Peninsula has nineteen boigine colubrids, whereas the much larger but temperate area of China has just six. And the Chinese species are found only in southern China. Three of Europe's

seventeen colubrids are rear-fanged, and again all are confined to the southern edge of the continent. As indicated on previous pages, the other minor subfamilies of colubrids are essentially limited to the tropics.

A quick tour of the world to survey the colubrid snake fauna should begin in northwestern Europe mainly because so few species are involved: England and the Scandinavian countries, for example, have only two species. Two more appear in Germany and Poland, although not the same two in each case. Southward, more species occur, but even so Spain, Italy, and the Balkan Peninsula each have only nine colubrid snakes. All told, Europe has just seventeen species of colubrids. Probably no other area of comparable size and climate (except Australia) has so few colubrids. It is not merely that there is a small number of species in European colubrid fauna, but that, since all seven genera represented are widely distributed outside of Europe, there actually is no distinctive European fauna.

At least part of the reason for this was the Ice Age. The great glaciers that then covered northern Europe prevented the survival of snakes there and must have made southern Europe a far less favorable habitat. Certainly the ice sheets are the explanation for the absence of snakes in Ireland. (We have no quarrel with Saint Patrick, who is usually given the credit, but the fact of the matter is that the Ice Age preceded him by thousands of years.) With the retreat of the glaciers, the snakes began to move northward. For a while, England was connected with the mainland, and so was invaded by the few species of reptiles that were tolerant of cool climates. It is unlikely that Ireland had the same connections. As a consequence, that island was never recolonized by the snakes.

Another explanation for the small number of European colubrids may be extermination by man. Just how important a role man has played we do not know. At least one species, the Aesculapian snake, *Elaphe longissima* (Plate 96), occurred in Denmark in historic times but is now extinct there. Presumably man's activities have accounted for its disappearance. Other snakes, however, have done quite well in densely populated rural Europe.

Among the successful species are the only two colubrids in England and Scandinavia, the smooth snake, *Coronella austriaca,* and the common European water snake, *Natrix natrix* (Plate 81). The distribution and habits of the smooth snake have been dealt with earlier. The common water snake occurs throughout Europe and has many local names. Known in England as the "grass snake" and in Germany as the *"Ringelnatter"* because of the ringlike yellowish mark behind the head, it has the somber coloration and keeled body scales typical of the genus all over the world. It shows a great deal of color variation, the typical coloration in England, France, and western Germany being olive-green with several rows of black spots on the back and a row of vertical black bars low on the side. Like all its relatives, the common water snake lives along bodies of water and is an excellent swimmer. Its food consists chiefly of frogs and secondarily of newts, fish, tadpoles, and lizards. In order to catch fish and tadpoles, it must, of course, be a good diver. Individual snakes have been observed to remain submerged for twenty minutes while they poked about under rocks and sunken debris for food. The water snake is active during the day and is known for its fondness for basking in sheltered sunny places.

Though reaching a maximum length of nearly six feet, the common water snake is mature at two to three feet, which size in England and Germany is probably attained in three or four years. Mating takes place in the spring, and the eggs are laid about two months later. The female commonly selects a pile of decaying vegetation or even a manure heap for the egg site—the simple depression is

scarcely worthy of the term "nest." The customary number of eggs is thirty to forty, but much larger clutches have been reported. After an incubation period of about ten weeks, the young, measuring from six to eight inches, hatch out.

Ordinarily, the common European water snake is much less confined to water than its Central European relative, the checkered water snake, *Natrix tessellata,* so named because of its rows of square black spots. This snake, from three to four feet long, always remains in water or on banks. Apparently most of its hunting is done in the water, for the chief item in its diet is fish. The correspondence between habitat and diet is a common thread running through the animal kingdom, and even minor differences between the diets of two related species—as, for example, the change from an emphasis on frogs to an emphasis on fish in these two water snakes—reflect subtle changes in habits and habitats.

Another widely distributed genus is met in France, the whip snakes (*Coluber*), a conspicuous element in the fauna of southern Europe, North Africa, Asia, and North America. The green whip snake of southern Europe, *Coluber viridiflavus,* like all members of the genus, is a slender,

Green Whip Snake (*Coluber viridiflavus*)

active terrestrial snake feeding on lizards, snakes, mice, and sometimes frogs. This particular species, which is dark green or black, marked with crossbars of yellow spots, is average in size for the group, about five feet long when mature, though sometimes six feet or more. One of the five whip snakes of Europe, *Coluber jugularis,* enters southern Poland, but that is as far north as they go in Europe.

The chicken snake genus (*Elaphe*) is also represented in Europe by five species, the best known being the Aesculapian snake, *E. longissima.* Except for Dione's snake, *E. dione,* which is an inhabitant of sandy grasslands, these snakes are found in woods and around farm buildings, where they prey on mice and rats. Favorite haunts are sunny patches in rather open woods and on walls. The Aesculapian snake is the only species living so far north as southern Germany and Poland.

The three rear-fanged snakes of Europe—the Montpellier snake, *Malpolon monspessulana,* the hooded snake, *Macroprotodon cucullatus,* and the European cat snake, *Telescopus fallax*—belong to genera that occur in North Africa and in Southwest Asia. In general, warmth-requiring creatures like snakes have been able to migrate into Europe only by means of three southern routes: one from Morocco to Spain, the second from Asia Minor into the Balkans, and the third a series of steppingstones from Tunisia to Sicily to Italy. The first two routes are interrupted by only very narrow strips of water (the Straits of Gibraltar and the Bosporus) and have therefore been the easiest for land animals to cross. This fact shows up immediately in the European distributions of these rear-fanged snakes. Two of them occur in Spain (the Montpellier snake also living on the Mediterranean coast of France), and two in the Balkans. No rear-fanged snake is found in Italy.

The only European genus that does not occur in North Africa is the chicken-snake group (*Elaphe*), which is essentially Asiatic and North American.

In fact, the European colubrid fauna looks like a diluted version of the North African colubrid assemblage. This is a relationship we have referred to before in discussing various groups of lizards such as the geckos, skinks, and lacertids. As is to be expected in a larger fauna, North Africa has several genera not present in Europe. Two characteristics of this arid and semiarid region stand out. In the first place there are no arboreal snakes. To be sure, certain of the terrestrial types, for example the whip snakes (*Coluber*) and sand snakes (*Psammophis*), occasionally climb into bushes, but no North African species shows any arboreal specialization such as keeled ventrals, green coloration, or extreme slenderness of body. Here, in this essentially treeless region, is a clear example of a way in which the environment affects the composition of the fauna.

A second feature of the North African fauna is the appearance of the auger type of burrowing snake. The two species of the genus *Lytorhynchus* occurring in this region are able to loosen soil with the rostral shield, which has free lateral edges. This represents a parallel with snakes in other semiarid areas of the world, for example the leaf-nosed snakes (*Phyllorhynchus*) of southwestern United States. Both species of *Lytorhynchus* are small—about one and a half feet long—and secretive. They are usually found under stones.

The most conspicuous colubrid snakes of North Africa are the whip snakes (*Coluber*) and sand snakes (*Psammophis*), the former with seven species and the latter with three. All are slender, long-tailed, big-eyed, active, diurnal snakes feeding on lizards, snakes, birds, and small mammals. The parallel between these two genera extends to breeding habits—both lay eggs—and to size—both average roughly four feet in length. But at this point the parallel ends, for, while *Coluber* has no grooved teeth or venom and ends its African distribution in North Africa and Somaliland, *Psammophis* is a rear-fanged snake and continues its African distribution to the Cape of Good Hope.

Farther southward in East Africa the colubrid fauna expands enormously. Whereas only twelve genera occur in North Africa, over thirty are found in the region composed of Kenya, Uganda, Tanganyika, and the northern half of Mozambique. But more than numbers have been added, for here are arboreal snakes spilling out of their true homes in the rain forest, more nocturnal snakes, and additional kinds of burrowers. Several species of North African ground snakes are among the common snakes of East Africa. One of them, the sand snake, *Psammophis sibilans,* a brown five-footer, lives in gardens, grasslands, bushy areas, and along streams.

Mole Snake (*Pseudaspis cana*)

Because it is diurnal, this active snake is often seen, and for the same reason often falls victim to many birds of prey, including harrier eagles, buzzards, and fish eagles.

Another ground snake found from Egypt to the Cape of Good Hope, the Cape wolf snake, *Lycophidion capense,* is abundant in East Africa. Unlike the sand snake, which is a rear-fanged colubrid, the wolf snake is a nonvenomous species reaching a maximum length of much less than three feet. This purplish brown or black snake has a flat, broadly rounded snout and a rather slender form. It feeds very largely on skinks, and, in the absence of venom to quiet its victims, it depends on several long teeth to maintain a grip on the hard-scaled, squirming lizards. The females lay about seven eggs at a time.

The file snakes (genus *Mehelya*) are also common and terrestrial. These nonvenomous snakes acquire their common name from the shape of their bodies, which are triangular in cross section, and their coarsely keeled scales. The Cape file snake, *Mehelya capensis,* which may be olive-gray or black and up to five feet long, feeds mainly on snakes. Like most of the snake-eaters, its appetite is frequently larger than its stomach, for one five-footer was discovered in the process of digesting a sand snake (*Psammophis*) that was longer than itself. About ten inches of the prey's tail was protruding from the file snake's mouth, and presumably would have been swallowed as soon as digestion of the head end had proceeded sufficiently. It attacks venomous snakes with the same impunity as the North American king snakes (genus *Lampropeltis*). The file-snake genus is primarily a forest group, and the species such as *capensis* that do inhabit the savanna country of East Africa usually live in the denser clusters of trees. The eggs, numbering about six, are laid in decaying vegetation.

Probably the terrestrial colubrid most often seen in East Africa is the house snake, *Boaedon lineatum,* so named because it is commonly found in and around houses—under mats, in heaps of rubbish, and in roof thatching. It is a small snake (rarely over three feet long), dark olive-brown or blackish in color, and with an elliptical pupil. Normally it feeds on rodents, and despite its slender form it can engulf full-grown rats. The house snake does, however, eat birds on occasion, and one was trapped in a canary's cage after it had eaten the bird.

The burrowing colubrids of East Africa, as we have defined that region here, do not include any leaf-nosed snakes such as *Lytorhynchus* of Egypt. But several chisel- or shovel-snouted burrowers are present. One of these, *Prosymna ambigua,* is a bluish gray snake about a foot long. Its snout projects be-

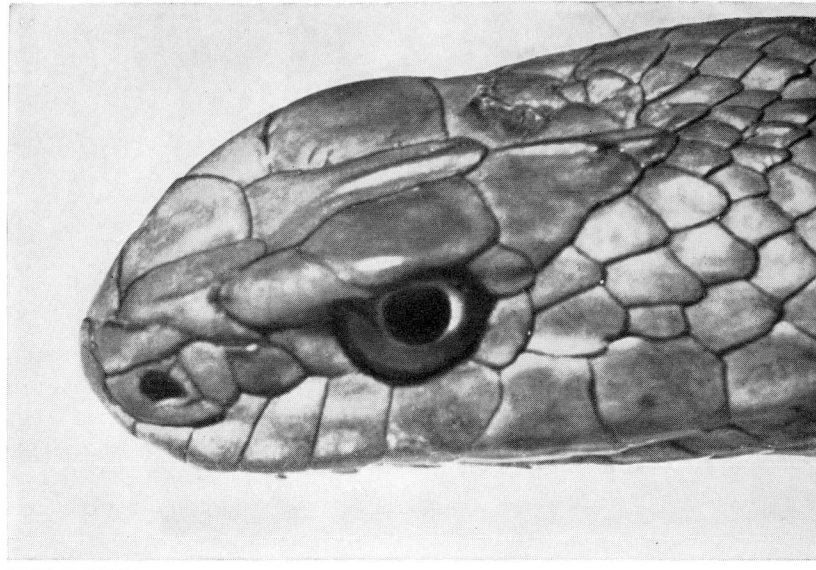

ERICH SOCHUREK

Montpellier Snake (*Malpolon monspessulana*)

yond the lower jaw, which is somewhat countersunk in the manner of the sand skink (*Neoseps*) described earlier. The rostral shield at the tip of the snout has a sharp horizontal edge, and the internasals and prefrontals behind the rostral are represented by a single broad shield each instead of being paired as in nonspecialized colubrids. The other chisel-snouted burrower, the beaked snake, *Scaphiophis albopunctata,* has to be seen to be appreciated, for this snake has a peculiar downward-sloping head ending in an extremely sharp horizontal edge. The lower jaw is countersunk as in *Prosymna,* but none of the head shields are combined or lost. Both of these snakes apparently chisel their way through the earth with the modified rostral. Burrowers of this type are not usually encountered in dense forests, and these two species are restricted to the open savanna country. The small *Prosymna* is insectivorous, but nothing is known about the diet of the beaked snake, which sometimes reaches a length of five feet.

The African sharp-nosed snakes (genus *Rhamphiophis*) compose a group of rear-fanged snakes with heads very similar to those of the beaked snakes. Their snouts slope downward to a large and sharp-edged rostral; the usual number of head shields is present. These oviparous snakes grow to about five feet. Their food consists of small rodents, lizards, snakes, and frogs.

The other type of burrowing colubrid found in East Africa is characterized by a blunt, small head, short tail, and fused head shields. Though this kind of burrower, which is typified by the reed snakes (*Calamaria*) described on previous pages, is characteristic of humid forested regions, at least one genus is restricted to open country. This genus, *Chilorhinophis,* includes three small, beautiful species, none of which is more than eighteen inches long. The internasals have fused with the prefrontal shields so that the top of the snout has only two scales instead of the usual four. The loreal shield on the side of the snout has been lost, and so have some of the scales on the temple. Butler's snake, *Chilorhinophis butleri,* is a bright lemon yellow with a black head and neck, a narrow black stripe down the center of the back, and a similar black stripe on each side. The underside is yellowish orange. Gerard's snake, *C. gerardi,* with similar coloration, curls its tail in the air when disturbed in a defensive posture common among brightly colored snakes (see description of *Maticora* in cobra section).

These burrowing snakes are not well known because of their secretive habits. Far more commonly seen and far more widespread is the curious egg-eating snake, *Dasypeltis,* which is found all over Africa. This grayish or brownish snake rarely becomes longer than three feet. As we have noted already, it feeds exclusively on eggs, which it hunts on the ground and in trees. Ornithologists frequently discover it at bird nests, or even in them.

Ornithologists might also surprise true arboreal snakes at bird nests in this savanna region. One of these tree- or bush-dwelling snakes, the boomslang, *Dispholidus typus,* could give a man looking for birds an unpleasant shock, for, as we have mentioned earlier, it is a large rear-fanged snake and is the only one considered dangerous to man. Its diet includes birds, their eggs, frogs, and especially chameleons. Other arboreal rear-fanged colubrids of East Africa include the African vine snake, *Thelotornis,* a grayish, curiously mottled species with an elongate head. Although it does eat small birds, it feeds on lizards and frogs to a much larger extent than its relative the boomslang.

Another group of arboreal snakes, the green tree snakes (*Chlorophis*), has several representatives in the savannas of East Africa. Besides their green coloration, most of these snakes have another arboreal adaptation in the form of keeled ventral scales. These nonvenomous snakes are oviparous and feed mainly on frogs and lizards. Since about half of the species live in the rain forest, the green tree snakes form an introduction to this area of Central Africa.

As anyone might guess, the rain forest of Africa is rich in arboreal snakes, many of them green and many with keeled ventral and caudal plates. Falling in this category, in addition to the green tree snakes, are the colubrine genera *Gastropyxis* and *Hapsidophrys.* However, not all of the tree-dwelling colubrids are green, for the largest, the six-foot *Thrasops jacksoni,* is appropriately named the "black tree snake." Because of its color and large size, *Thrasops* is often erroneously identified as a black mamba, a truly dangerous relative of the cobras.

A number of the colubrid genera found in the rain forest also live in the surrounding less humid areas. In addition to the green tree snakes (*Chlorophis*), this wide-ranging category includes the small terrestrial wolf snakes (*Lycophidion*) and the large snake-eating file snakes (*Mehelya*). Both of the last two genera are rather plain in color and contrast sharply with the striped ground snake, *Bothrophthalmus lineatus,* a black-and-red-striped species with a flaming red belly. This four-foot oviparous snake exists in two color phases, the red phase just described and one in which the red is replaced by bright yellow. Rodents and other small mammals are the main items in its diet. Although much less conspicuous, the genus *Geodipsas* is also confined to the floor of dense forests. These small (less than two feet long) rear-fanged snakes have the peculiar habit of flattening their bodies and becoming extremely rigid when disturbed. They also emit a strong-smelling anal secretion.

The colubrid fauna of the African rain forest also includes aquatic snakes. The most conspicuous of these are the rather wide-ranging African water snakes (genus *Grayia*). Several of these fish-eating snakes follow rivers out of the forest into the savanna country. They are generally brownish or grayish and range between three and five feet in length. The black-bellied water snake, *Hydraethiops melanogaster,* a fish-eater from two to three feet long, is confined to the rain forest.

Though separated from East Africa by a relatively short distance, Madagascar has a reptile fauna strikingly different from the African. We have already commented on this distinction in discussing some of the lizard families—such as the agamids, iguanids, and gerrhosaurids—and now come to it again in the colubrid snakes. None of the twenty genera of colubrid snakes found on Madagascar and adjacent islands is dangerously venomous. Only one, the rear-fanged terrestrial *Geodipsas,* also occurs in Africa (see above), but is represented there by different species. With one possible exception, the Madagascan genera are found nowhere else in the world. Despite its unique quality, this fauna includes many types. Roughly two-fifths of the species are boigine rear-fanged snakes. Slender, elongate arboreal forms (*Stenophis*) as well as shovel-nosed burrowers (*Heteroliodon*) are present. And there is even one genus (*Lioheterodon*) with three species that have upturned snouts remarkably like the hog-nosed snakes of North America.

The most peculiar-looking snakes on Madagascar

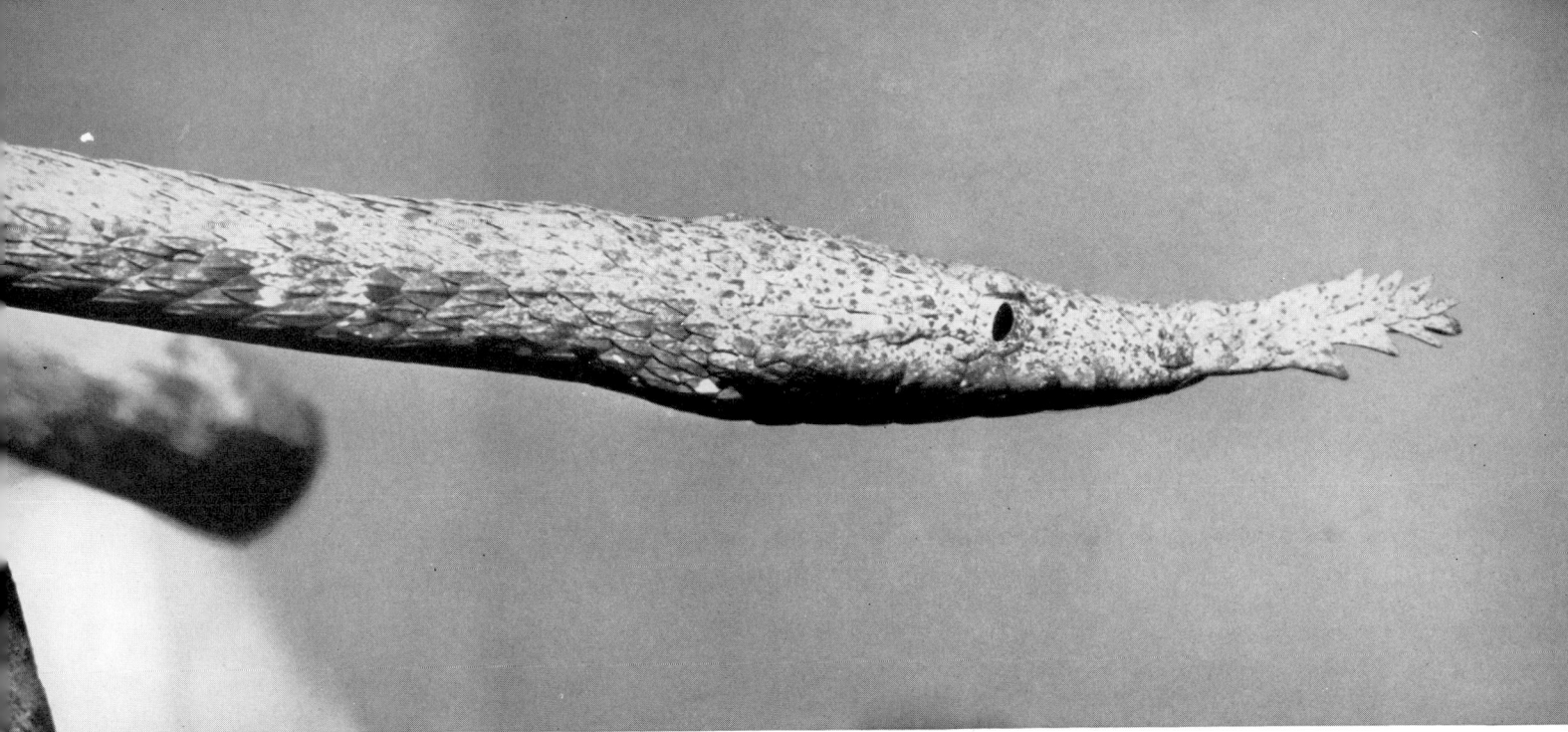

Madagascan Rear-fanged Snake (*Langaha intermedia*)

are the rear-fanged species of the genus *Langaha*. These three-foot, brownish snakes have long, scaly appendages projecting from the snout. Many arboreal snakes, of which apparently *Langaha* is one, have long, drawn-out heads with the nostrils and ends of the jaws in the usual positions at the tips. But in *Langaha* the nostrils and chin are at the base of the projection. Even stranger, the male has a simple conical appendage, whereas in the female the appendage is broad and leaflike. At one time the males and females were thought to be separate species, so that four species were recognized instead of the two we now know.

One of the conspicuous differences between the colubrid snakes of the savanna and forest areas of Africa is the absence of the chisel-snouted and leaf-nosed burrowers from the rain forest. Evidently the hard, dry soil of the savannas, grasslands, and semideserts can be dug into more effectively by sharp-nosed snakes, whereas the blunt-headed burrower is more efficient in the moist and relatively soft soil and rotting vegetation of the forest. The leaf-nosed snakes of the genus *Lytorhynchus*, abundant in the dry area from the Sudan northward, are part of the fauna common to North Africa and Southwest Asia. The relative uniformity of the fauna throughout this vast arid and semiarid region stretching from the Atlantic coast of Africa to northern India has been mentioned repeatedly in our discussions of various lizard families. Besides *Lytorhynchus,* the conspicuous colubrids ranging across this region are the whip snakes (*Coluber*), the sand snakes (*Psam-*

mophis), the diadem snakes (*Spalerosophis*), and the water snakes (*Natrix*).

Genera characteristic of other regions spill over into Southwest Asia. Several chicken snakes (*Elaphe*), which are distributed mainly in eastern Asia and North America, occur in Asia Minor. However, only one species, *Elaphe hohenackeri,* is confined to this region. Boigine rear-fanged snakes are represented by a few types, thus pointing up

Arabian Leaf-nosed Snake (*Lytorhynchus diadema*)

Arabian Rear-fanged Snake (*Malpolon moilensis*)

again their essentially tropical distribution, for southwest Asia has a temperate climate. The active terrestrial sand snakes (*Psammophis*) are the most abundant of the rear-fanged snakes of this region, although the cat-snake genus (*Telescopus*) has four species here.

Another genus of rear-fanged snakes, much more common in the tropics of Africa and Asia, has one species, the Indian gamma, *Boiga trigonata*, living at the edge of this arid region in Baluchistan and northwestern Pakistan. This brownish snake, from three to four feet long, feeds mainly on lizards, especially the bloodsuckers (*Calotes*), but also eats birds and small mammals, which it catches in trees. It is reported to kill its prey by constriction, but this seems odd because we would expect the venom to have some effect on the small prey. Like many members of this genus, the Indian gamma is quick to defend itself. Facing the enemy, it raises the fore part of its body in an "S" curve and inflates its body while at the same time vibrating its tail. From this posture, it strikes repeatedly with open mouth; it can, however, do little harm to a man. The Indian gamma ranges southward into peninsular India, where other species of *Boiga* also occur. All are oviparous and, while they are mainly arboreal, are often seen on the ground.

It is in India that we first encounter other subfamilies of Colubridae. The rear-fanged water snakes of the subfamily Homalopsinae include three Indian species, all of which are rather docile. They feed primarily on fish but also catch frogs. One of them, the dog-faced water snake, *Cerberus rhynchops,* is itself sometimes caught on fishing tackle. More homalopsine snakes, and several additional subfamilies, occur slightly farther to the east in Burma, Thailand, and Indo-China. The Xenoderminae, for instance, are represented in this tropical region by several genera, such as *Achalinus* and *Fimbrios,* which were mentioned earlier in these pages.

The slug-eating dipsadine snakes also make their appearance here. Their large eyes, set in a short but wide head, seem all out of proportion to the slender body. The slug-snake genus, *Pareas,* has several terrestrial species that have cylindrical bodies rather than the compressed form of the arboreal species. Besides the compressed bodies, the arboreal species have enlarged scales down the mid-line of the back and thus approach the I-beam form of the South American *Imantodes* (see above).

Other specialized arboreal colubrids occur in Southeast Asia. Some, for example the chicken snakes (*Elaphe*), are only slightly modified for this type of existence. However, even among the chicken snakes, there are green species, for instance, the red-tailed chicken snake, *Elaphe oxycephala*. Still other tree-dwelling colubrids have sharply keeled ventral and caudal plates, as in the rear-fanged bronze-backs (*Ahaetulla*). The vine snakes of the genus *Dryophis* (Plates 117, 123), which combine green coloration with an excessively slender body and elongate head, also live in this tropical area, and differ from the bronze-backs and chicken snakes in being viviparous.

Terrestrial snakes also abound in the Orient. Besides the big Oriental rat snakes (*Zaocys* and *Ptyas*), this category includes the smaller kukri snakes (genus *Oligodon*), whose common name refers to the resemblance of the large hind teeth to the shape of a Gurkha knife. Though enlarged, the teeth at the rear of the upper jaw are not grooved. About half of the fifty or sixty species live in Southeast Asia. Most of them are less than three feet long, and all seem to be egg-layers. Bird eggs and reptile eggs form an important part of their diet.

In a region with abundant rainfall and many streams, both large and small, one expects many aquatic snakes. Not only are there many species of the water-snake genus (*Natrix*), but there are also several other genera with the same habits. One of these, the mountain water snakes (*Opisthotro-*

pis), has the nostrils almost on the top of the snout, thus departing from the norm in snakes but approaching the ideal condition for aquatic animals. The mock vipers (*Psammodynastes*), small rear-fanged snakes, are also associated with water but are most often seen on twigs overhanging small forest streams where they are likely to catch their principal food—frogs. Their relatively large head, elliptical pupils, and astonishingly courageous disposition have earned them their common name.

A very large percentage of the genera found in Southwest Asia also inhabits the East Indies. In fact, all of those referred to above, except *Achalinus* and *Fimbrios,* occur in Borneo and Sumatra, the largest land areas in the East Indies. This similarity in colubrid faunas is the reflection of a more general affinity of these two areas, a relationship that the study of animal geography has formalized by combining Southeast Asia and the East Indies into the *Oriental Region.* The main difference between the colubrids of Borneo and Sumatra on the one hand and those of Thailand and Burma on the other is a change in the species representing the various genera. To be sure, certain genera are found in only one area or the other, but these genera are usually small in numbers of species. For example, the peculiar *Xenodermus* is known only from the East Indies and has just one species.

Some genera may have more species in one or another subdivision of the Oriental Region. The reed snakes (*Calamaria*), highly specialized burrowers described above, are good examples. Seven species of these earthworm-feeders live in Southeast Asia, whereas about seventy are found in the East Indies, including the Philippine Islands. Specially modified blunt-headed burrowing colubrids are quite common in the humid East Indies. In addition to *Calamaria,* there are at least six genera of small, secretive snakes with smooth cylindrical bodies, short tails, small eyes, reduced head shields, and rather blunt snouts. Not a single leaf-nosed or shovel-nosed burrowing colubrid is found in this extremely rich fauna, thus contrasting sharply with the North American and East African faunas.

Water snakes of various genera, specialized tree snakes (including the so-called flying snake, *Chrysopelea*), and terrestrial snakes are all present in numbers in the Philippines, Borneo, Sumatra, and Java. But as we proceed eastward through the Indies, the fauna diminishes in size and variety until in New Guinea it has almost disappeared. It seems incredible that this gigantic tropical island should have only 22 species of colubrids. For comparison, consider that Borneo, which is about the same size as New Guinea, has roughly 120 colubrids, and that Kansas, about one-third as large, has 33. This extreme impoverishment is a consequence of the long geological time during which New Guinea, together with Australia (which has only 12 colubrids), was separated from the continent of

Oriental Rat Snake (*Ptyas mucosus*)

Asia. This separation also explains the peculiar development of the elapid snakes (to be discussed in a subsequent section) and the pouched mammals in New Guinea and Australia.

Returning to Asia, elements of the tropical Southeast Asian colubrid fauna range northward into the not-quite-tropical but still mild climate of southern China. Most of these tropical snakes are rear-fanged —such snakes as the painted bronze-back, *Ahaetulla ahaetulla,* and the mock viper, *Psammodynastes.* The same group of snakes accounts for most of the arboreal species of China, the forests of which are concentrated mainly in the extreme south and southwest. Chicken snakes (*Elaphe*) are the only other Chinese colubrids that commonly climb bushes and trees, and they are widely distributed throughout the country. Dione's snake, *Elaphe dione,* which is found all the way from southeastern Europe, is one of the commonest snakes in northeastern Asia, where it lives in fields, ditches, forests, and farm buildings and searches for rodents and birds. It lays about ten eggs at a time.

The dearth of arboreal snakes in Northeast Asia is balanced by the abundance of species of aquatic colubrids. The water snakes (*Natrix*) are, as usual, the most numerous and are represented by sixteen species. As in other parts of the Old World, they are dark, medium-sized snakes with keeled scales. Frogs are the most important element in the diet, with fish usually a secondary element. The other aquatic groups are the mountain water snakes, *Opisthotropis* (see also above).

Most Chinese colubrids are terrestrial snakes belonging to genera that are widespread. For example, there are several species of big rat snakes (genera *Ptyas* and *Zaocys*), about five kukri snakes (*Oligodon*), and four Oriental wolf snakes (*Lycodon*); these genera are found throughout Southeast Asia. The green snakes (*Opheodrys*) are present not only in China and Southeast Asia, but also in eastern North America. However, the genus *Dinodon,* a group of four species, is confined to northeastern Asia, from southern China to Manchuria and Korea, and from Formosa to Japan. These snakes, though somewhat larger (about four feet long), resemble the Oriental wolf snakes (*Lycodon*) in having an enlarged but nongrooved tooth in the upper jaw, an elliptical pupil, and a rather flat, blunt head. *Dinodon* is at home in fields, along streams, and near farmhouses, and feeds almost exclusively on cold-blooded prey (frogs, fish, snakes, and lizards), which it hunts at night. Like its relative *Lycodon,* it is oviparous, laying about ten eggs in a clutch.

The relatively few colubrid genera common to both Eastern and Western Hemispheres have been referred to many times in the preceding pages: the water snakes (*Natrix*), the chicken snakes (*Elaphe*), the whip snakes (*Coluber*), and the green snakes (*Opheodrys*). With the exception of the whip snakes, these genera are confined, in North America, to the portions of the continent east of the Rocky Mountains. The similarity of the fauna of southeastern North America to that of eastern Asia has been commented on in discussing the emydid turtles, and these colubrids extend that relationship.

The restriction of these widespread genera to southeastern North America brings up another point, namely, that the fauna of this continent consists of quite distinct subdivisions, corresponding to climatic, and therefore vegetational, subdivisions. For example, we speak of a southeastern fauna, an assemblage of reptiles (and amphibians and fishes as well) found primarily in the southeastern United States as far west as the northeastern coast of Mexico and thus associated with a mild, humid climate that formerly supported one of the great hardwood forests of the world. In this rich area live all but one of the ten North American species of water snakes, including the mangrove water snake, *Natrix sipedon compressicauda* (Plate 80), with its flattened tail; the bright red-bellied water snake, *Natrix erythrogaster* (Plate 82); and the small, two-foot, striped queen snake, *Natrix septemvittata.*

The chicken snakes, too, are well represented here. The American rat snake, *Elaphe obsoleta*— its many races including the black rat snake, *Elaphe obsoleta obsoleta,* and the yellow rat snake, (*Elaphe obsoleta quadrivittata,* Plates 97, 98, 99)—is the largest and often reaches a length in excess of five feet. Another species, the fox snake, *Elaphe vulpina,* ranges farther to the north and west, to northern Wisconsin and Nebraska. When encountered in a pasture, this brown-blotched snake frequently coils into a threatening defensive posture and vibrates its tail furiously. Such tail vibration is a rather common behavior of many harmless snakes. In the United States, where rattlesnakes occur over a wide area, this nervous but harmless activity of nonvenomous snakes leads to a great deal of confusion, especially if the tail happens to touch dry leaves.

Many persons do not distinguish at all between harmless and venomous snakes, and a surprising number of harmless snakes are brought to museums for identification under the misapprehension that they are (or were) rattlesnakes, copperheads, or water moccasins. To recount but one example out of many, a Chicago man, recently returned from northern Wisconsin, telephoned the museum in Chicago to say that he thought he had obtained the skin

North American Smooth Green Snake (*Opheodrys vernalis*)

of a rattlesnake. We asked him to bring the skin to the museum, and on his arrival found that he had a fresh skin of a fox snake. To our question as to how he could have mistaken so harmless a creature for a rattlesnake, he told us that he thought it was a rattlesnake because it had rattled. When we pointed out that the tail had no rattles, he said that he had assumed that the snake had snapped them off, and he had even searched for the rattles in the dry leaves for half an hour. What he thought was "rattling" was of course the sound of the tail vibrating in the leaves.

Two species of green snakes occur in the United States, the smooth green snake, *Opheodrys vernalis* (Plate 95), and the more arboreal rough green snake, *Opheodrys aestivus* (Plate 93), which ranges southward to northern Mexico. A third species lives in southern Mexico. The whip snakes (*Coluber*) are represented in the United States by five species, all of them slender and handsome (Plates 89, 91, 92, 94).

As an indication of how rich and distinct the fauna of southeastern United States is, eight genera are known only from this corner of the world. Several of these, the rainbow snake (*Abastor*) and the mud snake (*Farancia*), are moderate-sized (about four feet long), brightly colored burrowers. The rainbow snake has three longitudinal stripes on a black ground color, a yellow stripe where the side meets the ventral plates, and a red belly with a double row of dark spots. The food and reproductive habits of this strikingly colored snake are unknown. Fortunately, information on the habits of the mud snake, a red-marked black creature, is available. This oviparous snake lays anywhere from 22 to 104 eggs at a time, which makes it one of the most prolific snakes known. It feeds primarily on frogs, fish, and big salamanders, such as the mud eel (*Siren*) and the congo eel (*Amphiuma*).

One of the strangest snake myths is attached to the rainbow snake and the mud snake, for these are the creatures famous as "hoop snakes." Accord-

[227]

ing to the stories, the snake forms its body into a hoop by grasping its tail in its mouth, so it can roll over the ground. And, wonder of wonders, if it should bump against any living thing in the course of these peregrinations and stick the "poisonous" stinging tail into that object—even a tree—that thing dies instantly. The sole nugget of truth in this snake story is the fact that these snakes do have a hard, sharp tip to the tail. We once lived in Louisiana with a crew of oil riggers and were regaled by horrendous stories of the potency of the "stinging" tail by the boardinghouse owner. By great good luck we caught a mud snake and brought it in alive coiled around our arm to ask the gentleman if this were his "stingin' " snake and why it did not sting. Unfortunately the poor man had described the brilliant coloration of the mud snake too accurately, for, though he wanted to say it was not the right species, the tough oil men made him admit that it evidently was.

The remaining six genera peculiar to southeastern United States are small, the largest, the striped swamp snake, *Liodytes alleni,* being a scant eighteen inches. The striped swamp snake is aquatic and feeds largely on crayfish. Another native of this area, the black swamp snake (*Seminatrix*) is also aquatic. This little black snake is only a foot long, and like the striped swamp snake is viviparous. The secretive earth snakes (*Haldea*) mentioned earlier are also viviparous. The other genera in this group of six—the worm snake, *Carphophis amoena,* the short-tailed snake, *Stilosoma extenuatum,* and the scarlet snake, *Cemophora coccinea*—are secretive or subterranean species that lay eggs. Both the short-tailed snake and the worm snake are blunt-headed burrowers with certain of the head shields fused.

Other genera confined to North America are not restricted to southeastern United States. The foot-long brown snakes (*Storeria*), for instance, are

Scarlet Snake (*Cemophora coccinea*)

found from Maine and southern Canada to Minnesota, southward to Florida and Louisiana. Both species are viviparous and both eat quantities of snails and slugs, the red-bellied snake, *Storeria occipitomaculata* (Plate 83), to a greater extent than DeKay's snake. Incidentally, the latter is one of the few snakes that survive in the suburbs of our northern metropolitan areas. We find these little brown snakes right up against the foundations of our own homes in the suburbs of Chicago and New York. Evidently they hibernate in cracks in the soil close to the buildings and benefit by some of the heat that passes through the foundation.

DeKay's snake is often accompanied through the winter by the plains garter snake, *Thamnophis radix* (Plate 105), which is if anything more abundant in suburbs around Chicago. This two-foot snake is distributed, as its common name indicates, in the plains from Illinois westward to the Rockies. Other species extend the range of this viviparous genus to every one of the United States, into the southern tier of Canadian provinces, and southward through Mexico to Costa Rica. One, the red-striped San Francisco garter snake, *Thamnophis sirtalis tetrataenia* (Plate 88), is especially handsome.

Almost equally widespread in the United States and Central America are the king snakes (*Lampropeltis;* Plate 116) and bull snakes (*Pituophis*). Contrasting sharply with these two large constricting snakes, the ring-necked snakes (*Diadophis;* Plate 90) are small, never growing more than two feet long, and are secretive. They are frequently found under rocks and logs and usually deposit their eggs in such places. When disturbed, a ring-necked snake usually hides its head under a coil of the body and curls its tail upward to show the bright reddish or yellowish underside. We have referred to this type of behavior before, and it will be mentioned again in a subsequent section.

Before turning to another faunal region of North America, we want to point out one striking feature of the fauna described so far, and that is the relatively large number of viviparous genera. Live-bearing is unusual among colubrid snakes, and, although only seven of the thirty-six American genera have this form of reproduction, this represents a high proportion. Northeast Asia, for instance, has twenty-seven colubrid genera, but only two are viviparous.

The second major faunal region of the United States is the arid or semiarid Southwest, a region extending down into Mexico. Within this portion of the United States are fourteen colubrid genera that reach the northern limits of their ranges there. The ten occurring only in Central America, Mexico, and southwestern United States have some peculiar

Western Patch-nosed Snake (*Salvadora hexalepsis*)

characteristics in common. In the first place, seven of the ten have modified snouts for burrowing. Though the patch-nosed snakes (*Salvadora*), the leaf-nosed snakes (*Phyllorhynchus;* Plate 101), the glossy snake (*Arizona;* Plate 110), and the long-nosed snakes (*Rhinocheilus;* Plate 106) are active, terrestrial snakes, their rostral shields are specialized for augur-type burrowing. The leaf-nosed snakes are the smallest, being only about one and a half feet long, and are perhaps the most subterranean. Except for the patch-nosed snakes, these primarily lizard-eating genera are nocturnal, and all are oviparous.

Three other genera are smaller in length, reaching a maximum of around eighteen inches. The banded sand snakes (*Chilomeniscus;* Plate 122) and the shovel-nosed snakes (*Chionactis*) have sharp-edged snouts and countersunk lower jaws, enabling them to "swim" under the surface of sand like certain skinks (for example, the Florida sand skink, *Neoseps*). The hook-nosed snake (*Ficimia*) recalls the hog-nosed snakes (*Heterodon*) but has an even more sharply turned up snout and presumably burrows in the manner of the hog-nosed snakes. Like the four larger types, these three are egg-layers. In correspondence with their smaller size, they feed on invertebrates; spiders, insects, and centipedes.

The intensity of the sun's rays forces nocturnal habits on many of the reptiles inhabiting this arid region. Besides the seven genera just mentioned, three nocturnal rear-fanged groups occur. All are oviparous and feed on animals appropriate to their respective sizes. The black-headed snakes (*Tantilla*), which reach a maximum of eighteen inches but are usually much shorter, eat invertebrates. Lizards and frogs are the principal items in the diet of the night snakes (*Hypsiglena*), rather blunt-headed creatures averaging one and a half feet in length. The lyre snakes (*Trimorphodon*) are more slender

Mexican Rear-fanged Snake (*Conophis lineatus*)

and longer, reaching a length of about three feet, but like *Hypsiglena* have blunt heads and elliptical pupils. They eat lizards and small mammals.

Twenty-seven of the colubrid genera found in the United States range across the border into Mexico, several of them going as far as South America. Northern Mexico and southwestern United States have a similar climate and vegetation, as we have said before, so that a similarity in the fauna is to be expected. But southern Mexico is radically differ-

ent—it is tropical, and as a consequence many snakes that are restricted to the tropics can live there. The addition of a tropical faunal element raises the total of colubrid genera found in Mexico to sixty-five.

These tropical snakes include several that just barely enter the United States. The vine snakes (*Oxybelis*), with their extremely slender bodies, long tails, and long-drawn-out snouts, manage to reach Arizona. But these snakes, which resemble the Oriental genus *Dryophis* to an extraordinary degree, have their center of distribution in northern South America, though they range as far south as northern Argentina. The nocturnal American cat-eye snakes (*Leptodeira;* Plate 119), a partly arboreal, partly terrestrial group of oviparous rear-fanged snakes, have roughly the same geographic distribution.

The fact that Central America has a number of native genera (no less than eighteen) is obscured for two reasons. In the first place, the native forms such as *Geatractus* and *Leptocalamus* are small and secretive snakes and not often seen. The other reason for their relative obscurity is the abundance of large snakes that spill over into Central America

Mountain Patch-nosed Snake (*Salvadora grahamiae*)

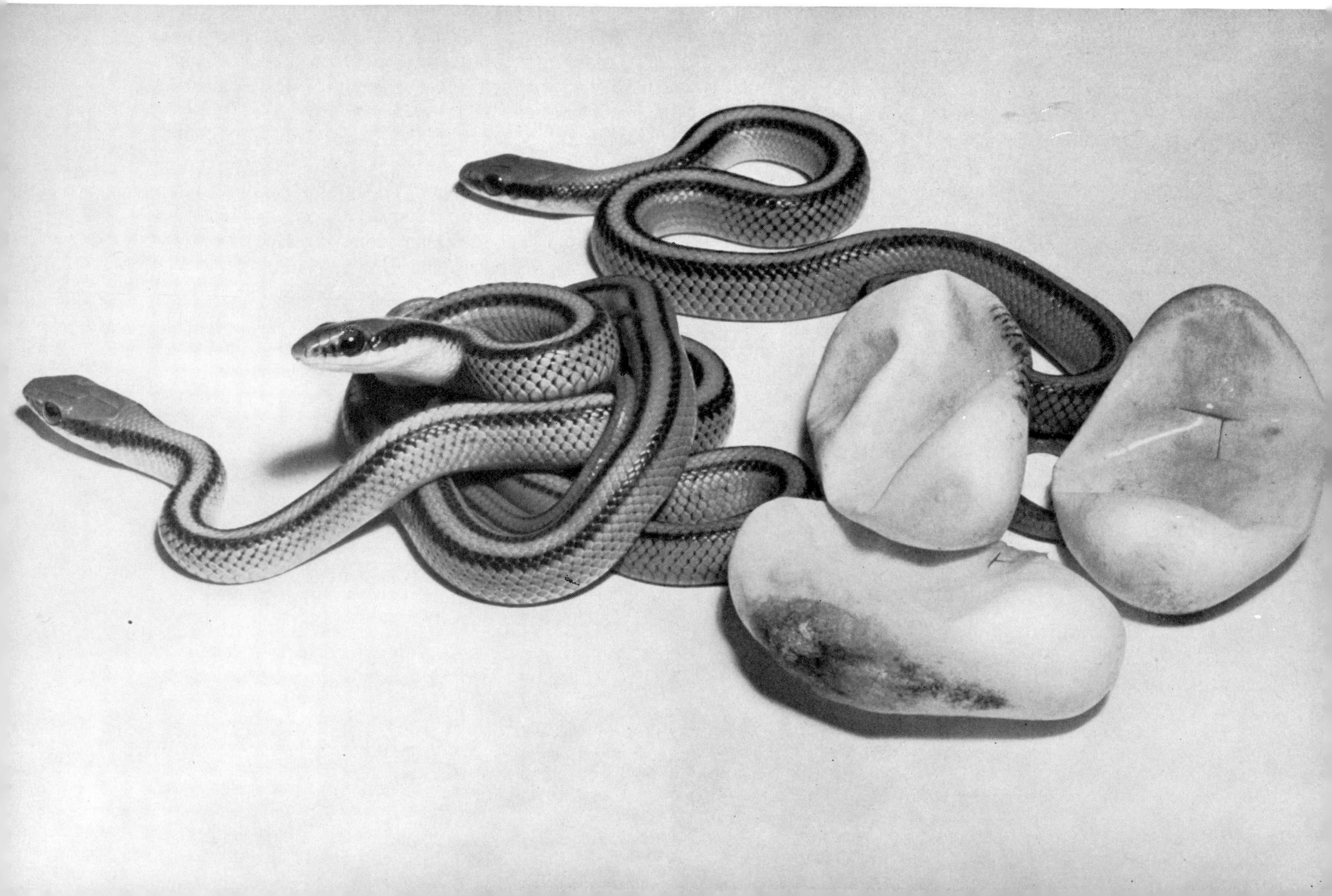

South American Green Tree Snake (*Thalerophis richardi*)

from northern South America. Conspicuous among these are the green tree snakes (*Thalerophis*), the snake-eater *Clelia,* and the big arboreal black-and-white *Spilotes.* Smaller South American colubrids in Central America are the banded, rear-fanged *Oxyrhopus,* the snail-eating *Sibon,* and the equally harmless *Xenodon.* This last genus has enlarged but nongrooved rear teeth similar to those of the hog-nosed snakes (*Heterodon*), to which *Xenodon* is probably closely related.

When we turn our attention to South America, we find the headquarters of forms known in Mexico by only a few species. This is especially noteworthy in such forms as the vine snakes (*Oxybelis*), which are spread all over northern South America, and in the large snakes of the genera *Drymarchon* (the indigo snake and its relatives), and in *Spilotes.* Central America, for reasons obscure in the history of the Tertiary Era, has a richer fauna of lizards than South America, reckoned by number of families. The snakes, however, with the exception of the rattlesnakes, are richer in variety of generic types

in South America, though without the addition of any families. About fifty genera of colubrine and boigine snakes are mainly or exclusively South American, not counting those that, though present in northern South America, are mainly Central American.

With such a wealth of types it is not surprising that the colubrid snakes of northern South America have adopted all ways of life open to snakes. Arboreal types include extremely slender, slow-moving forms such as the snail-eater (*Sibon*) and the vine snakes (*Oxybelis*), as well as less slender but swift-moving groups such as the green tree snakes (*Thalerophis*). Heavy-bodied terrestrial colubrids, like the brown snake (*Drymarchon*), as well as swifter, more slender ground-dwellers, such as *Drymobius,* are also represented. When disturbed, one of the terrestrial snakes, *Leimadophis,* flattens its body so that the scales are spread to expose the bright red skin. Rear-fanged false coral snakes (*Erythrolamprus*), red with black rings, are occasionally seen on the forest floor.

[231]

Another terrestrial species, the wide-ranging, snake-eating musurana, *Clelia clelia,* changes color with age, a phenomenon far more common among lizards than snakes. Young musuranas have brownish or blackish heads with a broad cream-colored band on the nape of the neck. The general body color is pinkish above the white below, and each body scale is tipped with black. As they grow, the color darkens until at maturity the musurana is a uniform bluish black except for a whitish band down the center of the belly.

The spindle snakes (genus *Atractus*) are the most numerous of the South American burrowing colubrids at least in number of species, for no less than fifty have been described thus far. Most of the secretive or burrowing colubrids of tropical America exhibit the tendency mentioned earlier to strengthen the head by fusing certain head scales and by losing others. The genus *Geophis,* for example, has no preocular scale or temporals. The rear-fanged *Stenorhina* has the internasal on top of the snout fused with one of the nasal scales on the side of the snout; frequently the loreal shield is lost. One of the aquatic groups, the fish-eating genus *Helicops,* has a single shield in place of the usually paired internasals. But in this instance the result is to bring the nostrils closer to the top of the head and into a position similar to that of the rear-fanged water snake *Enhydris* of the Orient.

Like Madagascar, the larger West Indian islands have no dangerously venomous snakes. There is a considerable variety of harmless forms. In addition to the blind snakes, *Typhlops* and *Leptotyphlops,* and the boas, the fauna includes several colubrid genera that also occur in Central and South America as well as some that are found nowhere else. Among these native genera are the terrestrial *Alsophis* and *Dromicus,* the secretive *Arrhyton* of Cuba, and the arboreal *Uromacer* of Hispaniola.

As has already been mentioned, the snakes of Australia are mainly venomous members of the family Elapidae, and even New Guinea, which is a part of the Australian Region of zoogeographers, adds only very few more colubrines and boigines. A few species of water snakes (*Natrix*) spill over from their rich variety in the East Indies; a unique genus, *Stegonotus,* with several species in New Guinea, has only one species that reaches northern Australia; and the genus *Ahaetulla* (or *Dendrophis*), the common harmless tree-snake type of the Oriental Region, ranges into New Guinea and tropical Australia. The genus *Boiga* is the only boigine representative. The Homalapsinae, the rear-fanged water snakes, are well represented on the tropical coasts.

The Cobras and Coral Snakes and Their Relatives

(*Family Elapidae*)

The dangerously venomous snakes are grouped into four sharply distinct families. These in turn represent two very distinct types, with two families in each; those with the venom-conducting fangs fixed at the front end of the jaw are the Proteroglypha, or front-fanged snakes; and those with much larger perforated fangs that fold backward out of the way when not in use are the Solenoglypha. The two front-fanged families are the Elapidae, in which the best known forms are the cobras (Plate 127) and coral snakes and the mambas; and the Hydrophidae, the true sea snakes.

The elapids include the very large king cobra, which reaches a length of almost twenty feet, with an extremely powerful venom, and some small Australian forms that scarcely reach fifteen inches, and whose bite is said to be essentially no more dangerous than the sting of a wasp. In coloration the elapids range from earth-resembling desert forms to the pure green of one of the arboreal mambas and to the brilliantly ringed coral snakes, with alternating bands of black, yellow, and red.

The only front-fanged snakes within the borders of the United States are the common coral snake of the Southeast and the much smaller and quite different Arizona coral snake, *Micruroides euryxanthus* (Plate 125), which is ringed with the same alternating black, yellow, and red bands. The two snakes are referred to distinct genera, *Micrurus* and *Micruroides,* because the latter, the small Arizona form, has a small solid tooth on the maxillary bone in addition to a venom-conducting fang that is like a hypodermic needle. In *Micrurus* there are no teeth left on the maxillary other than the hollow fang. This difference corresponds with an evolutionary series in the family. A number of Australian types have several solid or sometimes grooved teeth on an elongate maxilla, whereas the more highly evolved genera, like *Micrurus* (and like the cobras), have only the venom-conducting fang on a much shortened maxillary bone. The North American coral snake, *Micrurus fulvius,* has brilliant red rings alternating with black and yellow ones, the yellow bordering the black rings, and thus bordering the red zones also. The snout is black. This arrangement of colors distinguishes the venomous coral snake

Brazilian Coral Snake (*Micrurus frontalis*)

from other red-yellow-and-black-ringed harmless snakes in the southeastern United States. In them the yellow ring is wedged between two black ones, and the snout is light. This latter distinction, however, does not hold even for the closely related western coral king snakes, and in Central America there are other types of harmless snakes that resemble the coral snakes even in the arrangement of the rings.

The true coral snakes (genus *Micrurus,* Plate 126) range from the Mexican border, which is reached by *Micrurus fulvius,* to Paraguay and northern Argentina. The Brazilian giant within the genus, *Micrurus spixi,* reaches the astonishing length (for a coral snake) of five feet. This species has an elaborate development of the black, red, and yellow rings in which the black rings are arranged in threes, or "triads," the middle black ring being separated from the two outer ones by broad yellow zones, so that the red zones separate the triads. This arrangement may be completely obscured in old specimens in museum collections, in which the red and yellow and black zones are of nearly equal width and the yellow and red fade (in preservative) to the same color. The genus *Micrurus* has altogether about forty species in tropical America. A remarkably

colored coral snake, found notably on the Amazonian side of the Andes from Peru to Colombia, has a much more elongate and slender body, with as many as four hundred ventral plates. In this form, which has been named *Leptomicrurus,* meaning "slender *Micrurus,*" the bright color is yellow and is arranged in spots on the ventral surface. There is no red. The yellow comes to the upper side as a ring only on the neck and at the base of the tail; the tail is exceptionally short and blunt, and thus resembles the small narrow and rounded head very closely. What makes this resemblance of head and tail still more remarkable is that the snake hides its head beneath its coils when molested by a large animal and waves its tail above them as if it were the threatening head. We find that this is a quite general rule among snakes with bright ventral colors—harmless ones as well as venomous ones. They tend to hide the head and wave the tail, which is often raised in a tight watch-spring coil. Our common North American ring-necked snakes do this (Plate 90), and so does the mud snake of the Southeast. So do many of the coral snakes besides *Leptomicrurus.* It is thus not surprising that there has been much discussion of the brightly ringed harmless snake coloration as representing mimicry of the venomous types by the

[233]

harmless ones. Such development of both coloration and behavior is quite independent of the principle of mimicry, the main objection to the mimicry interpretation being that both venomous coral snakes and harmless mimics are mostly secretive, and often are burrowers or are nocturnal in habits.

Turning to the Old World, we find a much greater variety of front-fanged snakes. It is somewhat astonishing that the headquarters of the family is in the Australian Region, and that Australia itself has more kinds of venomous snakes than of nonvenomous ones. Furthermore, Australia has neither vipers nor pit-vipers. The Australian mammals are of such remarkably primitive types that the snakes, one might think, should also be mainly primitive. One might even suspect that the snake-eating front-

fanged snakes could have exterminated the smaller ground-dwelling harmless snakes, leaving only the larger pythons, the blind and subterranean burrowers, and a few arboreal forms. The Australian elapids, however, must have been ancient inhabitants of that continent, for they include a great diversity of forms, and these include what must be regarded as the primitive types of the family, genera like *Glyphodon, Pseudelaps, Diemenia, Pseudechis,* and *Denisonia,* in which the elongate maxillary bone, with fangs in front, bears a number of teeth posteriorly. The enlarged fangs are often paired, and the smaller teeth on the rear part of the jaw may be either grooved or solid. The fact that the hollow venom-conducting fang is derived from a tooth grooved on its anterior face is shown by the presence of a median line, where the two sides of the ancestral groove have met. These snakes can be arranged in a series from those with numerous solid teeth on the maxilla, through those with fewer grooved teeth, to the final stage, in which the maxillary teeth are reduced to the enlarged fangs only.

Many of the smaller Australian elapid snakes have only a weak venom, which might be either a primitive condition, or might be derived secondarily with decrease of size and change of food habits, these snakes being mainly insect-eaters. Representative types are various species of *Pseudelaps* and *Rhynchoelaps.* Their venom is said to be no more dangerous than that of the sting of a wasp or bee. One of the smaller Australian forms, known as the "bandy-bandy," is boldly ringed with black and yellow.

The larger Australian elapid snakes have extremely powerful venoms. Death of a human being from the bite of a large tiger snake or of a twelve-foot-long taipan (*Oxyuranus*) may result in a few minutes. The taipan, fortunately, is rare and found only in northeastern Australia. The tiger snake, unlike the cobras and coral snakes, bears living young. It is extremely prolific, producing as many as seventy-two young at a birth. Most of the Australian elapid snakes are viviparous, only the various species of the genus *Demansia* being uniformly oviparous. One of the widespread Australian species, *Acanthophis antarcticus,* is remarkable for its viperlike body form, with a wide head and short tail. This, next to the taipan, is the most feared of the venomous snakes of Australia. The mortality from its bite is about 50 per cent.

There is, fortunately, a small popular handbook describing the Australian snakes, illustrated in color, by J. R. Kinghorn, Curator of Reptiles at the Australian Museum at Sidney and for many years the leading herpetologist of Australia. From this book

Indian Cobra (*Naja naja*), **front view**

one may gain a good view of the general nature of the unique Australian snake fauna, which includes no less than eighty-five species and varieties of elapid snakes.

Southeastern Asia is rich in elapid snakes, including cobras; king cobras; kraits; the Oriental coral snakes variously patterned in black, yellow, and red; and the vividly colored lengthwise-lined *Maticora* of the East Indies. The Oriental coral snakes are appropriately named *Calliophis,* meaning "beautiful snake," and *Hemibungarus,* meaning "half a krait."

The genus *Maticora,* also referred to in the Orient as a coral snake, is more familiar in reptile literature as *Doliophis.* It is one of the most remarkable types among the bright-colored elapid snakes. These creatures are yellow or red beneath, with or without black bars, and are striped above with light yellow or bluish lines on a brown or black ground color. The details of this coloration may vary strikingly within each of the three species, and this has led to their description and redescription under a multitude of scientific names. As in so many species of snakes with a vivid coloration of the underside, the tail is raised and waved while the head is hidden beneath the coils. One of the East Indian species, *Maticora bivirgata,* has four sharply defined pale blue lines on a purplish black ground color, with a bright red belly unmarked with black. *Maticora intestinalis,* found in the same region, has three pale yellow lines on a brownish ground color, with a yellow or red belly heavily barred with black except beneath the tail, where the color is a bright red. The Philippine species has two longitudinal lines and has the tail barred beneath.

These snakes of the genus *Maticora* all have enormously developed venom glands that extend backward into the body for about a third of its length, room being provided for them by a backward displacement of the heart. In the only known case of a human being being bitten by one of these snakes, Dr. Jacobsen, of Java, records the following symptoms: A single fang penetrated the skin between his index and middle finger; only mild local pain was experienced until some two hours after the bite. Then he was attacked suddenly by giddiness and difficulty in breathing; and there were five or six successive attacks, each lasting five to ten minutes. He speculates that if he had received the full dose of venom, from both fangs, "the result would probably have been serious."

No venomous snake is more widely known than the Oriental common cobra, *Naja naja,* whose Indian subspecies again duplicates the generic "naja" to the designation *Naja naja naja.* The word "naja"

Death Adder (*Acanthophis antarcticus*)

Indian Cobra, rear view

King Cobra courting (*Ophiophagus hannah*)

is derived from the Sanskrit word "naga" for snake. The hood of this Indian form can spread wider than the hood of any other cobra; it ranges throughout Africa as well as tropical Asia. The hood is spread by means of elongate ribs that force out the loose skin of the neck; when it is extended, it is a curved disk of several times the diameter of the body, and black markings on the skin between the scales become visible as a conspicuous figure in the shape of the eye of a hook-and-eye fastener, or of circular or other form. This cobra assumes a defensive and warning posture when it is approached, with a third of the body raised vertically above the flat coil on the ground, the hood widely expanded, and the head directed forward. The danger from cobra bite is primarily from treading upon one at night, and is greatly multiplied by the fact that the majority of country people in India and the East Indies go barefoot. The widely quoted figure of thirty thousand deaths a year in India from cobra bite is an estimate only, and recent figures bring this down to about ten thousand. This amounts to about one in thirty thousand of the population, as compared with the current estimate of four or five deaths per annum in Brazil, scarcely one per million. It must be emphasized that these estimates are little more than guesses, for, in the more remote regions, whether of Brazil or India, there is no source of information.

The danger of the cobra's bite to man has never been set forth more vividly than in Kipling's story *Rikki-Tikki-Tavi,* which concerns the fight between cobra and mongoose and the enmity between man and cobra. As in a folk tale, the Indian animals speak English; but as in any good piece of folklore, the story is based on fact as well as on misinterpretation of fact. Cobras do enter houses; birds do lead

snakes and other enemies away from their nests by the pretense of having a broken wing, and mongooses do attack and kill cobras, which lay eggs and guard them. What does not appear is that only about 10 per cent of cobra bites are fatal; but the danger from the bite of the krait is scarcely exaggerated.

The common cobra is the stock in trade of Oriental snake charmers, who live by presenting a show in street or market place with venomous snakes and pythons, profiting from the same morbid interest in snakes that makes the reptile house in any zoo second only to the monkey house in popular appeal. The cobra is suited to the snake charmer's purpose because of its vast reputation as a dangerous creature, and by the fact that with its spread hood it is immediately recognizable. Cobras kept in a basket, when the top is removed, will rear up a third of their length, spread their hoods widely, and face the performer, who plays some simple melody on a flutelike instrument, swaying his body in time to the music. This the snake cannot hear, but it appears to, since the snake sways back and forth with the movements to and fro of the snake charmer's body. The mere handling of dangerous snakes thrills the spectator, who does not know that the cobras may have had their fangs removed, or may have had their lips sewn shut, or that, alternatively, the snake charmer may be immune to the venom from repeated inoculations and may present his show with snakes which have their venom apparatus intact.

The Indian cobra is an especially favorable animal for these shows because it apparently is not capable of aiming its strike accurately during the day. Furthermore these daytime strikes are usually made with the mouth shut. All in all, it is not an aggressive creature. In fact the young are far more likely to strike than the adults. It is interesting to note that the habit of spreading the hood, rearing, and facing a larger animal is fully developed in the egg; for a hatching cobra, when only its head and the front of the body have emerged from the egg, will rear, spread its hood, and strike like any adult.

The largest of the cobra group is the king cobra, usually set off as a distinct genus, *Ophiophagus,* a name that refers to its snake-eating habits. Although ordinarily the king cobra makes off when disturbed, it sometimes stands its ground. To be walking along a jungle trail and suddenly to be confronted by a big king cobra with about four feet of its twelve-foot length reared up is a nerve-wracking experience. It is not very surprising, then, that the king cobra should have the reputation of being aggressive. Attacks on man are reported, and we believe them to be authentic, though most probably provoked by an approach to the nest. The king cobra is the only member of this group that habitually makes its own nest. By forming a crook with the fore part of her body, the female drags dead leaves and decaying sticks into a heap. The nest is a two-chambered affair, a lower compartment for the eggs and an upper one for the female who remains on guard. In some cases the male also guards the nest.

One of the erroneous ideas derived from the Kipling story is still widely current in the minds of nonzoologists. This is that the krait is a tiny dust snake, even more deadly than the cobra. Actually there are many kinds of kraits and several small species. The common krait, however, distributed from South China to India, reaches a length of at least five feet. It is a brown-and-white-banded snake, and is certainly very dangerous if it is stepped on at night. When encountered by day it has the seemingly stupid habit of coiling up with its head beneath its coils; it may be kicked, and even killed with a stick without defending itself. All of the kraits have an extremely potent venom.

Cobras and their relatives are even more diversified into distinct species in Africa than in India and the East Indies. The most famous of the African true cobras (i.e., members of the genus *Naja*) is the Egyptian asp, the snake with which Cleopatra committed suicide. Herpetologists have argued as to whether Cleopatra's serpent might not be one of the various deadly vipers of Egypt. The bite of the asp was known as a relatively painless mode of death in ancient times, and was a familiar means of offering death to a political prisoner as an alternative to torture. This seems to make it extremely likely that Cleopatra's suicide was by asp bite. None of the African cobras has so wide-spreading a hood as the Indian cobra. It is the asp whose head appears in the headdress of familiar sculptures of ancient Egypt.

Several species of rather narrow-hooded cobras in Africa have developed the capacity to spit their venom to a considerable distance, and do so with alarming accuracy, directing the venom at the face and eyes of an approaching large animal. The venom acts on the eyes as a powerful irritant, producing a strong burning sensation; permanent injury to the eyes can be avoided only by prompt washing with water. Dr. C. M. Bogert, of the American Museum of Natural History, has shown that the venom is ejected by muscular pressure on the gland, and that the stream of liquid is directed forward by a narrowed and forwardly facing opening on the fang, very well distinguished from the downwardly directed opening in the fangs of cobras that do not spit. The "ringhals" or "spuy-slang" of South

[237]

Africa (*Hemachatus*) spits so regularly at approaching visitors in a zoo that it spatters the glass front of its cage with venom until it becomes accustomed to captivity.

An aquatic species of front-fanged snake, the water cobra, banded black and brown, lives in the large lakes of Central Africa and feeds on fishes. It is named *Boulengerina,* after the famous Belgian-British herpetologist who reviewed the amphibians and reptiles of the world in a tremendous work, the nine volumes of the *Catalogues* of the British Museum collections, published over the years 1882 to 1896.

The African relatives of the cobras known as mambas (genus *Dendroaspis,* Plate 118) are so active and aggressive, so large (the largest is fourteen feet long), and have so deadly a venom that they have given rise to a considerable folklore and to legendary or partly legendary stories of attacks on man. The venom is known to be exceedingly potent, for in an experiment on himself with a minute quantity, Dr. Eigenberger (of Sheboygan, Wisconsin) nearly died. The unpredictable nature of snake bite

Desert Cobra (*Walterinnesia aegyptia*)

is vividly illustrated by the experience of Louis Agassiz Fuertes, the famous animal artist, while in Abyssinia on his last expedition. While on horseback he shot a large snake at the roadside, firing the auxiliary cartridge and dust shot used for collecting birds. He was familiar, of course, with the wide-headed rattlesnakes at home in the United States and with the equally broad-headed common puff adder of Africa; and seeing that the snake he had shot had a very slender head and neck, he did not think it could be venomous. He dismounted and picked it up, and the snake, which unfortunately turned out to be a mamba and not yet dead, turned and bit him on the finger, puncturing the skin with a single fang. The astonishing result was that no symptoms of poisoning developed! Either the snake had somehow exhausted its venom, or the fang was stopped up with dirt, or for other reasons unknown no venom had been ejected with its bite. The snake was properly preserved, and it documents the story as Specimen Number 12738 in the Chicago Natural History Museum's research collections.

Another account of an experience with a mamba is given by Mr. Arthur Loveridge, by far the most active student and collector of snakes who has worked in Africa. He relates that while descending a mountain path the porters behind him called out to warn him that they had stirred up a mamba; he turned too late to do anything but stand still. The snake dashed down and between his legs, and disappeared. Had he seen it in time to shoot it, or had this incident occurred to any other than a very cool-headed herpetologist, there would have been still another story of an aggressive attack on man by a mamba.

The mambas (*Dendroaspis*) are characterized by much-enlarged teeth at the front of the lower jaws, in addition to the large venom-conducting fangs above. In the arboreal green mamba, these teeth may be of service in keeping hold of a bird or lizard that has been struck, just as we suppose to be the case with the elongate front teeth of the arboreal pythons and boas.

The smaller elapid snakes of Africa include the small black-and-white-banded *Elaps* from which the family Elapidae takes its name. By an unfortunate confusion, and lack of clairvoyant knowledge of the rules of zoological nomenclature on the part of the herpetologists whose work was accomplished before the rules were made, the name *Elaps* was applied to the South American coral snakes for more than a hundred years. The little African snake had meanwhile come to be known under the name *Homorelaps*. Much more widespread in Africa is *Elapsoidea*, with a single widespread species with numerous geographic races.

One relative of the cobras, *Aspidelaps,* confined to the sandy deserts of South Africa, must be mentioned for its remarkably shortened head, in which the snout is covered by a broadly expanded rostral shield, which has free lateral edges. This startlingly resembles the form of snout in various burrowing and even only partly burrowing harmless snakes of Asia and North America that have been mentioned in an earlier section. In these snakes, burrowing is accomplished by sidewise thrusting and hooking back of the head. The free edges of the rostral shield appear to be developed in response to this functional use, certainly one of the most clear-cut examples of parallel evolution in snakes.

The Sea Snakes
(*Family Hydrophidae*)

One may not hope on any ordinary voyage to see anything like the sea serpent of mythology, but there are extraordinary sights at sea that are the more vivid for the usual monotony of the surface—like a whale spouting, a row of porpoises in their endless jumping, most rarely a whale clear out of water in his incredible vertical leap. These conspicuous creatures are examples of the return to the sea of land animals, which has been going on from the time of the earliest animals that left the sea to become adjusted to the land. The sea offers so vast an abundance of life, and thus so inexhaustible a food supply, that land animals (even our own ancestors) were tempted into living along its shores, and more rarely took the remarkable evolutionary step of a return from land life to aquatic life, and from the form of a land animal to the streamlined fish form, as in the whales and porpoises, which are derived from early mammals.

During the great Age of Reptiles, group after group returned in part or as a group to the sea. Among the most ancient of reptile groups, the turtles produced the familiar sea-dwelling forms. So did the crocodiles (in the teleosaurs), and so did the lizards (in mosasaurs). Most completely marine of the extinct groups were the ichthyosaurs and the plesiosaurs, the former with a startlingly fishlike body form, and the latter like gigantic turtles with vastly elongated necks. Among existing reptiles, the snakes have in their turn produced a true sea snake; but as this is confined to the tropics, it is little known outside of zoological circles. Far more remarkable even than the sight of a whale is the occasional encounter of an ocean liner in the Pacific or Indian Ocean with an aggregation of sea snakes. Some species are fond of basking on the surface of the water, and on calm days may be seen in hundreds from the bow of a steamer, especially in early morning or late afternoon. When the wash of the steamer disturbs them, they dive vertically down and disappear.

These sea snakes form a very well-marked family, characterized by adjustment for life in the water. These adjustments are evident in the flattening of the body from side to side; the still greater flattening of the tail, which is oarlike and used as a scull; the valvelike closure of the nostrils and their upward direction. Almost all of the sea snakes bear living young. There is a series within the family leading from the ordinary type of overlapping (imbricate) scales of the primitive types to small juxtaposed scales entirely without imbrication.

It is strange indeed that these snakes should be so abundant on the coasts of Asia and Australia and totally absent in the Atlantic. One species, *Pelamis platurus,* the common black-and-yellow sea snake, overlaps the range of all the other species, and is the one form that reaches the west coast of the Americas. In the other direction it has found its way to Madagascar. This snake is often dark brownish black on the upper half of the body and brilliant yellow on the lower side, the two colors meeting in a sharp line. This coloration appears in most parts of the range of the species, and is the normal one in the Bay of Panama. In other regions a great variety of variant patterns appear, sometimes with an extra brown-and-yellow stripe on the sides, sometimes with the colors broken into alternating crossbars. It helps to explain the remarkably wide distribution of this species to learn that it swims freely out to the open sea. A voyager in the Philippine seas writes, "I have seen it in the seas of Mindoro and Sulu, swimming by thousands on the top of the water." Small fishes have an instinct to assemble beneath any floating object such as a coconut husk or a stick, and thus the sea snake, floating quietly at the surface, quite automatically attracts its natural food.

Various authors have commented on the extreme potency of the venom of the sea snakes. This is fortunately matched by extreme reluctance to strike except at the small fishes, especially eels, that form its food. Dr. Albert W. C. T. Herre, with whom the senior author made a long voyage through the Pacific, often told us of his experiences with sea snakes in the Manila Aquarium. When an eel of appropriate size was put in the tank with a hungry sea snake, the snake promptly struck the eel, which could be seen to stiffen out and die in a few moments. The importance of a powerful venom to prevent the escape of its prey into crevices in coral seems very evident. Nevertheless, some of the sea snake types seem to have a relatively weak venom. As to the inoffensiveness of sea snakes in general, Colonel Wall, from long experience in India, writes: "There are scarcely any records of casualties, even among the fishermen who haul them in by the dozen every day in their nets. The snakes so caught are handled fearlessly by those drawing in the nets, who throw them back into the sea." Other accounts, from the Malayan coasts, speak of frequent casualties; but it is almost impossible to obtain any critical accounts from the Malay fishermen.

It is most interesting that there are two levels of adjustment to life in the sea within the family. The members of the subfamily Laticaudinae have broadly overlapping dorsal scales and ventral plates (like those of most snakes) extending across the belly about a third the width of the body. The three types, *Laticauda, Aipysurus,* and *Emydocephalus* (these lack English vernacular names), are also evidently among the more primitive types of sea snakes, since some of them come ashore on the coral reefs to lay their eggs.

Laticauda semifasciata is the largest form in this primitive subfamily, reaching a length of more than six feet and a diameter of at least three inches. This form was formerly found in great abundance in Philippine waters and was made the object of a special fishery by Japanese fishermen, some being taken for their skins only, others being kept alive in sacks and shipped to Japan for food. The snakes for food are spitted on a pointed bamboo stick, roasted and smoked, and eaten with soy sauce. One may speculate that so prepared they must be at least as palatable as the rattlesnake meat prepared in Florida and sold in cans, presumably to provide tidbits at cocktail parties. It is remarkable that these Philippine sea snakes gathered by the thousands at the island of Gato, north of Cebu, to breed in the large caves open to the sea. The numbers collected may have reached thirty thousand per annum; an estimate of ten thousand snakes, not less than a meter in length, as the proper number for a continuing fishery was made by our friend D. S. Rabor, of Silliman University on Negros Island.

In the second subfamily of sea snakes, there are no records of the snakes coming ashore, and in them the ventrals are reduced to a degree that makes them barely wider than the adjacent scales. All of them produce living young while at sea. A few of the twenty-three species of *Hydrophis* reach a length exceeding eight feet. It is remarkable that some of the longest of the sea snakes have a small head and slender neck and anterior half of the body, with a bulky abdominal portion that is very much larger in diameter. This curious body form, which recalls that of the extinct marine plesiosaurs, seems to be associated with the mechanical requirements for striking at prey in the water. Without any fixed fulcrum from which to launch its stroke, the free-swimming venomous snake makes use of the inertia of the heavy abdomen, while the great resistance of the water is made less by the slenderness of the head and neck. In the normal sea snakes, the head and neck are about half the diameter of the rear part of the body. In those with the more obvious plesiosaur form, like the banded slender-necked sea snake, *Hydrophis fasciatus,* or the small-headed slender sea snake, *Microcephalophis gracilis,* the abdomen is four or five times the diameter of the neck.

Most sea snakes are creatures of the shallow seas, whose vast extent in the East Indian region provides suitable waters for them and a suitable abundance of fishes, and especially eels, for their food. Only the black-and-yellow sea snake is completely pelagic, and absent even from the estuaries of the great Malayan rivers, where other sea snakes abound. One species has become adjusted to life in fresh water, living in Lake Taal in southern Luzon in the Philippine Islands. This species, *Hydrophis semperi,* is actually little more than a landlocked race of the widespread blue-banded sea snake, *Hydrophis cyanocinctus,* which is distributed along the coasts of Asia and the East Indies from the Persian Gulf to Japan. Lake Taal occupies an ancient volcanic crater, and in its center is the small active volcano of Taal. The modern lake is about twelve miles in diameter and overflows to the sea through a narrow, swift-flowing stream five or six miles long.

There are fifteen genera and about fifty species of sea snakes. Their failure to swim across wide areas of the sea has isolated the Asiatic forms from the Australian to a considerable extent, and most of the shallow-water forms are different in the two areas. Their wonderful adjustments to their environment, and the steps to be discerned toward that adjustment in the living forms, make them one of the most significant evidences concerning the evolution of the order of snakes.

The sea-serpent stories of mythology are not even based on snakes, but on elongate fishes or on giant cuttlefish, and "sea monster" might be a better term. There is now a report of a gigantic eel larva in the Pacific, the adult of which is unknown. It might well prove to be the most serpentlike of all the sea serpents. The numerous true sea snakes of the Pacific do not count as "sea serpents" because of their small size. Mythology refuses to be satisfied by mere facts, and the belief in unknown gigantic monsters is more attractive than the prosaic facts about the snakes that really do live in the sea.

The True Vipers
(*Family Viperidae*)

In the highest development of the venom apparatus in snakes, the hypodermic fangs injecting the venom are greatly enlarged, so much so that they are folded back when not in use, and erected in the mouth only when the actual strike is made. The two families with this elaboration of the jaws and teeth are the vipers and pit-vipers, the Viperidae and the Crotalidae, which together are referred to as the Solenoglypha, and contrast with the front-fanged Proteroglypha (cobras and allies and sea snakes) with fixed teeth, the rear-fanged Opistho-glypha, and the harmless snakes without venom-conducting teeth, the Aglypha. The pit-vipers are a step in advance of the true vipers in their possession of a special sense organ, the facial pit, which enables them to detect warm-blooded prey.

The vipers are confined to the Old World, where they are found throughout most of Europe, Asia, and Africa, with a remarkable variety of small and large forms, from the small Orsini's viper, *Vipera ursini* of southern Europe, which rarely reaches a length of even twelve inches, to the truly horrendous Gaboon viper, which may be nearly six feet long, with a body six inches in diameter.

The vipers are almost all terrestrial, and the normal body form is short and stocky, with a short tail. Modifications of this form consist mainly in great widening of the head (to contain enlarged venom glands) and extreme shortening of the tail. The great majority of vipers have lost the large head shields characteristic of the colubrine snakes and have replaced them with numerous small scales.

In general the vipers have not exploited a variety of habitats. Their heavy-bodied form appears to be an ancient characteristic, and one that, in terms of evolution, committed them to a few particular modes of life. Basically, vipers lie in wait for their prey, strike it, wait for it to die, track it down, and then swallow it. The perfected venom-injecting device probably gave rise to this behavior, and this in turn permitted the development of the stocky form. A snake that must pursue active prey must itself be relatively swift and therefore rather slim.

[continued on page 257]

116. Milk Snake
(*Lampropeltis doliata annulata*)

[ROY PINNEY

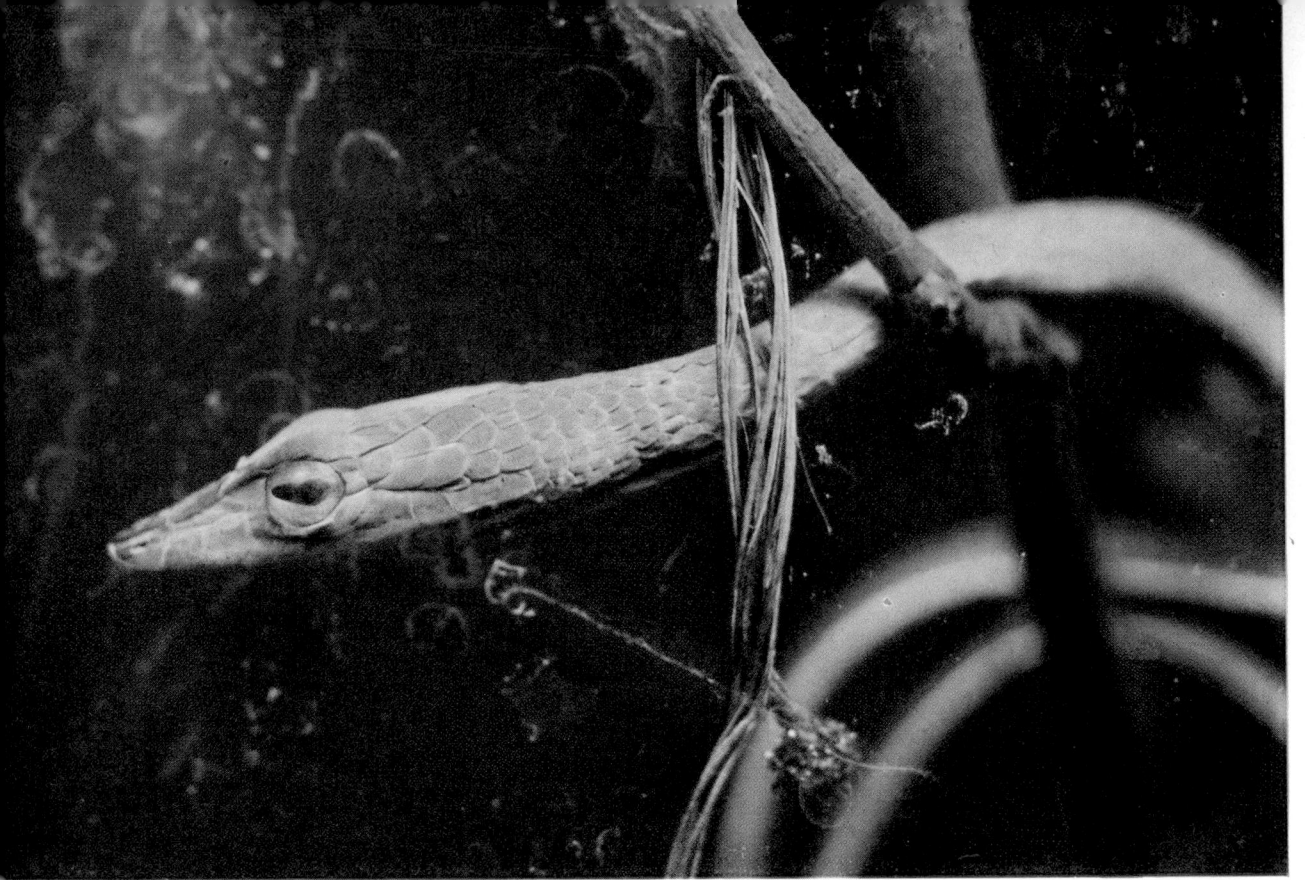

117. Long-nosed Tree Snake (*Dryophis nasuta*)

[JOHN MARKHAM]

118. Black Mamba (*Dendroaspis polylepis*)

[JOHN MARKHAM]

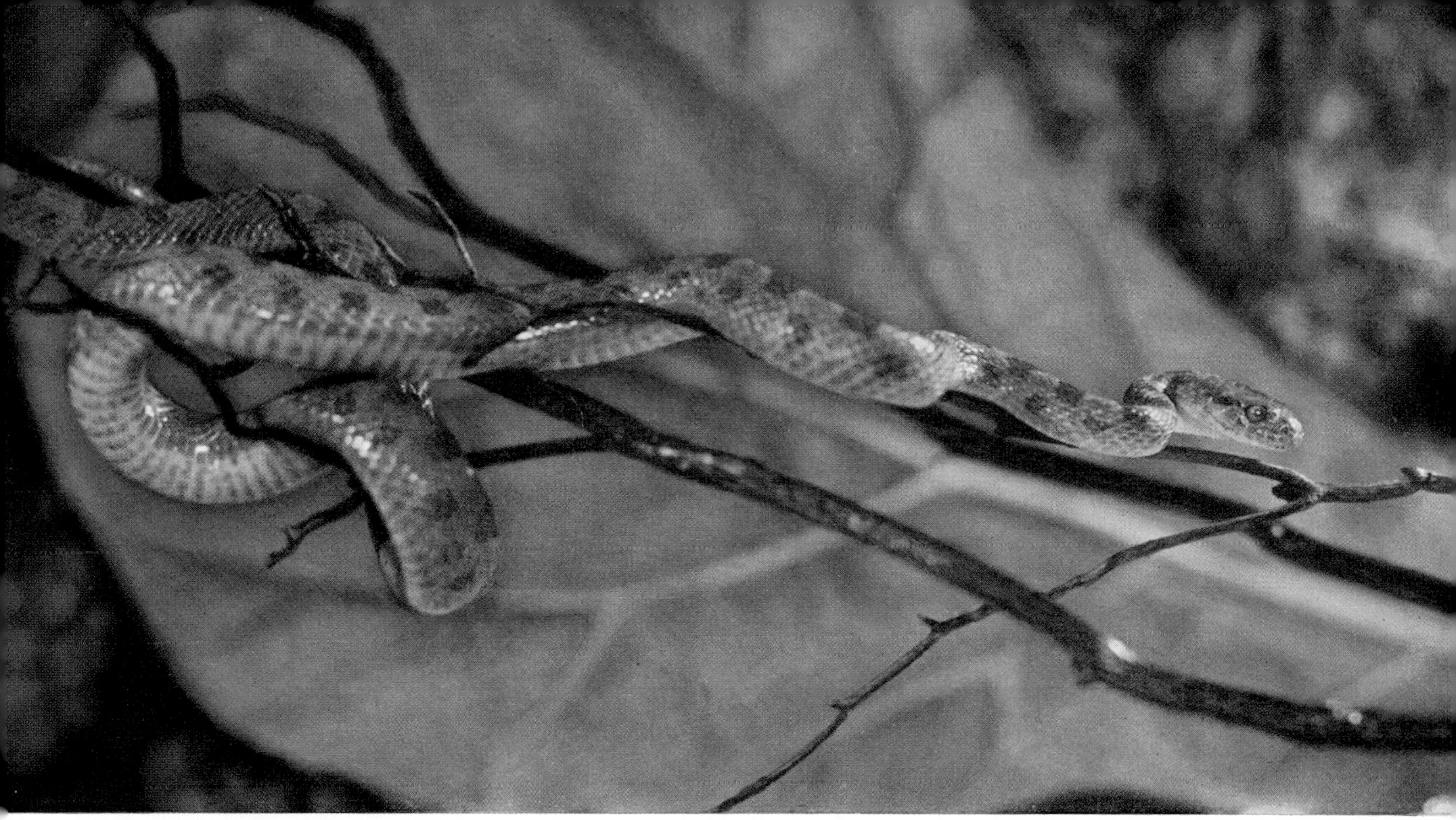

119. Cat-eye Snake (*Leptodeira annulata*)

[ROY PINNEY AND PHILADELPHIA ZOO]

120. Mangrove Snake (*Boiga dendrophila*)

[JOHN MARKHAM]

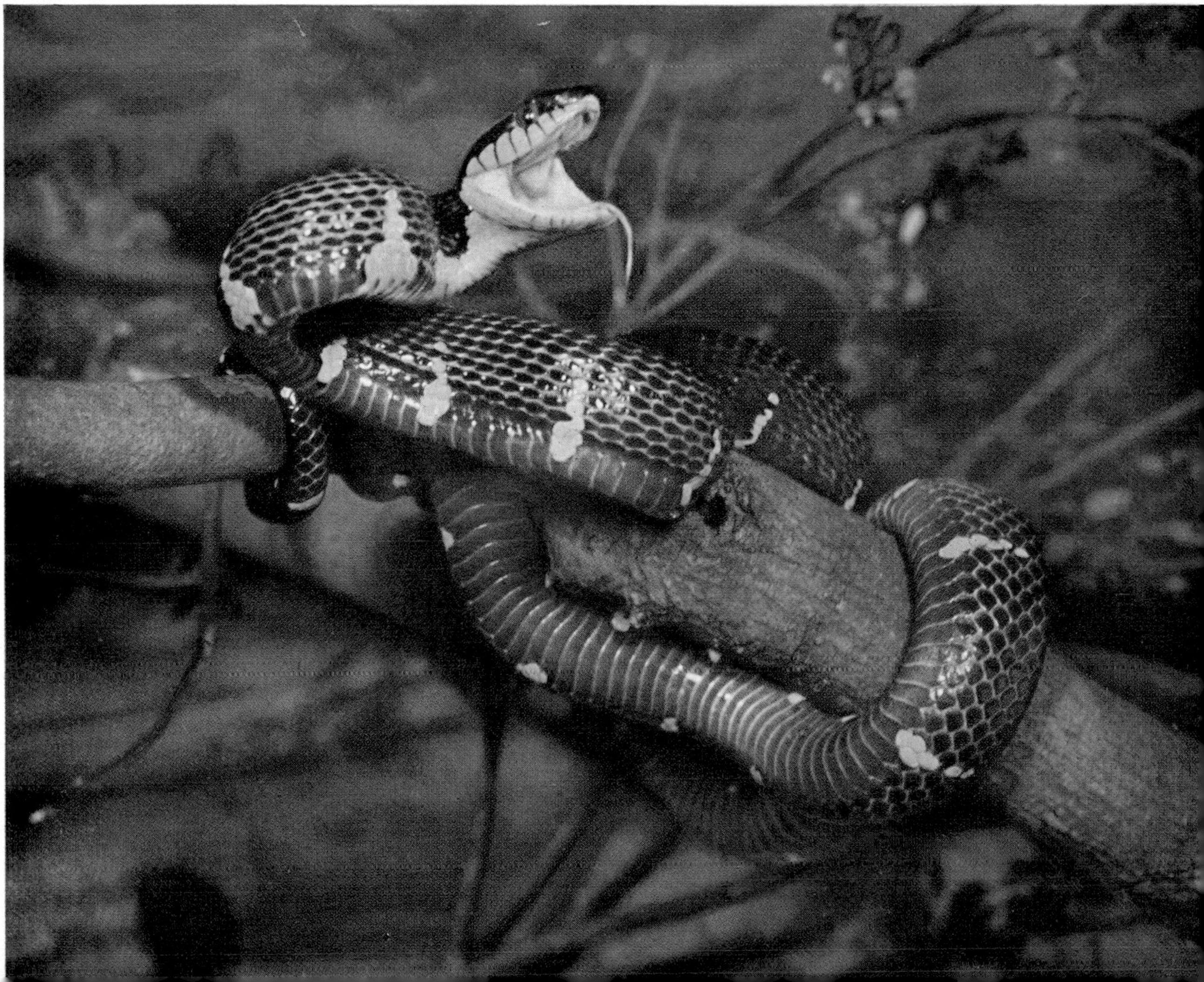

121. Boomslang
(*Dispholidus
typus*)

122. Banded
Sand Snake
(*Chilomeniscus
cinctus*)

123. Long-nosed
Tree Snake
(*Dryophis nasuta*)

124. Flying Snake (*Chrysopelea*)

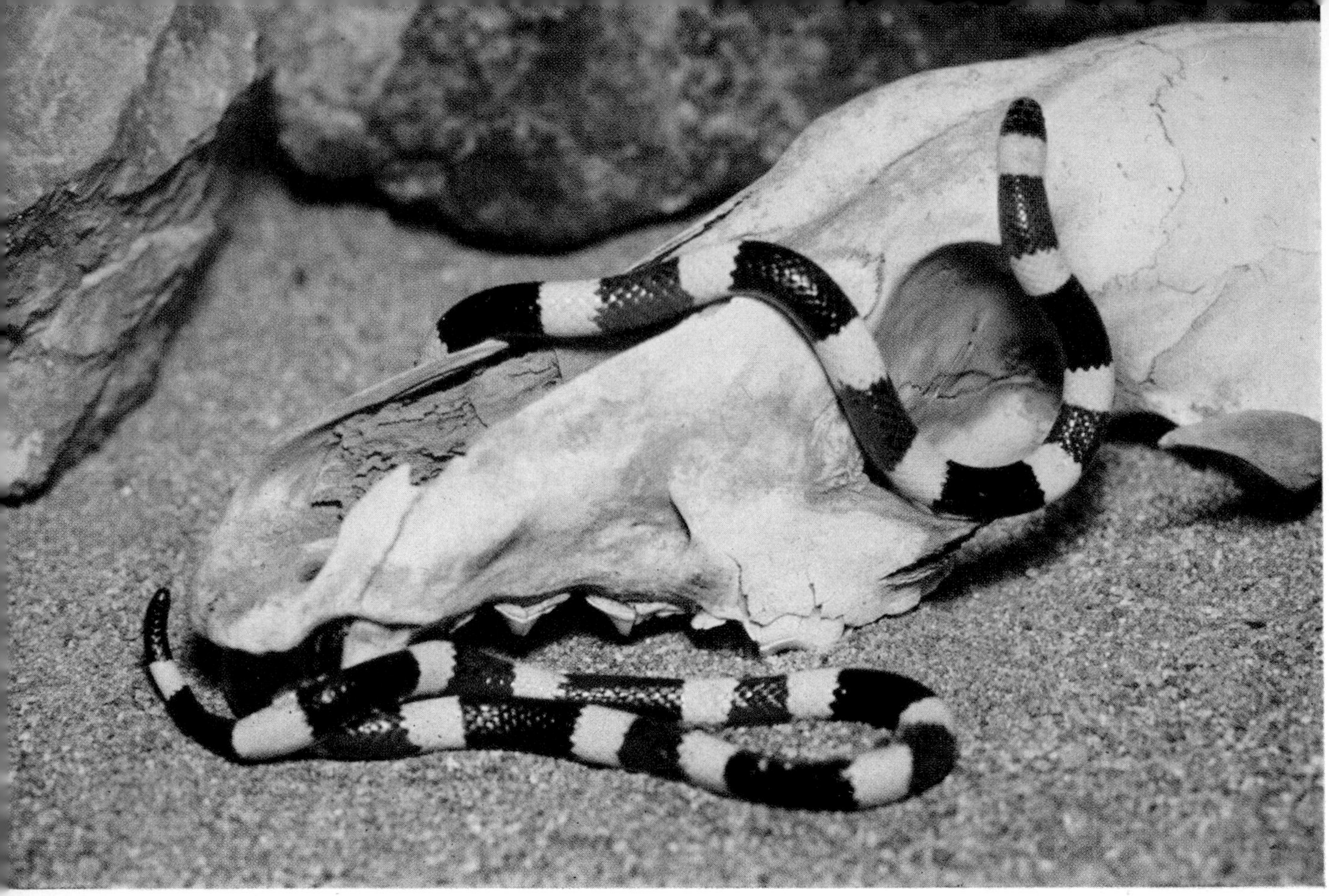

125. Arizona Coral Snake (*Micruroides euryxanthus*)

[HAL H. HARRISON : NATIONAL AUDUBON]

126. Eastern Coral Snake (*Micrurus fulvius*)

[ALLAN D. CRUICKSHANK: NATIONAL AUDUBON]

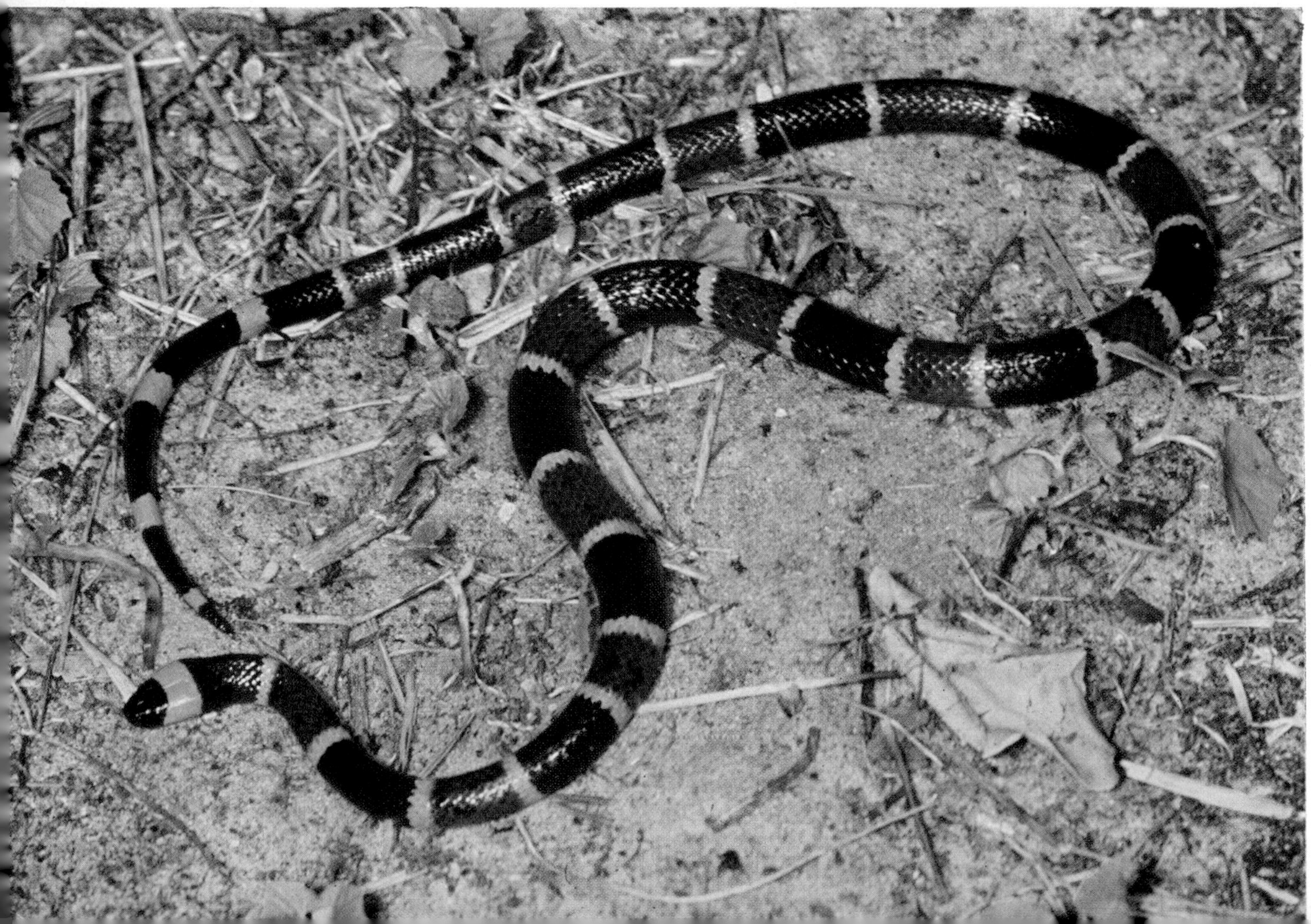

128. Common European Viper (*Vipera berus*)

[JOHN MARKHAM]

**130. Gaboon Viper
(*Bitis gabonica*)**

[ROY PINNEY AND
STATEN ISLAND ZOO]

**129. Puff Adder
(*Bitis arietans*)**

[JOHN MARKHAM]

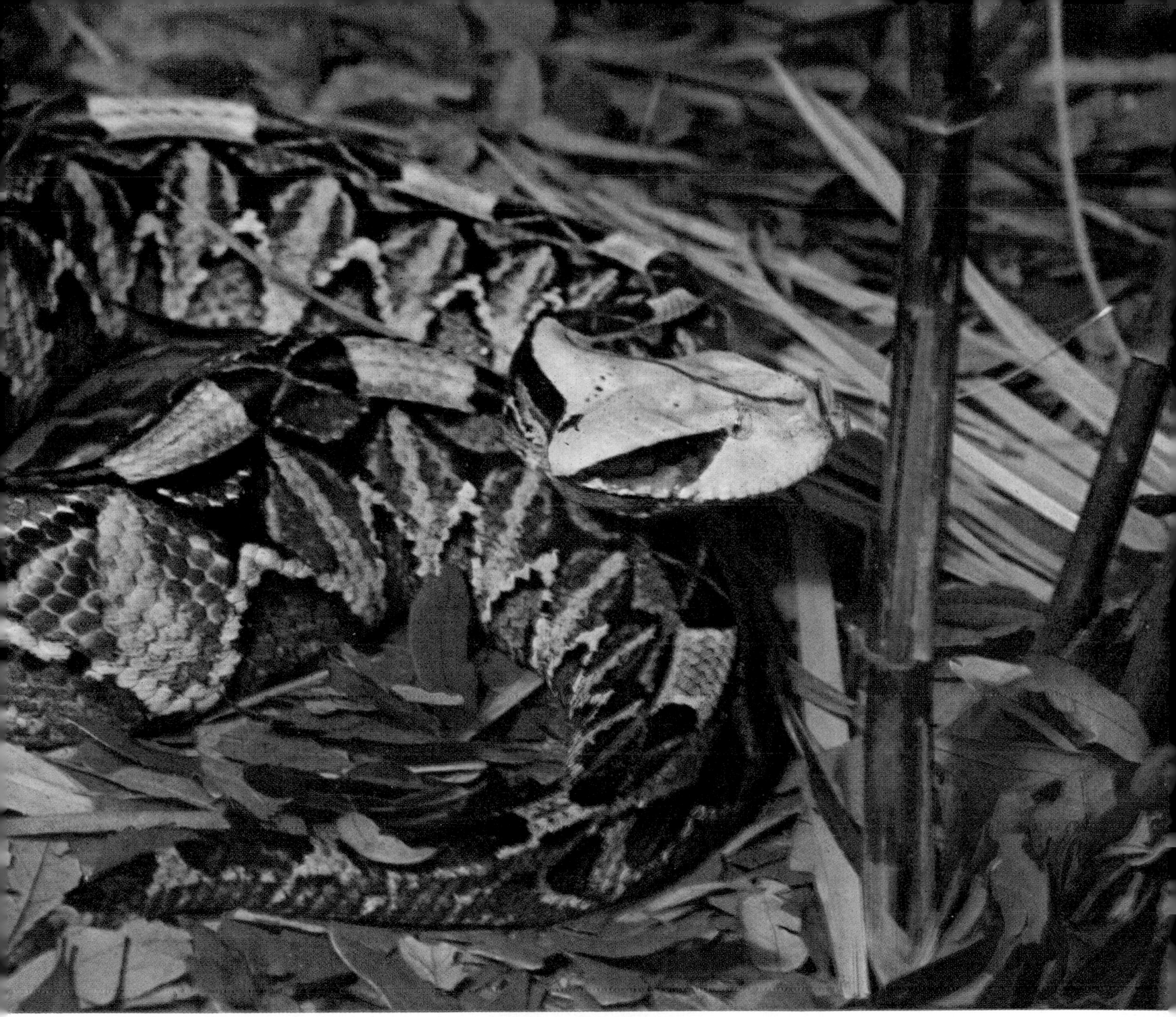

131: Gaboon Viper (*Bitis gabonica*)

[CHARLES HACKENBROCK AND STATEN ISLAND ZOO]

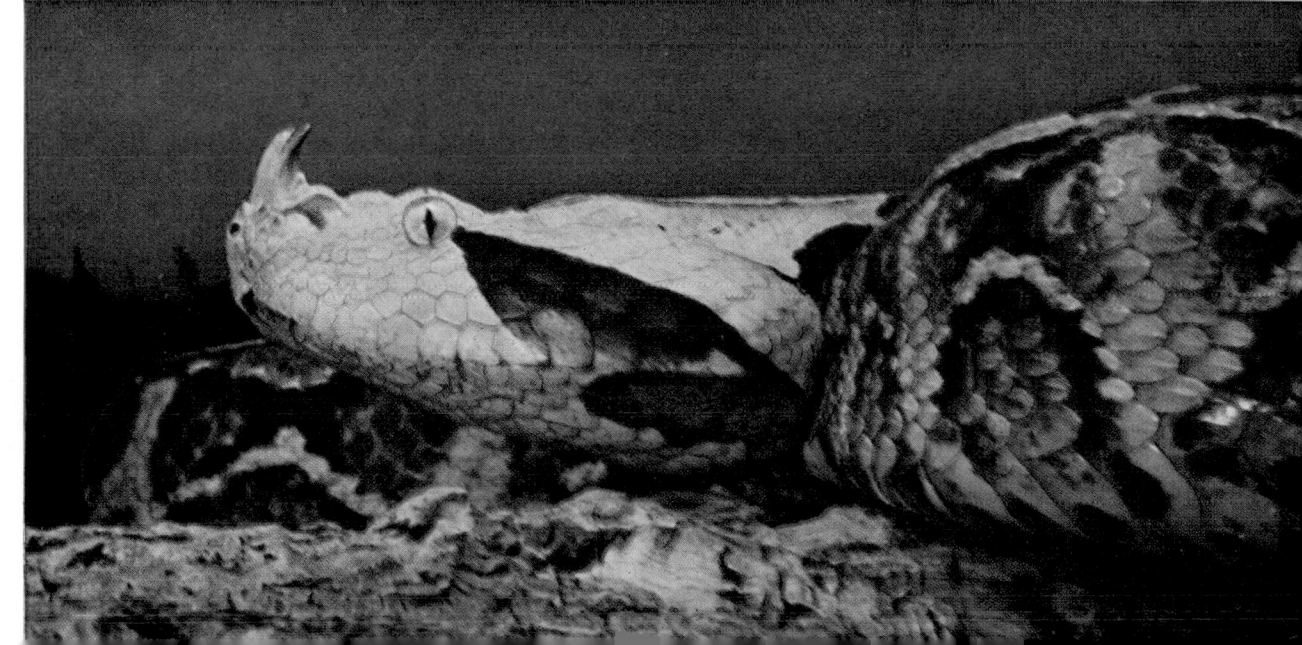

132. Broad-banded
Copperhead
(*Ancistrodon
contortrix
laticinctus*)

[JOHN MARKHAM]

133. Rhinoceros
Viper
(*Bitis
nasicornis*)

[JOHN MARKHAM]

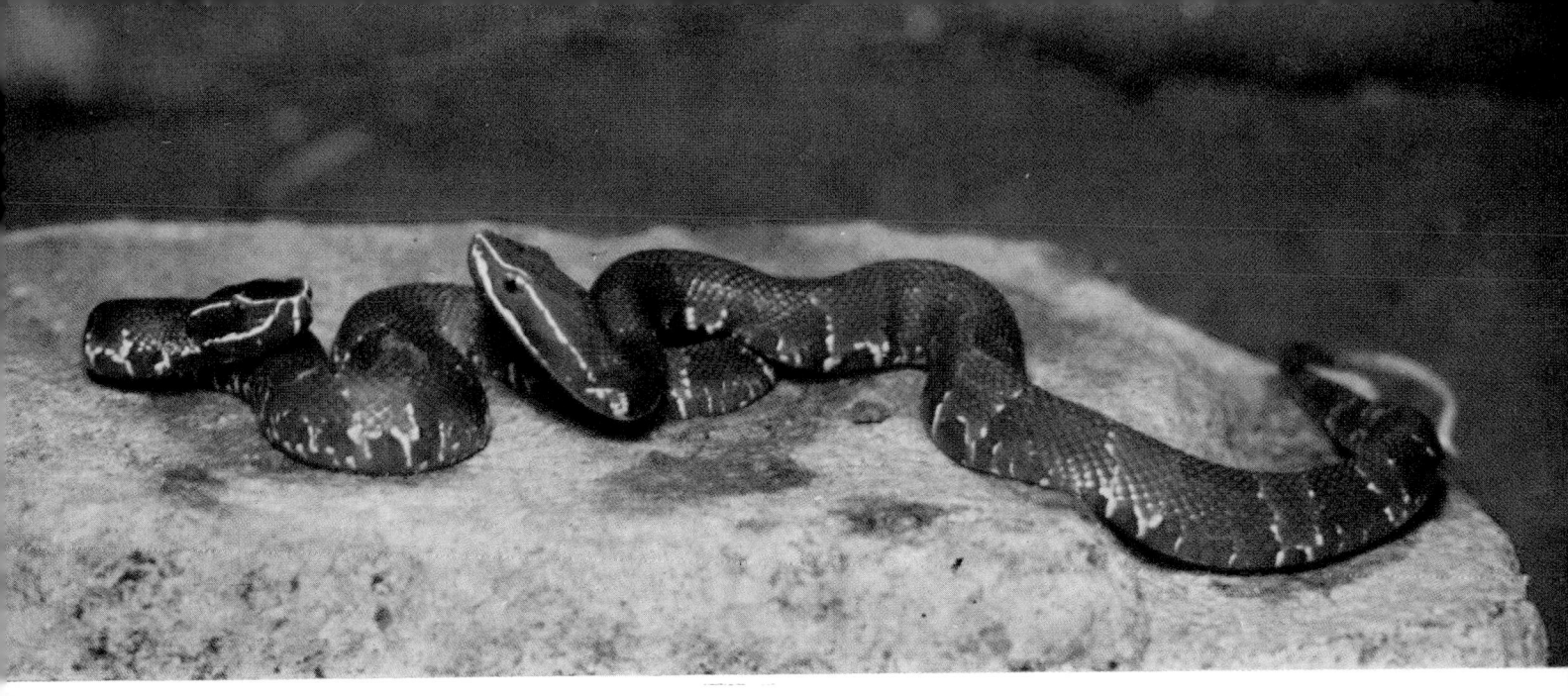

134. Mexican Moccasin (*Ancistrodon bilineatus*)

[HAL H. HARRISON : NATIONAL AUDUBON]

135. Water Moccasin (*Ancistrodon piscivorus*)

[JOHN MARKHAM]

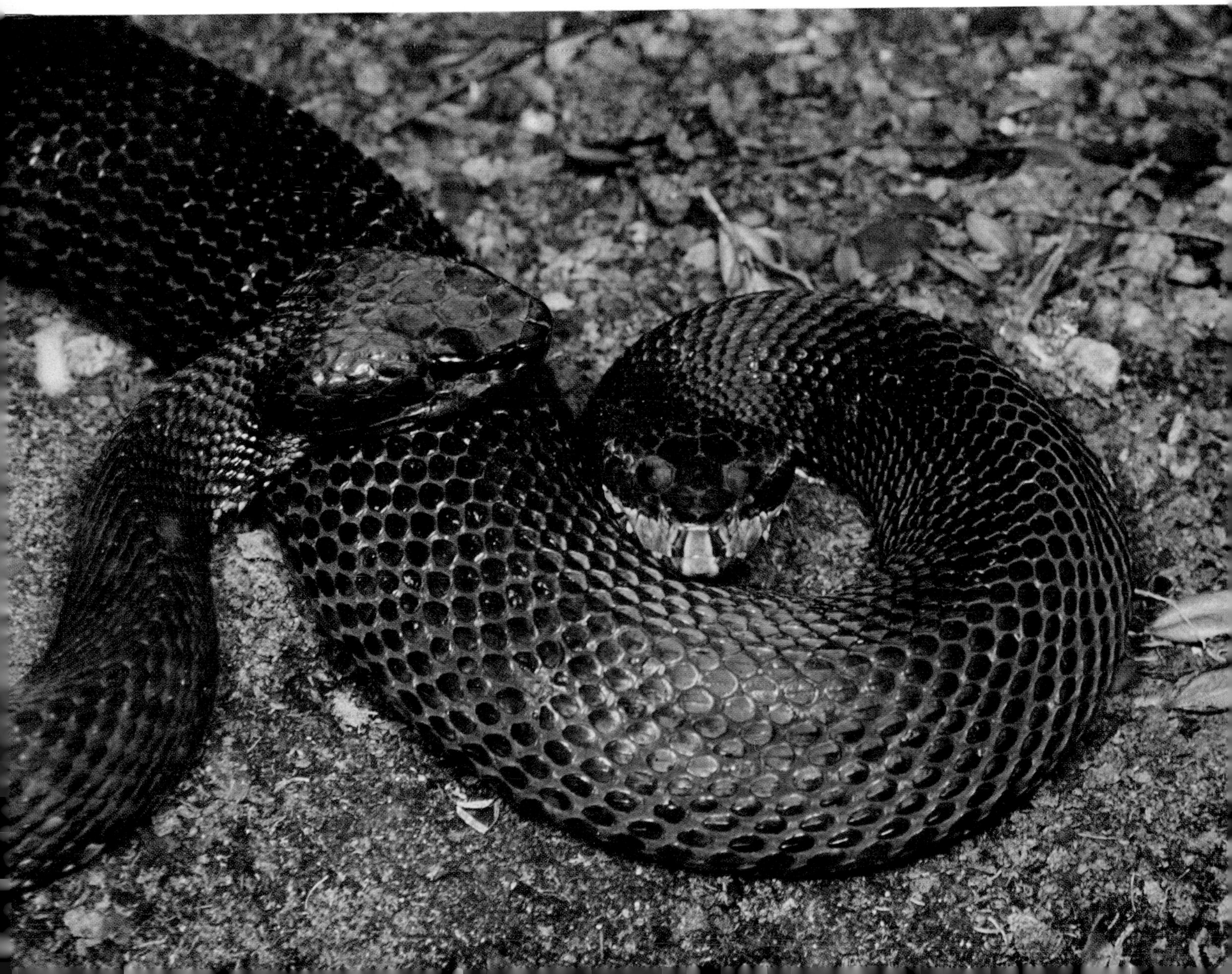

137. Wutu (*Bothrops alternatus*)

[JOHN MARKHAM]

138. Pigmy Rattlesnake (*Sistru*

[ROY PINNEY AND STATEN ISLAND ZOO]

136. Sidewinder
(*Crotalus cerastes*)

[HAL H. HARRISON :
NATIONAL AUDUBON]

iarius)

139. Eastern Massasauga (*Sistrurus catenatus*)

[CHARLES HACKENBROCK AND STATEN ISLAND ZOO]

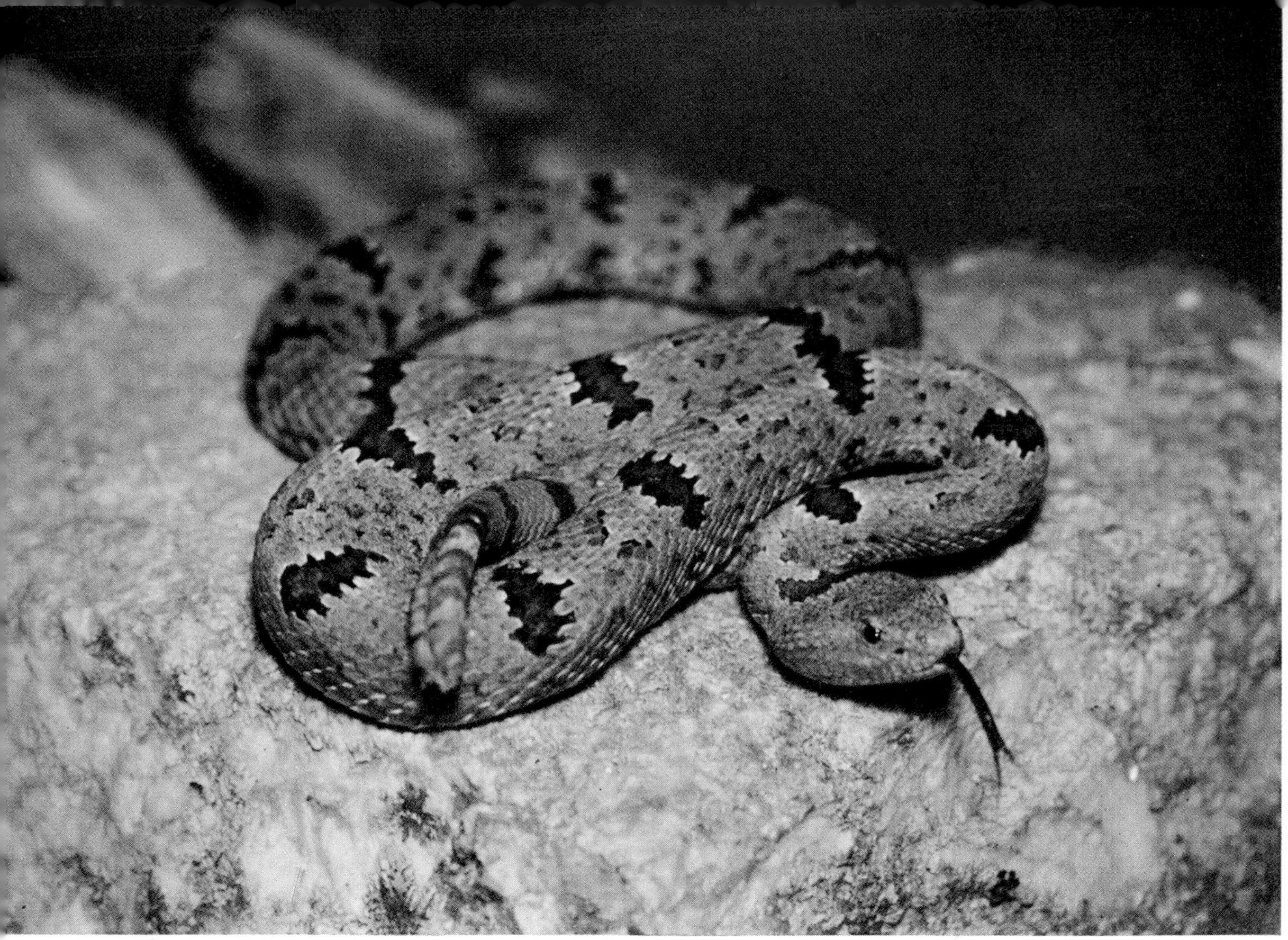

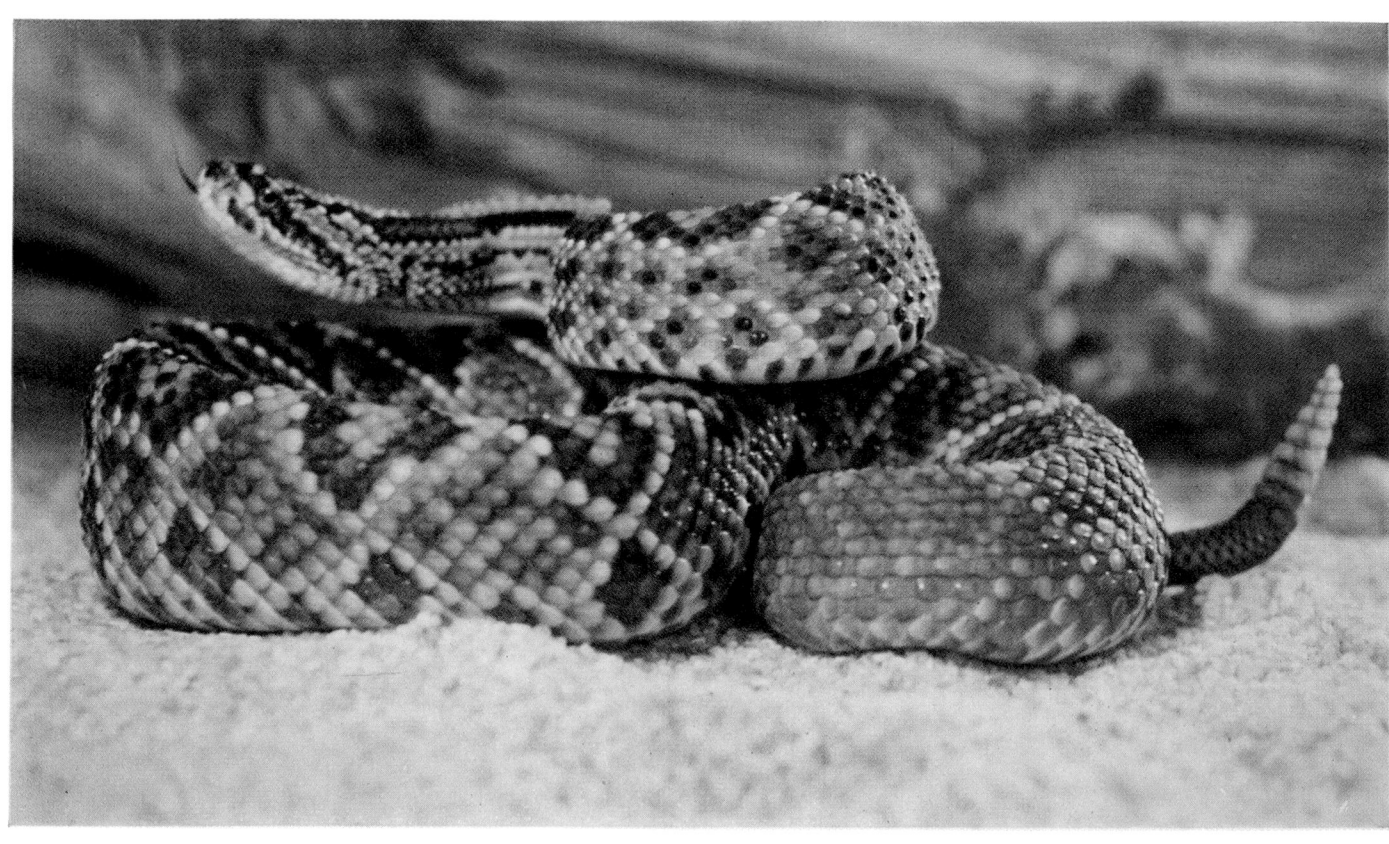

140. Rock Rattlesnake (*Crotalus lepidus*)

[HAL H. HARRISON : NATIONAL AUDUBON]

141. South American Rattlesnake (*Crotalus durissus*)

[ROY PINNEY AND STATEN ISLAND ZOO]

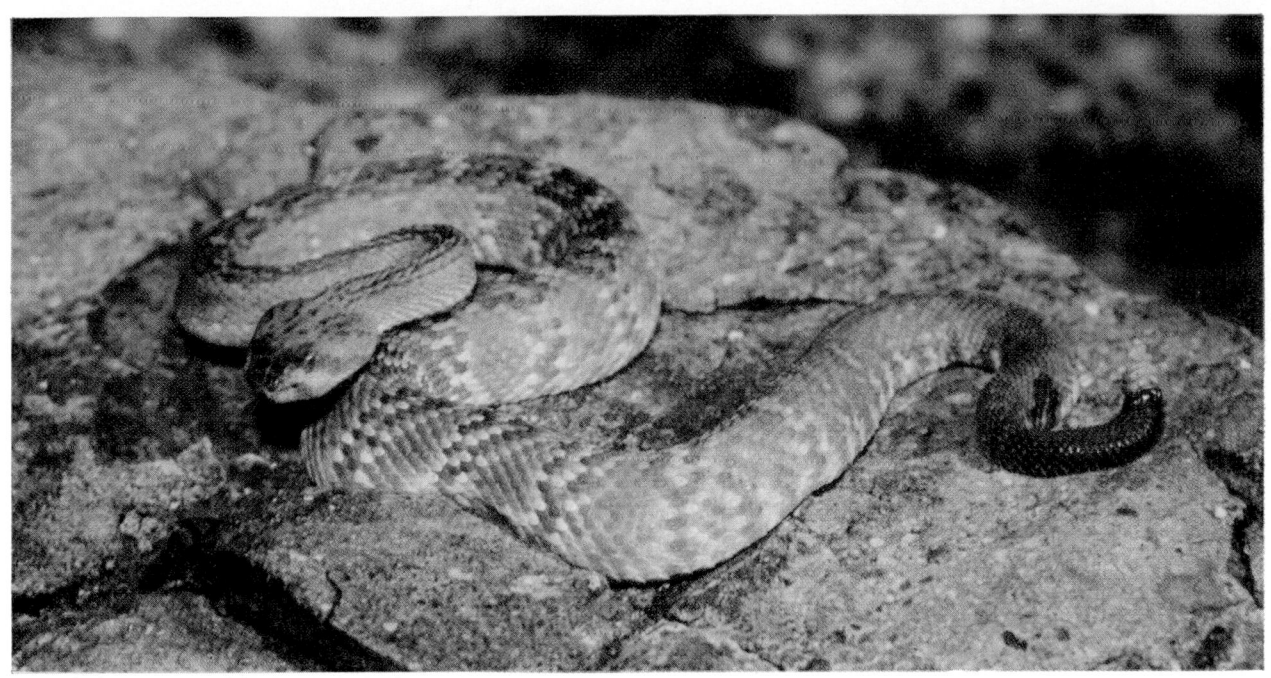

142. Black-tailed Rattlesnake (*Crotalus molussus*)

[HAL H. HARRISON : NATIONAL AUDUBON]

143. Red Diamond Rattlesnake (*Crotalus ruber*)

[ROY PINNEY AND STATEN ISLAND ZOO]

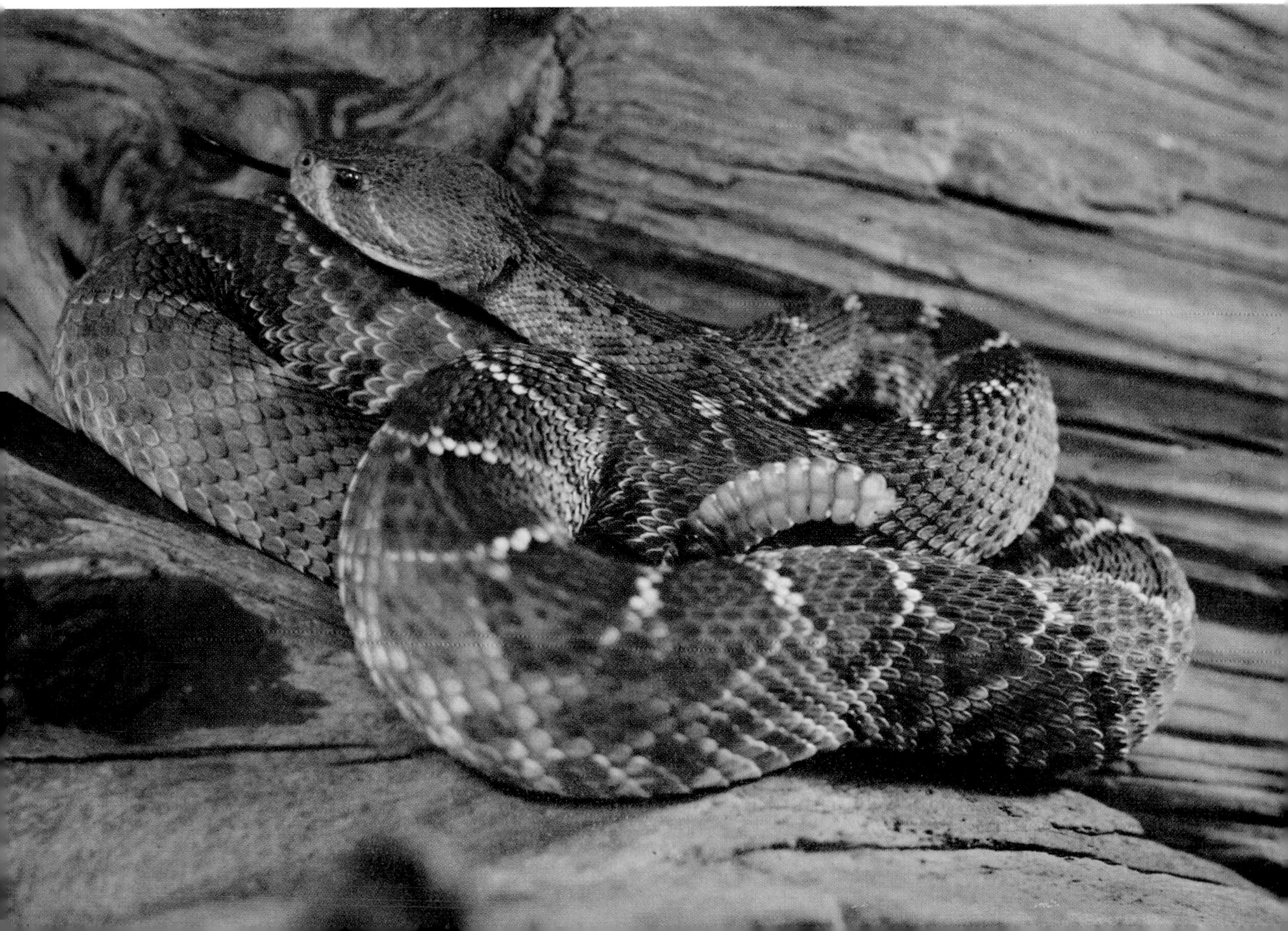

144. Arizona Black Rattlesnake
(*Crotalus viridis cereberus*)

145. Northern Pacific Rattlesnake
(*Crotalus viridis oreganus*)

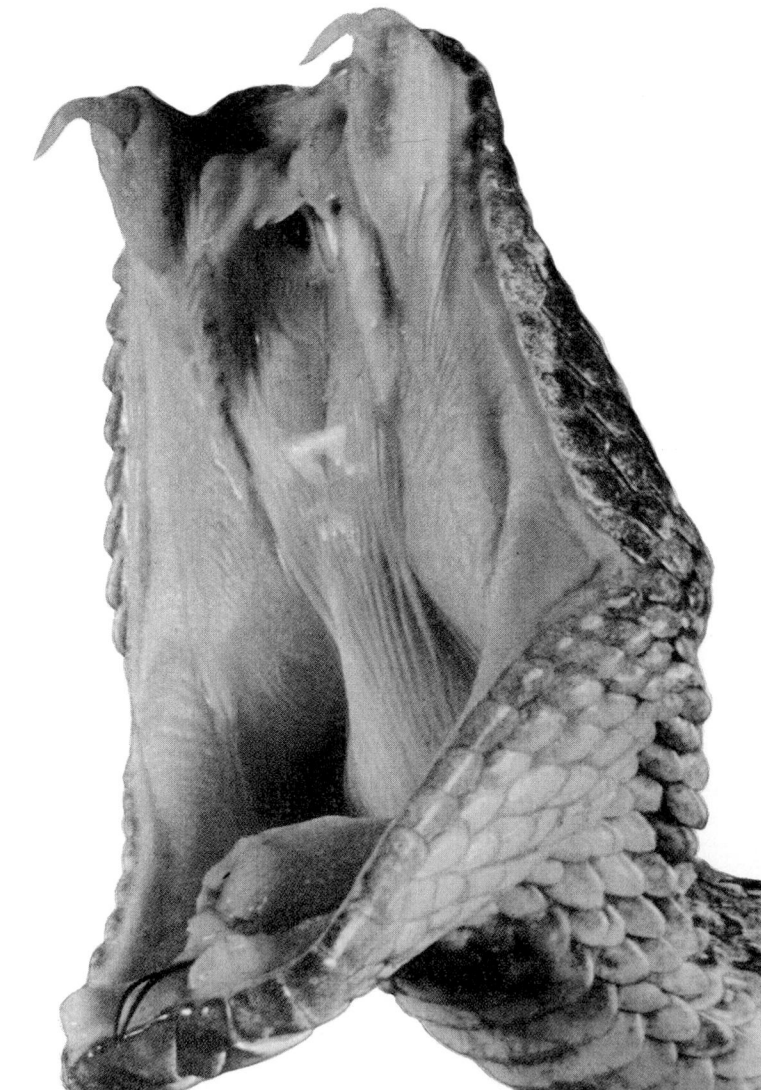

[continued from page 240]

But if a snake can lie camouflaged, like, for example, the enormous Gaboon viper (see below), its body form may be slender or stocky.

A heavy body form is most effective on the surface of the ground, and the great majority of vipers are terrestrial. The few that have adopted an arboreal life use the same adaptation as the heavy-bodied arboreal boas and pythons, namely, a prehensile tail. Many vipers live in loose sand and have acquired sidewinding locomotion and a special method of burying themselves, neither of which is handicapped by a stocky body. Only one group, the mole vipers (genus *Atractaspis*), have adopted a true burrowing existence and have modified the family body form in the course of evolution. Vipers swim well, but are essentially dry-land snakes; no species has become aquatic in habits.

The best known of the vipers is the common European viper, *Vipera berus* (Plate 128), known in England as the adder; this species is found throughout Europe and ranges all the way across northern Asia to Sakhalin Island north of Japan. In Great Britain it is found in considerable numbers throughout England, Wales, and Scotland, and is familiar, in consequence, in literary allusions. The largest specimens on record from England are a

male twenty-five and one-half inches in length and a female of twenty-eight and one-half inches. The record length in Europe is about thirty-two inches. The venom of this species is an effective one for obtaining its normal food of lizards, field mice, and shrews. Even a full bite of the adder is rarely fatal to man, for only seven cases of death are on record in England and Wales for a period of fifty years, and at least four of these were of children. The effect of venom is roughly a relation between the amount of venom injected and the size of the victim. Thus for a small lizard or mouse a given dose of venom may be fatal in a few minutes, or even in as short a time as thirty seconds, whereas the same amount may just make a child severely ill.

The European viper is very variable in coloration, sometimes wholly black, more usually dark gray with a zigzag black marking along the back all the way to the tip of the tail. This may be broken up into black spots, or the band may be more nearly straight-sided. There is usually a series of smaller spots along each side. The lips are light, and a more or less distinct X-shaped pattern may appear on the head.

In spite of agelong persecution by man, the adder is much the most abundant species of snake in

Orsini's Viper (*Vipera ursini*)

ERICH SOCHUREK

Asp Viper (*Vipera aspis*)

England and Wales, and is the only kind of snake to be found in Scotland. It survives, no doubt, because its food animals, field mice and meadow mice, persist in agricultural regions as well as in wild terrain, and because of the abundance of excellent refuges in the way of stone walls and thick hedgerows.

Adders come out of their winter hibernation early in March, and bask in sunny places until the weather is warm enough for greater activity. They return to hibernation in October, after the temperature has dropped to about 46 degrees Fahrenheit. Hibernation takes place in holes or burrows made by other animals, at depths of a foot or more, and often in association with lizards and sometimes toads. They may hibernate singly or in small aggregations, the largest number reported from a single den being forty.

In April the mating season is at its height, but mating may take place also at other seasons, especially in the fall. During courtship the male tongues the female and vibrates his body along hers, while she remains entirely passive. The posturing of pairs of male adders with the fore part of the body raised, and sometimes intertwined, was long thought to be an act of courtship, but has been shown to be a part of the preliminaries. The two males push each other about but do not bite. This "dance of the adders" recalls that similar ritual fighting takes place between rival males of other kinds of snakes, and presumably is the origin of the caduceus, the intertwined symbol of medicine derived from the Aesculapian snakes in the Greek worship of the god of medicine. It is usual for more than one male snake to attend a female, and this is the explanation of masses of snakes being seen intertwined in a "ball" in spring.

The broods of living young of the adder are produced in August and early September. The number of young at a birth averages about a dozen, varying from six to twenty. The young vary in length from about six to eight inches. The adder ranges as far north as any reptile, going beyond the Arctic Circle in Norway and elsewhere. In the northern part of its range the shorter summer and the lower temperatures slow down the development of the embryos so much that it takes two seasons for them to develop.

In captivity adders are often difficult to keep because they may refuse food. This is especially true if they have been caught by the neck with an iron snake stick or are held down too firmly in any way, since injury of the neck usually inhibits normal feeding. The adder is not likely to bite when handled unless it is frightened by a sudden movement. Once adjusted to taking food in confinement or in the larger outdoor moated snake pits at zoological gardens, adders live well, but for a relatively short time.

No species of snake is more frequently the bearer of the fable that the mother snake takes her young into her throat and stomach for protection when a human being approaches. The adder, in fact, is one of the first snakes of which this was reported in print. In *The British Amphibians and Reptiles*, Malcolm Smith quotes an account by William Harrison that appeared in Holinshed's *Chronicle*s in 1577. The statement there is:

> I did see an Adder once myselfe that laie (as I thought) sleaping on a moalehill, out of whose mouth came eleven yoong adders of twelve or thirteen inches in length apiece, which plaied to and fro in the grass one wyth another, tyll some of them espyed me. So soone therefore as they sawe me they ran againe into the mouth of their damme whome I killed, and then founde eache of them shrowded in a distinct cells or pannicle in hyr belly much like unto a shoft white jelly.

We have quoted this in full because it shows so exactly the basis of fact on which the story is based, namely, that a mother viper about to produce her young contains them in her belly, each enclosed in the membrane and fluid quite as stated. William Harrison's account, furthermore, almost word for word, has been repeated unnumbered times in newspapers, popular magazines, and even in scientific journals. The return into the mother's body by way of her open mouth is either an embroidered story or actual hallucination. The story is probably world-wide, for it is told in America of garter snakes, rattlesnakes, and numerous other species.

The species belonging to the genus *Vipera,* in addition to the adder, include Orsini's and Renard's vipers in southern Europe, which are the smallest forms. In three larger species from southern Europe, the asp viper, Lataste's viper, and the sand viper (*Vipera aspis, V. latasti,* and *V. ammodytes*), the snout shows three degrees of development of an upturned appendage, and the head shields are much more broken up than in the adder. To the southeast, three large species of true vipers appear, *xanthina, lebetina,* and *palestinae,* the first in northern Asia Minor, the second widespread in northwestern Africa and southwestern Asia, and the third confined mainly to Palestine. The Palestinian viper produces the largest number of cases of snake bite of all the venomous snakes of that country, presumably because it is found in well-populated agricultural districts. The distribution of the true vipers is so much a connected one that it is somewhat surprising to find an isolated species, Hind's viper, in far-off Kenya Colony.

The common viper of the Indian Peninsula, Russell's viper, *Vipera russelli,* is a pretty snake with a bold and bright-colored pattern of reddish brown spots, outlined with black and outlined again with white, arranged in three lengthwise rows along the back and sides. It is a large snake, for it may reach a length of more than five feet. Beyond India, this viper ranges eastward to Siam and appears in Java and some other East Indian islands. Known also as the daboia and as the tic-polonga, Russell's viper is one of the most feared snakes of India, Burma, and Siam, and is made the more dangerous by the high proportion of barefoot children and adults in the dense populations of these lands. Small mammals are its main food, but it also eats frogs, birds, and lizards. Like other species of *Vipera,* Russell's viper is a live-bearer and is said to give birth to twenty to sixty-three young at a time.

Africa is the home of the majority of vipers and contains numerous types. In certain areas individuals of many forms occur in extraordinary numbers. The night adders of the genus *Causus,* its four species found only south of the Sahara, are strictly terrestrial and are noteworthy among vipers for having the unmodified head shields of colubrine snakes. This characteristic suggests that the night adders are a primitive group, whereas in another respect they are extremely specialized. Two of the species have greatly elongated venom glands that extend backward into the trunk for about one-fourth the length of the body. Another primitive feature of

Sand Viper (*Vipera ammodytes*)

Palestinian Viper (*Vipera palestinae*)

this genus is its habit of laying eggs. Their diet, too, is unusual among vipers and consists mainly of frogs and toads. The four species are remarkably well defined; the common night adder, *Causus rhombeatus,* and the green night adder, *Causus resimus,* have the elongate venom glands, whereas the two remaining species have oval glands in the temple region of the head, as do other venomous snakes. Loveridge describes the fighting of a pair of males of Lichtenstein's night adder, posturing with the fore parts of their bodies erect very much as in the fighting of male adders in England.

Another group of African vipers, the well-named mole vipers (genus *Atractaspis*), also has the large colubrine-type head shields, and the species are oviparous like the night adders. But these primitive features are combined with extreme specialization for subterranean life. The mole vipers have the typical cylindrical body form, narrow head, small eye, and short tail that characterize the burrowing snakes of other families throughout the snake group. Most subterranean colubrid snakes have only thirteen to seventeen scale rows and have the same number from neck to end of body. But the mole vipers, alone among these specialized burrowers, have many scale rows (nineteen to thirty-seven) and vary the number along the length of the body. This sharp distinction reflects the family history; all

vipers (with one exception) have many scale rows and a reduction in the number along the body.

Despite the smallness of a mole viper's head, the fangs are startlingly long. It seems almost as if they had been developed to a size beyond functional use, for the mouth is scarcely large enough for them to be erected when it is opened. It turns out that the fangs can be erected by passing them outside the lower jaw when the mouth is closed. No one has reported the details of their action in obtaining food, which consists of snakes, lizards, and, preponderantly, small mammals. The mammals are probably hunted down in their burrows, for we have found five rodents in the stomach of one mole viper.

It has often been suspected that the venom of the mole vipers might be especially powerful, but this suspicion seems to have been based merely on the size of the fangs. The evidence now available is inconclusive. In most of the recorded cases of human beings bitten by one of these snakes, the symptoms have been moderate and the patient has recovered. However, at least one human fatality has been reported.

The genus *Atractaspis* is represented by about a dozen species in the region from the Sahara Desert to South Africa, without counting the numerous geographic races. A species has recently been found to exist in the Sinai Peninsula and in Palestine.

[260]

The genus of puff adders, *Bitis,* includes the species most characteristic of Africa, with a great range of size from the huge Gaboon viper to the very small South African Peringuey's viper, which is little more than a foot in maximum known length. The species of *Bitis* are quite sharply divided into those that inhabit the Central African forest (the rhinoceros and the Gaboon vipers), which are among the most brilliantly colored of snakes, and the various species of savannas and deserts, which are all colored in browns and grays, in resemblance to the soils where they occur. All of the species have a head very wide relative to the neck, enabling them to accomodate the large venom glands, and a relatively very short and wide body, followed by a very short tail. A curious feature of these snakes is a pocket, open at the front, in the skin above the nostrils. The use of this structure is entirely unknown.

By far the most abundant and widely distributed of these vipers is the puff adder, *Bitis arietans* (Plate 129), which has crescentic yellow markings on the back, the general color varying from brown to gray. The species ranges over all of the open country of Africa from the southern border of the Sahara to the Cape of Good Hope, and it spills beyond even these limits, into Morocco to the northwest and Arabia to the northeast. The usual length is from three to four feet, but specimens nearly five feet long are on record. The number of young produced at a birth may be as high as seventy or even more. The venom of the puff adder is a most potent one. A rat dies within a few seconds to a few minutes after being struck. In man, death occurs much less rapidly than from a cobra or mamba bite, the neurotoxic properties of the venom being much less immediately effective, and the blood-dissolving effect the more dreadful. A full charge of

Russell's Viper (*Vipera russelli*)

venom from a large puff adder is almost certain to be fatal unless antivenin is available. As with all venomous snake bites, however, so many factors are involved that a relatively large number of victims recover from the bite even of this species.

The usual food of the puff adder consists of rodents about the size of a house rat. In the typical mode of feeding of vipers and pit-vipers, the prey is struck with a lightninglike stab of the large erected fangs, and permitted to run off to die. After an interval of some minutes, the snake takes up the trail of the dying rodent, following it by repeated testing of the ground with the tips of its tongue, which are withdrawn after each movement to enter the pits of the Jacobson's organ on the roof of the mouth. Careful examination of this trailing of the food, using various species of snakes, both in the field and in the laboratory, shows that the trail of the prey, no matter how complicated, is accurately followed. A curious and unexpected use of the very large fangs is made by the puff adder. It employs them to hook the food animal into the mouth until it is far enough down for the throat muscles to begin their powerful swallowing action.

Larger than even the largest puff adder, the Gaboon viper, *Bitis gabonica* (Plates 130, 131), is made the more striking by its gaudy color pattern of yellow, pale purple, and brown, the colors being arranged in a geometrical pattern. There is a pair of enlarged scales between the nostrils. The breaking up of the plates of the head has reached the extreme at which even the supraocular plates are replaced by small scales. The head at the temples is twice as wide as the neck, and the fangs are extremely long, in large specimens reaching the formidable length of more than an inch and a half. It is somewhat surprising to find that so appropriately named a snake should prove to be exceptionally inoffensive. There is no question of the extreme potency of the venom of the Gaboon viper, for R. Marlin Perkins, now well known for his zoological television broadcasts, nearly lost his life from a Gaboon viper bite while he was curator of reptiles at the St. Louis Zoological Park. The symptoms that developed, and the final saving of his life by a blood transfusion, are dramatically described in the case report in the *Bulletin of the Antivenin Institute of America*. It is therefore the more remarkable to read how a tiny Negro urchin dragged a five-foot living specimen into camp, by the tail, for the purpose of selling it to Mr. Herbert Lang. Native Africans are much more afraid of harmless geckos than of the Gaboon viper, which employs its fangs and venom to obtain its food and can scarcely be driven to defend itself.

The rhinoceros viper, *Bitis nasicornis* (Plate 133), is even more brilliantly colored than the Gaboon viper and shares the forest habitat with it. In the rhinoceros viper, purple and blue are more extensive, with the addition of green triangles, margined with black and blue, on the sides. The common and scientific names both refer to large pointed and erectile scales at the tip of the snout. This species does not reach the size of the Gaboon viper, a four-foot specimen being exceptionally large.

The vivid coloration and striking color patterns of these two forest snakes at once suggest that this might constitute warning coloration to prevent the snake's being stepped upon by larger animals or molested by smaller ones. Experience in their native forest, as well as the simple experiment of placing a captive specimen on a leaf-mold background, shows plainly that, in fact, the disrupted and angular pattern blends astonishingly with the dry and green leaves of the forest floor.

Among the smaller species of *Bitis* in South Africa, those of sandy terrain progress by the spiral rolling motion known as sidewinding, which will be described in discussing the small American rattlesnake known as the sidewinder. Like this rattlesnake, both *Bitis cornuta* and *Bitis caudalis* have raised, hornlike scales over each eye. This is a feature that appears repeatedly among the species of vipers and pit-vipers.

Several of the smaller species of *Bitis* are able to climb into bushes. But the only truly arboreal vipers in Africa, and indeed in the whole world, are the tree vipers (genus *Atheris*). As indicated earlier, they retain the stocky body characteristic of the family but utilize a prehensile tail to maintain themselves in their arboreal surroundings. The tree vipers have strongly keeled body scales, head scales completely broken up and resembling those of the body, and green or green-and-black coloration. And, of course, all have the hallmark of arboreal habits, the prehensile tail. The tree vipers are relatively small snakes as vipers go, for even the largest females do not reach a length of thirty inches. Their food may include any arboreal vertebrate, but only frogs and small mammals have thus far been recorded from their stomachs.

Association of a stocky body and a short tail among the vipers reaches an extreme in the genus *Cerastes*. Its two species are found in the deserts of North Africa, notably in Egypt, and in Arabia and adjacent parts of southwestern Asia. Both are small snakes, rarely exceeding two feet. Adaptation to life in sand is evident in their sidewinding locomotion and in a peculiar method of burying themselves. The scales along their sides have sawlike keels set obliquely. By shimmying movements of the body, these scales work the sand away from beneath them and draw it over their backs. Thus the snakes sink vertically and, since they do this when coiled, leave a characteristic representation of their coils modeled in the sand above them. Some individuals of one species, *Cerastes cerastes,* have a sharp hornlike scale over each eye, which make these snakes so much more interesting to Egyptian snake charmers that they often supply a horn for hornless snakes by inserting a hedgehog spine in the proper place. Another genus with hornlike knobs of scales over the eyes, the false cerastes (*Pseudocerastes*), has a species in Palestine and one in Persia. It is thought that the Palestinian one, *Pseudocerastes fieldi,* which received its scientific name only in 1930, may be the horned viper mentioned in Genesis. Essentially a desert group, the false cerastes have a valvelike structure inside the nostril and especially tight closure of the lips, all of which appear to be a defense against wind-blown sand.

The most powerful venom of any of the vipers, milligram for milligram, seems to be that of the saw-scaled viper, *Echis carinatus,* a snake that ordinarily reaches a length of no more than about two feet. It is found throughout the desert region of North Africa, and eastward through the Indian Peninsula to Ceylon. In India and Ceylon it is essentially confined to the drier semidesert areas. In northwestern India it is astonishingly abundant, for it is reported that bounties were paid on more than 200,000 specimens per year for six years in one district of northwestern India alone. The saw-scaled viper seems able to bear much more heat and much more intense sun than other desert snakes. When excited it has the habit of rubbing the sides of its coils against one another, forming almost a figure eight, with the head at the center. The rough scales rasping against each other produce a sharp hissing sound. The lightninglike strike and the nervous aggressiveness of this creature, combined with an especially potent venom, make it one of the most dangerous of all venomous snakes.

McMahon's viper, *Eristocophis mcmahoni,* known only from a small area in Baluchistan, combines certain characteristics of several other desert genera but has a few peculiarities of its own. Among these are a pair of winglike scales on the snout and keeled ventral plates. Unfortunately so little is known of this species' habits that the functions of its distinctive structures are unknown. The winglike scales may possibly be burrowing aids, but the keeled ventrals, characteristics usually associated with arboreal snakes, are puzzling. For not only would this viper find little to climb on in its native

Horned Viper (*Cerastes cornutus*)

desert, but it also acts like a sand burrower, lying buried during the day with only its head exposed. It has a very loud and deep hiss, so far heard only at night. The specimens collected by the Afghan-Baluchistan boundary commission seemed to have an unusually delicate skin, so much so that it was difficult to obtain an uninjured specimen.

The last of the types of the vipers to be mentioned, Fea's viper, *Azemiops feae,* has the head shields of an ordinary harmless snake, as in the night adders (*Causus*) and mole vipers (*Atractaspis*). Fea's viper occurs in Upper Burma, northern Indo-China, and adjacent parts of China and southeastern Tibet. It is a handsomely colored snake, dark above, with about fifteen narrow light crossbands, which may be interrupted on the mid-line; the head is yellow with two dark lengthwise stripes above. Nothing is known about its habits or about its venom. Fea's viper is one of the least known of all venomous snakes, which is unfortunate, because, being the only viper with so few scale rows (only seventeen) and almost no scale reductions along the body, it represents a radical departure for the family. The relatively short fangs are also unusual among the vipers.

The Pit-Vipers

(*Family Crotalidae*)

The pit-viper family seems to be so much like the viper family that it has taken herpetologists a hundred years to reach the conclusion that, having gone their own ways in so long an evolution, the two groups must be recognized as fully distinct. There can be no doubt that the two solenoglyph types, with erectile and fold-back fangs, have had a common origin. However the sensory pit behind the nostril, which gives the pit-vipers their name, must have been developed very early in their evolutionary history, and it quite evidently added so much to the efficiency of the snakes that possessed it that they could undergo their own adaptive radiation into the principal habitats, independent of the parallel evolution of the viper family. The pit-vipers have developed a variety of terrestrial habits; some have become arboreal with prehensile tails (quite like the African viper *Atheris*), and some have taken to the water, but without much specific adaptation to aquatic habits. However, no pit-viper forms have become as completely adapted to burrowing as the mole vipers (*Atractaspis*).

The two families meet in southeastern Asia and the East Indies, though not with types that actually compete. The great majority of the pit-vipers, and the most extraordinary of the genera and species, are American. Nonetheless, eastern Asia has a variety of species of pit-vipers, more or less closely related to the American forms, and they range through temperate Asia to extreme southeastern Europe (*Ancistrodon halys*) and through southeastern Asia to Ceylon (*Ancistrodon* and *Trimeresurus*). Africa, the great center of diversification of the true vipers, is entirely without pit-vipers.

In the Western Hemisphere the pit-vipers have undergone a great and independent development of species in North America and quite independently in South America, North America being the home of the rattlesnakes, and South America the center for the fer-de-lance genus *Bothrops,* the New World representative of the Old World *Trimeresurus*. The copperhead and moccasin genus *Ancistrodon*, which

has nine species in the Old World, has only three in the Western Hemisphere.

The facial pit on the side of the head is a hollow with a membrane across it at some depth. It is larger than the nostril, situated on the side of the face between the nostril and the eye, and thus in the area of the "lores," hence sometimes known as the "loreal pit." The membrane at the bottom of the external pit closes off an internal cavity, which is connected with the outside air by a narrow opening below the edge of the lower preocular scale. The whole structure is contained in a large excavation in the maxillary bone. The membrane has been shown to be richly supplied with nerve endings. The function of the pit has for more than two hundred years been the subject of rather wild speculation, including theories that it served as an organ of smell, or of hearing, or for the detection of low-frequency air vibrations, or finally that it produced some kind of secretion. As early as 1892, it had been observed that a rattlesnake was especially excited by a lighted match held near it. Then, guided by an earlier discovery that the pits in the lips of pythons are sensitive to heat, G. K. Noble and Arthur Schmidt (in 1937) reported extensive experiments with covered electric light bulbs moved in front of rattlesnakes in which the other sense organs has been blocked off, their nostrils having been plugged, their eyes covered, and their tongues cut off. The snakes struck accurately at the light bulbs, and it thus became evident that the pits were an aid in locating warm-blooded prey. These studies have been extended and confirmed by subsequent experiments. Thus the facial pit is a genuine "sixth sense," a peculiarly effective aid to the snakes that kill warm-blooded prey by means of venom injected during a sudden strike, and the more essential because the snakes hunt primarily at night.

The fact that snakes lack a normal sense of hearing has been mentioned. Experimentation to determine that snakes do not hear has been carried out especially with rattlesnakes, in which the usual response to any strong stimulus is to rattle, or to protrude the tongue, or both. In a series of experiments, sounds from 43 to 1376 cycles per second were produced in a telephone receiver about a foot above the snake's head in a cage covered with black cloth. The sounds were of such intensity as to be heard by a human being a hundred yards away. The snake did not respond, except when the lower frequencies caused vibration of the floor of the cage.

The sensitivity of snakes to vibrations sensed through the ground has been mentioned in connection with the behavior of the snakes in the snake charmer's performance. The remarkable complica-

Water Moccasin (*Ancistrodon piscivorus*)

tion of the senses of smell and taste by means of the Jacobson's organ in lizards and snakes has also been mentioned. It is equally as important to the pit-vipers as to the vipers in tracking down their prey after it has been struck.

Experiments with the vision of rattlesnakes, the results of which apply well to all snakes with eyes of similar size, indicate that a rattlesnake may detect movements of an object at a distance of fifteen feet. The absence of lids, the vertical pupils, and the overhanging supraocular scale give the pit-viper eye a peculiar appearance, often referred to as "sinister." In fact, the snake's eyes express nothing, for they look just the same whether the snake is sleeping, approaching food, or angered by an approaching person.

It will be necessary to discuss the venom of some of the individual kinds of pit-vipers under the several species headings, for the species differ greatly in this respect. Supposing that so remarkable an apparatus as the rattle of the rattlesnake must indicate an advance in structural type, the pit-vipers without a rattle are evidently the more primitive. These include a group with large head shields of the colubrine type, the copperheads and moccasins (*Ancis-*

trodon), a gigantic South American form (*Lachesis*), and the fer-de-lances (*Trimeresurus* and *Bothrops*). We may examine the principal genera in order.

The copperheads, water moccasins, and some nine species of Old World pit-vipers are assembled in the genus *Ancistrodon,* often written as *Agkistrodon* or *Agkishodon* in rather barbarous transliterations from the Greek. The American forms, the copperhead and water moccasin, are well known by these vernacular names. The copperhead, *Ancistrodon contortrix* (Plate 132), is found in eastern North America in two distinguishable forms, one ranging from southern New England through New York and Pennsylvania to the Middle West, and the other distributed on the Atlantic and Gulf coastal plains. Farther to the west, on the Edwards Plateau of Texas and northward into Kansas, there is a distinct subspecies in which the reddish brown crossbands characteristic of *contortrix* are very wide; a fourth subspecies, with a more distinctly black-mottled belly, is found in trans-Pecos Texas and in adjacent northern Mexico. The copperhead is one of the best known of the venomous snakes of the eastern United States, partly because it is venomous, partly because its coloration is extremely distinctive.

Its venom, in man, produces a painful case of snake bite, with much discoloration of the flesh and skin, but usually without a fatal result. The copperhead is a snake of the east American forest region, and its harmonious pink, gray, and brown coloration quite distinctively resembles the dead-leaf ground cover of the hardwood forest. Its food consists mainly of small mammals, but when large insects, like some caterpillars, are available, they are regularly taken. Stomachs of copperheads have been found crammed with seventeen-year cicadas in the year and season when these insects were emerging. The young are produced alive, the broods averaging no more than six, with ten a maximum.

The water moccasin, *Ancistrodon piscivorus* (Plate 135), often called the cottonmouth moccasin, or just cottonmouth, is a much larger snake than the copperhead, and is found throughout the southern part of the range of the copperheads. It does not occur much south of the mouth of the Rio Grande, along the Gulf Coast, for in Mexico it is replaced by a much more boldly colored and quite distinct species, the Mexican moccasin, *Ancistrodon bilineatus* (Plate 134). The name "cottonmouth," for the species in the United States, refers to the white inside of the mouth, which is conspicuous when the snake stands its ground with mouth open and fangs erect, ready to strike. This seems actually to be a warning posture, for we have seen a "cottonmouth" with its head raised and mouth open hold this posi-

Water Moccasin

tion without movement for several minutes. The water moccasin is dark brown or even black in color when adult. The young are brightly banded, in a pattern somewhat like that of the copperhead, with a bright yellow tail tip, also as in the juvenile copperhead. This yellow tail tip is waved about in a peculiar manner and has been thought to serve as a lure. The water moccasin reaches a length of nearly five feet, with a great girth in large specimens. The young are born alive, in broods of five to fifteen. The food includes fish and animals of lake shores and stream banks, especially frogs, with a smaller proportion of small mammals and birds. This species is especially hardy in captivity. It breeds freely in confinement and has been known to reach an age of twenty years.

In the Old World, the representatives of *Ancistrodon* range from China and Japan to the Himalayan region and Ceylon. There are about nine species, three times as many as in North America. One of these, *Ancistrodon halys,* ranges from the steppe region of southeastern Russia through a chain of races in Central Asia to Japan, where the subspecies is *Ancistrodon halys blomhoffi.* The Himalayan species, *Ancistrodon himalayanus,* produces living young, while *rhodostoma,* the Malayan moccasin, lays from a dozen to thirty eggs in a nest and guards them until they are hatched.

The next series of snakes of the pit-viper family, with head shields more or less completely broken up into scales, but without a rattle, is also found both in the eastern part of the Old World and in tropical America. It has been conventional to employ the generic name *Bothrops* for the American species and *Trimeresurus* for the Asiatic ones, but the supposed differences between the two series are neither adequately investigated nor, at best, more than trivial. Both names are used in this book for the convenience of the reader, who may find them so distinguished in other works.

The breaking up of the head shields, with enlarging venom glands and thus widened head, appears to be one of the directions of evolution in venomous snakes, for several series of forms with progressive stages of this condition may be demonstrated among both vipers and pit-vipers. Thus the genus *Trimeresurus,* for which much the most frequent name is the French term fer-de-lance, or lance-head, represents an evolutionary stage in advance of the copperhead-moccasin tribe. There are about twenty-five Old World species, ranging from China and Formosa to Ceylon, with a few mainly arboreal species in the East Indies. This compares with about thirty-five species in tropical America. We shall discuss the Oriental species first. Perhaps

it may be explained why we must say "about" twenty-five and "about" thirty-five species. A large proportion of described species prove, when further studied, and especially as fresh collections are made, to be in fact geographic forms that fall into well-defined species groups. The Philippine lance-heads have not been sufficiently compared with others from the East Indies; and it seems clear that some American forms now listed as full species would fall into more intelligible order if grouped in a smaller number of subspecies. Many additional new subspecies remain to be discovered or discerned; very few fully distinct "new species" are to be expected.

The Asiatic species fall into two quite natural ecological groups—those with prehensile tails, evidently with arboreal habits, which may be either brown or green; and the brown or spotted or variously colored kinds that are primarily ground-dwelling and do not have prehensile tails. One species in Ceylon, the large-scaled lance-head, *Trimeresurus macrolepis,* differs sharply from all other members of the genus *Trimeresurus* (including the American *Bothrops*) in having strongly enlarged head scales, somewhat like those of *Ancistrodon,* though with various additions. It also has the lowest number of dorsal scale rows, twelve to fifteen.

The Asiatic species without prehensile tails are on the whole much larger than the arboreal forms, and none of them has the vivid green coloration of the tree-dwellers. An exception to this rule is Jerdon's mountain viper, *Trimeresurus jerdoni,* a terrestrial species having a dark green color with strong black markings. It is an inhabitant of high mountains from Tibet to western China and south into Burma. The largest and perhaps the best known of these species is the habu, *Trimeresurus flavoviridis,* the much-feared species of Okinawa Island that became well known to the American occupying troops during World War II. The heavy-bodied habu reaches a length of at least five feet. It is astonishingly abundant, for in a random collection of forty-three snakes from a limited area seven specimens were habus, and seven more the smaller kufah, *Trimeresurus okinavensis.*

The largest of the prehensile-tailed species is *Trimeresurus cantori,* of the Nicobar Islands, which is on record as reaching the length of forty-five inches in female specimens. Most of these species are green, and many have a sharply marked light line, yellow or white, along each side, as is curiously frequent in arboreal snakes. One may recall that the harmless West Indian *Uromacer* and the South American rear-fanged *Oxybelis* both have species with this feature. About two-thirds of these arboreal species are green, the others brown or brown-blotched, both colorations with a high degree of protective resemblance to the human eye, the green ones in green foliage, the brown ones against branches or vines. The little brown *puniceus,* which may be found just above the forest floor in Borneo, has been seen with its red prehensile tail anchored to a little plant, its brown body in a flat coil, and its pointed head projecting like the pointed end of a leaf. The red tail is a feature of the coloration in several species. In Wagler's pit-viper, *Trimeresurus wagleri,* which reaches a length of three feet, the coloration is especially vivid. Young individuals are bright green with a regular row of half-white, half-red spots along the back. The full-grown snake is very different, black above with scattered green spots, becoming green on the sides with the scales outlined in black; to this are added numerous narrow crossbars, which are green above and yellow on the sides. The belly is greenish white with irregular yellow patches, and the ventral plates are black-bordered; the head is black above with greenish markings; and the tail is black speckled with green.

Wagler's pit-viper, especially abundant in the lowland jungles of the Malay Peninsula and Borneo, is distributed nearly throughout the East Indies, from Sumatra, Borneo, and Celebes through the Philippines, but it does not seem to occur in Java. It is markedly arboreal, most often seen in low bushes, and is very sluggish and gentle during the day, not at all prone to bite unless quite roughly handled. It feeds on birds, small mammals, and lizards. The bite is not dangerous to man, though it produces severe pain and local swelling. Venom relatively innocuous to man appears to characterize all of the arboreal pit-vipers of the Asiatic region, contrasting with the dangerous terrestrial habu of the Ryukyu Islands. Wagler's pit-viper is kept in considerable numbers at the "Snake Temple" in Penang, and in Sumatra and Borneo it is kept in the trees near houses, since it is supposed to bring good luck.

When we turn to the consideration of the numerous American kinds of pit-vipers with reduced head shields and without a rattle, we find a sharp disagreement among professional herpetologists as to whether they belong in the same genus with the Old World forms or not; those who separate them on the two sides of the Pacific refer the American species to *Bothrops.* Since relatively few American students concern themselves with Oriental fauna, and the distinction of the two groups has been in fashion for nearly half a century, most of the popular literature employs the generic name *Bothrops.* It is employed here, but we wish to point out that the question is by no means adequately settled. It is a problem of comparative anatomy, complicated by the large number and great diversity of the species involved in the two widely separated faunas. No one has raised much question as to the occurrence of the genera *Natrix* for the common water snakes, *Elaphe* for the rat snakes, or *Ancistrodon* for the pit-vipers related to the copperhead, which occur in both Asia and America; but the lance-head snakes have been the subject of an active controversy marked by more opinion than adequate study.

The fer-de-lance itself, by far the best known of the species of *Bothrops* (or *Trimeresurus*), became widely known in the early accounts of travel in the Americas because of its abundance on the island of Martinique, in the southern West Indies, which was the site of a French colony as early as 1635. The fact that the bite of the fer-de-lance (the snake reaches an extreme length of about eight feet) is very often fatal makes it of serious interest to man. When studied with care, the large pit-viper of Martinique, long known under the name of *Bothrops lanceolatus,* proves to be no more than one of the many populations of *Bothrops atrox,* which is distributed from southern Mexico to southern Peru and through all of northern South America. Wherever this snake occurs, it is likely to be abundant, well known to the resident human beings, and thus to have a great variety of common names. The Spanish "barba amarilla," referring to its yellow chin, is perhaps the best-known name in Central America. In Brazil it is not distinguished locally from other large lance-heads, and these are widely known under the names "jararaca" and "jararacussú."

The conspicuous pattern of the back of the fer-de-lance consists of black-edged light diamond markings on a brown or grayish ground color. The sharply triangular head is correlated with large venom glands and the associated muscles. The venom is a powerful one, and from a full dose of it death may result in a very short time. The symptoms include a rather horrifying blackening of the skin and flesh of the part bitten, resulting from loss of blood through the walls of the capillaries. This effect spreads through the body, so that the eyes of the victim become bloodshot, and much blood is lost by internal bleeding. The prompt administration of antivenin appears to be the only certain remedy, though the first-aid measures of crosscuts at the fang punctures and continued application of suction are to be recommended. As in the bites of other venomous snakes, the amount of venom injected is unpredictable, and thus even the untreated bite of so formidable a snake is not surely fatal.

A clue to the numbers of the barba amarilla in

Panama is supplied by the record of more than 800 heads in a collection of 10,690 snakes received by the late E. R. Dunn through the efforts of Dr. Herbert C. Clark, of the Gorgas Memorial Laboratory in Panama City. Dr. Clark employed laborers who were engaged in clearing land for plantations. Their effectiveness as snake collectors is shown by the heads of 62 bushmasters, for which snake Dr. R. L. Ditmars, of the New York Zoological Gardens, once made an unsuccessful expedition to Panama. Unfortunately, the Clark collection does not supply what would be the most interesting figure, namely, the numbers of snakes of all kinds per acre, as well as the numbers of the venomous ones.

The numbers of the fer-de-lance in nature are in part the result of high fecundity, for as many as seventy-one young have been produced by a single mother snake. The ability of the young to defend themselves with a fully formed venom apparatus, in an agile body, a few minutes after they are born, may well contribute to the survival of a higher proportion of the young produced than would be the case for nonvenomous snakes.

Other large species of lance-heads are found in Brazil. The true jararacussú, *Bothrops jararacucu*, may reach a length of about five feet. It is much like the fer-de-lance in pattern, but has a distinctively low number of ventrals. The true jararaca, *Bothrops jararaca*, reaches about the same dimensions. The wutu, *Bothrops alternatus* (Plate 137), is a snake of similar size, with an extraordinarily vivid pattern of chocolate-brown crescentic markings on the sides. The somewhat smaller Wied's lance-head, *Bothrops neuwiedi*, is also a boldly marked species, with a series of transverse hour-glass-shaped markings along the back. It is found through most of Brazil and adjacent Uruguay, Paraguay, Bolivia, and Argentina, and its geographic variation has been emphasized by naming subspecies for seven of the states of Brazil, in addition to *Bothrops neuwiedi boliviana* and *Bothrops neuwiedi meridionalis* for Bolivia and the Argentine respectively.

The most stocky-bodied lance-head is the very rough-scaled "tommygoff" (a corruption of the Honduran tamagasse), *Bothrops nummifera*, of Central America. This three-foot-long species is especially aggressive, and it is perhaps better named the "jumping viper," for it may completely clear the ground in its strike. The little dark *Bothrops godmani* occurs only at relatively high altitudes in Guatemala and Honduras and adjacent Mexico. Other small lance-heads in Central America, *Bothrops lansbergi* and its subspecies, have an up-turned snout, which is a feature found in the

Central American Prehensile-tailed Pit Viper
(*Bothrops schlegeli*)

snouted lance-head, *Bothrops ammodytoides*, the southernmost species of the genus, of the Argentine.

The prehensile-tailed species of the American lance-heads form a smaller proportion of the list than they do in the Orient. There are eight species, and six of these are green with much or a little black or yellow speckling. One, Schlegel's pit-viper, *Bothrops schlegeli*, is mainly green, but remarkably variegated with gray, brown, and black; it has the red tail that is so widespread in the Asiatic forms of *Trimeresurus*. In another species the tail is equally brightly colored, but lemon yellow. Schlegel's pit-viper has the "horns" over the eyes—really a series of little raised scales—that are so frequently found in terrestrial vipers and pit-vipers. It hangs from any suitable branch by its prehensile tail, with a free-hanging flat coil from which to strike. It is

[269]

Bushmaster (*Lachesis muta*)

found from Costa Rica to Ecuador. The green arboreal pit-vipers seem all to be confined to the Central American and the Andean forest regions, from southern Mexico to southern Peru.

The largest, or at least the longest, of the American pit-vipers is the bushmaster, *Lachesis muta,* of northern South America, Panama, and parts of Costa Rica. The bushmaster is reputed to grow to a length of twelve feet. With its large venom glands, enormous fangs (which have been found to measure an inch in length in a six-foot specimen), and the great potential length of its strike, the bushmaster must count as one of the most dangerous of venomous snakes. Its name, *Lachesis,* is taken from that one of the Fates who was believed to determine the length of life in human beings. It might be added that the names of the other fates, Clotho and Atropos, the spinner of the thread of life and the inflexible one who cut it, have been favorite names for venomous snakes (given to certain African vipers) among the early herpetologists, all of whom were familiar with classical mythology.

The bushmaster has received much publicity because of its desirability as an attraction in zoological gardens, combined with the fact that it does not live well in captivity. Whereas it is relatively rarely encountered, the sixty-two specimens collected in Panama through workmen engaged in clearing land are sufficient to indicate a considerable population. It is by no means confined to forests, for William Beebe reports that the species was more abundant at Caripito, Venezuela, than at his British Guiana station of Kartabo, where he obtained a specimen eight and one-half feet long and sent it alive to the New York Zoo. He has given a vivid account of this capture in *Jungle Peace.*

The bushmaster is a mainly gray-and-brown snake, with a bold pattern of large diamond-shaped blotches along the back. Its food is mainly small mammals, for which it lies in wait along the forest or scrub-land trails. Unlike most American pit-vipers, the bushmaster lays eggs, and it is believed that the nest is guarded by the female. The number of eggs produced is about a dozen.

The last of the genera of pit-vipers, the two very distinct types of rattlesnakes, plainly represent the last word in the evolution of the whole snake group. They are evidently also the most recently developed types, for they do not have any Old World representatives. It is highly remarkable that *Sistrurus,* the pigmy rattlers, should so clearly represent an ancestral stage in rattlesnake development, with their primitive type of colubrid head shields, very small rattles, and feebly developed venom supply.

The true rattlesnakes, *Crotalus,* exhibit several further intermediate stages leading to forms with very large rattles, very large venom glands, extreme potency of venom, and highly developed senses and behavior patterns.

The parallel evolution from the normal nine dorsal head shields to head shields broken up as the head becomes enlarged, within the two groups of the pit-viper family, has been mentioned. It may be diagramed simply as follows:

	Snakes without a rattle	Snakes with a rattle (rattlesnakes)
With large head shields:	*Ancistrodon*	*Sistrurus*
With head shields broken up:	*Trimeresurus* *Bothrops* *Lachesis*	*Crotalus*

Two species of *Sistrurus,* the rattlesnakes with the primitive style of colubrid head shields, occur in the United States, with a third in southern Mexico. One is extremely small, usually no more than one and one-half feet in length, and only rarely reaching two feet. This is the pigmy rattler, *Sistrurus miliarius* (Plate 138), confined to the southeastern United States from North Carolina to Florida, westward to central Texas, and northward in the Mississippi Valley to southern Missouri.

The little pigmy rattlers have a distinctive pattern: there is a row of dark blotches along the back, with a row of smaller ones on each side, in which the individual spots are opposite the larger ones. Smaller and less distinct markings may alternate with the others.

When a person is bitten by a rattlesnake there is usually so much excitement that more than one remedy is applied, and no very clear record of either symptoms or recovery is available. Even though the venom of the pigmy rattler is thought to be relatively innocuous, we are fortunate to have an objective report, from an able naturalist, about a bite on his finger. The entomologist W. T. Davis, of Staten Island, was engaged in searching for insects in southeastern North Carolina, with an entomologist friend. In turning over some loose bricks and boards, he found a small snake that he took to be a juvenile hog-nosed snake. So small a creature seemed harmless; Mr. Davis took no precautions in trying to catch it, and was promptly stabbed on the third finger of his left hand, near the nail. Two small drops of blood appeared at once, and he experienced immediate and considerable pain. As the hand began to swell, the pain in the finger lessened. The snake having meanwhile disappeared, the two naturalists had to move nearly every piece of brick and board to find it. It proved to be a pigmy rattler, as suspected, about nine inches long. Concluding that so small a creature could not produce very serious poisoning, Mr. Davis continued collecting with his friend. They suspended work early in the afternoon. The bite had taken place at about ten in the morning, and the hand and arm had continued to swell during the afternoon; at six o'clock it was decided to consult a doctor. The doctor agreed that there could not be any danger from the bite of so small a snake and gave no treatment beyond painting the finger with iodine. There were no systemic symptoms. It was difficult, however, for Mr. Davis to remove his undershirt when he went to bed, but though the hand gave him some pain, he slept fairly well; when he got up in the morning he felt faint, and had to go back to bed. He took some ammonia in water, and he presently felt well enough to get up and go out collecting. The finger turned partly black, and a fingerstall was fitted on because blood and serum were now oozing from the punctures. Mr. Davis again felt faint. Nearly twenty-four hours had passed before any systemic effects were felt. The following morning, forty-eight hours later, the two entomologists returned to Wilmington, North Carolina, and again engaged in collecting.

Rattlesnake fangs

That night, when he took off his clothes, Mr. Davis' left side was swollen, the whole underside of his arm was black and blue, and a flabby swelling had developed under the arm. On the third day the swelling under the arm was reduced, the hand was less painful, and blood and serum had almost stopped oozing from the finger. The swelling increased again that evening, but on the fourth day it had gone down. The finger looked hideous, but gradually improved. The general swelling disappeared on about the eighth day. But the finger was not fully usable even eighteen months later!

This account of the symptoms from the bite of so small an individual, and from a snake species not thought to be very dangerous at worst, gives ample introduction to the truly horrendous effects of the venom of a larger rattlesnake of a more dangerous species.

The larger relative of the pigmy rattler, the eastern massasauga, *Sistrurus catenatus* (Plate 139), is the only rattlesnake to be found in wide areas in Indiana, Illinois, Michigan, and Wisconsin. It is found as far east as the Finger Lakes region of Central New York. This snake seems to be a prairie rattlesnake, derived probably from the populations of the Great Plains. The two western massasaugas are now divided into the desert massasauga of Texas and New Mexico and the western massasauga of Kansas and adjacent areas.

The common eastern massasauga, especially in the eastern part of its range, is confined to sphagnum swamps, to which it seems to have retreated when the hardwood forest re-established itself after the Ice Age. In northeastern Illinois this species is found in isolated colonies on hardwood ridges. It is remarkable that it is able to persist in the vicinity of the spreading suburban communities of Chicago; and it seems certain that these survivors of the prairie fauna are doomed to imminent extermination. No fatality is known from a massasauga in the Chicago area, but the bite is certainly a serious one, and the death of a child from the bite of a large individual is possible, though not probable. Fortunately this inhabitant of regions with considerable human populations is one of the least aggressive of venomous snakes, defending itself only when actually molested. Its temperament is sharply different from that of the pigmy rattlers, which are irritable and prone to strike out at any approaching object. Perhaps it is well to point out that bites from venomous snakes in general are mostly received by persons handling specimens without due precautions. The chances of being bitten in the field, before one has seen the attacking snake, are small even where venomous snakes are abundant.

Before going on to the discussion of the principal rattlesnake genus, *Crotalus,* we must discuss the nature of the rattle, the unique organ that gives the universally used name to these snakes. The series of hard, dry, horny segments at the end of the tail, which constitute the rattles of rattlesnakes, are in fact segments of unshed skin, one added with each shedding. The skin at the end of the tail, where the rattles are to be formed, is much modified and thickened, and the tip of the tail changed in form. The newly born rattlesnake has a large rounded scale at the tip of the tail, the prebutton, and this is shed with the first shedding of the skin. Beneath it the first rattle has taken shape, and this differs from the prebutton in having a strong constriction, foreshadowing the two constrictions in the next rattle; the strongly constricted base of the first rattle fits into the constriction near the middle of rattle number two and holds it in place, though there is no attachment. The baby rattler with only a prebutton, or with only the first rattle segment, cannot rattle. It is only when several loose segments have developed with successive skin sheddings that the movement of these dry hollow shells against each other produces a characteristic high-pitched buzz when the tail is vibrated. The fact that so many harmless snakes vibrate the tail when molested forms an evident setting of the stage for the evolution of the rattle. The three-lobed segments of the rattle increase in size to about the tenth segment, after which they become approximately equal, as the snake itself increases in length (and in width of tail) more slowly. The fact that rattlesnakes shed their skins three or four times a year during the first years of their lives completely disposes of the widely held popular idea that the number of rattles corresponds to the years of a snake's age. When the rattle is complete, with the button, the number of rattles divided by three does give an approximate age. But as the rattle grows, the terminal rattles tend to break off; only exceptionally are there more than eight rattles when the button is present; and this remains the average number of rattles in older snakes, with the terminal rattles worn off or broken off. The fact that the number of rattles has become an integral part of every story of an encounter with a rattlesnake (fatal, of course, to the rattlesnake) has led to extraordinary stories of the number of segments in individual snakes—up to fifty in fact—and even more when imagination has had full freedom. The longest authentic series found in nature appears to be twenty-three; there are innumerable longer strings on record, but exaggeration in reported strings and faking in actual ones seems to explain at least the great majority of such stories. Long strings of rattles can be lengthened by putting two or more series together, by softening the basal rattle of the string that is to be added. In captivity, in individual rattlers that become completely accustomed to human beings and are never in contact with enemies, the segments in a natural rattle have been known to reach twenty-nine. The loss of the terminal rattle segments is beneficial so far as sound production is concerned, since longer series tend to deaden rather than increase the sound. The most effective rattle is an eight-segment one, or just about the average. A rattle of this length is not dragged on the ground, as the rattlesnake carries his tail slightly elevated.

The best reason to be found for the evolution of so effective a sound-producing apparatus in a creature that has no sense of hearing is that it serves as an advertising device by which larger animals are warned away, so that they neither tread upon the snake nor molest it. The evolution of the rattlesnake seems to have taken place in the western United States during the evolution of the great variety of hoofed animals of the Middle Tertiary Period, which included rhinoceroses, horses, and camels, as well as various ruminants, in addition to types of large creatures now wholly extinct. An animal as large as a bison or horse, even if bitten by a venomous snake, would not be likely to die (its size being large in proportion to the dose of venom). But the experience would be an extremely painful one, far more so than any ordinary wound. One of the large flesh-eaters could easily kill a rattlesnake, but not without receiving a charge of venom, which, if it did not kill, would leave a most indelible mark on his memory. The rattlesnake for its part, by advertising that it is indeed the instrument of painful experiences, secures freedom from molestation. The usual behavior of the rattlesnake in standing his ground and rattling vigorously indicates all this clearly. This behavior promoted the whole evolution of the rattle, by differential selection of those individual snakes that had a more effective noisemaker and noisemaking habit. The evolution went far beyond the primitive development of a noisemaking rattle, for the rattle exhibits various completely built-in features, like those for strengthening the chain, for keeping it from dragging, and for making a louder and more startling noise. These are testimony to the continuing evolution in this organ, which must continue to the present day, for there is no indication that rattlesnakes have passed the peak of their successful evolutionary development and diversification. The persistence of various small and primitive forms is further testimony to the effectiveness of the rattle in establishing the rattlesnake's role in his environment.

As part of the introduction to the true rattlesnakes, we may give some account of their venom; some of this information will apply to the venom and venom apparatus of the vipers and of the proteroglyph elapid snakes as well.

The venom is a somewhat cloudy liquid, readily clarified to a clear yellow by centrifuging, which removes cellular debris. Chemical analysis of venom has shown proteins, mainly enzymes, to be the principal constituents. The list includes proteins (albumin and globulin), proteases and peptones, mucin and mucinlike substances, ferments, fats, detritus (in uncentrifuged venom), and certain inorganic salts. Physiological analysis of the venom, from the study of its effects, mainly upon mammals, has always been more meaningful. It was at first thought that venoms could be grouped as neurotoxic and hemorrhagic, the first acting destructively mainly upon nerve tissue, the second on the blood and other tissues. It is found, however, that venoms are not ordinarily of one type or the other, but rather are composed of varying mixtures of both. Following the analysis of N. H. Fairley, the eminent Australian authority on snake bite, there are: (1) neurotoxic elements that act on the bulbar and spinal ganglion cells of the central nervous system; (2) hemorrhagins that destroy the lining of the walls of the blood vessels; (3) thrombose, producing clots within the blood vessels; (4) hemolysins, destroying red blood corpuscles; (5) cytolysins that act on the leucocytes and on the cells of other tissues; (6) elements that retard the coagulation of the blood; (7) antibactericidal substances; and (8) ferments that prepare the food animal for pancreatic digestion. Elapid snakes have venoms usually richer in elements 1, 4, and 6; viperids and crotalids are especially noted for elements 2, 3, and 5. This is not an invariable arrangement, for some venoms are especially lethal to birds, others to amphibians, and the venom of the sea snakes primarily to eels or to fishes in general. A remarkable example of the adaptation of venom occurs in a race of the common lance-head of Brazil on an offshore island, where the only food available is birds. The vipers climb into the low bushes that cover the island, and failure to kill their prey very quickly would usually mean losing it, since it could not be trailed on the ground. As if in response to this need, the venom has become especially powerful and effective against birds. In rattlesnakes, the principal variation from the usual mainly hemorrhagic and cytolytic type is in the tropical American *Crotalus durissus,* and especially its principal race *terrificus,* which is widespread in South America. In these forms the neurotoxic component is so highly developed that a special antivenin must be provided for their bite. It is interesting that the little massasauga has a considerable neurotoxic component in its venom.

The symptoms of snake bite when a large quantity of venom is injected are horrifying. Almost all cases report swelling and discoloration of the skin and flesh near the bite from loss of blood into the tissues. The swelling may become so great as to rupture the skin. Lymphatic glands are soon involved, as in the case of the pigmy rattlesnake bite reported above. Pain is instantly felt from the injection of venom of the hemorrhagic type. It may be unnoticed in the bites of the tropical rattlesnakes (as of the elapids), with their neurotoxic venoms. General faintness and nausea may be a relatively early symptom. The hemorrhage, beginning with the loss of blood into the tissues near the wound, may spread to the internal organs. There is likely to be a rapid pulse, with general lowering of the body temperature and lowered blood pressure. The smaller component of neurotoxic elements seems to come into action last. In spite of all these possible effects, the number of recoveries from snake bite in the United States is in the high proportion of 90 per cent of the total recorded.

The treatment of a snake-bite case consists of prompt first aid to reduce the amount of venom and delay its spread through the body, and secondly of the use of antivenin. Dr. L. M. Klauber, in his recent monumental work on the rattlesnakes, gives a critical summary of recommended treatment. First of all, he suggests that the victim should be reassured by the fact that most cases of snake bite do not result fatally. With proper treatment, the fatalities appear to be less than 3 per cent. The nature of the bite should also be confirmed, for the bites of harmless snakes may be severe but no more harmful than any scratch, and should require no different treatment than ordinary disinfection. It is necessary to warn that no alcoholic stimulant should be given, contrary to popular belief. The idea that brandy or whisky is a remedy for snake bite grew out of wishful thinking—plus the fact that, as most snake-bite victims recover, many also recover from both snake bite and an overdose of whisky. Actually the stimulant, by increasing circulation, speeds the absorption of the venom, which is just what should be prevented. This leads to the next advice—that is, to lie down and rest and certainly not to run.

Then a tourniquet should be applied between the bite and the heart (most bites being on the extremities) about two inches above the bite. Any strip of cloth, such as a necktie or a strip torn from a shirt, will serve. Rubber tubing is supplied in the snake-bite kits that are often carried by hunters and fishermen for this emergency. The tourniquet must not be too tight. One should be able to force a finger beneath it, and there should be a pulse below it. It is important to loosen the tourniquet for twenty seconds every fifteen minutes.

The next step is the difficult one of making incisions at the fang punctures. The skin should be sterilized with iodine or alcohol, and the razor blade or knife should be sterilized as well. Then a lengthwise cut should be made at each puncture to the depth of about three-fourths the width between the fang marks (when both are present). If available, a local anesthetic should be injected. It is very difficult to cut oneself with quarter-inch cuts without anesthetic. A drop of full-strength carbolic acid will anesthetize the skin and sterilize it as well; but it must be wiped off promptly, or the difficulty of healing will be increased by the carbolic burn. Do not cut at all if the snake is a small one or if the patient can be taken to a doctor within a few minutes, say a quarter of an hour.

The further emergency treatment consists in applying suction to the wound, by mouth or by a suction device (as supplied in snake-bite kits). Sucking by mouth is not dangerous if one keeps spitting out the blood and venom. Keep sucking for at least half an hour, and suck even if no cuts are made.

When a field kit of antivenin is available, follow the instructions on the label. Do this only if a doctor cannot be reached within an hour or two. If the patient's reaction to horse serum is not known, make the test as the field kit instructs. Do not use the antivenin if there is serious sensitivity to horse serum. It is essential to reach a doctor, and the doctor reached should be one who has some experience with snake-bite treatment. If the patient is alone, he should drive only as far as the nearest highway, and then get someone to take him farther. If a physician has not had experience with snake bite, he should telephone to the county hospital for advice. If the patient has a copy of Dr. W. H. Stickel's "Wildlife Leaflet No. 339" (which may be obtained from the Fish and Wildlife Service, Washington, D. C., for the asking), he should give it to his attending physician to read.

The prohibitions are important. Do not use potassium permanganate (which was a recommended remedy for many years); do not burn or cauterize the wound, which would interfere with the all-important drainage; and do not give whisky or use other folklore remedies.

The whole subject of snake bite and snake venom

has a somewhat morbid interest, and it is well to recall that snake bite is actually an extremely rare accident. It is worth remembering that the number of fatalities from snake bite in Panama in a year is about the same as the number of persons killed by lightning. We suspect that more are killed by lightning than by snake bite in the United States. The number of cases of bite from poisonous snakes in the United States is roughly estimated to be about 1500 (including 1000 from rattlesnakes) annually; the number of deaths is probably less than 40 (30 from rattlesnakes); and the mortality rates are about 3 per cent of bites, or 0.02 per 100,000 of population. The whole fascinating subject is reviewed at length in Klauber's two volumes published in 1956: *Rattlesnakes; Their Habits, Life Histories, and Influence on Mankind.*

The fact that some animals seem to be immune to the venom of snakes, and this to varying degrees, and that immunity may be acquired by human beings from being repeatedly bitten, suggested research in this direction as early as 1887. The discovery that immunity even to many times the ordinary lethal dose of venom could be produced without evident harm to an experimental animal led naturally to the employment of the blood serum of an immunized animal as an antidote to poisoning from snake bite. As soon as this proved possible, there was a burst of interest in the whole subject, for recoveries from very serious cases of snake poisoning were spectacular when antivenin was injected into the patient's blood, even when the prognosis, without antivenin, had been imminent death. The stage was set for the development of institutes for the production of antivenins and for their distribution for general use in countries where large numbers of venomous snakes occur. Because of A. Calmette's pioneer work on antivenins at the Pasteur Institute at Lille, France, and because their production was related to the whole field of immunization, Pasteur's name was often attached to these institutes, as at Calcutta and Bangkok. The Instituto Butantan, in São Paulo, Brazil, became an especially important center of research in the immunization of the source animals for the serum and in the production of antivenin. The establishment of the Antivenin Institute of America in the 1920's, with a published *Bulletin,* coincided with the beginning of antivenin production in the United States. A major improvement in antivenin came with the

Eastern Diamondback Rattlesnake (*Crotalus adamanteus*)

Red Diamondback Rattlesnake (male combat dance)

discovery that its qualities were preserved in the dry state, and with the further recognition that caution was necessary in the matter of the patient's sensitivity to horse serum, with full directions accompanying each kit.

All rattlesnakes produce living young. In the southern United States a brood is born annually. In the northern range of the prairie rattlesnake, *Crotalus viridis,* the development of the young is so much slowed down by lower summer temperatures that it takes two years before the young are ready to be born. This may be the case in New England for northern populations of the timber rattlesnake, *Crotalus horridus.* The sexually mature adults mate

in the spring, soon after emergence from hibernation, and may mate again in the autumn. The fact that the spermatozoa of the male may be retained in the tissues of the female oviduct (as in other snakes) makes it possible for successive broods to appear in captivity after the sexes have been separated. The number of young varies with the size of the mother snake, from a single one to the maximum record of 60. The usual numbers in the best-known North American species are 10 for the timber rattler, about the same number for the western diamondback, a somewhat higher average (not yet well known) for the Florida diamondback, and 10 (with a maximum of 21 in 307 cases) in

(*Crotalus ruber*)

the typical subspecies of the prairie rattlesnake. Larger numbers seem to be the rule in the Mexican West Coast rattlesnake, *Crotalus basiliscus,* and in the Central and South American species *Crotalus durissus.*

There is naturally very great diversity in the food habits of the various species of rattlesnakes (twenty-nine in all) ranging from Saskatchewan to Argentina. Warm-blooded prey forms the more usual food of all the larger species, and any sort of mammal or bird of suitable size in the region inhabited may be attacked. The smaller forms take a much larger proportion of lizards, and some frogs and salamanders are eaten, especially by the massasaugas and pigmy rattlers. Mammals, including animals to the size of a cottontail rabbit or half-grown jack rabbit, are more frequently fed upon than birds.

The locomotion of rattlesnakes is at first, in the juveniles of most species, by the typical lateral (or horizontal) undulation of most snakes, and all rattlesnakes employ this mode of progression. The heavy-bodied adults of the larger species adopt the rectilinear mode of movement, in which the muscles draw the skin forward and the free edges of the ventral scales supply the purchase on the ground necessary for forward progress. This mode of locomotion leaves an essentially straight track in

[277]

sand or dust. The extraordinary locomotion of the "sidewinder" is discussed below.

Several of the North American species of rattlesnakes are widely known by name. The timber rattlesnake, also known as the banded rattlesnake, was the first species to become known to English colonists, for they encountered it when they reached Virginia and New England. Rattlesnakes had been known much earlier to the Spanish in South and Central America. The timber rattlesnake, *Crotalus horridus horridus,* has dark angular crossbands or chevrons across the back, and thus differs from the more widespread rattlesnake pattern of diamond-shaped markings formed by the light borders of dark blotches. This species is found from southern New England southward to northern South Carolina, Georgia, and Alabama, and westward to eastern Kansas and Oklahoma. On the Atlantic and Gulf coastal plains and in the lower Mississippi Valley it is represented by the canebrake rattler, *Crotalus horridus atricaudatus.*

An even wider range of territory and a somewhat greater range of latitude is covered by the chain of subspecies that composes the species *Crotalus viridis,* the prairie rattlesnake. This species barely reaches the range of the timber rattlesnake in eastern Kansas, but occurs thence westward to the Pacific; it reaches the northern limits of rattlesnake distribution in British Columbia, Alberta, and Saskatchewan. The subspecies of the prairie rattlesnake include: *concolor,* the faded rattlesnake of eastern Utah; *lutosus,* the Great Basin subspecies; *cerberus,* black form of central Arizona (Plate 144); *oreganus,* of most of California and interior Oregon (to British Columbia); *helleri,* of southwestern California; *nuntius,* the pinkish form of northern Arizona, contrasting with the black *cerberus; abyssus,* of the Lower Sonoran Zone at the bottom of the Grand Canyon; and *caliginis,* of South Coronado Island, off the northern coast of Lower California. Most of these forms exhibit intergradation where they meet, but essential uniformity over their main range. They afford a most instructive example of what is meant by the concepts "species" and "subspecies."

The two largest of the rattlesnakes are the eastern and western diamondback rattlesnakes, *C. adamanteus* and *C. atrox,* and there has been no little discussion both as to their maximum size and as to which is the larger. The size of a rattlesnake is of great interest in any story about an encounter with one; it is also of real importance in cases of snake bite, for the dose of venom and the depth to which it is injected are essentially proportional to the size of the snake. Klauber's table of rattle-snake lengths includes average size at birth, smallest gravid female, a large adult male (the largest in a group of one hundred), the largest measured specimen, and the maximum length believed to be valid. Eleven species reach lengths exceeding forty inches; seven may exceed sixty inches; and only three exceed eighty inches. The eastern diamondback is a little larger than the western in every category. The maximum length thus far reliably reported is eight feet two inches. The longest western diamondback record is almost exactly seven feet. The next largest forms are the western Mexican rattlesnake and the South American rattlesnake, respectively with records of six feet eight inches and a trifle under six feet.

Measurements of skins are quite unreliable, for, even without stretching, a snakeskin turns out to be much longer than the snake in the flesh. It should be mentioned that the standard measurement of a rattlesnake does not include the rattle.

The small rattlesnakes of the genus *Sistrurus* have already been mentioned. The largest known specimen of the pigmy ground rattler measures thirty-one inches, and this is much longer than some of the small Mexican species of the genus *Crotalus. Crotalus pricei miquihuanus,* the Miquihuanan twin-spotted rattlesnake, appears to be much the smallest of all; the longest specimen known measures less than sixteen inches.

No less than eighteen species of true rattlesnakes are found in Mexico, and several of these are represented by two or more subspecies. Nine of the species are small, rarely reaching thirty inches in length. Perhaps the most distinctive of all is Stejneger's rattlesnake, which is remarkable for its extremely long and slender tail, tipped with a very small rattle. The rock rattlesnakes, *Crotalus lepidus* (Plate 140), are distinctive in both forms, one with greenish ground color and dark crossbands being found in southern Arizona, the other, mottled pink and black, being found in western Texas. Both forms extend southward on the Mexican plateau, but do not meet and intergrade except at the south. As its name may imply, the rock rattlesnake is mainly a mountain form. We have, in fact, never encountered it except in rock slides.

The South American rattlesnake, *Crotalus durissus* (Plate 141), and the West Mexican *Crotalus basilicus* are remarkable for the fact that their venom has a much more powerful neurotoxic action than that of most species of *Crotalus;* the fact that these are large snakes makes them still more dangerous. Special antivenin is available for them, and its use is essential in the case of a severe bite from these forms. The South American species has a remarkably wide distribution, extending from the northern Argentine and Uruguay through Paraguay, lowland Bolivia, most of Brazil, and along the northern part of the continent through the Guianas and Venezuela to eastern Colombia. Its range barely touches Peru, but that its reputation extended far beyond the regions in which it was actually present is charmingly shown by a pre-Inca artist, who shows a coiled rattlesnake on one of the beautiful Peruvian burial pots; the fact that a rattlesnake is being depicted from hearsay is shown by the artist's concept, for the tail in the figure ends in a child's rattle, like a small gourd.

The red diamondback rattlesnake, *Crotalus ruber* (Plate 143), is one of the most colorful of the larger species of rattlers. It is found in southwestern California and in most of the peninsula of Lower California. It appears to be closely related to the Texas diamondback. This form now may count as one of the best-known kinds of rattlesnakes, for it has been studied for many years at the San Diego Zoo in California, where various individuals have become so well adjusted to captivity that they have engaged in the male combat dance, which proves to be so widespread a phenomenon among snakes. The rattlesnake performance, which closely resembles that of the common European viper, was first successfully photographed at the San Diego Zoo. The same zoo has been successful in getting individual pairs to mate and to produce young in their cages; and this has gone so far as to include records of hybridization with other species. Several age records for the red rattlesnake at San Diego have now passed fourteen years.

The black-tailed rattlesnake, *Crotalus molossus* (Plate 142), is another rather large species found in the southwestern United States and on the Mexican plateau. As its common name indicates, its black tail distinguishes it at once from the western diamondback, the Mojave rattlesnake, and the prairie rattlesnake, all of which are found in the same general territory, and all of which have boldly banded tails.

One of the most interesting of the rattlesnakes, unique in its perfected mode of locomotion over loose sand, is the sidewinder, *Crotalus cerastes* (Plate 136), which is further distinctive in the hornlike scaly projections above the eyes. It is a relatively small species, rarely as much as thirty inches in length, in which the females tend to be larger than the males, reversing the usual relation of other species. The remarkable feature of a method of progression over loose sand was mentioned in connection with the small vipers of the genera *Cerastes* and *Bitis,* respectively of northern and southern African deserts. Any snake placed on a smooth surface on which it cannot obtain adequate traction with its ventral plates will throw loops of its body forward to assist its progress. In "sidewinding" this becomes an effective and perfected means of locomotion over loose sand, which offers little more traction than a sheet of glass. The snake rolls off at a direction oblique to that in which it seems to be going if judged by the axis of the body. Actually, the body becomes a helical coil, and in rolling along leaves most characteristic straight tracks in a parallel series, modified by a loop (shaped like the letter "J") made as the head is set over, and a cross mark (T-shaped) when the tail is lifted off the sand. The directions for following a sidewinder include the statement, "Follow the 'J' and not the 'T.' " That the locomotion is only by vertical pressure on the sand is shown, in a fresh track, by the distinctness of the marks made by each ventral plate. Why this one species of rattlesnake should have developed sidewinding to such an elaborate degree, whereas the other rattlers that invade sandy regions have not (they move by the rectilinear method) is not at all clear; but they do in fact preempt an ecological niche. Other rattlesnakes may pursue their prey into the loose-sand areas, but they cannot efficiently compete with the side-winder.

Index

NOTE: Numerals in bold face type refer to color plates. All other numbers refer to pages; page numbers followed by an asterisk indicate black-and-white illustrations.

abacura, Farancia, 215
Abastor, 227
Ablepharus, 125, 126, 132
  boutoni, 129, 130
  pannonicus, 131
abyssus, Crotalus viridis, 278
Acanthodactylus, 143, 144
  boskianus, 137, 142 *
  cantoris, 141
Acanthophis antarcticus, 234, 235 *
acanthurinus, Uromastix, 86
Achalinus. 187, 224, 225
Acontias, 125, 131
Acrantophis, 178
Acrochordidae, 186
Acrochordus, 186
  javanicus, 187
acutus, Crocodylus, 66
adamanteus, Crotalus, 275 *, 278
adder, 257, 258
  death, 235 *
  night, 259, 263
    common, 260
    green, 260
    Lichtenstein's, 260
  puff, 135, 213, 238, 261, **129**
aegyptia, Walterinnesia, 237 *
aenea, Chamaesaura, 136
aeneus, Oxybelis, 216
aestivus, Opheodrys, 211, 227
Agama, 85, 86, 89, 119
  agama, 79, 85
  atricollis, 80, 81 *
  mutabilis, 85
  stellio, 85, **28**
agama, *Agama,* 79, 85
agama, common, 79, 85
  desert, 85
  South African, 81 *
agamid, 77, 79, 91, 93, 96, 116, 122, 125, 128, 140, 141, 144, 222
  angle-headed, 79, 83, 87
    Bell's, 87 *
  deaf, 83
  hook-nosed, 87
  horned, Ceylonese, 86
  lyre-headed, 86
  smooth-scaled, 86
  spiny-tailed, 78, 81, 83, 86, 96, 113, 140, **26**

agamid (continued)
  toad-headed, 77, 81, 83, 86, 124, 125
    Arabian, 83 *, 84 *
Agamidae, 77, 96, 116, 137
agilis, Lacerta, 140, 141, 188
Agkistrodon, 265
Aglypha, 240
Ahaetulla, 224, 232
  ahaetulla, 226
Aipysurus, 239
alba, Amphisbaena, 162
albopunctata, Scaphiophis, 221
algirus, Psammodromus, 143 *
alleni, Liodytes, 228
Alligator mississippiensis, 45 *, 66
alligator, American, 45 *, 46, 66
  Chinese, 46, 67
Alligatoridae, 44, 66
Alsophis, 232
alternatus, Bothrops, 269
ambigua, Prosymna, 221
Amblyrhynchus cristatus, 117, 122, 124
amboinensis, Cuora, 25
  Hydrosaurus, 78 *
Ameiva, 137, 138, 139
ameiva, 137, 138, 139, 140
amethystinus, Liasis, 181
ammodytes, Vipera, 259 *
ammodytoides, Bothrops, 269
amoena, Carphophis, 214, 228
Amphibolurus barbatus, 80 *, 88
  muricatus, 88
Amphisbaena alba, 162, **57**
  fuliginosa, 162
amphisbaenid, 161
Amphisbaenidae, 77, 161
Amphiuma, 227
anaconda, 176, **74**
  Paraguay, 177
anchietae, Python, 179
Ancistrodon, 264, 268, 271
  bilineatus, 266, **134**
  contortrix, 265
    laticinctus, **132**
  halys, 264, 267
  himalayanus, 267

Ancistrodon (continued)
  piscivorus, 265 *, 266 *, **135**
  rhodostoma, 267
Anelytropsidae, 134
Anelytropsis, 134
Anguidae, 163
Anguis, 163
  fragilis, 163, 165 *
angulifer, Epicrates, 176 *, 177
angustatus, Claudius, 17
Anilidae, 185
Anilius scytale, 185
annandalei, Hieremys, 25
Anniella geronimensis, 167
  pulchra, 166
Anniellidae, 166
annulata, Boa, 176
anole, 90, 115, 117, 120, 122
  false, 115
  green, 116, 118, 120, **32**
  Haitian, 122 *
  knight, 120, **29, 30, 31**
  leaf-nosed, 120
  Sagra's, 118
  water, Cuban, 122
Anolis, 115, 120
  carolinensis, 90, 115, 116, 118, **32**
  chlorocyanus, 122 *
  equestris, 120, **29, 30, 31**
  phyllorhinus, 120
  sagrei, 118
Anomalepis, 184
Anomochilus, 185
antarcticus, Acanthophis, 234, 235 *
apodus, Ophisaurus, 164
Aporoscelis, 86
Aprasia pulchellus, 77
argus, Morelia, 181, 182 *
arietans, Bitis, 261
Arizona, 229
  elegans, **110**
arizonae, Xantusia, 124
Arrhyton, 232
asp, 237
Aspidelaps, 238
Aspidites, 183
aspis, Vipera, 258 *, 259
Atheris, 262, 264
Atractaspis, 257, 260, 263, 264
Atractus, 215, 232

atricaudatus, Crotalus horridus, 278
atricollis, Agama, 80, 81 *
atrox, Bothrops, 268
  Crotalus, 278
attenuatus, Ophisaurus, 163
austriaca, Coronella, 188, 218
Azemiops feae, 263

Bachia cophias, 139
bandy-bandy, 234
barbatus, Amphibolurus, 80 *, 88
Barkudia insularis, 133
Basiliscus, 96, 119
  basiliscus, 113
  plumbifrons, 115 *
  vittatus, 113 *
basiliscus, Crotalus, 277, 278
basilisk, 96, 113, 116, 119, 124
  banded, 113 *
  double-crested, 115 *
baska, Batagur, 27
Batagur baska, 27
Batrachemys, 40
beak-heads, 41
bealii, Clemmys, 26
belli, Gonyocephalus, 87 *
belliana, Leiolepis, 86
bengulensis, Varanus, 171
berlandieri, Gopherus, 27 *
berus, Vipera, 257
bibroni, Pelochelys, 37
bilineatus, Ancistrodon, 266
Bipes, 162
bipes, Scelotes, 126
bitaeniatus, Chamaeleo, 95
Bitis, 261, 279
  arietans, 261, **129**
  caudalis, 262
  cornuta, 262
  gabonica, 262, **130, 131**
  nasicornis, 262, **133**
bivirgata, Maticora, 235
bivittatus, Python molurus, 180
blandingi, Emys, 18, 19 *
blanfordi, Ophiomorus, 132
Blanus, 162

bloodsucker, 83, 224
  Australian, 88
  Indian, 79, 86, 126
Boa, 178
  annulata, 176, **68**
  canina, 177, **70**
  cooki, 177, **69**
  hortulana, 177, **75**
boa, 232, 175, 209
  annulated, 176, **68**
  constrictor, 176, **73**
  Cuban, 176 *
  rainbow, 177
  rosy, 178, **72**
  rubber, 178
  sand, 177 *, 178
  tree, Cook's, 177, **69**
    emerald, 177, 178, **70**
    garden, **75**
Boaedon lineatum, 221
bocourti, Enhydris, 216
Boidae, 175
boid, 191
Boiga, 215, 224, 232
  dendrophila, 215, **120**
  trigonata, 224
Boiginae, 187, 215, 218
bojeri, Scelotes, 126
Bolyeria, 178
Bolyerinae, 178
boomslang, 215, 222, **121**
borneensis, Lanthanotus, 173
boskianus, Acanthodactylus, 137, 142 *
Bothrophthalmus lineatus, 222
Bothrops, 264, 267, 268, 271
  alternatus, 269, **137**
  ammodytoides, 269
  atrox, 268
  godmani, 269
  jararaca, 269
  jararacucu, 269
  lanceolatus, 268
  lansbergi, 269
  neuwiedi, 269
  nummifera, 269
  schlegeli, 269 *
Boulengerina, 237
boutoni, Ablepharus, 129, 130
Brachylophus, 123
Brachymeles, 126, 133
braminus, Typhlops, 184
brevicauda, Varanus, 169, 172
brevicornis, Chamaeleo, 93

bronze-back, 224
  painted, 226
Brookesia, 91, 93, 95
buccata, Homalopsis, 216
Bufo marinus, 172
bushmaster, 270 *
butleri, Chilorhinophis,
  222

Cabrita, 161
Caiman, 67
  latirostris, 67
  sclerops, 67, **19**
  yacare, 67
caiman, 66, 67
  black, 46, 67
  broad-nosed, 46
  Central American, 46
  dwarf, 46
  Paraguay, 46, 67
  smooth-fronted, 46, 67,
    68
  spectacled, 46, 67, **19**
Calabaria reinhardti, 183
Calamaria, 215, 221, 225
californiae, Lampropeltis
  getulus, 190 *, 191 *
caliginis, Crotalus viridis,
  278
Calliophis, 235
Callisaurus draconoides,
  115, 116, 117, 119, **38**
Calliscincopus, 137
Callopistes maculatus,
  140
Calotes, 78, 83, 86, 124,
  224
  cristatellus, 80
  versicolor, 79
cana, Pseudaspis, 220 *
canina, Boa, 177
cantori, Trimeresurus,
  267
cantoris, Acanthodacty-
  lus, 141
capense, Lycophidion,
  221
capensis, Mehelya, 221
Caretta, 33
Carettochelys, 37
carinata, Mabuya, 128
carinatus, Echis, 263
  Sternotherus, 16
  Zaocys, 210
carolina, Terrapene, 19
  bauri, 20
  major, 20
  triunguis, 20
carolinensis, Anolis, 90
Carphophis amoena, 214,
  228
Casarea, 178
caspica, Clemmys, 25
cataphractus, Cordylus,
  135
  Crocodylus, 47, 66
catenatus, Enyalius, 121 *
  Sistrurus, 272
caudalis, Bitis, 262
Causus, 259, 263
  resimus, 260
  rhombeatus, 260
Celestus montanus, 164
  plei, 164
Cemophora coccinea,
  228 *
cenchoa, Imantodes, 212,
  214 *
cenchris, Epicrates, 177

Cerastes, 262, 279
  cerastes, 263
  cornutus, 162, 263 *
cerastes, Cerastes, 263
  Crotalus, 279
Ceratophora, 86
Cerberus, 216
  rhynchops, 224
cerberus, Crotalus viridis,
  278
Chalarodon, 123
Chalcides, 131, 132
  chalcides, 131 *
Chamaeleo bitaeniatus,
  95
  brevicornis, 93
  chamaelon, 90 *
  dilepis, 93, 95, **63**
  fischeri, 94 *
  furcifer, 93
  gallus, 93
  ituriensis, 90
  jacksoni, 95 *, **61**
  labordi, 93
  melleri, 91, **62**
  oshaugnessyi, 91
  oustaleti, 91
  oweni, 91, 93, 94
  pumila, 92 *
  zeylanicus, 93, 94
Chamaeleolis, 122
  chamaleontides, 123 *
chamaeleon, Chamaeleo,
  90 *
Chamaeleonidae, 90
chamaleontides, Chamae-
  leolis, 123 *
Chamaelinorops, 122
Chamaesaura, 135, 136
  aenea, 136
  macrolepis, 136
chameleon, 79, 90, 115,
  122, 128, 141, 166, 222,
  60
  armored, 95
  common, 90 *
  dwarf, 96
  false, 122, 123 *
  Fischer's, 94 *
  flap-necked, 93, **63**
  forked-nosed, 93
  Indian, 93, 94
  Ituri, 90
  Jackson's, 94, 95 *, **61**
  Labord's, 93
  Madagascar, 91
  Meller's, 91, **62**
  O'Shaugnessy's, 91
  short-horned, 93
  South African, 92 *
  stump-tailed, 91, 93, 95
  three-horned, 91, 93, 94
  two-lined, 95
Charina, 178
cheechak, 69
Chelidae, 38
Chelodina longicollis, 38
Chelone imbricata, 31
Chelonia, 12
Chelonia, 31
  mydas, 32 *, 33 *, 35 *
Chelonidae, 31
Chelydra serpentina, 12 *,
  14 *, 15 *
Chelydridae, 14
Chelys fimbriata, 39 *
Chersydrus, 186
  granulatus, 187

Chilomeniscus, 229
  cinctus, **122**
Chilorhinophis, 221
  butleri, 222
  gerardi, 222
Chinemys kwangtungen-
  sis, 26
  reevesi, 26
Chionactis, 229
Chitra indica, 37
Chlamydosaurus, 88
  kingi, 81, 82 *, 88 *
chlorocyanus, Anolis,
  122 *
Chlorophis, 212, 222
Chondropython viridis,
  183
Chrysemys, 22, **8**
  picta belli, 22
    dorsalis, 22
    marginata, 22
    picta, 22, **8**
Chrysopelea, 216, 225,
  124
  paradisi, 215 *
  pelias, 216
chuckwalla, 116, 119, **44**
cinereus, Sphaerodactylus,
  74
clarki, Sceloporus, **46**
Claudius angustatus, 17
Clelia, 231, 232
  clelia, Clelia, 191, 232
Clemmys, 18, 24, 25, 26
  bealii, 26
  caspica, 25
  guttata, 18, **6**
  insculpta, 18, **5**
  japonica, 26
  leprosa, 25
  marmorata, 18, 24
  muhlenbergi, 18
  mutica, 26
Cnemidophorus, 137, 138,
  139
  inornatus, 138
  lemniscatus, 140
  sacki, 138
  sexlineatus, 138
  stictogrammus, 138
coachwhip, western, 209
coahuila, Terrapene, 20
cobra, 168, 232, 261
  common, 235, 236
  desert, 237 *
  Indian, 234 *, 235 *,
    236, **127**
  king, 232, 235, 236 *
  spitting, 237
  water, 237
coccinea, Cemophora,
  228 *
coctaei, Macroscincus,
  127
coeruleus, Gerrhonotus,
  164
Coleonyx variegatus, 74 *,
  25
collaris, Crotaphytus, 118
Coluber, 188, 209, 219,
  220, 223, 226, 227
  bilineatus, **92**
  constrictor flaviventris,
    209 *, 210 *
  flagellum flavigularis,
    209
  piceus, **94**
  gemonensis, 209
  jugularis, 220

Coluber (continued)
  lateralis, **91**
  taeniatus, **89**
  viridiflavus, 219 *
Colubridae, 187
Colubrinae, 187, 188, 218
compressicauda, Natrix
  sipedon, 226
concolor, Crotalus viridis,
  278
Conolophus, 118
Conophis lineatus, 230 *
Constrictor, 178
  constrictor, 176, **73**
contortrix, Ancistrodon,
  265
cooki, Boa, 177
cophias, Bachia, 139
Cophotis, 83
copperhead, 226, 264, 268
  broad-banded, **132**
corais couperi, Drymar-
  chon, 209
Cordylidae, 135
cordylid, 136
  club-tailed, 135
  false, 135
Cordylus, 135
  cataphractus, 135, **47**
  cordylus, 135
  giganteus, 135
coriacea, Dermochelys,
  30 *
cornuta, Bitis, 262
  Cyclura, 123 *
cornutus, Cerastes, 162,
  263 *
  Phyllurus, 76
coronatum, Phrynosoma,
  43
Coronella austriaca, 188,
  218
Corucia zebrata, 124, 127,
  133
Corythophanes, 96, 113,
  119, 124
couperi, Drymarchon co-
  rais, 209
Cricosaura typica, 124
cristatellus, Calotes, 80
cristatus, Amblyrhynchus,
  117, 122, 124
crocodile, 44
  African, 47, **20**
    slender-snouted, 46
  American, 46, 65
  Australian, 46
  Cuban, 46, 66
  dwarf, Congo, 46
    West African, 46,
      48 *
  marsh, 46
  Morelet's, 46, 66
  mugger, 46, 48, 65 *
  New Guinean, 46, 65
  Nile, 46
  Orinoco, 46, 66
  Philippine, 46
  salt-water, 46, 47
  Siamese, 46, 65, **21**
Crocodilia, 44
crocodilurus, Shinisaurus,
  167
Crocodylidae, 47
Crocodylus, 47
  acutus, 66
  cataphractus, 47, 66
  intermedius, 66
  johnstoni, 65, 66

Crocodylus (continued)
  mindorensis, 65
  moreleti, 66
  niloticus, 47, **20**
  novae-guineae, 65
  palustris, 48, 65 *
  porosus, 47
  rhombifer, 66
  siamensis, 65, **21**
Crotalus, 271, 272
  adamanteus, 275 *, 278
  atrox, 278
  basiliscus, 277, 278
  cerastes, 279, **136**
  durissus, 273, 277, 278
    terrificus, 273, **141**
  horridus, 276, 278
    atricaudatus, 278
  lepidus, 278, **140, 145**
  molossus, 279, **142**
  pricei miquihuanus, 278
  ruber, 276 *, 277 *, 279,
    143
  viridis, 276, 278
    abyssus, 278
    caliginis, 278
    cerberus, 278, **144**
    concolor, 278
    helleri, 278
    lutosus, 278
    nuntius, 278
    oreganus, 278
Crotalidae, 240, 264 ff
Crotaphytus, 113, 115,
  117
  collaris, 118
    baileyi, **48**
    collaris, **49**
  wislizeni, 119, **37**
Ctenosaura, 118, 119
cucullatus, Macropro-
  todon, 220
cunninghami, Egernia,
  134 *
Cuora, 25
  amboinensis, 25
curtus, Python, 179, 181
cyanurum, Lygosoma,
  128, 129
Cyclanorbis, 37
Cyclemys, 25
Cycloderma, 37
cyclopion, Natrix, 191 *
Cyclura, 122
  cornuta, 123 *
  macleayi, **33, 34**
Cylindrophis, 185
Cyrtodactylus, 72
  pulchellus, 72 *

Damonia subtrijuga, 25
darwini, Diplolaemus,
  121 *
Dasypeltinae, 216
Dasypeltis, 218, 222
  scaber, 217 *
Deirochelys reticularia,
  24 *
Deiroptyx, 122
delalandi, Nucras, 142
Demansia, 234
Dendroaspis, 237
  polylepis, **118**
dendrophila, Boiga, 215
Denisonia, 234
dentata, Elseya, 38
denticulata, Testudo, 28
Dermatemydidae, 17
Dermatemys mawi, 17

Dermochelys coriacea, 30 *
diadema, Lytorhynchus, 223 *
Diadophis, 185, 229
amabilis, **90**
diardi, Typhlops, 184
Dibamidae, 134
Dibamus, 134
Dicrodon, 140
coarse-scaled, 140
fine-scaled, 140
guttulatum, 140
heterolepis, 137, 140
Diemenia, 234
dilepis, Chamaeleo, 93, 95
Dinodon, 226
dione, Elaphe, 220, 226
Diplodactylus spinigerus, 76 *
vittatus, 76
Diploglossus, 163
Diplolaemus darwini, 121 *
Diplometopon zarudnyi, 162 *
Dipsadinae, 216
Dipsas, 212, 213, 216
Dipsosaurus, 119
dorsalis, 116, 118
Dispholidus typus, 215, 222, **121**
Dogania, 37
doliata, Lampropeltis, 188
dorsalis, Dipsosaurus, 116, 118
douglassi, Phrynosoma, 115 *, 119
Dracaena, 138
guianensis, 138, 139
Draco, 83, 87, 124
draconoides, Callisaurus, 115, 117, 119
Dromicus, 232
Drymarchon, 231, **102, 103**
corais couperi, 209
Drymobius, 231
Dryophis, 224, 230
nasuta, 215, **117, 123**
dulcis, Leptotyphlops, 184
dumerili, Varanus, 171, 172, 173
durissus, Crotalus, 273, 277, 278

echinata, Lacerta, 140, 142
Echinosaura, 139
Echis carinatus, 263
eel, Congo, 227
mud, 227
Egernia, 127, 133
cunninghami, 134 *
stokesi, 134
Elachistodon westermanni, 218
Elaphe, 210, 220, 223, 226, 268
dione, 220, 226
guttata, 211 *, **87**
hohenackeri, 223
longissima, 211, 218, 220, **96**
obsoleta, 210, 211, 212 *
obsoleta, 226, **100**
quadrivittata, 226, **97, 98, 99**

Elaphe (continued)
oxycephala, 224
prasina, 211
vulpina, 226
elapid, 226
Elapidae, 185, 232
Elaps, 238
Elapsoidea, 238
elegans, Sphaerodactylus, 73
Testudo, 28
elephantopus, Testudo, 29
Elseya, 38
dentata, 38
Emydidae, 18
Emydocephalus, 239
Emydura, 39
macquari, 39 *
Emys, 38
blandingi, 18, 19 *
orbicularis, 18, 25, **4**
Enhydris, 216, 232
bocourti, 216
Enyalius catenatus, 121 *
Enygrus asper schmidti, 178
Epicrates angulifer, 176 *, 177
cenchris, 177, **71**
equestris, Anolis, 120
Eremias, 143, 144
nitida, 141
Eretmochelys, 34
Eristocophis mcmahoni, 263
erythrogaster, Natrix, 226
Erythrolamprus, 231
Eryx, 177
johni, 177 *
Eumeces, 128, 129, 130, 132
fasciatus, 128, 129, **67**
obsoletus, 127, 128
skiltonianus, 128
taylori, 128
Eunectes murinus, 176, **74**
euryxanthus, Micruroides, 232
Evoluticauda, 96
exanthematicus, Varanus, 170
expansa, Podocnemis, 38
extenuatum, Stilosoma, 215, 228

fallax, Telescopus, 220
Farancia, 227
abacura, 215
fasciatus, Eumeces, 128, 129
feae, Azemiops, 263
fer-de-lance, 191, 264, 267
fernandi, Lygosoma, 130
ferox, Trionyx, 36
Feylinia, 134
Ficimia, 229
fieldi, Pseudocerastes, 263
fimbriata, Chelys, 39 *
Fimbrios, 187, 224, 225
fischeri, Chamaeleo, 94 *
flavigularis, Coluber flagellum, 209
Gerrhosaurus, 136
flavipunctatus, Tejovaranus, 140
flaviventris, Coluber constrictor, 209 *, 210 *

flavoviridis, Trimeresurus, 267
floridana, Rhineura, 161, 162
Fordonia, 216
fragilis, Anguis, 163, 165 *
frenatus, Hemidactylus, 69, 71, 75
frontalis, Micrurus, 233 *
fulgidus, Oxybelis, 216
fuliginosa, Amphisbaena, 162
fulvius, Micrurus, 232
furcifer, Chamaeleo, 93
fuscus, Gonatodes, 74

Gaigeia, 124
galliwasps, 163, 164, 166
gallus, Chamaeleo, 93
gamma, 224
gangeticus, Gavialis, 68
garrulus, Ptenopus, 73
Gastropyxis, 222
Gavialis gangeticus, 68
gavial, 44, 46, 68
false, 46, 65
Gavialidae, 44, 68
Geatractus, 230
gecko, Gekko, 69, 70 *, 71, **22, 23**
gecko, 69, 79, 91, 115, 124, 125, 140, 144, 220
ashy, 74
banded, 74 *, **25**
bent-toed, 72 *
day, 75
flat-tailed, 75
fan-footed, 73 *
fat-tailed, 76
flying, 72
garrulous, 73
half-toed, 71
common, 75
house, common, 73
kidney-tailed, 76
leaf-fingered, 74
leaf-tailed, 75
Australian, 75 *, 76
naked-toed, 73
oceanic, 71
Pacific, 71
reef, 74
scaly-toed, 71
spiny-tailed, Australian, 76 *
stone, 76
Turkish, 73
turnip-tail, 73
waif, 71
wall, 73, **24**
Wall's, 73
yellow-headed, 74
Gehyra oceanica, 71
Gekko gecko, 69, 70 *, 71, **22, 23**
Gekkonidae, 69
gemonensis, Coluber, 209
Geniochersus, 28
Geoclemys hamiltoni, 25, 26
Geodipsas, 222
Geoemyda, 18, 24, 25
grandis, 25
trijuga, 25
geographica, Graptemys, 22
Geophis, 232

gerardi, Chilorhinophis, 222
geronimensis, Anniella, 167
Gerrhonotus, 163, 166
coeruleus, 164
principis, 166
liocephalus, 166 *
multicarinatus, 164, 166, **50**
scincicauda, 163
gerrhosaurid, 136, 222
keeled, 137
Gerrhosauridae, 136
Gerrhosaurus, 137
flavigularis, 136
major, 136
validus, 137
getulus, Lampropeltis, 191, **111, 112**
Lampropeltis getulus, 191, **111, 112**
gharial, 68
gigantea, Testudo, 28
giganteus, Cordylus, 135
Varanus, 172
Gila monster, 91, 167, 168, 173, **54**
gilleni, Varanus, 170
Glyphodon, 234
godmani, Bothrops, 269
Gonatodes fuscus, 74
Gonyocephalus, 83, 87
belli, 87 *
liogaster, 79
Gopherus, 28
berlandieri, 27 *
polyphemus, 28 *
gouldi, Varanus, 172 *
gracilis, Microcephalophis, 240
Ophisaurus, 164
graeca, Testudo, 28
grahamiae, Salvadora, 230 *
grandis, Geoemyda, 25
granulatus, Chersydrus, 187
Graptemys geographica, 22
Grayia, 222
griseus, Varanus, 171 *, 173
guentheri, Holaspis, 140, 142
Leiocephalus, 117
guianensis, Dracaena, 138, 139
guttata, Clemmys, 18
Elaphe, 211 *
guttulatum, Dicrodon, 140
Gymnodactylus, 73
Gymnophthalmus, 138

habu, 267
Haldea, 228
striatula, 214, 215
halys, Ancistrodon, 264, 267
hamiltoni, Geoclemys, 25, 26
hannah, Ophiophagus, 236 *
Haplopeltura, 216
Hapsidophrys, 222
Hardella thurgi, 27
hardun, 85, **28**
Harpesaurus, 87

harti, Ophisaurus, 164
hasselquisti, Ptyodactylus, 74 *
Helicops, 232
helleri, Crotalus viridis, 278
Helminthophis, 184
Heloderma horridum, 167, **53**
suspectum, 167, **54**
Helodermatidae, 167, 173
Hemachatus, 237
Hemibungarus, 235
Hemidactylus frenatus, 69, 71, 75
mabouia, 73
turcicus, 73, 74
Hemiphyllodactylus, 71
henshawi, Xantusia, 124
Herpeton, 216
Heterodon, 191, 213, 215, 229, 231, **85, 86**
platyrhinos, 213 *
Heteroliodon, 222
heterolepis, Dicrodon, 137, 140
hexalepis, Salvadora, 229 *
Hieremys annandalei, 25
himalayanus, Ancistrodon, 267
hohenackeri, Elaphe, 223
Holaspis guentheri, 140, 142
holbrooki, Lampropeltis getulus, 191
Holbrookia, 97, 113, 118, 119
maculata, **40**
texana, 119
Homalopsinae, 216, 224, 232
Homalopsis buccata, 216
Homopus, 28
Hoplocercus, 122
spinosus, 113, 116
Hoplurus, 123
horridum, Heloderma, 167
horridus, Crotalus, 276, 278
Moloch, 88, 89 *, 96
hortulana, Boa, 177
humilis, Leptotyphlops, 184
Hydraethiops melanogaster, 222
Hydraspis, 40
Hydromedusa maximiliani, 40
tectifera, 40
Hydrophidae, 186, 232, 238
Hydrophis, 239
cyanocinctus, 240
fasciatus, 240
semperi, 240
Hypsiglena, 229
Hydrosaurus, 77, 87, 96
amboinensis, 78 *

Iguana iguana, 96, 113, 118, 120, 122, 124, **35, 36**
iguana, 167, 178
black, 118, 119
common, 96, 113, 118, 120, 122, 124, 133, **35, 36**

iguana (continued)
crested, 118
desert, 116, 118, 119
ground, 122
Cuban, **33, 34**
marine, 117, 122, 124
rhinoceros, 123 *
iguanid, 79, 91, 93, 95, 96, 124, 125, 128, 140, 141, 166, 222
Brazilian, 121 *
casque-headed, 119
Fijian, 123
fringe-toed, 119, 143, **42**
helmeted, 96, 113, 119, 124
long-legged, 96, 113, 115, 122, 124
narrow-tailed, 113, 115
Patagonian, 121 *
smooth-headed, 117
smooth-throated, 118, 122
spiny-tailed, 113
sword-tailed, 113, 122
weapon-tail, 122
Iguanidae, 96, 137
Imantodes, 212, 224
cenchoa, 212, 214 *
imbricata, Chelone, 31
indica, Chitra, 37
indicus, Varanus, 172
inornatus, Cnemidophorus, 138
Scelotes, 126
insculpta, Clemmys, 18
insularis, Barkudia, 133
intermedia, Langaha, 223 *
intermedius, Crocodylus, 66
intestinalis, Maticora, 235
ituriensis, Chamaeleo, 90

jacksoni, Chamaeleo, 95 *
Thrasops, 222
Japalura, 86
japalures, 86
japonica, Clemmys, 26
jararaca, 269
jararaca, Bothrops, 269
jararacucu, Bothrops, 269
jararacussú, 269
javanicus, Acrochordus, 187
Xenodermus, 187
jerdoni, Trimeresurus, 267
jicari, Lialis, 77
johni, Eryx, 177 *
johnstoni, Crocodylus, 65, 66
jugularis, Coluber, 220

Kachuga tectum, 27
Kentropyx striatus, 137
kingi, Chlamydosaurus, 81, 82 *, 88 *
Kinixys, 28
erosa, **11**
Kinosternidae, 16
Kinosternon scorpioides, 17
subrubrum, 17
kirtlandi, Thelotornis, 216
komodoensis, Varanus, 169 *

krait, 235, 236
common, 237
kufah, 267
kwangtungensis, Chinemys, 26

labordi, Chamaeleo, 93
Lacerta, 140
agilis, 140, 141, 188
echinata, 140, 142
langi, 140, 142
lepida, 137, 141, 144, **56**
muralis, 144
albanica, 144 *
viridis, 141, 144 *
vivipara, 141, **58**
lacerta, common, 140
green, 141, 144 *
jeweled, 137, 141, 144, **56**
Lang's, 142
spiny, 142
viviparous, 141, 144, **58**
lacertid, 136, 140, 166, 220
blunt-headed, 142
Delalande's, 142
desert, 143, 144
bright, 141
fringe-tailed, 140, 142
fringe-toed, 143, 144
Bosc's, 142 *
Cantor's, 141
grass, 137, 161
six-lined, 161
Indian, 161
plated, 143 *
snake-eyed, 141, 144
Lacertidae, 137, 140
Lachesis, 265, 271
muta, 270 *
Laemanctus, 115, 119
serratus, 120 *
Lampropeltis, 188, 221, 229
doliata, 188, **107**
annulata, **116**
getulus, 191, **111, 112**
californiae, 190 *, 191 *
getulus, 191
holbrooki, 191, **113**
pyromelana, **114**
lance-head, 267, 269
snouted, 269
Wied's, 269
lanceolatus, Bothrops, 268
Langaha, 223
intermedia, 223 *
langi, Lacerta, 140, 142
lansbergi, Bothrops, 269
Lanthanotidae, 173
Lanthanotus, 173
borneensis, 173
latasti, Vipera, 259
laterale, Lygosoma, 125 *, 128, 129, 130
laticauda, Phelsuma, 75
Laticauda semifasciata, 239
latirostris, Caiman, 67
Leandria perarmata, 95
lebetina, Vipera, 259
Leimadophis, 231
Leiocephalus, 122
guentheri, 117
schreibersi, 117

Leiolepis belliana, 86
lemniscatus, Cnemidophorus, 140
lepida, Lacerta, 137, 141, 144
Lepidochelys olivacea, 34
Lepidodactylus lugubris, 71
Lepidophyma, 124
lepidus, Crotalus, 278
leprosa, Clemmys, 25
Leptocalamus, 230
Leptodeira, 230
annulata, **119**
Leptomicrurus, 233
leptotyphlopid, 184
Leptotyphlopidae, 183
Leptotyphlops, 232
dulcis, 184
humilis, 184
macrolepis, 184
septemstriata, 185
lesueuri, Physignathus, **27**
Lialis jicari, 77
Liasis amethystinus, 181
Lichanura roseofusca, 178
trivirgata, 178, **72**
lineatum, Boaedon, 221
lineatus, Bothrophthalmus, 222
Conophis, 230 *
liocephalus, Gerrhonotus, 166 *
liogaster, Gonyocephalus, 79
Lioheterodon, 222
Liolaemus, 113, 115, 118, 122
Liotyphlops, 184
Lissemys, 37
lizard, 69
alligator, 163, 166
northern, 166
Oregon, 163
southern, 164, 166, **50**
Texas, 166 *
anguid, 163
armadillo, 135, **47**
beaded, 167, 168, **53**
bearded, 80 *, 88
bunch grass, 118
caiman, 138, 139
casque-headed, 115, 120 *
collared, 113, 115, 116, 117, 118, 119, 124
eastern, **49**
western, **48**
earless, 96, 118, 119
lesser, **40**
Texas, 119
fence, 116, 117, 118, **41**
European, 140, 141, 144
Fernand's, 130
flap-footed, 76, 116, 163
pretty, 77
flat, 135
Florida scrub, 118
flying, 83, 87, 96, 126
frilled, 81, 82 *, 88 *, 124
fringe-toed, 120
girdled, 137
girdle-tailed, 135
common, 135
glass, 165

lizard (continued)
grass, 140
gridiron-tailed, 119, **38**
Komodo dragon, 169 *, 172
legless, 166
California, 166
Geronimo, 167
leopard, 119, **37**
night, 124
Arizona, 124
Cuban, 124
granite, 124
island, 124
yucca, 124
plated, 137
rock, 137
Sudan, 136, **59**
yellow-throated, 136
sand, 188
scaly-foot, 76
side-blotched, **39**
Sita's, 86, 126
smooth-throated, 113, 115
snake, 136, 163
large-scaled, 136
Transvaal, 136
spiny, 115, 117, 119, 120, 122
Clark's, **46**
desert, **45**
tree, 115
wall, 144 *
water, 77, 87, 96
East Indian, 78 *
island, 78
whip, African, 136
worm, 77, 116, 140, 161
Arabian, 162 *
Central African single-shield, 161
Florida, 161, 162
red, 162, **57**
sharp-tailed, 162
spotted, 162
zebra-tailed, 115, 116, 117
loggerhead, 31, 33
longicollis, Chelodina, 38
longissima, Elaphe, 211, 218, 220
Loxocemus, 186
lugubris, Lepidodactylus, 71
lutosus, Crotalus viridis, 278
Lycodon, 226
Lycophidion, 222
capense, 221
Lygosoma, 126, 129, 132, 133
cyanurum, 128, 129
fernandi, 130
laterale, 125 *, 128, 129, 130
travancoricum, 125
vittatum, 133
Lyodytes alleni, 228
Lyriocephalus scutatus, 86
Lystrophis, 213
Lytorhynchus, 220, 221, 223
diadema, 223 *

mabouia, Hemidactylus, 73
mabouya, Mabuya, 130

Mabuya, 125, 126, 128, 129, 130, 131, 132
carinata, 128
mabouya, 130
multifasciata, 126, 128, 129, 133
quinquetaeniata, 126, 130, 131
mabuya, 125, 126, 130, 131
brown-sided, 133
common, 130
Indian, 128
macquari, Emydura, 39 *
Macrochelys schmidti, 15
temmincki, 15
macrolepis, Chamaesaura, 136
Leptotyphlops, 184
macrolepis, Trimeresurus, 267
Macroprotodon cucullatus, 220
Macroscincus coctaei, 127
maculatus, Callopistes, 140
magister, Sceloporus, **45**
major, Gerrhosaurus, 136
Malaclemys, 20 *, 21 *
Malacochersus, 28
Malpolon moilensis, 224 *
monspessulana, 220, 221 *
mamba, 232, 237, 261
black, 222, **118**
marginata, Testudo, 28
marinus, Bufo, 172
marmorata, Clemmys, 18, 24
massasauga, 272
eastern, **139**
matamata, 39 *
Maticora, 222, 235
bivirgata, 235
intestinalis, 235
mauritanica, Tarentola, 73
mawi, Dermatemys, 17
maximiliani, Hydromedusa, 40
maximus, Zonosaurus, 137
m'calli, Phrynosoma, 119
mcmahoni, Eristocophis, 263
megacephalum, Platysternon, 17
Mehelya, 221, 222
capensis, 221
melanogaster, Hydraethiops, 222
Melanophidium, 185, 186
melanopleura, Scelotes, 126
Melanosuchus niger, 67
melleri, Chamaeleo, 91
Mesoclemmys, 40
mexicana, Terrapene, 20
Microcephalophis gracilis, 240
Micruroides euryxanthus, 232, **125**
Micrurus, 232, 233
frontalis, 233 *
fulvius, 232, **126**
spixi, 233
miliarius, Sistrurus, 271

mindorensis, Crocodylus, 65
miquihuanus, Crotalus pricei, 278
mississipiensis, Alligator, 45 *, 66
moccasin, 264
  cottonmouth, 266
  Mexican, 266, **134**
  water, 226, 265 *, 266*, **135**
moilensis, Malpolon, 224 *
moloch, 88, 89 *, 96
Moloch horridus, 88, 89 *, 96
molossus, Crotalus, 279
molurus, Python, 179, 180
monitor, 91, 167, 169, 174
  desert, 171 *, 173
  Duméril's, 171, 173
  earless, 173
  false, 140
  Gillen's, 170
  Gould's, 172 *
  Indian, 171, 173
  lace, 172
  Malayan, 170, 173
  Nile, 170, 172, 173
  Pacific, 172
  perentie, 172
  rough-necked, 171, 173
  savanna, 170, **52**
  short-tailed, 169, 172
  Timor, 172
Monopeltis, 161
monspessulana, Malpolon, 220, 221 *
montanus, Celestus, 164
moreleti, Crocodylus, 66
Morelia argus, 181, 182 *, **77**
Morenia ocellata, 26
  petersi, 26
mucosus, Ptyas, 225 *
muhlenbergi, Clemmys, 18
multicarinatus, Gerrhonotus, 164, 166
multifasciata, Mabuya, 126, 128, 129
muralis albanica, Lacerta, 144 *
  Lacerta, 144
muricatus, Amphibolurus, 88
murinus, Eunectes, 176
musurana, 191, 232
muta, Lachesis, 270 *
mutabilis, Agama, 85
mutica, Clemmys, 26
muticus, Trionyx, 36
mutilatus, Peropus, 71
mydas, Chelonia, 32 *, 33 *, 35 *

Naja, 234 *, 237
  naja, 235 *, 236, **127**
Nardoana, 183
nasicornis, Bitis, 262
nasuta, Dryophis, 215
Natrix, 192, 210, 223, 224, 226, 232, 268
  cyclopion, 191 *
  erythrogaster, 226, **82**
  natrix, 192, 218, **81**
  septemvittata, 226

Natrix (continued)
  sipedon, 192 *
    compressicauda, 226, **80**
  taxispilota, 192, **84**
  tessellata, 218
  trianguligera, 192
nejdensis, Phrynocephalus, 83 *, 84 *
nelsoni, Terrapene, 20
Neoseps, 127, 129, 221, 229
  reynoldsi, 126, 130
Nephrurus, 71, 76
Nessia, 127, 133
Neusticurus rudis, 139
neuwiedi, Bothrops, 269
niger, Melanosuchus, 67
nigropunctatus, Tupinambis, 138, 139
niloticus, Crocodylus, 47
  Varanus, 170, 172, 173
nitida, Eremias, 141
notatus, Sphaerodactylus, 74
Notochelys platynota, 26
novae-guineae, Crocodylus, 65
Nucras delalandi, 142
nummifera, Trimeresurus, 269
nuntius, Crotalus viridis, 278

obesus, Sauromalus, 116, **44**
obsoleta, Elaphe, 210, 211, 212 *
  obsoleta, 226
obsoletus, Eumeces, 127, 128
Ocadia sinensis, 26
occipitomaculata, Storeria, 216, 229
oceanica, Gehyra, 71
ocellata, Morenia, 26
odoratus, Sternotherus, 16 *
Oedura, 76
okinavensis, Trimeresurus, 267
Oligodon, 226
olivacea, Lepidochelys, 34
Opheodrys, 226
  aestivus, 211, 227
  vernalis, 227 *, **95**
Ophidia, 175
Ophiodes striatus, 163
Ophiognomon, 138
Ophiomorus, 127, 132
  blanfordi, 132
Ophiophagus, 236
  hannah, 236 *
Ophioscincus, 125, 127
Ophisaurus, 163, 164
  apodus, 164, **51**
  attenuatus, 163
  gracilis, 164
  harti, 164
  ventralis, 166
Ophisops, 141, 144
Opisthoglypha, 215, 240
Opisthotropis, 224, 226
orbicularis, Emys, 18, 25
oreganus, Crotalus viridis, 278
ornata, Terrapene, 20
  Uta, 96, 115, 141

oshaugnessyi, Chamaeleo, 91
Osteolaemus, 47
  tetraspis, 48 *
oustaleti, Chamaeleo, 91
oweni, Chamaeleo, 91, 93, 94
Oxybelis, 216, 230, 231, 267
oxycephala, Elaphe, 224
Oxyrhopus, 231
Oxyuranus, 234

Paleosuchus, 67
palestinae, Vipera, 259, 260 *
palustris, Crocodylus, 48, 65 *
pannonicus, Ablepharus, 131
paradisi, Chrysopelea, 215 *
Parasibynophis, 188
Pareas, 216, 224
Pelamis platurus, 239
pelias, Chrysopelea, 216
Pelochelys bibroni, 37
Pelomedusa, 37
  subrufa, 38
Pelomedusidae, 37
Pelusios, 38
perarmata, Leandria, 95
Peropus mutilatus, 71
petersi, Morenia, 26
Phelsuma laticauda, 75
Phenacosaurus, 115
philbyi, Scincus, 132 *, 133 *
Phrynocephalus, 77, 81, 83, 86, 124
  nejdensis, 83 *, 84 *
Phrynops, 40
Phrynosoma, 96, 113, 116, 117, 118, 119, 124
  coronatum, **43**
  douglassi, 115 *, 119
  m'calli, 119
Phyllodactylus tuberculosus, 74
phyllorhinus, Anolis, 120
Phyllorhynchus, 220, 229
  browni browni, **101**
Phyllurus cornutus, 76
  platurus, 75 *
Physignathus, 87
  lesueuri, **27**
picta belli, Chrysemys, 22
  dorsalis, Chrysemys, 22
  marginata, Chrysemys, 22
  picta, Chrysemys, 22
piscivorus, Ancistrodon, 265 *, 266 *
Pituophis, 213, 229
  catenifer, **115**
    affinis, **108**
    sayi, **109**
Platemys, 40
platurus, Pelamis, 239
  Phyllurus, 75 *
platynota, Notochelys, 26
platyrhinos, Heterodon, 213 *
Platysaurus, 135
Platysternidae, 17
Platysternon megacephalum, 17

Plectrurus, 185
plei, Celestus, 164
plumbifrons, Basiliscus, 115 *
Podocnemis expansa, 38
poinsetti, Sceloporus, 116
Polychrus, 96, 113, 115, 122, 124
polyphemus, Gopherus, 28 *
ponticeriana, Sitana, 86
porosus, Crocodylus, 47
porteri, Testudo, 29 *
prasina, Elaphe, 211
pricei miquihuanus, Crotalus, 278
principis, Gerrhonotus coeruleus, 166
Prosymna ambigua, 221
Proteroglypha, 232, 240
Psammodromus, 143
  algirus, 143 *
Psammodynastes, 225, 226
Psammophis, 216, 220, 221, 223, 224
  sibilans, 220
Pseudaspis cana, 220 *
Pseudechis, 234
Pseudelaps, 234
Pseudemydura, 39
Pseudemys, 18, 22, 24
  scripta, 22 *
    elegans, 22, **10**
    gaigeae, 22
    troosti, 22
Pseudocerastes fieldi, 263
Pseudocordylus, 135
Ptenopus garrulus, 73
Ptyas, 210, 224, 226
  mucosus, 225 *
Ptychozoon, 72
Ptyodactylus hasselquisti, 73 *
pulchellus, Aprasia, 77
  Cyrtodactylus, 72 *
pulchra, Anniella, 166
pumila, Chamaeleo, 92 *
punctatus, Sepsophis, 133
  Sphenodon, 41
puniceus, Trimeresurus, 268
Pygopodidae, 76
Pygopus, 76
Python, 179
  anchietae, 179
  curtus, 179, 181
  molurus, 179, 180, **76**
    bivittatus, 180
    molurus, 180
  regius, 179, 181, **79**
  reticulatus, 179, 180
  sebae, 179, 180, **78**
  spilotes, 181
  timorensis, 179
python, 175, 179, 191, 209
  African, 179, 180, 181, **78**
  Angolan, 179
  Australian, 181
  ball, 179, 181, 183, **79**
  blood, 181
  carpet, 181, 182 *
  diamond, 181
  green tree, 183
  Indian, 179, 180, 181, **76**
  reticulated, 179

python (continued)
  rock, 181
    amethystine, 181
    short-tailed, 179, 181
    Timor, 179, 181
Pythonidae, 175, 179
Pyxis, 28

quadrivittata, Elaphe obsoleta, 226
quinquetaeniata, Mabuya, 126, 130, 131

racer, 209
  blue, 209 *, 210 *
  red, **94**
  Sonoran, **92**
  striped, **91**
racerunner, 137, 139, 140
  six-lined, 138
  strand, 140
radix, Thamnophis, 229
rapicaudus, 71
  Thecadactylus, 73
rattlesnake, 188, 191 226, 227, 265, 270, 271 *
  black, Arizona, **144**
  black-tailed, 279, **142**
  canebrake, 278
  diamondback, eastern, 275 *, 278
    Florida, 276
    red, 276 *, 277 *, 279, **143**
    western, 278
  faded, 278
  pigmy, 270, 271, 278, **138**
  prairie, 276, 278
  rock, 278, **140**
  sidewinder, 279
  South American, 278, **141**
  Stejneger's, 278
  timber, 276, 278
reevesi, Chinemys, 26
regius, Python, 179, 181
reinhardti, Calabaria, 183
resimus, Causus, 260
reticularia, Deirochelys, 24 *
reticulatus, Python, 179, 180
reynoldsi, Neoseps, 126, 130
Rhamphiophis, 221
Rhineura floridana, 161, 162
Rhinocheilus, 215, 229
  lecontei, **106**
Rhinophis, 185
rhodostoma, Ancistrodon, 267
rhombeatus, Causus, 260
rhombifer, Crocodylus, 66
Rhynchocephalia, 41
Rhynchoelaps, 234
rhynchops, Cerberus, 224
richardi, Thalerophis, 231 *
Ringelnatter, 218
ringhals, 237
Ristella, 132
riversiana, Xantusia, 124
roseofusca, Lichanura, 178
ruber, Crotalus, 276 *, 277 *, 279

rudicollis, Varanus, 171, 173
rudis, Neusticurus, 139
rugosa, Tiliqua, 129
russelli, Vipera, 259, 261 *

sacki, Cnemidophorus, 138
sagrei, Anolis, 118
Salvadora, 229
  grahamiae, 230 *
  hexalepsis, 229 *
salvator, Varanus, 170, 173
sand fish, 132 *, 133 *
Sanzinia, 178
Sauria, 69
Sauromalus, 119
  obesus, 116, **44**
sawback, 22
scaber, Dasypeltis, 217 *
scalaris, Sceloporus, 118
Scaphiondontophis, 187
Scaphiophis albopunctata, 221
Sceloporus, 115, 117, 119, 120, 122
  clarki, **46**
  magister, **45**
  poinsetti, 116
  scalaris, 118
  undulatus, 117, 118, **41**
  woodi, 118
Scelotes, 126, 131
  bipes, 126
  bojeri, 126
  inornatus, 126
  melanopleura, 126
scheltopusik, 164, **51**
schlegeli, Bothrops, 269 *
  Tomistoma, 65
schmidti, Enygrus asper, 178
  Macrochelys, 15
schreibersi, Leiocephalus, 117
scincicauda, Gerrhonotus multicarinatus, 163
Scincidae, 124
scincoides, Tiliqua, 129
Scincus, 133
  philbyi, 132 *, 133 *
Scolecosaurus, 138
sclerops, Caiman, 67
scorpioides, Kinosternon, 17
scripta, Pseudemys, 22 *
  elegans, 22
  gaigeae, 22
  troosti, 22
scutatus, Lyriocephalus, 86
scytale, Anilius, 185
sebae, Python, 179, 180
Seminatrix, 228
seps, Tetradactylus, 137
Sepsophis punctatus, 133
septemstriata, Leptotyphlops, 185
septemvittata, Natrix, 226
Serpentes, 69, 175
serpentina, Chelydra, 12 *, 14 *, 15 *
serratus, Laemanctus, 120 *

sexlineatus, Cnemidophorus, 138
  Takydromus, 137, 161
shinisaurid, 167
Shinisaurus crocodilurus, 167
siamensis, Crocodylus, 65
sibilans, Psammophis, 220
Sibon, 212, 216, 231
Sibynophinae, 187
Sibynophis, 187
sidewinder, 279, **136**
sinensis, Ocadia, 26
sipedon, Natrix, 192 *
Siren, 227
Sistrurus, 270, 271, 278
  catenatus, 272, **139**
  miliarius, 271, **138**
Sitana ponticeriana, 86
skiltonianus, Eumeces, 128
skink, 124, 136, 140, 144, 163, 220
  black-sided, 126
  blind, 126, 131
    dart, 127
  blue-tailed, Polynesian, 128, 129
  blue-tongued, 129, 133, **66**
  Bojer's, 126
  Bouton's, 129, 131
  brown-sided, 126
  Cape Verde, 127
  casque-headed, 133
  cat, 132
  cylindrical, 131 *, 132, **64**
  dart, 125, 126, 131
  five-lined, 128, 129, **67**
  African, 126, 130, 131
  giant, 124, 133
  Great Plains, 127, 128
  keeled, 124, 126, 133
  lidless, 125, 126, 130, 132
  little brown, 125 *, 128, 129, 130
  Pecos, 128
  plain, South African, 126
  sand, 126, 221
    Asian, 127, 132
    Blanford's, 132
    Florida, 127, 129, 130, 229
  short-legged, 133
    Philippine, 126
  slender, 126, 129, 132, 133
    striped, 133
  snake, 125, 127
  spiny-tailed, 133
    Cunningham's, 134 *
  stump-tailed, 129, **65**
  Travancore, 125
  western, 128
sliders, 22
slowworm, 163, 164, 165 *
snake, 69, 170, 174, 175
  Aesculapian, 211, 218, 220, 258, **96**
  beaked, 221
  black-headed, 218, 229
  blind, 183, 232
    Diard's, 184
    slender, 183

snake (continued)
    Texas, 184
    western, 184
  brown, 228
  bull, 213, 229, **109, 115**
  Butler's, 222
  cat, 224
    European, 220
  cat-eye, 230, **119**
  chicken, 210, 220, 223, 226
    red-tailed, 224
  colubrid, 187
  coral, 185, 232, 233
    Arizona, 232, **125**
    Brazilian, 233 *
    common, 232
    eastern, **126**
    false, 185
    Oriental, 235
  corn, 211 *, **87**
  DeKay's, 229
  diadem, 223
  diamond, **77**
  Dione's, 220, 226
  earth, 228
    rough, 214, 215
  egg-eating, 217 *, 222
    African, 218
    Indian, 218
  elapid, 232
  file, 221, 222
    Cape, 221
  flowerpot, 184
  flying, 216, 225, **124**
  fox, 226, 227
  garter, 191
    black-necked, **104**
    plains, 229, **105**
    San Francisco, 229, **88**
    Gerard's, 222
  glass, 136, 163, 164
    eastern, 166
    slender, 163
  glossy, 229, **110**
  gopher, Sonora, **108**
  grass, 218
  green, 226
    African, 212
    rough, 211, 227, **93**
    smooth, 227 *, **95**
  ground, striped, 222
  hog-nosed, 191, 213 *, 215, 222, 229, 231, **85, 86**
  hooded, 220
  hook-nosed, 229
  hoop, 227
  house, 221
  indigo, 209, 231, **102, 103**
  king, 188, 209, 221, 229, **111, 112**
    Arizona mountain, **114**
    California, 190 *, 191 *
    common, 191
    speckled, **113**
  kukri, 224, 226
  leaf-nosed, 220, 229
    Arabian, 223 *
    Pima, **101**
  long-nosed, 215, 229, **106**
  lyre, 229
  mangrove, 215, **120**

snake (continued)
  milk, 188, **107**
    Mexican, **116**
  mole, 220 *
  Montpellier, 220, 221 *
  mud, 215, 227
  night, 229
  patch-nosed, 229
    mountain, 230 *
    western, 229 *
  pipe, 185
  queen, 226
  rainbow, 227
  rat, 210
    black, 210, 211, 212 *, 226, **100**
    keeled, 210
    Oriental, 224, 225 *
    yellow, 226, **97, 98, 99**
  rear-fanged, Arabian, 224 *
    Madagascan, 223 *
    Mexican, 230 *
  red-bellied, 216, 229, **83**
  reed, 215, 221, 225
  ring-necked, 229
    western, **90**
  sand, 216, 220, 221, 223, 224
    banded, 229, **122**
  scarlet, 228 *
  sea, 186, 232, 238
  sharp-nosed, 221
  shield-tailed, 185
  short-tailed, 215, 228
  shovel-nosed, 229
  slug, 224
  smooth, 188, 191, 209, 218
  spindle, 215, 232
  sunbeam, 186
  swamp, black, 228
    striped, 228
  tiger, 183, 234
  tree, barred, 216
    blunt-headed, 214 *
    green, 222, 231 *
    long-nosed, 215, **117, 123**
    paradise, 215 *
  vine, 224, 230
    African, 216, 222
  water, 192, 210, 223, 224, 226, 232
    African, 222
    black-bellied, 222
    brown, 192, **84**
    checkered, 218
    common, 192 *
    European, 192, 218, **81**
    dog-faced, 224
    green, 191 *
    mangrove, 226, **80**
    mountain, 224, 226
    Oriental, 186
    red-bellied, 226, **82**
    triangular, 192
  whip, 209, 220, 223, 226, 227
    European, 188, 209, 219
    green, 219 *
  wolf, 222
    Cape, 221
    Oriental, 226

snake (continued)
  worm, 214, 228
    Oriental, 214
snake bite, effects of, 271, 273
  treatment of, 274
Solenoglypha, 232, 240
Spalerosophis, 223
Sphaerodactylus cinereus, 74
  elegans, 73
  notatus, 74
Sphenodon punctatus, 41, **18**
Spilotes, 231
spilotes, Python, 181
spinifera, Trionyx, 36
spinigerus, Diplodactylus, 76 *
spinosus, Hoplocercus, 113, 116
spixi, Micrurus, 233
Squamata, 69
Staurotypus, 17
Stegonotus, 232
stellio, Agama, 85
Stenocercus, 113, 115
Stenophis, 222
Stenorhina, 232
Sternotherus, 38
  carinatus, 16
  odoratus, 16 *, **3**
stictogrammus, Cnemidophorus, 138
Stilosoma extenuatum, 215, 228
stinkpot, **3**
stokesi, Egernia, 134
Stoliczkaia, 187
Storeria, 228
  occipitomaculata, 216, 229, **83**
striatula, Haldea, 214, 215
striatus, Kentropyx, 137
  Ophiodes, 163
subrubrum, Kinosternon, 17
subrufa, Pelomedusa, 38
subtrijuga, Damonia, 25
sungazer, 135
suspectum, Heloderma, 167

taipan, 234
Takydromus, 140, 161
  sexlineatus, 137, 161
Tantilla, 218, 229
Tarentola mauritanica, 73, **24**
taxispilota, Natrix, 192
taylori, Eumeces, 128
tectifera, Hydromedusa, 40
tectum, Kachuga, 27
tegu, 138, 139, **55**
teiid, 137
  Chilean, 140
  Guiana earless, 139
  rough, 139
  snake, 137
  spectacled, 138
  water, 139
  worm, 138
Teiidae, 137
Teius, 140
  teyou, 139
Tejovaranus flavipunctatus, 140

Telescopus, 224
  fallax, 220
temmincki, Macrochelys,
  15
Terrapene, 19, 38
  carolina, 19, **1**
    bauri, 20
    major, 20
    triunguis, 20, **7**
  coahuila, 20
  mexicana, 20
  nelsoni, 20
  ornata, 20, **2**
  terrapin, 18, 24
    diamondback, 20 *,
      21 *
    red-eared, 22 *, **10**
*terrificus, Crotalus duris-
  sus,* 273
tessellata, Natrix, 218
Testudinidae, 27
Testudo, 28
  denticulata, 28, **14**
  elegans, 28, **9**
  elephantopus, 29
  gigantea, 28, **15**
  graeca, 28, **12**
  hermanni, 28, **13**
  marginata, 28
  porteri, 29 *
Tetradactylus, 136
  seps, 137
tetraspis, Osteolaemus,
  48 *
*tetrataenia, Thamnophis
  sirtalis,* 229
texana, Holbrookia, 119
teyou, Teius, 139
teyu, 139, 140
Thalerophis, 231
  richardi, 231 *
Thamnophis, 191
  cyrtopsis, **104**
  radix, 229, **105**
  sirtalis tetrataenia, 229,
    88
*Thecadactylus rapicau-
  dus,* 73
Thelotornis, 222
  kirtlandi, 216
Thrasops jacksoni, 222
thurgi, Hardella, 27
Tiliqua, 127, 133
  rugosa, 129, **65**
  scincoides, 129, **66**
timorensis, Python, 179
  Varanus, 172
toad, horned, 85, 96, 113,
    116, 117, 118, 119,
    124, 125
  coast, **43**
  flat-tailed, 119
  short-horned, 115 *,
    119
tokay, 69, 70 *, 71, **22, 23**
Tomistoma schlegeli, 65
tommygoff, 269
tortoise, 13
  common European, 28,
    12

tortoise (continued)
  Galapagos, 29 *
  gopher, 28 *
    Texas, 27 *
  Hermann's, 28, **13**
  hinge-back, **11**
  Marion's, 28
  South American, 28,
    14
  star, **9**
Tracheloptychus, 137
Trachischium, 214
Trachyboa, 177
*travancoricum, Lygo-
  soma,* 125
trianguligera, Natrix, 192
Tribolonotus, 133
trigonata, Boiga, 224
trijuga, Geoemyda, 25
Trimeresurus, 264, 267,
    271
  cantori, 267
  flavoviridis, 267
  jerdoni, 267
  macrolepis, 267
  okinavensis, 267
  puniceus, 268
  wagleri, 268
Trimorphodon, 229
Trionychidae, 36
Trionychoidea, 36
Trionyx, 36
  ferox, 36
  muticus, 36
  spinifera, 36, **16, 17**
  triunguis, 36
triunguis, Trionyx, 36
trivirgata, Lichanura, 178
Trogonophis, 162
  wiegmanni, 162
Tropidodipsas, 212
Tropidophis, 177
Tropidophorus, 124, 126,
    133
tuatara, 41, **18**
*tuberculosus, Phyllo-
  dactylus,* 74
*Tupinambis nigropuncta-
  tus,* 138, 139
  teguixin, **55**
turcicus, Hemidactylus,
    73, 74
turtle, 12
  big-headed, 17
  Blanding's, 18, 19 *
  box, 18, 19
    common, 20
    eastern, 18, **1**
    Malayan, 25
    three-toed, 20, **7**
    western, 20, **2**
  Central American river,
    17
  chicken, 24 *
  cryptodire, 36
  emydid, 18
  flap-shelled, African, 37
    Indian, 37
  green, 31, 32 *, 33 *,
    35 *

turtle (continued)
  hawksbill, 31
  hidden-necked, 37
  leatherback, 30 *
  map, 22
  mud, 16, 17
    eastern, 17
    narrow-bridged, 17
    South American, 17
    three-keeled Central
      American, 17
  Muhlenberg's, 18
  musk, 16 *, **3**
    common, 16
    keel-backed, 16
  olive-backed, 31
  otter, 40
  painted, 22, **8**
  pond, 18, 25
    black, 26
    European, 18, 25, **4**
    Pacific, 18
  ridley, 34
  river, 38
  sea, 31
  snake-necked, 37, 38
    Australian, 39 *
  snapping, 12 *, 14 *,
    15 *
    alligator, 15
    common, 14
  soft-shelled, 36
    Florida, 36
    long-headed, 37
    Malayan, 37
    New Guinean, 37
    Senegal, 37
    spineless, 36
    spiny, 36, **16, 17**
  spotted, 18, **6**
  tortoise-shell, 31, 34
  wood, 18, **5**
Typhlacontias, 127
Typhlophis, 184
typhlopid, 184
Typhlopidae, 183
Typhlops, 184, 185, 232
  braminus, 184
  diardi, 184
Typhlosaurus, 126, 131
typica, Cricosaura, 124
typus, Dispholidus, 215,
    222

Uma, 116, 119, 120, 143
  notata, **42**
undulatus, Sceloporus,
    117, 118
Ungaliophis, 177
unicolor, Xenopeltis, 186
Urocentron, 96, 113
Uromacer, 211, 232
Uromastix, 78, 81, 83,
    86, 96, 113, 140
  acanthurinus, 86, **26**
Uropeltidae, 185
Uropeltis, 185
Uroplatus, 75
ursini, Vipera, 240, 257 *

Uta, 113
  ornata, 96, 115, 141
  stansburiana, **39**
uta, 113
  tree, 96

validus, Gerrhosaurus,
    137
Varanidae, 169, 174
Varanus, 170
  bengalensis, 171
  brevicauda, 169, 172
  dumerili, 171, 172, 173
  exanthematicus, 170, **52**
  gilleni, 170
  giganteus, 172
  gouldi, 172 *
  griseus, 171 *, 173
  indicus, 172
  komodoensis, 169 *
  niloticus, 170, 172, 173
  rudicollis, 171, 173
  salvator, 170, 173
  timorensis, 172
  varius, 172
variegatus, Coleonyx,
    74 *
varius, Varanus, 172
ventralis, Ophisaurus, 166
vernalis, Opheodrys,
    227 *
versicolor, Calotes, 79
vigilis, Xantusia, 124
viper, 168, 188, 240
  asp, 258 *, 259
  common European,
    257, **128**
  Fea's, 263
  gaboon, 240, 257, 261,
    262, **130, 131**
  horned, 162, 263 *
  Lataste's, 259
  McMahon's, 263
  mock, 225, 226
  mole, 257, 260, 263
  mountain, 267
  Orsini's, 240, 257 *,
    259
  Palestinian, 259, 260 *
  Peringuey's, 261
  pit, 240, 262, 264
    Central American
      prehensile-tailed,
      269 *
    Schlegel's, 269 *
    Wagler's, 268
  Renard's, 259
  rhinoceros, 262, **133**
  Russell's, 259, 261 *
  sand, 259 *
  saw-scaled, 263
  tree, 262
Vipera, 259, 267
  ammodytes, 259 *
  aspis, 258 *, 259
  berus, 257, **128**
  latasti, 259
  lebetina, 259
  palestinae, 259, 260 *

Vipera (continued)
  russelli, 259, 261 *
  ursini, 240, 257 *
  xanthina, 259
Viperidae, 240
viridiflavus, Coluber,
    219 *
viridis, Chondropython,
    183
  Crotalus, 276, 278
  Lacerta, 141, 144
vittatum, Lygosoma, 133
vittatus, Basiliscus, 113 *
  Diplodactylus, 76
vivipara, Lacerta, 142
vulpina, Elaphe, 226

wagleri, Trimeresurus,
    268
Wallsaurus, 73
Walterinnesia aegyptia,
    237 *
*westermanni, Elachisto-
  don,* 218
whip snake, striped, **89**
whiptail, 138
  Arizona, 138
  spotted, 138
  striped, 138
wiegmanni, Trogonophis,
    162
wizlizeni, Crotaphytus,
    119
woma, 183
woodi, Sceloporus, 118
wutu, 269, **137**

xanthina, Vipera, 259
Xantusia, 124
  arizonae, 124
  henshawi, 124
  riversiana, 124
  vigilis, 124
Xantusidae, 124
Xenoderminae, 187, 224
Xenodermus, 225
  javanicus, 187
Xenodon, 231
Xenopeltidae, 185, 186
Xenopeltis unicolor, 186
Xenopholis, 187
xenosaurid, 167
Xenosauridae, 167
Xenosaurus, 167
Xiphocercus, 113, 122

yacare, Caiman, 67

Zaocys, 210, 224, 226
  carinatus, 210
zarudnyi, Diplometopon,
    162 *
zebrata, Corucia, 124,
    127, 133
zeylanicus, Chamaeleo,
    93, 94
Zonosaurus maximus, 137